From Action to Ethics

Also available from Bloomsbury:

Advances in Experimental Philosophy of Action, edited by Paul Henne and Samuel Murray
Certainty in Action, by Danièle Moyal-Sharrock
Wittgenstein's Lion, by Constantine Sandis
Reframing Ethics Through Dialectics, by Michael Steinmann

From Action to Ethics

A Pluralistic Approach to Reasons and Responsibility

Constantine Sandis

BLOOMSBURY ACADEMIC
LONDON • NEW YORK • OXFORD • NEW DELHI • SYDNEY

BLOOMSBURY ACADEMIC
Bloomsbury Publishing Plc, 50 Bedford Square, London, WC1B 3DP, UK
Bloomsbury Publishing Inc, 1385 Broadway, New York, NY 10018, USA
Bloomsbury Publishing Ireland, 29 Earlsfort Terrace, Dublin 2, D02 AY28, Ireland

BLOOMSBURY, BLOOMSBURY ACADEMIC and the Diana logo are
trademarks of Bloomsbury Publishing Plc

First published in Great Britain 2024
This paperback edition published 2025

Copyright © Constantine Sandis, 2024

Constantine Sandis has asserted his right under the Copyright,
Designs and Patents Act, 1988, to be identified as Author of this work.

For legal purposes the Acknowledgements on p. ix constitute
an extension of this copyright page.

Cover design by Constantine Sandis and Louise Dugdale

All rights reserved. No part of this publication may be: i) reproduced or transmitted in
any form, electronic or mechanical, including photocopying, recording or by means
of any information storage or retrieval system without prior permission in writing from
the publishers; or ii) used or reproduced in any way for the training, development or
operation of artificial intelligence (AI) technologies, including generative AI technologies.
The rights holders expressly reserve this publication from the text and data mining
exception as per Article 4(3) of the Digital Single Market Directive (EU) 2019/790.

Bloomsbury Publishing Inc does not have any control over, or responsibility for,
any third-party websites referred to or in this book. All internet addresses given
in this book were correct at the time of going to press. The author and publisher
regret any inconvenience caused if addresses have changed or sites have
ceased to exist, but can accept no responsibility for any such changes.

A catalogue record for this book is available from the British Library.

A catalog record for this book is available from the Library of Congress.

ISBN: HB: 978-1-3502-3511-3
PB: 978-1-3502-3515-1
ePDF: 978-1-3502-3512-0
eBook: 978-1-3502-3513-7

Typeset by Deanta Global Publishing Services, Chennai, India

For product safety related questions contact productsafety@bloomsbury.com.

To find out more about our authors and books visit www.bloomsbury.com
and sign up for our newsletters.

For Calypso
*who can act for reasons but hasn't quite made it all
the way to ethics.*

But what first, Debbie, attracted you to the millionaire Paul Daniels?

Mrs Merton

Contents

List of figures   viii
Preface and acknowledgments   ix

Introduction: Actions, reasons, and ethics   1

Part I Action

1. Action cubes and traces   9
2. What is it to do nothing?   22
3. Are we superhuman or are we dancer? Action and will in the novels of Anthony Powell   35
4. Reasoning to action   49
5. How to act against your better judgement   55

Part II Reasons

6. Dretske on the causation of behaviour   67
7. The objects of action explanation   78
8. Verbal reports and 'real' reasons: Confabulation and conflation   88
9. Can action explanations ever be non-factive?   101
10. Are reasons like shampoo?   113

Part III Ethics

11. Gods and mental states: The causation of action in ancient tragedy and modern philosophy of mind   127
12. Motivated by the gods: Compartmentalized agency and responsibility   146
13. The man who mistook his *Handlung* for a *Tat:* Hegel on Oedipus and other tragic Thebans   158
14. The doing and the deed: Action in normative ethics   175
15. Ethics and action theory: An unhappy divorce   188

Appendix: Basic actions and individuation   203
Notes   209
References   237
Index   265

Figures

1	Action Necker Cube (Abstract)	12
2	Action Necker Cube (Concrete)	14
3	Moving my body	72
4	Turning my head	74
5	Raising my arm	76
6	Indicating stimuli	77

Preface and acknowledgments

The essays in this book draw on material previously published between 2008 and 2022. I should like thank all of the publishers for their permission to re-use the relevant material. I hereby acknowledge their original sources in chronological order, which tells a different story from the one presented in the book:

'**How to Act Against Your Better Judgement**', *Philosophical Frontiers*, 3 (2) (2008): 111–24.

'**Dretske on the Causation of Behaviour**', *Behavior and Philosophy*, 36 (2008): 71–85. © Cambridge Center for Behavioral Studies. Reprinted with permission from CCBS.

'**Gods and Mental States**', in Constantine Sandis (ed.), *New Essays on the Explanation of Action*, 358–85, Basingstoke: Palgrave Macmillan, 2009. © Springer Nature. Reprinted with permission from Springer Nature.

'**Basic Actions and Individuation**', in Timothy O'Connor and Constantine Sandis (eds.), *A Companion to the Philosophy of Action*, 10–17, Oxford: Wiley-Blackwell, 2010. ©Wiley-Blackwell; reprinted with kind permission.

'**The Man Who Mistook his *Handlung* for a *Tat***', *Bulletin of the Hegel Society of Great Britain*, No. 62 (2010): 35–60. © The Hegel Society of Great Britain 2010; reprinted with kind permission.

'**The Objects of Action Explanation**', *Ratio*, 25 (3; Sep 2012): 326–44. ©Wiley-Blackwell; reprinted with kind permission.

'**Can Action Explanations Ever Be Non-Factive?**', in Brad Hooker, Margaret Little, and David Backhurst (eds.), *Thinking about Reasons: Themes from the Philosophy of Jonathan Dancy*, 29–49, Oxford: Oxford University Press, 2013. © Oxford Publishing Limited. Reproduced with permission of the Licensor through PLSclear.

'**Verbal Reports and "Real Reasons": Confabulation and Conflation**', *Ethical Theory and Moral Practice*, 18 (2), 267-80. © Springer Nature. Reproduced with permission from Springer Nature.

'**Motivated by the Gods**', in Andrei Buckareff, Carlos Moya, and Sergi Rosell (eds.), *Agency and Responsibility*, 209–25, Basingstoke: Palgrave Macmillan, 2015. © Springer Nature. Reproduced with permission from Springer Nature.

'**Are We Superhuman or Are We Dancer?**', *Proceedings of the 7th Biennial Anthony Powell Conference*, AP Society Press, 2016, 25–41. First published by The Anthony Powell Society; reprinted with kind permission.

'**The Doing and the Deed**', *Royal Institute of Philosophy Supplement*, 80 (July 2017): 105–26. © The Royal Institute of Philosophy and the contributors 2017; reprinted with kind permission.

'**Are Reasons Like Shampoo?**', in Gunnar Schumann (ed.), *Explanation in Action Theory and Historiography: Causal and Teleological Approaches*, 146–64, Abingdon: Routledge, 2019. © Taylor & Francis Group. Reprinted by permission of the publisher (Taylor & Francis Ltd.).

'**Reasoning to Action**', *Philosophical Explorations*, 23 (1; 2020): 180–6. © Taylor & Francis Group. Reprinted by permission of the publisher (Taylor & Francis Ltd.).

'**What Is It to Do Nothing?**', in Veronica Rodriguez-Blanco and George Pavlakos (eds.), *Negligence, Omissions and Responsibility: Reflecting on Philosophy of Action*, 187–204, Cambridge: Cambridge University Press, 2021. © Cambridge University Press 2022; reprinted with kind permission.

'**Action Cubes and Traces**', in Carla Bagnoli (ed.), *Time in Action: The Temporal Structure of Rational Agency and Practical Thought*, 32–51, Abingdon: Routledge, 2021. © Taylor & Francis Group. Reprinted by permission of the publisher (Taylor & Francis Ltd.).

'**Ethics and Action Theory**', in Roger Teichmann (ed.), *The Oxford Handbook of Elizabeth Anscombe*, 469–489, Oxford: Oxford University Press, 2022. © Oxford Publishing Limited. Reproduced with permission of the Licensor through PLSclear.

While I've tried to keep any repetition of ideas to a minimum, some inevitable overlap remains so as to enable the reader to dip into any given essay without prerequisites.

I have avoided the inclusion of any essays that are readily available online via free open access, or which appear in other English collections of my work. I have also chosen not to include any co-written essays. Modified versions of nine of the essays listed above have been published (alongside six others) in a French translation by Rémi Clot-Goudard as *Raisons et responsabilité - Essais de philosophie de l'action* (Ithaque, 2021; reprinted Éliott 2023). I cannot thank Rémi enough for his philosophical and organizational help.

I would also like to thank Colleen Coalter, Becky Holland, Suzie Nash, Ben O'Hagan and Liza Thompson at Bloomsbury, for all their help and patience; four anonymous referees for the press for their encouragement and invaluable feedback; my wife Louise Chapman for standing by me in sickness and in health; and our fellow Lex Academic team members, Jennifer Swift and Jessica Oliver, for their unflinching support.

The raw material for this volume was published over a period of fifteen years, having first been presented at more than one hundred seminars, workshops and conferences. I hope that all of those who helped me to improve it will forgive me for not collating all of my original acknowledgments here. I would be remiss, however, to not mention Andreas Lind for his ongoing encouragement and advice during this time. I also benefited from Visiting Fellowships at the Helsinki Collegium for Advanced Studies (2009 and 2014), Centre de Recherche en Ethique in Montréal (2014–15 and 2018–19) and the Center for Ethics and Public Affairs at the *Murphy Institute* at Tulane University (2018–19), as well as from sabbaticals at Oxford Brookes University and the University of Hertfordshire, financial support from the Spanish Ministry project 'Modal Aspects of Materialist Realism' (2007–10), the NOMOS Network for Applied Philosophy projects 'Alternatives, Belief and Action' (2010–12) and 'Perspectival Thoughts and Facts' (2010–14), and the 'Santander Research Project Award' (2012–13).

The book is dedicated to Calypso, who will not read it.
CS
Poole, July 2023

Introduction

Actions, reasons, and ethics

Prologue

Action theory without ethics is empty; ethics without action theory is blind. The essays collected here accordingly stand for a symbiotic approach to philosophical and psychological accounts of (i) actions, (ii) their explanation and (iii) their moral status. Each individual essay takes us from action to ethics, broadly construed. But the essays also move collectively in this direction.

The book is divided into three corresponding parts. The first, 'Action' (Chapters 1–5), concerns the nature of action and its relation to agents. The second, 'Reasons' (Chapters 6–10), considers the reasons for which we act and how these relate to other explanatory factors. The final part, 'Ethics' (Chapters 11–15), turns to questions in moral psychology and normative ethics, approaching them from the perspective of the book's earlier discussions. A brief appendix, 'Basic Actions and Individuation', presents a critical overview of the main positions on action individuation and the search for the most basic form of action. These enquiries are not conducted ahistorically, but via an intertwining with an eclectic history of ideas, from *The Bhagavad Gītā* and Sophocles to Freud, Anthony Powell, Anscombe and Ricœur. It is tempting to describe the result as a kind of applied philosophy of action, but the influence between action theory and that which is extraneous to it runs in both directions.

Given how strongly interconnected I take the book's main topics to be, it should come as no surprise that its three parts are not so much divided by thematic boundaries as they are united through investigatory fluidity. How can we offer accounts of either reasons or rightness without a solid grasp of action concepts? Conversely, if an ontology of action is to have any merit, then it needs to accommodate certain psychological and ethical constraints.

On the one hand, we can conceive of actions as repeatables that can be done intentionally or unintentionally; voluntarily or involuntarily; rationally or irrationally; rightly or wrongly; individually or collectively; and so on. On the other, there exists an equally valid conception according to which they are spatio-temporal particulars with concrete causes and effects. What is the connection between these two senses of 'action', and how should it inform motivational psychology and ethical theory? These are the questions that this book seeks to answer.

I. Action

Part I develops a distinctive understanding of the relation of doings to things done. This serves as a *leitmotif* throughout the rest of the book. In doing so, it also carves out a space for agency and volition within the natural order of things. The first chapter, 'Action cubes and traces', considers Paul Ricœur's powerful suggestion that we should understand things done as marks left on *time* by the events of our acting, just as things written down are residual traces of writing events. While his resulting account of actions as cubical volumes in space-time, which may be reached from a plurality of perspectives, is an insightful one, I maintain that we would do better to conceive of our deeds not as traces but as the *leaving* of traces, a distinction with surprisingly important repercussions in both moral psychology and normative ethics.

One corollary of the cubical account of action may be traced back to the Bhagavadian view that all action contains inaction, and vice versa. Guided by this, Chapter 2 ('What is it to do nothing?') argues that we should reject any theory that rests on the metaphysical assumption that actions—or even their characterizations—can be neatly divided into positive acts of doing and so-called 'negative' acts of omitting, refraining and neglecting. I proceed to re-evaluate the doctrine of doing and allowing and related puzzles concerning moral responsibility in the light of this rejection.

Chapters 3–5 explore the relation between actions and their agents. 'Are we superhuman or are we dancer?' does so by way of the novels of Anthony Powell. Powell's characters are satirically partitioned between agents and patients, with many of those who at first appear to belong to the former set *par excellence* being ultimately shown up. Powell's novels serve as a comic warning of the perils – both theoretical and practical – of overestimating our agential capacities.

'Reasoning to action' considers Jonathan Dancy's recent defence of an 'actionalist' conception of practical reasoning. This has its roots in Aristotle's thought that we can equally reason from our current beliefs to action as we can to a new belief. In recent decades this has been challenged by cognitivists and intentionalists who, respectively, claim that practical reasoning can only result in either normative beliefs or intention. My own version of the 'actionalist' conclusion holds that the aim and issue of practical reasoning are logically connected in such a way that reasoning cannot result in action without also resulting in some form of belief *in* action. This raises questions about the very possibility of akrasia, which is the topic of Chapter 5, 'How to act against your better judgement'. Those who object to Davidson's understanding of how akrasia is possible tend to argue that he is committed to claiming that akratic agents must *in some sense* hold contradictory judgements in deliberation. I try to show that while there is nothing paradoxical in what Davidson says, his 'solution' only deals with that form of akrasia that Aristotle calls *propeteia* (rashness), at the expense of the more puzzling case of *astheneia* (weakness). I conclude that, despite certain failings stemming from its motivational internalism, Davidson's theory is essentially equipped with the right distinctions to demonstrate the possibility of genuine *astheneia*.

II. Reasons

This part of the book moves from reasoning to reasons. Debates about the ontology of reasons are frequently conducted with surprising independence from questions concerning the nature of action and its explanation. This leads to a number of unfortunate conflations between the reasons we act for, the reasons that explain why we acted as we did, and the reasons that motivated us to so act. The chapters in Part II may be viewed as an exercise in analytic deconstructivism. They aim to demonstrate why there can be no coherent analysis of 'reason for action' whereby it can simultaneously act as a consideration, *explanans*, and motive or motivational force. Put more positively, we should be conceptual pluralists about both actions and their reasons. I argue for this explicitly in 'The objects of action explanation', which serves as a transition between the first two parts of the volume. The chapter begins by distinguishing between different conceptions of behaviour before exploring an accompanying variety of things that 'action explanation' may plausibly amount to.

Chapter 6, 'Dretske on the causation of behaviour', introduces Fred Dretske's unjustly neglected distinction between the triggering and structuring causes of behaviour. Dretske maintains that intentional human action is triggered by perceptual events ('causes') but structured by representational facts ('reasons'). On this view, actions are not events but, rather, causal *processes* of one event triggering another. This chapter seeks to show that while Dretske's causalism is considerably more persuasive than the standard Davidsonian alternative, it ultimately fails to capture what is distinctive about *intentional* action and its explanation.

If, however, we altogether abandon causalist accounts of action explanation, then does this not render reasons epiphenomenal? The remaining chapters in the middle section of the book seek to address this question from different angles. 'Verbal reports and "real reasons"' (Chapter 8) examines the relation between the various forces that underlie human action and our verbal reports about our reasons for acting as we did. Its unabashed conclusion is that much of the psychological literature on confabulations conflates a number of distinct motivational factors. The most interesting part of the confabulation literature, then, is that many experimental psychologists are themselves guilty of confabulation in their accounts of why their subjects behaved as they did. I contend that subjects frequently give correct answers to questions about the considerations they acted upon, while remaining largely unaware of why they take themselves to have such reasons to act. Pari passu, experimental psychologists are wrong to think that they have shown our everyday reason talk to be systematically confused. This is significant because reason-ascriptions can affect characterizations of action that are morally and legally relevant (a theme I return to in Part III). But far from rendering empirical research on confabulations invalid, my re-interpretation of it unclouds its true insights into human nature.

Chapter 9, 'Can action explanations ever be non-factive?', suggests that, although anti-psychologists such as Dancy are right to contest the commonplace view that agential reasons are psychological states, they throw the baby out with the bathwater in concluding that reason-giving explanations must therefore be non-factive. An apparent corollary of this view is the paradoxical thesis that the reasons for which we act are actually incapable of explaining why we act. I revisit this thesis in 'Are reasons like shampoo?' (Chapter 10). Debates in 'reasonology' typically arise when theorists, in the grip of different pictures, enforce Procrustean constraints on attempts to carve nature at its proverbial joints. One such picture is that of a reason as a consideration we act in the light of. Another is that of a reason as something that motivates us. A third is that of reasons as explanations of processes or events. It is an illusion to think that these distinct conceptions can be united under a single concept of a reason: one whose correct analysis reveals a hidden triple formula. We would do better to embrace a pluralism that allows for different concepts of a reason for different purposes: psychological, socio-historical and ethical. Once we come to accept this, the vexed question of whether reasons are causes dissolves.

III. Ethics

The chapter in the previous section have been guided by the thought that we cannot sensibly divorce theories of action explanation from accounts of what it is to act in the first place. In this final part of the book, I make the parallel suggestion that one cannot simply plug in one's favourite account of action into ethical debates without seriously affecting the plausibility of any given theory.

The first three chapters of Part III (11–13) concentrate on the relation between action explanation and moral responsibility. 'Gods and mental states' argues that, contrary to popular opinion, ancient tragedy presents us with a percipient understanding of human agency and responsibility that is preferable to most contemporary accounts. This is because the ancients were wise to separate the motivation of action from its causal production. 'Motivated by the Gods' looks to both Greek tragedy and Theodore Dreiser's *An American Tragedy* for insights into the ownership of motivational factors that are not fully under our control. The liability for actions performed under such alien influences, I maintain, is not merely causal but moral and psychological. 'The man who mistook his *Handlung* for a *Tat*' acts as a bridge between the previous two papers and the final pair (which focus on the importance of action theory for normative ethics). This chapter compares the aforementioned distinction between doings and things done to Hegel's tripartite presentation of action under the aspects of *Handlung*, *Tat* and *Tun*. I try to show that the latter anticipates the complex moral epistemology of H. A. Prichard and W. D. Ross in its pluralistic approach to luck and imputation.

Chapter 14, 'The doing and the deed', makes a case for the importance of the aforementioned distinctions to central questions in normative ethics. The lack of attention paid by moral theory to the philosophy of action is striking when compared, for example, to that paid by epistemology to the notion of belief. I demonstrate how much more effectively we can steer through the debates between consequentialism, deontology, virtue ethics and so on, once armed with a proper pluralistic understanding of action concepts. Consider, for example, the debate concerning whether or not intention matters to right action. It is prima facie unclear what it would mean for intention to matter to the rightness or wrongness of a (repeatable) thing done. By contrast, it is highly implausible that intention does not matter to the moral evaluation of an agent's particular *doing* of something. I contend, inter alia, that the notion of right action most amenable to virtue ethics is different from that used by, say, consequentialists.

The final chapter, 'Ethics and action theory', looks back at mid-twentieth-century attempts to think through issues in moral philosophy via questions about action. It is a sad irony that this approach was effectively as a result of Anscombe's influential 1958 article 'Modern Moral Philosophy', in which she explicitly makes a case for it. Having offered an analysis of how we got to where we are today, the chapter ends on a more optimistic note for the future of action in ethics, for which this book serves merely as a groundwork.

Epilogue

In a 2021 interview conducted by Chris Heath for *GQ* magazine's 'Happiness Project', filmmaker David Lynch found himself distinguishing between the doing of things, and the work done:

> I'm just kind of happy in the doing of things. [. . .] Getting an idea, or realizing an idea, working on a painting or working on a piece of sculpture, working on a film. [. . .] One thing I've noticed is that many of us, we do what we call work, for a goal, for a result. And in the doing, it's not that much happiness. And yet that's our life going by [. . .] It doesn't matter what your work is, you just get happy in the work, you get happy in the little things and the big things. And if the result isn't what you dreamed of, it doesn't kill you if you enjoyed the doing of it. It's important that we enjoy the doing of our life. (Heath 2021)

This is not a book about happiness, but for the most part I have enjoyed writing the essays it contains. It is unlikely that they have achieved all that I set out to do. I hope the reader will at least find some pleasure in perusing them, whatever the merits of the text.

Part I

Action

1

Action cubes and traces

Prologue

In Mary Torjussen's first novel, the narrator's boyfriend is said to be *Gone without a Trace*. As the novel reveals, however, all actions involve the leaving of a trace of some kind, if only in one's mind. While the leaving of traces is not an acknowledged part of any concept of action, I wish to argue that it is illuminating to conceive of our *doings* in such terms. In time, the material, psychological or digital traces that our actions result in may be faded, lost, forgotten, covered up or altogether vanished.[1] But they can also endure, remaining open to re-discovery at any moment. Like a moth-ridden bundle of letters discovered in an abandoned attic, some will only ever be of parochial interest, while others stand as marks on the history of the world (see Section 2).

Paul Ricoeur asks:

> To what extent may we say that what is *done* is inscribed? . . . We say that such and such an event *left its mark* on its time . . . in a metaphorical way, some actions are events that imprint their mark on their time. But on what did they imprint their mark? Is it not in something spatial that discourse is inscribed? How could an event be printed on something temporal? . . . Could we not say that history is itself the record of human action? History is the quasi 'thing' on which human action leaves a 'trace', puts its mark. Hence the possibility of 'archives' . . . like a text, human action is an open work, the meaning of which is 'in suspense' . . . the text may be reached from different sides. Like a cube, or a volume in space, the text presents a 'relief'. Its different topics are not on the same altitude.[2]

With the notable exception of Ricoeur's work, the philosophy of the trace exists entirely independently from the concerns of mainstream philosophy of action, and vice versa. This is partly an effect of the so-called analytic–continental divide, variations of which stubbornly persist despite the popularity of protestations against it. But it is equally due to the unfortunate way in which contemporary moral theory has divorced itself from the philosophy of action, which has in turn long abandoned the philosophy of history. This essay attempts to undo some of this damage by presenting a three-dimensional approach to action that is as much informed by Hegel, Levinas and Ricoeur as it is by Anscombe and Hornsby.

1. Aspects of action

On Hegel's view, 'the self-consciousness of heroes (like that of Oedipus and others in Greek tragedy) had not advanced out of its primitive simplicity either to reflection on the distinction between deed and action, between the external event and the purpose and knowledge of the circumstances, or to the subdivision of consequences' (Hegel [1820] 1991 – referred to as *PR* in the sequel – §118A). The Greeks thus 'accepted responsibility for the whole compass of the deed' (Hegel [1820] 1991), despite the fact that 'the right of the will to recognize as its action, and to accept responsibility for, only those aspects of its deed which it knew to be presupposed within its end, and which were present in its purpose' (*PR*: §117).[3]

While current action theory distinguishes between wilful, deliberate, intended and foreseen harm, on the one hand, and unforeseen harm, on the other, as well as between different motives and mitigating circumstances, in some ways not much has changed since the Greeks. We (perhaps cannot help but) confront action through some particular aspect, such as trace, consequence, motive, purpose or intention, but never all of them at once. Yet we continue to adopt the default of taking individuals to be responsible for actions *tout court*, whatever the mitigation.

The mereology of action suggests that there is no such thing as knowledge of or responsibility for action *tout court*. This is because the various 'inner' and 'outer' aspects of any given action are arranged in such a way that one may have knowledge of – or be responsible for – what one is doing *qua* one of them but not *qua* another. If action didn't contain divisions such as that between 'what is purposed and what is accomplished' (*PR*: §114A), then the relation between practical knowledge and what actually happens would not have presented such a challenge for philosophers, such as Anscombe, who wish to emphasize our non-observational knowledge of action.[4]

To keep to Hegel's own example, Oedipus is responsible for patricide *qua* external deed but only for striking an old man in self-defence *qua* intended action. The former constitutes one of the act's 'outer' aspects (such as its traces and consequences) and the latter one of its 'inner' ones.[5] Hegel thus distinguishes between the ancient ethical concern with objective deed (*Tat*) and our additional modern interest in subjective elements of action, including those of foresight, knowledge, motive, intention and purpose (*Handlung*).[6] These 'inner' and 'outer' aspects should not be understood as ontologically separable components. Indeed, in stating that '[t]he laurels of mere willing are dry leaves which have never been green' (*PR*: §124A), Hegel reveals himself to be an early enactivist for whom volition, intention and other psychological predicates gain meaning only insofar as they are made flesh in action. Charles Taylor summarizes this aspect of Hegel well when he writes that '[i]n order to understand mental life as something we have to achieve understanding of . . . we have to abandon the view of it as constituted of data. We have to understand it as action' (Taylor 1979: 85; cf. Taylor 1983: 24–5).

Robert Brandom also distinguishes between an externalist strand in Hegel (according to which actions are identified and individuated 'according to what is actually done') and an internalist one (according to which they are identified and individuated 'by the agent's intention or purpose' (Brandom 2019: 384)). He next suggests that it is on the first of these two views 'that the inner can be understood only in terms of its outer expression' (Brandom 2019: 384). But Brandom dissolves the apparent tension between the two views by declaring them to be two sides of the *same* concept of action (Brandom 2019: 374), despite the fact that Hegel clearly distinguishes between three concepts of action: *Tun* (act), *Tat* (deed) and *Handlung* (action).

It is telling that Brandom completely ignores the first of these, despite its function as a tertium quid that deals with conflicts between *Tat* and *Handlung*. Brandom takes '*Tat*' to refer to 'the deed done, with all of its accordioned descriptions' and '*Handlung*' to 'that same deed *as* the agent's doing', further characterizing the latter '*as* specifiable by the restricted set of descriptions under which it is intentional, and hence something *done* at all' (Brandom 2019: 389; all emphasis in the original). In so doing, he confuses Hegel's threefold understanding of action with a one-dimensional Davidsonian schema according to which '[w]hat makes an event, performance, or process an *action*, something *done*, is that it is *intentional* under *some* description' (Brandom 2019: 368).[7]

Hegel distinguishes between the notion of an act (*Tun*) from the 'internal' standpoint of the agent (behaviour in so far as it relates to one's own foreknowledge, purpose, intention and knowledge) and that from 'external' standpoints (e.g. legal, scientific, cultural). He terms the former *Handlung* (action) and the latter *Tat* (deed). This distinction should not be confused with the contemporary one between actions and mere bodily movements. For one, both *Handlung* and *Tat* are aspects of conduct that results from the will, namely, *Tun* (LA 1835: 1160f.). Moreover, Hegel's taxonomy is motivated by concerns relating to modes of perception. So, whereas theorists such as Davidson (and, following him, Brandom) assert that all actions are events that are intentional under some description, Hegel reserves the term '*Handlung*' for just those aspects of behaviour that are highlighted by a specific set of agent-related descriptions. This is not an ontological category, for there are no such objects as actions-under-specific-descriptions (see Anscombe [1979] 1981).

What thus first appear as two distinct one-dimensional views of one event are, for Hegel, two different sides or aspects of a single *three*-dimensional account comprising the inner, outer and extended (or environmental) aspects of acts. His enactivism thus consists in a holistic understanding of mind and behaviour as two different aspects of one thing that is both embedded within (but also indefinitely extended throughout) the agent's environment. This dynamic interaction between agent and world renders us hostage to luck: a stone thrown is the devil's (*PR*: §119A).[8] To act is to leave traces that stand in a fundamentally different relation to time from the ephemeral events of our producing them, namely, that of being left *on* time rather than occurring *in* it.[9] Any trace left will be imputable to us from *some* perspective, but not from others.

Hegel's writings on action form the roots from which Ricoeur's picture of actions as cubical volumes with inner/outer, surface/foundation and foreground/background perspectives grow (as illustrated in Figure 1, below). Ricoeur models actions on texts whose 'different topics are not on the same altitude' (Ricoeur [1986] 2008: 160). Accordingly, 'the reconstruction of the whole has a perspectivist aspect similar to that of perception' and 'a specific kind of one-sidedness is implied in the act of reading ... what we want to understand is not something hidden behind the text, but something disclosed in front of it' (Ricoeur [1986] 2008: 160).[10]

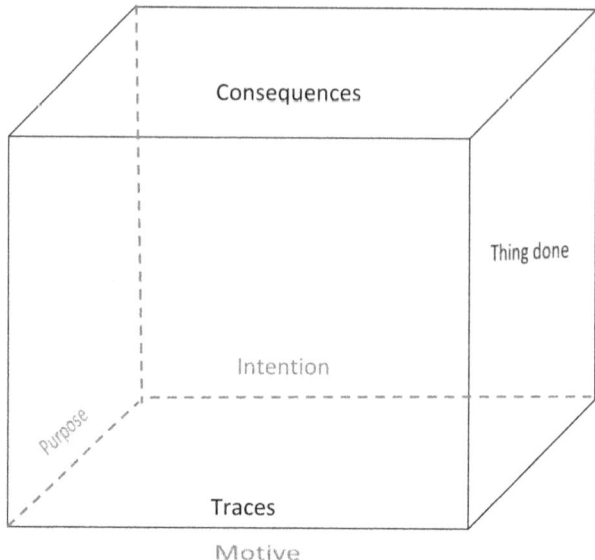

Figure 1 Action Necker Cube (Abstract) © Constantine Sandis.

When we observe someone acting, we typically do not see any one of the previously mentioned ('inner' or 'outer') aspects in isolation.

What we typically see (and react to) is an action *qua* some of its aspects, not any aspect in isolation. Some of the aspects will be at the foreground and others in the background, if not altogether unnoticed. On any given occasion, we may see some action as the expression of a particular intention, the means to achieving a specific goal, the cause of some grave consequence, or the result of some identifiable motive. The motives 'behind' any given action may be all too obvious or an utter mystery. Zooming in, we might view an action (e.g. someone's run on a particular occasion) as the moving of the individual's body ('She's panting!'). Stepping back, we might see the same act as the bringing about of a certain consequence ('She's raising money for a good cause'). When the consequence is intended, the latter description can also give us the agent's reason. When not, it serves to highlight something that the agent is unaware of ('She's left shoe marks').

Taylor ([1983] 2010: §2) puts forth an interpretation of Hegel as a proponent of a 'qualitative conception of action' shared by Anscombe (1957). This is to be contrasted with the more familiar causal one defended by Donald Davidson ([1963] 2001) but associated with Hegel by Knowles (2010) and Brandom (2019). On the latter view, actions are famously seen as 'external' events with an 'internal' cause. According to the qualitative conception, by contrast, agential knowledge is non-observational because 'the agent is the being responsible for the direction of action, the being for whom and through whom action is directed as it is' (Taylor [1983] 2010: 25). Since 'as agents we already have some sense, however dim, inarticulate, or subliminal, of what we are doing', knowledge of our own actions differs from that of external events for it is 'a matter of making articulate what we already have an inarticulate sense of' (Taylor

[1983] 2010: 25). But this misses a key part of Hegel's account; as already noted, actions for Hegel are neither 'internal' nor 'external', but are knowable via either aspect.

In the ideal case, the objective reality of our actions as performed in time will match up to what we set out to do. But things often go wrong, and not just in ways that we couldn't have foreseen. So, while agents have non-observational knowledge of their doings *qua* purpose and intention, ignorance of the external reality of their deeds *cannot* be remedied by making articulate something of which they already have some inarticulate sense of. Here we also find a crucial gulf between Hegelian and Freudian approaches to Greek tragedy. According to the latter, there are no mistakes and all actions performed 'in ignorance' are revelatory of unconscious desire. On the former, by contrast, 'unconsciously committed crimes' (Hegel [1835] 1993 – referred to as *LA* in the sequel – 1219) do not entail subconscious knowledge, intention, or desire, though they must nonetheless be accepted as the fruits of one's wider purpose.[11]

Anscombe approximates Hegel's view in allowing that there can be two ways of knowing one thing, namely, action.[12] For Hegel, however, knowledge of action *qua* purpose is to be contrasted with knowledge of action *qua* objectivity. While he doesn't conceive of these as two distinct ontological categories any more than Anscombe would,[13] he denies that it makes sense to talk of knowledge of action *tout court*. As with a Necker cube, we may bring about an aspect shift in an observer by asking them to see the action one way rather than another, by attending to a particular aspect. This is the case not only with actions occurring before us but equally with any behaviour we may recount and discuss, be it of a personal acquaintance, a character in a novel or something reported in the papers. We find a layered illustration of this in Luke (23.33-4):

> And when they came to the place that is called Calvary, there they crucified him, and the criminals, one on his right and one on his left. And Jesus said, 'Father, forgive them, for they know not what they do.' And they cast lots to divide his garments.[14]

What *were* they doing? What did they *think* they were doing? And what did they ultimately *do*? Had they no practical knowledge whatsoever? And who were 'they' anyhow? It's not my purpose to adjudicate over the historical accuracy of the report, let alone the question of whether 'they' is here intended to refer to 'the chief priests, the leaders, and the people' to whom Pilate has handed Jesus over, or to the Roman soldiers who divide his clothes among themselves.[15] How one answers it will affect which internal aspects of 'what they are doing' are brought to the foreground.

In the former reading, 'they' know that they are handing over Jesus to the Romans to be crucified and that, in so doing, they are condemning him to death.

On the latter (illustrated in Figure 2, below), 'they' know that they are following orders and putting this person (who is said to have claimed to be 'The King of the Jews') to death by nailing him to a cross. The 'internal' aspects of motives, purpose and intention will look rather different when considering the actions of the chief priests versus those of Roman soldiers, while the 'external' ones may remain constant. This is not to say that the two are unrelated, but though *some* key aspects of our doings are an

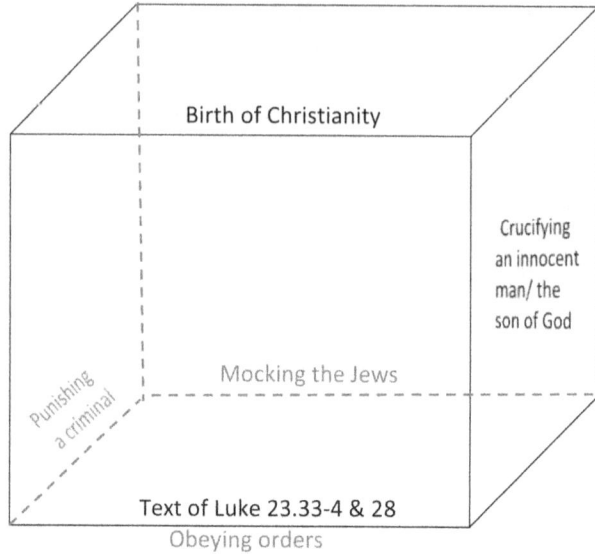

Figure 2 Action Necker Cube (Concrete) © Constantine Sandis.

expression of our motives and intentions, many are not.¹⁶ Either interpretation allows that 'they' can be said to know that they are killing someone. For it would be no excuse to say, 'I only intended to nail him to the cross, the rest was up to fate or God'.¹⁷ More to the point, 'they' don't know that they are giving birth to Christianity and thereby also setting in motion a particular unfolding of history. From within a Christian outlook, they are also killing the innocent Son of God, fulfilling the book, accomplishing God's will and creating the possibility for atonement. So understood, they might equally be forgiven *because* of what they unwittingly do, namely, performing the necessary evil required for the very reconciliation of God and mankind.

Whatever happened on Calvary left its mark on history, but its traces do not form a single track. Each new path gives rise to new ways of describing the original acts. To speak of action as having multiple descriptions and only being intentional under some of them camouflages the fact that this is only true about our doings and not the things we do. Indeed, in intentionally doing or not doing some given thing, one is invariably doing or not doing a number of other things (both intentionally and otherwise),¹⁸ including the leaving or erasing of various traces. Two or more people may even act together with perfect coordination *and* practical success, despite a near-absolute lack of shared motive, purpose or even (in highly comic or tragic scenarios) intention.

It is also commonplace nowadays to talk of acting as the (causal) bringing about of a bodily movement. But neither physical actions (such as standing very still) nor mental ones (such as reciting a poem to oneself) need to involve bodily movements.¹⁹ Moreover, even if we restrict ourselves to those that do, whether they are identical to the bringing about of the bodily movement in question is a moot point. The causal understanding of basic arm raisings as the bringing about of arm risings may be contrasted with a constitutive account according to which the agent, *in* raising her arm, makes it true that her arm rises in the sense that this occurs *in virtue of* her raising it. Such truth-making relations are constitutive rather than causal because, in the ordinary case of arm raising, there is nothing that the agent does in order to bring about her arm's rising; the agent's arm rises *in virtue of* her having raised it, much like a tablecloth is coloured in virtue of its being red. Whenever we act, we make any number of things true and, by the same token, a number of other things false. If to act *is* to leave a trace of some kind, then in acting we make it true that we have left a trace. As we shall see, this is so even when we are engaged in the act of eliminating traces.

2. Traces on time

While the philosophical concept of the trace can be traced at least as far back as Plato's memory impressions [σημεῖα ἐνσημαινομένους] (*Theaetetus* – abbreviated to '*T*' in the sequel – T191d) and their analogue in writing [γραφῆς] (*Phaedrus* (1995) – abbreviated to '*P*' in the sequel – 275a), the history of its historiographical incarnation arguably begins with Hegel's 1822-3 lectures (see Hegel [1837] 2011) and is followed shortly thereafter by Neander ([1826] 1854) and Macaulay (1828).[20] These foundations are built upon by Dilthey ([1860] 1996), Edmunds (1869), Nietzsche ([1874] 1980), Heidegger ([1927] 1962) and Arendt ([1958] 1998), although accounts of 'the trace' don't fully emerge until Levinas (1963, [1972] 2003), Derrida (1967a, b) and Ricoeur ([1985] 1988, [1986] 2008, [2000] 2004).[21]

The question of what makes any given trace *historical* goes hand in hand with that of what demarcates some particular fact as historical. E. H. Carr famously pronounced that 'not all facts about the past are historical facts, or are treated as such by the historian' (Carr 1961: 4). The claim is plausible, but there are no fixed criteria for determining which facts are of historical significance. Carr's own take was that past facts are transformed into historical ones by a process of selection that begins with a proposal for membership, after which they only become established as such if the nomination has been seconded and sponsored by other historians.[22] The view would come under the fire of Geoffrey Elton, who mocks Carr's distinction between facts of the past and historical facts.[23] In its place, Elton puts forward a trace theory of historical facts according to which any past event may count as a historical fact if it has left traces for historians to discover. The study of history is thereby considered to be dependent on the provision of such traces:

> Historical study is not the study of the past but the study of present traces of the past; if men have said, thought, done or suffered anything of which nothing any longer exists, those things are as though they had never been. The crucial element is the present evidence, not the fact of past existence . . . the surviving traces of the past are not confined to material survivals; evidence can to some extent be discovered where it appeared not to exist, and the historian's techniques at times enable him to reconstruct that which is lost from that which is still around. (Elton 1967: 20; cf. 81)

This outlook has more recently been defended by Richard Evans who writes that 'a historical fact is something that happened in history and can be verified as such through the traces history has left behind. Whether or not a historian has actually carried out the act of verification is irrelevant to its factuality: it really is there independently of the historian' (Evans 1997: 76).

It is not factuality that is up for dispute here, however, but what makes any given past fact *historical*. Even Elton must allow that the fact that I just put the kettle on is not (at least for now) a historical fact, no matter what traces I may have left behind. Like past facts, the present traces that provide evidence for them (be they buildings, documents, objects, carpet stains, etc.) can themselves become historical, but what makes them so surely comes down to degrees of interest rather than club membership. To complicate things, the very act of leaving a trace can itself be deemed historical and have that status independently of whether the trace in question remains present; it is sufficient that there exist traces of the traces.

Despite this vast historiographical concern with traces and the rise of action theory from the ashes of philosophy of history, the connection between kinds of everyday action and the leaving of traces has been little explored outside the work of Levinas, Ricoeur and their followers. Levinas writes:

> [T]he trace ... signifies outside of all intention of making a sign and outside of any project that would sight it. When one 'pays by check' in a commercial transaction so as to leave a trace of payment, the trace is inscribed in the very order of the world. However, the authentic trace disturbs the world's order. It is 'superimposed'... the imprint left by the one who wanted to erase his traces in an attempt, for example, to accomplish the perfect crime. The one who left traces while erasing his traces didn't want to say or do anything by the traces he leaves.... His trace does not *signify* his past, as it does not *signify* his labor, or his enjoyment in the world, it *is* disturbance itself (one is tempted to say *engraving*) with irrefutable gravity. (Levinas [1972] 2003: 41–4)

Action traces can be far removed from a person's intention and yet stand as firm evidence of their purpose and, at times, even motive. In Claude Lanzmann's monumental documentary *Shoah*, Holocaust survivor Abraham Bomba recollects that 'they told us to clean the whole place. ... And in no time this was as clean as though people had never been on that place. There was no trace, none at all, like a magic thing, everything disappeared' (Bomba, quoted in Lanzmann 1985: 45). Lanzmann explains that when he started the film he had to deal with the disappearance of the traces and 'make a film on the basis of this nothingness'. He describes the result as an 'originary event' constructed with 'traces of traces' (Lanzmann, as quoted in Liebman 2007: 3–4). These include the traces of Nazi attempts to 'obliterate all traces' of what they had done (de Beauvoir 1985: vii), for example, by planting pines that were three to four years old 'to camouflage all the traces' (Lanzmann [1985] 1995: 10).[24]

So, what is it for a person to leave a trace by acting or, indeed, suffering?[25] And how do traces differ from consequences? We might begin to answer by noting that we *leave* traces but not consequences and that we bring about or *cause* consequences but not traces, though consequences can leave behind traces of their own.[26] To act is, in effect, to leave a trace, even when the action is one of attempting to remove one's former traces. The footprint or fingerprint, stain, smoke, ink mark and so on that we leave are a trace of our action but not a consequence.[27] Traces are fragments of the past that have 'not yet passed away' (Ricoeur [1985] 1988: 77), hence Heidegger's (characteristically overdone) puzzlement over how it is that fragments of the past (e.g. a Greek temple) can remain present-at-hand ([1927] 1962 – referred to as *BT* in the sequel – §§72–7). These traces, be they physical or otherwise, are the vehicles through which that which is no longer may continue to have effects through time.

However, Ricoeur mistakenly identifies the trace with *what* is done and actions as the events of inscribing traces on time. This is because he understands the things we do as marks left on time by the events of our acting, much as the things written are the residual trace of the writing event. I quote from lines surrounding the text of this essay's epigraph:

> What in effect does writing fix? Not the event of speaking but the 'said' of speaking... what we write, what we inscribe, is the noema of the speaking.... It is not the speech *event*, it is speech itself insofar as it is *said*... the detachment of the *meaning* of the action from the *event* of the action.... We speak of marking events. Are there not 'marks' on time, the kind of thing that calls for a reading rather than for a hearing?... In the same way that a text is detached from its author, an action is detached from its agent and develops consequences of its own... our deeds escape us and have effects we did not intend.... Social time, however, is not only something that flees; it is also a place of durable effects, of persisting patterns. An action leaves a 'trace', it makes its 'mark' when it contributes to the emergence of such patterns, which become the documents of human action. (Ricoeur [1986] 2008: 142–9)

On this analogy, the things we do are in some (admittedly metaphorical) sense more permanent than the fleeting events that come and go. In the case of writing, the distinction comes closer to that between a process and its resulting product. The suggestion is that we might, by extension, hold the same to be true of the act of speaking what is spoken and, *a fortiori*, that of the doing and the deed.[28] Ricoeur is aware, however, of the difficulty that, when all is said and done, things imprinted on time itself do remain in the world in the literal way that a text can; even audio-visual recordings are souvenirs of the event itself and not its traces.

Ricoeur thus identifies deeds with action traces, when what we actually do in acting is to *leave* traces. While his characterization of doings as the leaving of traces is an insightful one, he conflates the traces we leave with what we do when we act, namely, leave a trace. The error is fuelled by the fact that the French verb 'faire' is used to denote both making and doing.[29] Crucially, this failure leads to further confusions about the relation of actions to their location and effects in space and time. Inspired by Ricoeur, I have previously stated that 'our deeds are but the ashes of our acts in time'.[30] But this isn't quite right, for what we do in acting is *to leave* traces. The ashes of one's life, then, are not one's deeds *per se* but only their results.

Ricoeur's ontology of action connects with Jennifer Hornsby's way of framing the distinction as one between (i) the spatio-temporally located events of our doing things and (ii) the things we do, the latter admitting to being done by different agents across more than one location or occasion, including the possible future (as in Lenin's *What is to be Done*?). Hornsby writes:

> The word 'action' is ambiguous. Where it has a plural: in ordinary usage what it denotes, nearly always, are the things people do; in philosophical usage, what it denotes, very often, are events, each one of them some person's doing something. (Hornsby [1993b] 1997: 142)

And, before her, John Macmurray wrote:

> The term 'action' is involved in the same ambiguity [as] terms like 'perception' or 'conception'. It may refer either to what is done or to the doing of it... either 'doing' or 'deed'. When we talk of an action we are normally referring to what is done. (Macmurray 1938: 74–6)

My own two cents is that in everyday English, the locution 'thing done' is ambiguous between the two senses of action that Hornsby and Macmurray distinguish. The context is usually sufficient for us to know what was meant; we understand expressions such as 'the hardest thing I ever did', 'look what you did' and 'see what I did there?' as easily as we understand assertions like 'the soup is always great at Gino's', 'tonight's soup is very good' and 'your soup looks nicer than mine, I wonder if you got a fresher batch'.

Whatever the linguistic facts, there is conceptual space for Hornsby's ([1993b] 1997) distinction between particular doings and repeatable things that you and I might both do.[31] Unsurprisingly, we find competing ontologies of doings and things done in the literature, with little consensus on whether the former are particulars, events, processes, instances of relations and so on, and the latter universals, types, results, products and so on. For example, Prichard ([1932] 2004), von Wright (1963: 39) and Charles (2018) conceive of the thing done as the bodily event that action results in. But one does not 'do' any bodily movements that one's actions may result in. Rather, *in* acting, one makes it the case that any such bodily movements occur.[32] *What* we do when we act, then, is make certain things true. Leaving traces is making it the case that traces are left, even if we don't typically do so knowingly. While we can act with the specific purpose of leaving certain traces if we so please, our control of them diminishes over time, if not always quite as rapidly as it did for poor Hansel and Gretel.[33]

When we deliberate about any given course of action, we typically consider it from the point of view of our purpose and, should we go forward with it, intention. This directedness does not preclude us from considering what the likely consequences might be or from pondering about the motive we'd be acting from, but it is our purpose that ultimately keeps everything else in check. In the present moment, by contrast, actions are typically encountered from the point of view of what one is doing and its immediate consequences. We often can't help but see the action as motivated by certain concerns, but at other times, we make an inference to the same effect. In acting, we move from considering things we *could do* to engaging ourselves in the process of doing them. After the fact, we can look back at the events (or incomplete processes) of our acting from the point of view, not just of their consequences, but also of their more general spatio-temporal situation. The further past an action is, the wider this context becomes, and the more likely we are to begin from distant traces and work backward. While we can *try* to consider action from as many points of view as possible, we cannot do so from all of them simultaneously. Instead, we switch our attention from one aspect to another and try to form a fuller picture. Actions contain multitudes, but there is no view outside of space and time from which we can encounter any given act through all its different aspects. That is the paradox of action.

3. Rightness and responsibility

The epistemic perspectivism (or lack of absolute standpoint) of action has implications for moral worth, luck and responsibility. We have already seen that a person may have knowledge of action *qua* some things and not *qua* others. Pari passu, they can be held responsible for them from, say, the point of view of intention without being responsible from the point of view of knowledge, let alone objectivity. Arto Laitinen and I have defended the view that this is the best way to make sense of the tension between Hegel's claims that (i) agents have the right to be held responsible *only* for those aspects of their deed that were in fact included in their conscious purpose, intention, or foresight (i.e. their actions) and yet (ii) are responsible not only for such actions but also for what *should* have been foreseen in the circumstances (namely, what *would have* been by a thinking agent).[34]

On this interpretation, the various aspects of right are the conceptual apparatus through which Hegel is able to make fine-grained moral judgements. As such, they mirror various combinations of subjective and/or objective aspects of action. Accordingly, the accountability of one who is guilty of failing to foresee certain consequences may be mitigated by their right of knowledge, and that of one who foresees (but does not intend) certain unfortunate consequences, by their right of intention. Such rights are real but not absolute; the full picture is determined by their interplay with other rights.

While Hegel's primary concern is to mark out different scopes of responsibility, he allows that one's action may be wrong *qua* deed but morally worthy *qua* intended action. For example, Oedipus acts rightly but (through bad luck) does the wrong thing. This preserves both the Kantian intuition that moral worth is not a matter of incident or resultant luck and the opposing view that what we end up doing is a matter of luck to the extent that it wasn't intended or rationally foreseeable.[35] Bernard Williams is thus only half right when he states that 'the aim of making morality immune to luck is bound to be disappointed' for the reason that it is 'deeply and disquietingly subject to luck'.[36] The objective aspects of action are not the whole story. As E. R. Dodds puts it:

> Suppose a motorist runs down a man and kills him, I think he ought to feel that he has done a terrible thing, even if the accident is no fault of his: he has destroyed a human life, which nothing can restore. In the objective order it is

his acts that count, not intentions. A man who has violated that order may well
feel a sense of guilt, however blameless his driving. (Dodds 1966: 183–4)[37]

To kill an innocent man is a terrible thing to do, but the unlucky motorist has not acted terribly in doing so. What about the inverse scenario in which the motorist is imprudent but doesn't run anybody over? The worst thing that this second driver does (namely, risking killing somebody with his reckless driving) is, in the objective order of things, not nearly as bad as the worst thing that the prudent but unlucky motorist does (kill an innocent man). Yet it is the second driver who acts wrongly. The wrongness here is not simply a matter of what they do (as in the case of an otherwise prudent driver who has unwittingly ingested a drug) but of their very doing of it.[38] The problem of moral luck as traditionally conceived is thus a product of the confused standard line that '[w]hen we say that *what he did* was wrong we mean that *he acted wrongly*' (Bennett 1995: 46, emphasis added).[39] Steven Sverdlik tries to improve the latter by suggesting that the moral properties (or at least deontic ones) of the things we do are dependent on our motives for doing them:

> There is an action X such that if X were performed from one motive it would fall into one deontic category and if X were performed from another motive it would fall into a second deontic category in virtue of these differences in motives. (Sverdlik 2011: 4; Cf. O'Neil 2013: 223ff.)

But if a deed can be performed from different motives, it cannot be that deed itself that ever belongs to a deontic category, only the performing of it from a certain motive.[40] The same is true for many cases of intention. Moreover, one can act wrongly with the best of intentions, even if the doing isn't intentional under the infraction-highlighting description. For instance, a white person's styling their hair as dreadlocks or cornrows may count as an instance of cultural appropriation, however benevolent their intention. To condemn them straight out for this would be to ignore what might be more virtuous aspects of their action – for example, they were seeking to pay tribute to another culture, or express solidarity with a specific group of people. But this does not *in itself* expunge them from the accusation that they could and should have known better.

It might be objected, at this point, that moral and legal philosophy already have at their disposal all the tools they need to deal with such cases. After all, they have a long history of distinguishing between intention and (mere) foresight, motive and consequence, recklessness and negligence, and so on. The problem is not with the distinctions themselves but with the uses they are put to. It is asked whether the rightness of an action depends on the motive or its consequences; it is asked whether or not morality is a matter of luck; and it is asked what the conditions for moral responsibility are, and how they differ from those of causal responsibility. These are all symptoms of an absolutist approach to action that fails to do justice to the proper structure of all its aspects. At the very least, normative theories owe us more detail about the sort of thing actions must be if they are to have the kinds of moral properties ascribed to them. It is no good to simply say that they are events that are intentional under some description or processes that progress across time.

Epilogue

To praise or blame people solely on the grounds of what they did or didn't do is to give in to what we might call the obituary view of moral appraisal.[41] Obituaries typically provide embellished lists of successes and failures – for example, she founded a charity, directed two Oscar-winning documentaries, wrote an influential book. Indeed, the very chronology of peoples' lives is typically offered as a sort of list of things done at various moments in time. This is the action event as fact:[42] she was born at t_1, went to school A at t_2–t_5, studied subject X at university B, graduating at t_6, took a job working for firm C at t_7 and so on. There is no attempt to reveal actions as three-dimensional objects whose 'inner' and 'outer' aspects unfold in time and whose traces persist long after the fleeting event has come and gone. Ronald Dworkin writes that the 'final value of our lives is adverbial, not adjectival' (Dworkin 2011: 197).[43] His view is the mirror contrast of that which Parfit would end up offering in *On What Matters*, according to which all that ultimately matters is what one achieves and not how one comes to do so. I have tried to show both doings and deeds matter in different objective and subjective respects. There is no competition between them, nor is there any sense in which it makes sense to ask whether someone was responsible for an action *tout court*. This is the hardest lesson to learn because the impetus comes to us so naturally.

2

What is it to do nothing?

People's actions, I know, are for the most part the things they do — but mine are all the things I don't do.

Gabriel Nash in Henry James's, *The Tragic Muse*

If you have nothing to do, please do not do it here.

Bengali 'no loitering' sign

What is action, what is non-action? Even inspired seers are confused about this [. . .] He who sees action in non-action, non-action in action, is wise among men.

Bhagavad Gītā, IV: 16, 18[*]

Prologue

For good reason, people are generally not very forgiving of the sort of behaviour captured in the following *Daily Mirror* headline:

> Tory MP *forgot* to declare £400k income, but *remembered* to claim 49p for milk . . . Geoffrey Cox *neglected* to *declare* his bumper payday within 28 days – but in the meantime he *put claims* in for milk and tea bags. (*Daily Mirror*, 4 February 2016)

We have no pre-theoretical problem grasping what it is to forget or neglect to do something and may sometimes judge the latter more harshly than the former. But we begin to lose our confidence as soon as we start asking ourselves in what sense neglectful behaviour counts as *action*. Is it a doing of something or a mere lack or absence, namely, a nothing? And isn't being responsible for nothing the same as not being responsible for anything at all? If I do something, such as send you an email, then it is not unreasonable to hold me responsible for what I did. But if *what* I did was nothing, does it follow that I am responsible for nothing? If so, then complete non-action would lay us off all hooks of responsibility. But this cannot be right, at least not for cases where there is a relevant sense in which I could have done something, but didn't. We are frequently right to hold people responsible for doing nothing. There

---

[*] W. J. Johnson translation (Oxford Publishing Limited, 1994). Reproduced with permission of the Licensor through PLSclear.

is an apparent asymmetry here that would be problematic if real: when we act we are responsible for what we do, whereas when we do nothing we are not responsible for *what* we do (namely, nothing) but for *doing* it.

It is tempting to think that the puzzle arises because of linguistic oddities of our negative pronouns, such as 'nothing' and 'nobody'. If so, then perhaps there is no serious worry here, just fodder for clever wordplay:

> 'Cyclops', I said, 'you ask my name. I'll tell it to you; and in return give me the gift you promised me. My name is Nobody . . .
>
> The Cyclops answered me from his cruel heart. 'Of all his company I will eat Nobody last, and the rest before him. That shall be your gift' . . .
>
> I went at once and thrust our pole deep under the ashes of the fire . . . drove its sharpened end into the Cyclops' eye. Hearing his screams they came up from every quarter . . . 'What on earth is wrong with you Polyphemus?' . . .
>
> 'O my friends, it's Nobody's treachery, not violence, that is doing me to death'.
>
> 'Well then', came the immediate reply, 'if you are alone and nobody is assaulting you, you must be sick.' (Homer, *The Odyssey*: 119–21)[1]
>
> 'Just look along the road, and tell me if you can see either of them.'
>
> 'I see nobody on the road', said Alice.
>
> 'I only wish I had such eyes', the King remarked in a fretful tone. 'To be able to see Nobody! And at the distance too!' (Carroll 1871)

We may of course think that something serious lurks behind these jokes, perhaps some awful paradox that takes us to the core of metaphysical psychology. Think of Funes the Memorious, who quite literally forgets nothing in the eponymous story by Jorge Luis Borges, or of Oliver Sacks' patient Rose R, who explains in great depth how she goes about thinking about both 'positive' and 'negative' nothings.[2] As the stranger in Plato's *Sophist* puts it (238d): '[T]he nonexistent reduces even one who is refuting its claims to such straits that, as soon as he sets about doing so, he is forced to contradict himself.' And so it is that Martin Heidegger famously asks:

> However, what trouble do we take concerning this nothing? The nothing is rejected precisely by science, given up as a nullity. But when we give up the nothing in such a way do we not concede it? Can we, however, speak of concession when we concede nothing? But perhaps our confused talk already degenerates into an empty squabble over words. The nothing – what else can it be for science but an outrage and a phantasm? Science wants to know nothing of the nothing. (Heidegger [1929] 1977: 96)

Either way, it may seem that whatever difficulties we encounter will have little to do with the philosophy of action and we must take a more general approach to overcoming them. Perhaps the problem isn't so much a linguistic one about the word 'nothing' but an ontological one about absences in general, of the sort evoked by Tyron Goldschmidt's 'A Demonstration of the Causal Power of Absences' (Goldschmidt 2016), whose 'content' is identical to Dennis Upper's 1974 paper 'The Unsuccessful Self-Treatment of a Case of "Writer's Block"'. An absence of action, in such a case, would be no different from other absences, such as those of people. If so, then whatever approach we take to their causes and effects should form part of a more general strategy. The simplest, and perhaps the most popular since Parmenides denied that we can sensibly speak of the void, is that of David Lewis (2004: 283): 'Absences are spooky things, and we'd do best not to take them seriously. But absences of absences are no problem.'[3]

The things we do include doing 'doing nothing', but we must not confuse this activity with that of doing no thing at all. Whether or not something counts as doing some particular thing – or, indeed, doing nothing – depends on what we are contrasting it with. But there is no thing called 'inaction' that we do when we are said to be doing nothing. *What* we don't do is – ontologically speaking – on a par with what we could or should have done.[4] So one thing I won't do in what follows is to indulge in thought concerning the absence of action.

The puzzle we began with, it shall transpire, has less to do with such matters and more to do with different conceptions of action. The question of whether negative actions are ontologically distinct from positive ones makes sense only as a question about doings and not things done. While doings may have both positive and negative descriptions, it makes no sense to conceive of things done in a similar fashion. We do, of course, talk loosely of being responsible for the things we do; this is but a colloquial way of expressing responsibility for our doings. Mutatis mutandis, when we do nothing, what we are responsible for is not *nothing* but *doing* nothing. The same goes for omitting, refraining, and so on.

The literature on negative actions or inactions fails to make proper use of the distinction between *what* one does and one's act of *doing* it. This is partly explained by the sorry truth that most philosophers working in normative ethics have little interest in the philosophy of action per se. Although what follows focuses on 'negative actions', it forms part of this book's wider plea for taking the philosophy of action more seriously when carrying out normative and practical ethics.

1. Inaction in action

Jeremy Bentham introduces the term 'negative acts' as follows:

> Acts . . . may be distinguished, in the first place, into positive and negative. By positive (acts) are meant such as consist in motion or exertion: by negative, such as consist in keeping at rest; that is, in forbearing to move or exert oneself in such and such circumstances. Thus, to strike is a positive act: not to strike on a certain occasion, a negative one. Positive acts are styled also acts of commission; negative, acts of omission or forbearance. (Bentham 1789: 72)[5]

Eric D'Arcy offers a plausible objection to the belief that the conditions Bentham offers are sufficient, although he doesn't question their necessity. To the question, 'What were you doing at two o'clock this afternoon?' any of the following could be appropriate replies: 'Taking a siesta', 'Relaxing in an arm-chair', 'Sun-bathing', 'Sitting for a portrait', 'Waiting for the Carfax traffic lights to change', 'Being X-rayed', 'Getting my hair cut', 'Sitting in Whitehall in Civil Disobedience', 'Hunger-striking'. Each of these replies would satisfy Bentham's definition of an omission as physical non-movement, keeping at rest; however, we should not call any of them an omission. Bentham's criterion is no doubt a negative necessary condition for an omission, but it is not a sufficient one.[6]

I return to why even the 'negative necessary condition' is problematic in due course. In preparation, it is worth examining Gilbert Ryle's use of 'negative "acts"' to refer to what he characterized as the 'intentional non-performance of some specifiable actions' (Ryle 1973: 81). His own list of examples is curious, at best:

This class of negative 'acts' (if they are acts) includes *refraining, abstaining, postponing, shirking, neglecting, disobeying, overlooking, condoning, forgiving, acquiescing, ignoring, idling, pausing, resting, hesitating, omitting, enduring, waiting, remaining, permitting, letting, keeping* (still or *a secret*), *holding* (one's tongue), *sparing, economising, relinquishing, yielding, relying, trusting*. (Ryle 1973: 81–2; emphasis in original)

One puzzling thing about Ryle's list is that many of his own examples are not obviously ever intentional (forgetting, overlooking, hesitating), while many others seem like obvious examples of negative 'acts' regardless of intention (neglecting, ignoring, pausing, yielding, remaining, etc.).[7] Another is that acts of forgiveness and trust are prima facie not negative at all. We must of course distinguish the actions of expressing trust or forgiveness from the trust or forgiveness expressed, but to the extent that the latter can be said to be acts, they can be accorded a positive status. Presumably, Ryle believes that to forgive is to let go of a grudge or refrain from resenting and to trust to refrain from suspect, but one could equally think that to grudge is to fail to forgive and to suspect is to refrain from trusting.

We here have no obvious criterion for determining which description is the positive one and which the negative. Where there is action there is always inaction, and vice versa; hence, the twist on the old adage, 'don't just do something, stand there!'[8] and Schopenhauer's insistence that it is evil which has positive existence in the world, good being nothing more than its negation (Schopenhauer 1851). Philosophy treats the question of the relation of action to omission as a metaphysical problem to be solved with clever thinking and distinctions. But we must not shun the truth in perspectivism concerning what is positive and what is not.

Contrasting views on this are considered by the protagonist of Ian McEwan's *The Children Act*.[9] Fiona Maye is a judge who views her ruling on a past medical case as a condemnation of action by omission – killing a twin by refusing to separate it, thereby 'obliterating the potential of a meaningful life' (McEwan 2014: 29). Those who subsequently send her death threats, by contrast, see her as condoning *neglect* by *action*: *ignoring* but equally *interfering with* both God's will and the interests of the other twin, in advocating for the exercise of active separation. Fiona's recollection of all this is neatly juxtaposed with a personal choice she has to make between *saving* her marriage by *accepting* an affair and *ending* it by *denouncing* it; her husband questions which one of them would be wrecking the marriage if she took the latter course (McEwan 2014: 22). Indeed, the novel is replete with characters who remain standing, say nothing, refuse treatment, give up, conceal, forget, let go and so on, but in so doing are also said to be doing favours, acting kindly, taking risks, and committing suicide. Factual conceptions of positive and negative actions are shown to be deeply intermingled with evaluative ones:

> Berner's client was... a somewhat dreamy young man whose chief fault was a degree of *passivity*. And a *failure to keep* appointments... the father... was mostly *absent* from Wayne's childhood, which was one of chaos and *neglect*.... She *never hit* him ... he *missed* a lot of school. He *left* at sixteen ... *never claimed* unemployment ... the police *declined to investigate*. (McEwan 2014: 184–5; emphasis added)[10]

A third, connected oddity with Ryle's examples is that many of them don't seem to be cases of acts at all (e.g. forgetting, trusting). Indeed, Ryle's choice of examples betrays the fact that neither action nor intention is necessarily required for responsibility. This is not to say that their presence makes no moral difference, but *that* question shall not detain us here.[11] What Ryle's examples actually mark is that there is a difference between merely not doing something and either *failing* to do or deliberately avoiding doing it. What is not done, in such cases, is something one was – for better or worse – expected to do, in some weakly normative sense. My not having finished this essay by a deadline imposed by myself or others is thus a negative doing in a sense in which my not having read the entire works of Jackie Collins isn't. As Kent Bach puts it (2010: 50): '[T]here is not much point in asking what it is not to do any of the countless things that you could conceivably be doing.' Bach and Ryle both maintain that negative 'doings' such as those listed by Ryle are not actions proper.[12] In this they are opposed not only by me, but also by Brand, Danto, Davidson and Goldman,[13] all of whom mark the difference(s) between merely not doing something and acting 'negatively' in one or more of the following ways:

Not *doing* φ vs. doing *not-*φ
Not doing φ vs. *not-*φ*-ing*
Intending not to φ vs. Intending to not-φ[14]

Thus, for example, Brand writes (1971: 46): 'The difference between refraining from performing an action and doing nothing at all with respect to performing an action is that, basically, refraining is itself a kind of action, but doing nothing at all is just doing nothing at all. The patrol man does something, namely, not shooting the fleeing youth.' Similarly, Davidson (1985b: 217–18) writes: 'One of the things I have done is fail to discuss the problem'; '[n]ot eating a persimmon is something I did.' On Brand's view, the difference between the two kinds of cases is one of intention, but we have already seen that this doesn't cut at any helpful joints. Davidson and

Vermazen, by contrast, simply apply the Davidsonian vision of actions as events caused by rationalizing belief-desire pairs. It is debatable whether either account can capture things like forgetting, but so much the worse for forgetting one might think. A tougher problem for both views is that we may wonder when exactly these negative events are meant to occur. Ryle presents the difficulty as follows (1973: 89): 'A person who, hearing that the friend had for years never blabbed the secret, now asks "How many blabbings did the friend not commit?" would be asking as ludicrous a question as "How many inhabitants does the desert island not contain?" There is no counting what is not there.' Vermazen, in turn, responds with an example of a man who is meant to do something at precisely 2 a.m. but fails to do so because he has fallen asleep: '[T]he omission took place when he was asleep' (Vermazen 1985: 97).

Perhaps the right thing to conclude from all this is that *some* negative 'actions' (such as failing to do something at a particular time) may sensibly be said to have a spatio-temporal occurrence while others (such as not telling a secret) do not. But Ryle's worry is not merely temporal. In promising to not do something, for example, I don't promise to perform some act of *not-doing*, be it at some or at no particular time. There are, in any case, independent reasons for doubting that qualifying for the former is a necessary condition of being an action.[15] More obviously, having a spatio-temporal location cannot be a sufficient condition of being an action, for all sorts of events occur that are not even contenders for being actions.[16]

This brings us to a bone of contention that divides those who think that negative actions exist into two distinct camps. The first maintains that negative actions are distinct events from positive ones: '[W]e must commit ourselves to at least some negative act-tokens: things like S's *not* turning his head (at *t*) or S's not raising his hand (at *t*) have as much claim to be considered basic act tokens as their positive counterparts' (Goldman 1970: 47).[17] By contrast, the second takes the negativeness of an action to be a matter of description and not of ontology: '[N]egative events do not, strictly speaking, exist' (Vermazen 1985: 100). Moreover, 'even when a negative act exists, being negative is not a characteristic of the act but of the *characterization* of the act' (Davidson 1985b: 219).

This division brings the first set unexpectedly closer to Bach (who is happy to talk of negative events but not actions) than they are to those who agree with them that negative actions exist, but deny that they are distinct events.

The debate is curious, for each side has come up with convincing examples of both (a) negative 'actions' that cannot be re-described in positive terms and (b) ones that can. For example, my neglecting to send a birthday card to my mother need not be identical with some positive action (such as punishing her or taking a risk). At least it need not have positive descriptions under which the doing is *intentional*, for it will always be possible for one's not doing something to be re-described as their contravening some code or other, annoying someone, marking some statistical truth or whatever. By contrast, someone's not buying a Kit-Kat may on some particular occasion be correctly re-described as their deliberately boycotting Nestlé and on some other as an instance of their adhering to veganism (vegan Kit-Kats notwithstanding). Some negative 'actions' have distinct existences from positive ones, and others do not.

It matters not here whether the former (e.g. boycotting) are *actions*, but that they are doings with both a positive and a negative description.

2. To do or not to do

We contrast acting to a number of things not mentioned so far including thinking, speaking, sitting and standing still. But, while one may say, in one register, things like 'actions speak louder than words' or 'thought causes action', this can hardly be taken to disprove that there are such things as speech-acts or mental acts. To ask whether omissions, for example, are actions is like asking whether sitting still or thinking is an action. The correct response is: 'It depends why you're asking'. To this extent, the question also resembles that of 'Are ice and steam both water?', though unlike water, actions are not candidates for natural kinds. As with the difference between action and inaction, we think of sitting down as both a case of something one does and a case of doing nothing. When one confesses to have 'done nothing all day', this is a figure of speech rather than the favoured 'strict-speak' of philosophers; but is talk of doing nothing ever *not* a figure of speech?

It is helpful here to consider the reception of Harvey Sacks's ethnomethodology in David Velleman's work on action. Sacks's work points to the range of things a person might consider doing as culturally constructed in the weak sense that there are various 'doables' (to use Velleman's term) that are only open to us conceptually because of the culture we inhabit: zoning out in front of the TV, hailing a cab, checking email, going to the cinema, cheating on one's taxes, preparing an anniversary meal, waiting for the bus, reading the Sunday papers, as well as brokering, joyriding, sulking, window-shopping, pub crawling, hustling, jiving and so on.

According to Sacks, one of the things we might do is *being* a certain way: 'Among the ways you go about doing "being an ordinary person" is to spend your time in usual ways, having usual thoughts, usual interests' (Sacks 1984: 415). In all these cases, we are not pretending but taking on a culturally identifiable role, project or action. Velleman suggests that one can do *being* a certain way by doing things that count as *ways* of being so: '[T]here are ordinary ways of doing "being bored" – flipping unseeingly through an old magazine or staring unhungrily into the fridge – and when you are bored, you do it in one of those ways. . . .What we call taking an action is actually making an action, by enacting some act description or concept' (Velleman 2014: 1–4).

One thing that we might do, on such a picture, is *doing nothing*. In this case, what one does or sets out to do is not nothing but the doing of nothing. To literally do *nothing* is to not do *any* thing, including *doing nothing*. The doing of doing nothing, by contrast, is the doing of something (namely, doing nothing). This could be a serious matter taking the form of an act of resistance, a way of punishing someone or a mere game one is playing.

We can similarly play at sitting still, not smiling, or staying silent for as long as we can. Here *what* one is doing is not doing nothing but not doing some particular thing. Failing to shoot is different from doing *not shooting*. Variations on the theme of doing *not doing something* may include a sponsored silence, a hunger strike, a boycott. . . . The primary activity in vegan restaurants is that of *not eating animal-based products*.

Similarly, in Carrie Fisher's autobiographical book *Postcards from the Edge*, what the rehab clinic inhabitants mainly focus on is not so much *not* doing drugs as *doing* not drugs:

> Drug addicts without drugs are experts on not doing drugs. I talked to this girl Irene at lunch who's been here two weeks, and she said that in the beginning your main activity is a nonactivity in that you simply don't do drugs. That's what we're all doing here: *Not Drugs* . . . Roger and Colin . . . They *really* know how to not do drugs now. (Fisher 1987: 7, 10, 12)

The narrator and other characters spend thirty days talking and thinking of such things as *using up all the Not Cry, quitting, stopping, giving it up, committing to not doing drugs, not playing an instrument* and *almost doing something*. One of them describes herself as 'a failed anorexic' to a date who's done some reading on Zen:

> Of course, if you go by Zen it always comes down to, "I could make the movie, or not." That whole "or not" thing. It's like, how many Buddhists does it take to screw in a light bulb? Fourteen – seven to do it, and seven not to. (Fisher 1987: 78–9)

By contrast, someone who just happens to be eating an apple, or is just not eating, or not doing drugs at all, is not *doing* not eating animal-based products or not taking drugs. Procrastination is another case in point: one thing I am doing when I am cleaning the house is 'not writing my paper'. This is a very different phenomenon from when I am (simply) not writing my paper because I am in the middle of lecturing. It is similarly possible to be *doing* avoiding, ignoring, refraining, neglecting and so on, although once we reach *doing forgetting*, we will have traversed from enacting to pretending.

Most cases of refraining and neglecting are *not* cases of *doing* these things, in the sense carved out by Sacks and Velleman. To build upon these negative beginnings of a taxonomy of 'inaction', we need to introduce the distinction between *what* one does and (the process or event of) one's *doing* – a distinction which has remained implicit throughout my discussion so far. I moved from talk of actions as *doings* in §1 to talk of them as *doables* in this section. The former, Anscombe and Davidson taught us, can have numerous descriptions. This renders plausible the supposition that a so-called negative act, for example, one's delaying or refraining from doing something may (but need not) be identical to one's doing something else. Such acts may be intentional under both descriptions, or not, and it is not always obvious which it is. Hamlet's notorious delay in exacting his revenge on Claudius, for example, has been described as 'the very attempt to organize one's life through inaction' despite the fact that 'Hamlet himself does not know why he hesitates' (Zamir 2007: 170–1).

Both Anscombe and Davidson casually switch between descriptions of *what* one did and ones of (the event or process of)[18] their doing it.[19] But suppose that we both pump water on different occasions and that *my* pumping the water – but *not yours* – can be described as poisoning the inhabitants. In such a case, there is no answer to the question of whether what we did (namely, pump the water) can be described as poisoning the inhabitants.

Davidson develops an argument for why we need not postulate entities such as things done, maintaining that all our talk of them only requires to quantify over events that are our *doings*, under some description.[20] I shall not argue directly against this project here,[21] but aim to nonetheless show that distinguishing between the things we do and the events of our doing them serves as a better guide through the various puzzles we have encountered concerning negative 'actions'.

The distinction between the *things we do* ('doables' in a sense not unrelated to that of Velleman) and our *acts of doing* them ('doings') is intended to be at least partly analogous to that between things we perceive, believe, or say and so on, and our perceiving, believing or saying them.[22] The most influential way of capturing it is that of Jennifer Hornsby. While the precise details of her view have evolved over the years, the following serves well as a clear statement of how it relates to the thesis that whether or not an action is intentional is a matter of description:

> Actions are particulars – unrepeatable things, named by phrases like 'Hyam's setting light to the petrol at two o'clock on the fateful day', and 'my reading this paper now', *Something done*, on the other hand, is not a particular: things done are named by phrases like 'inflict damage', or 'eat an egg', or 'throw a brick' . . . a person's doing one thing may be the same as her doing another thing . . . when a person does two things, she may do one intentionally and the other not intentionally . . . someone who inflicts damage by throwing a brick, might throw the brick intentionally, but not inflict damage intentionally. (Hornsby 1993a: 56)[23]

Hornsby is here explicitly stating that doables are not actions, even once we have done them. We should not get too distracted by whether she is right to reserve the term 'action' in this way.[24] What matters is that there is a relevant distinction to be made, whatever the correct nominal and ontological details. The point is that there can be one act of one's doing two different things and that different descriptions apply to the former, but not the latter.[25] Across two consecutive footnotes, Hornsby adds: '[T]he things – that agents do – unlike actions, are themselves as finely discriminated as (interpreted) descriptions of actions . . . where an agent does one thing in or by doing another, her doing the one thing is (identical with) her doing the other, so that "doing the one thing" and "doing the other" both apply to her action' (Hornsby 1993a: 56). It is only our do*ings* – and not our do*ables* – that are open to various descriptions. This may sound deeply counter-intuitive to some. Could we not, after all, describe what someone does as inflicting damage? It is certainly true that one can inflict damage in, say, throwing a stone at a window. But the former is not a description of the latter. Rather, we have one act of a person doing several things, only one of which is the infliction of damage.

In the case of 'negative acts', this requires distinguishing between doings that are *not-doings*, such as my neglecting, omitting, allowing, failing, doing *doing nothing* and so on (things that may – but need not – be identical with positive doings) and *what* I do in such cases, namely, neglect, omit, *do nothing*, and so on. In none of these cases is *what* I do a nothing or an absence. What I do in such cases must also be distinguished from *things-not-done*, such as those things that I fail to do, or otherwise refrain from doing. Such things are not weird, they are the very things that I would have done had I not been neglectful, forgetful, on strike and so on – namely, wash up the dishes, finish the paper and go to work. The things we fail to do or avoid doing are the doables we might have done, such as 'the exercises we list without doing'.[26]

3. Puzzles of responsibility

I have been arguing, inter alia, against the thought that there is an interest-free ontological distinction to be made between so-called positive and negative actions. If this is right, then it is a mistake to appeal to such a distinction when introducing philosophical doctrines and puzzles concerning responsibility or blame for omissions, inadvertent action, negligence and so on. Accordingly, I maintain that there is no generalizable moral difference between doing some harm and allowing some harm to happen. In this I am in agreement with O. H. Green:

> Moral generalisations such that it is worse to kill than to let die stand almost no chance of being true and in any case cannot be founded on such irrelevancies as the presence or absence of bodily movements. Simply to deny the importance of the distinction between killing and letting die, on the other hand, is to show gross moral insensitivity to actual cases. (Green 1980: 195–204)[27]

To cause a harm cannot be the same thing as to allow that very same harm to happen, but this is a truism from which nothing of any ontological or moral interest follows. For whatever else we do in allowing a particular harm to happen may be morally worse than causing the harm itself. To give an example: someone might hit their own child or stand back and allow someone else to do it. It is easy to imagine cases of the latter scenario where what ones does, in allowing another to hit one's child, is morally worse than doing so oneself. One might object that the harm *you* do to your child by letting, say, a stranger hit them, is psychologically (and thus also) worse than any harm you might have done by hitting them yourself, but this just shows the oddity of trying to compare harms that have been completely detached from action in the first place.

Consequentialists are thus right to be sceptical of the doctrine of doing and allowing, though not because of any purported truth in consequentialism. Consider four people eating the same green salad for dinner. One does so because she is not very hungry, having had suckling pig for lunch, the other because she is vegan 'for the animals', the third because he is fasting, and the fourth because she is vegetarian 'for our children's environment'. Who is responsible for what? Some of the details will undoubtedly depend on further (causal) truths. But we can agree, a priori, that their common refrainment from eating meat has very different positive descriptions to the point where each might deem the other's omission as immoral, despite the consequences of their particular isolated – perhaps even aggregated – doings being identical.

There are good reasons for not wishing to restrict responsibility for our actions to those done knowingly or intentionally.[28] The mere fact that an act or omission was *ours* is sufficient for us to take on some qualified responsibility for it. As Bernard Williams puts it, 'in the story of life there is an authority exercised by what one has done, and not merely by what one has intentionally done' (Williams 1993: 69).[29] If even the cautious driver is *in some sense* responsible, it would be perverse to free the negligent driver from all responsibility, on the grounds that negligence is an omission. All this is typically thought to be compatible with the view that blameworthiness progressively decreases from acting purposefully to acting (merely) knowingly, acting recklessly and acting negligently (the last of these characterized by a *lack* of awareness to the risk of wrong).[30] Such gradation relies on the assumption that we can assign blameworthiness for an action tout court, as opposed to blameworthiness *qua* one or more of its aspects. This assumption is one of the main targets of Hegel's *Philosophy of Right*.[31]

Arto Laitinen and I have argued elsewhere that we would do better to follow Hegel in asking not whether we are responsible tout court for any given act, but whether we are responsible for any given act *qua* intention, *qua* purpose, *qua* knowledge, *qua* objectivity and so on.[32] Thus, for example, if a surgeon foresees that she will most likely cause her patient some pain even though she is doing her best not to, she is responsible for doing so *qua* – what Hegel terms 'the right of'– knowledge and objectivity, but not *qua* intention or purpose. Things get complicated once we introduce passive descriptions of our doings. It would take a whole page to offer a decent overview of just the actions of the four salad-eaters, earlier. If I unintentionally offend you in my purposefully eating a plant-based meal, I am responsible for doing so *qua* objectivity,[33] but not *qua* knowledge or intention. Whether I have done so *qua* purpose is trickier and depends on whether I could have achieved my overall goal in some other way (e.g. by eating shrimp). We may wish to supplement the Hegelian panoply by adding a right of *negligence* that I am accountable towards, even if I get lucky and you happen not to be offended.[34]

Negligence is unwitting (namely, lacking relevant knowledge and intention) by definition, even when, in acting negligently, we are doing something else intentionally.[35] Negligent conduct thus includes both 'positive' actions and omissions.[36] An example of the former kind would be feeding the wrong kind of food to my cat. The latter kind of negligence is meant to be particularly negative, owing to the combination of unwittingness and omission. Ori Herstein notes that what makes an omission *negligent*, as opposed to some other form of unwitting 'negative action', is that it 'also has a normative component'.[37] He further elaborates (2019: 5): 'Negligence is conduct that is in some sense improper. It is conduct in violation of some standard.'[38] But negligence is more than mere neglect. It implies a lack of proper care, resulting in risk exposure, in some admittedly loose sense.

We may, then, distinguish between the following characterizations, bearing in mind that they do not pick out ontological categories:

(i) Intentional 'Negative Acts' (e.g. not declaring income to the tax office)
(ii) Unwitting 'Positive Acts' (e.g. running over a hedgehog)
(iii) Unwitting 'Negative Acts' (e.g. failing to smile back at someone)
(iv) Negative Negligence (e.g. forgetting to lock the shop up).[39]

Category (iii) is a blend of aspects of (i) and (ii). By establishing that assuming responsibility for (i) and (ii) is, assuming the relevant Hegelian qualifications, unproblematic, we are awarded with responsibility for (iii) for free, as it were. Category (iv) is just a subset of (iii), so is no harder to explain. Those who worry over how to settle the causal conditions of negative negligence may be reminded that, as with all action, causality is not the sole factor relevant to moral imputation,[40] though it has its place.[41] There is thus no serious philosophical difficulty in 'justifying the assumption that we are responsible for negligent conduct' (Herstein 2019: 1). On the contrary, the concept of negligence is parasitic on that of responsibility.

Epilogue

At the outset of the *Bhagavad Gītā*, the warrior Arjuna stands confused and hesitant in the middle of the battlefield, reluctant to engage in battle with his own people: 'fathers, grandfathers, teachers, maternal uncles, brothers, sons, grandsons, friends, fathers-in-law, and companions' (*Bhagavad Gītā*, Vol. 1: 26–7). Overcome by deep compassion, he tells Krishna that, when he sees his own people eager to fight, the bow falls from his hand: 'nothing good can come from slaughtering one's own family in battle' (*Bhagavad Gītā*, Vol. 1:31). The remainder of the text consists of Krishna's ultimately successful attempt to convince Arjuna to abandon all attachment, as this is causing him to *neglect* his duty to action. The *Gītā* is a cunning text. On its spiritual surface, it preaches the overcoming of suffering, casting away of egoism, practice of detachment and unification of the self with the Supreme Being through karma. But the very same tenets serve as rhetoric to convince Arjuna to kill his family in battle. Not doing so is selfish because there is no such thing as non-action. To not do so would be to let his feelings stand in the way of his duty. The undercurrent theme, that 'action [karma] is better than non-action [akarma]' (*Bhagavad Gītā*, Vol. 1:8–9.),[42] is a thinly veiled attack on the Buddhist ideal of doing nothing (with which the Zen-living character from *Postcards from the Edge* is enamoured). There is no such thing as doing nothing, because every inaction involves an action and vice versa. Thus, 'man does not attain freedom from the results of action by abstaining from actions' (*Bhagavad Gītā*, Vol. 3: 4).

Non-action has consequences and can accordingly be re-described as action in terms of bringing them about. Thus, 'the entire world is bound by actions' (*Bhagavad Gītā*, Vol. 1:8–9). Krishna approves the (true) renunciation of action but maintains that 'the practice of yogic action is superior to the renunciation of action' (*Bhagavad Gītā*, Vol. 5: 2). For while the two practices are said to be ultimately the same – there being no fundamental difference between action that has abandoned all attachment and inaction – it is easier to be fooled into thinking that one has avoided action (when one hasn't) than into thinking that one has failed to avoid action (when one has succeeded). In plainer English, we are more easily convinced that we have avoided action when we have done something, than vice versa. And the person whose actions are detached from any desire for gratification is 'as though he were not doing anything' (Bhaktivedanta Swami Prabhupada 1972: 208).

The real distinction, then, is not between action and non-action but between attachment and non-attachment. This is masked by the very natural temptation to distinguish between positive and negative action, doing and allowing, performing and refraining, fulfilling and neglecting, etc. The philosopher's knowledge of how our own various doings and not-doings relate is, like that of Arjuna (or, indeed, Oedipus) deeply fallible. We must thus conclude, with the *Bhagavad Gītā*, that the ability to see action in inaction, and vice versa, is hard-won.

3

Are we superhuman or are we dancer?

Action and will in the novels of Anthony Powell

O body swayed to music, O brightening glance,
How can we know the dancer from the dance?
W. B. Yeats, *Among School Children* (1928)

1. Agents and Patients

The worlds of Anthony Powell are populated with agents and patients. At their centre stand the so-called 'men of action', in seeming control of their life as a whole and imposing their will upon the world. These are surrounded by sufferers who are subordinate to the will of others, mere products of their time and place. The division, of course, is a satirical one, and those who worship at the altar of the will at best turn out to have been dancing to the music of their time. Powell's novels thus mock the eccentric Nietzschean philosophy of the will to power that peaked in popularity in the 1930s and 1940s. In this they form a sharp contrast to the works of a motley assembly of writers – from George Bernard Shaw to Ayn Rand – who drew moral inspiration from this philosophy.

It is possible to see the world in this way: one is either a *maker* or a *victim* of history. These oppositions are frequently explicit in the novels of Anthony Powell, almost all of which are populated with characters described in ways that make them easy to compartmentalize into either of these extremes. This distinction between doing and suffering has been traced at least as far back as Homer:

> the harper has sung truly of the fate of the Achaeans, of what things they did (ἔρξαν) and suffered (ἐμόγησαν) under the walls of Troy. (*Odyssey*: 8.490)

Powell follows suit by dividing his characters into those who seemingly maintain tight control of both their own lives and those who fail to act and have things *happen* to them instead. Paradigmatic of the latter set is Buster's announcement that he's been *told* that he is going to *be* divorced (*VB*: 165). (See the bibliography for details of novel titles.) In a similar vein, we hear that 'Maclintick's wife has walked out on him' (*CCR*: 203) and that 'Lowell . . . couldn't find a regular job' (*CCR*: 195). One important aspect of such passivity is revealed in expressions of one's will being paralysed, be it by circumstance or as the result of a man of will exercising his power:

> I suppose I could have had a meal by myself, thinking of some excuse later to explain my absence, but the will to take so decisive a step seemed to have been taken physically from me. (*BM*: 260)
>
> I saw that I was now in Widmerpool's power. (*VB*: 243)

The theme of power is still present in Powell's final novel, *The Fisher King*, in which the photographer is seen – if only by himself – as a person with power over the living and the dead, 'imposing his or her will in a manner unparalleled on the person photographed' (*FK*: 121).[1] It would be a mistake, however, to understand the distinction between agents and patients as one between those who act and those who omit to.[2] After all, omitting or refraining can be an expression of a strong will. Indeed, in Powell's view, they are actions of some sort:

> cutting appointments was a recognised element in his [Mark Members'] method of conducting life . . . to impose the will. . . . The person awaited deliberately withholds himself from the person awaiting. Mere absence is in this manner turned into a form of action, even potentially violent in its consequences. (*AW*: 35)

The other side of this token is that Powell's patients – including Jenkins himself – do, of course, act, but the thing to notice is that they invariably *find* themselves doing so:

> unexpectedly, I found myself married (*CCR*: 56)
> I found myself talking to Ann Umfraville (*KO*: 117)

Accordingly, they have trouble explaining their actions and themselves. Here is Jenkins again:

> I suddenly felt unable to explain what I did, what I was. (*KO*: 119)
>
> I had attended reunion dinners of one of the branches of the army in which I had served, usually deciding to do so at the last moment, even then never quite knowing what brought me there. (*TK*: 201)

Consciously or otherwise, Powell frequently uses the following phrases to capture these seemingly unmotivated actions:

> For no obvious reason (*BM*: 13)
> for some unaccountable reason (*BM*: 204)
> whatever the reason (*BM*: 217)
> for some reason (*AW*: 84)
> for one reason or another (*LM*: 165, 177; *VB*: 203)

for some reason (*CCR*: 154)
for the worst of reasons (*VB*: 61)
for obscure reasons of his own (*BDFR*: 41)
for some inexplicable reason (*FK*: 136)

These 'patients' are condemned to a life of banality, for example 'to eat amateur paella and drink Chelsea Médoc for ever' (*LM*: 221). When it comes to making decisions, they deliberate about mundane things, such as 'father, trying to make up his mind if he would eat another slice of walnut cake or whether that would spoil his dinner' (*FVD*: 16). But the passive agent par excellence is Hugh Moreland, who is fond of quoting Nietzsche's opinion that there is no action without illusion (*VB*: 114; cf. *WN*: 109 and *V*: 242).[3] Plagued by chronic indecision, his appeals to Nietzsche are a sort of last-ditch attempt to move himself to action:

To make up my mind is always a rare thing with me, but the moment for decision has arrived . . . Nietzsche advocates living dangerously (*CCR*: 6-7)

Moreland, who, still unable to come to a decision about food, accepted her [Matilda's] ruling on this matter without dissent (*CCR*: 55)

No use fighting against fate (*CCR*: 209)

The pathetically minuscule acts of Powell's patients could not be further removed from what we might call the wide-scope activities of his agents. The latter are reliably comprised of lifelong enterprises such as those of writing a significant book, plotting political advancement or carving out a career. Indeed, his men[4] of action (*FK*: 9, 17) who have a way of bringing off what they want (*FK*: 117) are not so much interested in how they should act at any particular moment as they are on how to live their lives as a whole, a preference frequently associated with the pursuit of virtue. Their activities include conducting a successful love-affair (*FVD*: 175), taking the plunge (*LM*: 54), and venturing forth into the night (*CCR*: 183). Their will to power and domination takes many forms, from bringing about reconciliation between enemies (*LM*: 53) to triggers which set world affairs into motion. Powell's contrast between macroscopic agency and microscopic passivity is embodied in Bracey's relationship to Albert:

International events took their swift, their ominous, course, Bracey, characteristically, being swept into a world of action, Albert, firm as ever in his fight for the quiet life, merely changing the locality of his cooking pots. (*KO*: 72)

The world of action is essentially that of Wagnerian heroes, Arthurian knights, Caesars and other archetypal figures (*FK*: 18–19, 23), comically updated by Powell to be a home to agents (secret, literary and Hollywood), psychoanalytic patients, men of military action, executors of wills and so on. This is not so much to find a joke in every truth as to find the truth in every joke:

> Gwatkin ... was even conscious of such moral aspects of the military life as the fact that the army is a world of the will, accordingly if the will is weak, the army is weak. (*VB*: 228; cf. *WN*: 73)

> Soldiers must be judged to a large extent not by intelligence, but by their will to power. (*WN*: 88; see also *WN*: 93; cf. *V*: 47)

For people such as Captain Gwatkin, 'the only reality is action' (*WN*: 75) and we can approach reality – indeed authenticity – only via individual acts of will. Hence Gwatkin's retort that 'what we call good manners are just a form of weakness ... there's a lot to be said for going straight to the point' (*VB*: 227).⁵ Expressions of this viewpoint are paramount across *Dance*, and not restricted to the 'strong' characters:

> In human life, the individual ultimately dominates every situation, however disordered, sometimes for better, sometimes for worse. . . . There was a place for action, a display of will ... action had been taken, will-power brought into play. (*KO*: 61)

> she was always accustomed to act, in principle, as if London were the country, an exercise of will she rarely relaxed. (*BM*: 18)

> let's decide to anyway. . . . As we've agreed, these things are largely a matter of will. (*VB*: 109)

The Nietzschean provenance of such remarks would have been obvious to most of Powell's original readers:⁶

> Life is merely a special case of the will to power. (Nietzsche [1901] 1968: §692)⁷

Less obvious to Powell's readers would have been the deterministic aspects of Nietzsche's work. Their tension with his remarks on the will to power renders Nietzsche's position considerably more nuanced:

> a thought comes when 'it' wants, not when 'I' want (Nietzsche [1886] 1973: §17)

> do not imagine that this thought can be separated from the 'willing' (Nietzsche [1886] 1973: §19)

> can rise or sink to no other 'reality' than the reality of our drives ... thinking is only the relationship of these drives to one another ... all mechanical occurrences, in so far as a force is active in them, are forces of will, effects of will. (Nietzsche [1886] 1973: §36; cf. *WN*: 75)

> From a psychological point of view the concept 'cause' is our feeling of power resulting from the so-called act of will – our concept 'effect' the superstition that this feeling of power is the motive of power itself – A condition that accompanies an event and is itself an effect of the event is projected as the 'sufficient reason' for the event. (Nietzsche 1901: §689)

Powell found comic use for the transposition of Nietzsche's ideas into typically English settings:

> There is something about him intensely shocking to the innate liberalism and love of compromise of the English, more inclined to accept as humanitarian a parallel ruthlessness cloaked with talk of 'the greatest good for the greatest number' than a severely intellectual pessimism that dismisses the notion of human equality as utter nonsense. (*TSN*; see also *FIMT*: 2)

At times, Powell's and Nietzsche's views come very close, both of them mocking those who try to live their lives as if willing were a matter of choice, something up to them. This shared stance goes against the toxic grain of an ongoing philosophical tradition, which, as Soran Reader has put it, is 'culturally biased towards thinking of persons as agents'. Both would have appreciated Reader's contention that 'patiency, far from being a privation of personhood, must metaphysically and conceptually define us as much as agency does' (Reader 2010: 201).

2. Ghost railways

Powell's specific interests immediately set himself apart from traditional philosophies of freedom and action. Historically, these focus on discrete actions of no particular importance, such as that of raising an arm. Philosophers of action quarrel over whether such acts are caused by agents (possibly via some prior act of trying or volition) or whether people are mere vehicles through which mental or neurological processes and states cause bodily movements. They ask questions such as whether actions are caused by the so-called psychological states thought to motivate them:

> My right Hand writes, whilst my left Hand is still: What causes rest in one, and motion in the other? Nothing but my Will, – a Thought of my Mind; my Thought only changing, the right Hand rests, and the left Hand moves. This is matter of fact, which cannot be denied: Explain this, and make it intelligible, and then the next step will be to understand Creation. (Locke [1689] 1975: 629)

Such questions concerning mental causation were popular within Powell's seventeenth- and eighteenth-century literature, such as Samuel Richardson's *Clarissa* or Alexander Pope's *The Rape of the Lock*. As Jonathan Kramnick puts it

> In restoration and eighteenth-century Britain . . . writers described what precedes and constitutes an agent's doing something, whether writing a letter or fleeing a kingdom. The topic gathered new attention during the period because it opened the possibility for a causal theory of behaviour in line with causal theories applied elsewhere in the natural world. If desires, fears, beliefs, and so on and actions were like effects, some said, then minds were similar to other things in the environment; if minds represent the world in motion, others responded, they

were in some sense distinct from everything else. The discussion animated genres as diverse as the treatise, the lyric, and the novel. Sometimes it concerns matters as ordinary as lifting one's feet; other times it engaged topics as broad as what it means to be a person. In each case, the concern was how states of mind might prompt, accompany, or follow the movement of physical bodies. (Kramnick 2010: 2; cf. J.A. Smith 2016)

Be that as it may, Powell's interests converge with those of such earlier writers on the topic of free agency. *Agents and Patients* begins with the following epigram from John Wesley:

So in every possible case; He that is not free is not an Agent, but a Patient. (*AP*: i; cf. *WN*: 34)

This is derived from Wesley's Sermon 62 (9 December 1758), although Powell misattributes it to Sermon 67 (3 March 1786). In the passage immediately preceding the line which Powell quotes, Wesley is arguing that there is evil in the world because God gave people the freedom to choose good over evil, and vice versa:

He was endued also with a will. . . . He was likewise endued with liberty; a power of choosing what was good, and refusing what was not so. Without this, both the will and the understanding would have been utterly useless. Indeed, without liberty, man had been so far from being a *free agent*, that he could have been no *agent* at all. For every *unfree being* is purely passive; not active in any degree. Have you a sword in your hand? Does a man, stronger than you, seize your hand, and force you to wound a third person? In this you are no agent, any more than the sword: The hand is as passive as the steel. So in every possible case. He that is not free is not an agent, but a patient.

Controversially, Wesley is here arguing that liberty is not only required for *free* agency but is a necessary condition for agency *tout court*. For our Powellian purposes, however, the important point to note is that in Wesley's view the will and liberty are something possessed by all humans, strong *or* weak. Pari passu, possession of a will is not something that deserves praise but that in virtue of which we must assume responsibility for our actions. In the later sermon that Powell cites (but fails to quote from), Wesley adds that, without will and liberty, we would not be capable of vice or virtue:

He could not be a moral agent, any more than a tree or a stone. . . . Were human liberty taken away, men would be as incapable of virtue as stones. (Wesley, Sermon 67, §15)

Even if Wesley were right to think that virtue requires liberty of will, it would not follow that those who impose their will on others are more virtuous than those who suffer as a consequence. As Georgia Ronan Crampton reminds us, the renaissance celebration of agency contrasts sharply with the medieval conception of the suffering hero:

> Spenser the Renaissance poet celebrates action; Chaucer the medieval poet, sufferance. (Crampton 1974: 178)

> Spenser ... is the poet of action ... the medium for the heroes' good golden chain of virtues ... deeds are a true index to the man. ... The best are marked for brave pursuit of honourable deeds. (Crampton 1974: 181)

> To Chaucer, action simply does not seem to stand in need of so much recommendation. (Crampton 1974: 189)

> suffering is the most salient fact of the poem's universe. (Crampton 1974: 194)

The distinction between acting and suffering melts away to the degree that the hero suffers by *choice* (consider Moreland's 'allowing' Matilda to divorce him and marry Donners). The will is no less active in the sufferer than it is in he who causes suffering; both are open to vice and virtue, praise and blame. Moreover, Powell's agents do not possess a will in the Wesleyan sense in which *all* of us do so but in the sense of having a unified and directed set of drives which they harness towards power and domination (Birns 2004: 58). On Nietzsche's view, the will is not an instrument of ambition aimed at satisfying life-goals such as that of furthering a career. On the contrary, these apparent ends are mere channels for the ultimate aim of exercising power. Powell's characters can be divided into those who use power as a means and those who will it as an end:

> Quiggin, of course, liked power too; though perhaps less for its own sake. ... Erridge's will was a strong one ... at his words Smith had bowed his head as one who, having received the order of the bowstring, makes for Bosphorus. (*LM*: 132; cf. *WN*: 57)[8]

Contra Nietzsche, he finds little virtue in either. As we shall see in due course, he mocks those who see themselves as strong individual men of will and action. Powell's own sympathies clearly lie with the victims of luck, rather than with those who have difficulty in crediting their luck (*FK*: 132). Perhaps this is a partial recognition of the fact that, as Graham Greene puts it in his essay on Walter de la Mare,

> (e)very creative writer worth our consideration ... is a victim: a man given to an obsession. (Greene 1970: 108)

We are now better equipped to investigate the details of Powell's interest in agency and the will. This manifests itself from the opening lines of *Dance*:

> The men at work at the corner of the street had made a kind of camp for themselves ... swinging arms against bodies and rubbing hands together. ... For some reason, the sight of snow descending on fire always makes me think of the ancient world – legionaries in sheepskin warming themselves at a brazier. ... These classical projections, and something in the physical attitudes of the men

themselves as they turned from the fire, suddenly suggested Poussin's scene in which the seasons, hand in hand and facing outwards, tread in rhythm to the notes of the lyre that the winged and naked greybeard plays. The image of time brought thoughts of mortality: of human beings, facing outward like the Seasons, moving hand in hand in intricate measure: stepping slowly, methodically, sometimes a trifle awkwardly, in evolutions that take recognizable shape: or breaking into seemingly meaningless gyrations, while partners disappear only to reappear again, once more giving pattern to the spectacle: unable to control the melody, unable, perhaps, to control the steps of the dance. Classical associations made me think, too, of days at school, where so many forces, hitherto unfamiliar, had become in due course uncompromisingly clear. (*QU*: 1-2; cf. *FK*: 98)

Powell found the painting 'curiously hypnotic' and the figure of time 'extremely sinister' (Barber 2004: 169; cf. Birns 2004: 69).[9] One may impose upon it a structure according to which the painting represents the various destinies of man: poverty, luxury and so on. The strong-willed dancer surfaces most clearly in Powell's last novel (*FK*: 70-1, 180-1). The loss of power is there symbolized by 'dancers who can no longer dance', like photographers whose photographic powers run dry and find that they can take no more photographs (*FK*: 93). In *Dance*, Powell's interest lies in the forces that carry us away, under which we are more danced than dancer. These forces of circumstance surreptitiously guide every aspect of our lives and actions:

Nothing in life can be entirely divorced from myriad other incidents; and it is remarkable, though no doubt logical, that action, built up from innumerable causes, each in itself allusive and unnoticed more often than not, is almost always provided with an apparently ideal moment for its final expression. So true is this that what has gone before is often, to all intents and purposes, swallowed up by the aptness of the climax, opportunity appearing, at least on the surface, to be the sole cause of fulfilment. The circumstances that had brought me to Barnby's studio supplied a fair example of this complexity of experience. (*BM*: 254)

Other metaphors used by Powell to capture this lack of control over our lives include that of the Ghost Railway. Everyday life is compared to a Ghost Railway rushing downhill in total darkness and crashing through closed doors:

and the body lying across the line . . . once . . . we had been on a Ghost Railway . . . slowly climbing sheer gradients, sweeping with frenzied speed into inky depths, turning blind corners from which black, gibbering bogeys leapt to attack, rushed headlong towards iron-studded doors, threatened by imminent collision, fingered by spectral hands, moving at last with dreadful, ever increasing momentum towards a shape that lay across the line. (*CCR*: 219, 229)

Before we really know where we are, life seems to have begun in earnest at last, and we ourselves, scarcely aware that any change has taken place, are careering uncontrollably down the slippery avenues of eternity.(*BM*: 274)

Powell also uses real-life analogies to express a similar lack of control over one's life:

> There was every reason to think that before long now the tenor of many persons' lives, my own, among them, would indeed be regulated by those draconic, ineluctable laws, so mildly, so all embracingly defined in the Commission as 'the Rules and Discipline of War'. How was it going to feel to be subject to them? (*KO*: 159)

Indeed, Jenkins's tribute to Burton's *Anatomy of Melancholy* at the end of *Dance* (see also *WN*: 128; Spurling 1977: 216–17) leaves the reader feeling that we are all mere pawns, forever destined to be what Burton called 'a sea of ills so vast that to swim clear seems impossible' (Burton [1628] 2001: 273):[10]

> war, plagues, fires ... thefts ... peace, leagues. ... A vast confusion of vows, wishes, actions, edicts, petitions, lawsuits ... are drearily brought to our ears. New books every day, pamphlets ... whole catalogues of volumes of all sorts, new paradoxes, opinions ... controversies, in philosophy ... weddings. (*HSH*: 271–2; cf. Burton [1628] 2001: 18–19 and Brecht 1936: 71)

In the case of Jenkins – who writes his book *Borage and Hellabore* about Burton – passivity is accompanied by an explicitly fatalistic stance which – in jest or otherwise – is coated in Nietzsche, one touch of which 'makes the whole world kin' (*WN*: 129; *SAAG*: 86):

> We parted company, agreeing that Nietzschean Eternal Recurrences must bring us together soon again. (*SA*: 106)

> That was one of the reasons why I had made no effort to keep in touch with him (Widmerpool) ... knowing, as one does with certain people, that the rhythm of life would sooner or later be bound to bring us together again. (*CCR*: 102–3)

> Perhaps it was just Fate. (*SA*: 103)

> There seemed no justice in the fact that fate had willed this duty to fall on myself. (*KO*: 147)

> I'm just made that way. (*BM*: 248)

In his *Writer's Notebook*, Powell himself flirts with this sort of fatalism about character:

> One of the maddest things is to suppose that people could be 'different'. (*WN*: 88)

He seems to have espoused a related view of self-control, which he took to be rare but not impossible:

> Nothing irritates people more than self-control. (*WN*: 108)
> Self-control is so rare as to be little understood. (*WN*: 126)
> People usually do what they want. (*WN*: 91)

But Powell is no more a fatalist than he is a Wesleyan:

> Life would be all right, if you could say it was always people's fault, or alternatively if it was all fate. As it is both work unfairly.(*WN*: 108; cf. *WN*: 155)

> The margin between success and failure is a narrow one, Uncle Giles etc. (*WN*: 58)[11]

This view is far closer to that of Nietzsche himself, as opposed to that of his eccentric followers:

> (T)he desire for 'freedom of will' in that metaphysical superlative sense which is unfortunately still dominant in the minds of the half-educated, the desire to bear the whole and sole responsibility for one's actions and to absolve God, world, ancestors, chance, society from responsibility for them, is nothing less than the desire to be precisely that *causa sui* (self-cause) and, with more than Münchhausen temerity, to pull oneself into existence out of the swamp of nothingness by one's own hair. . . . Unfree will is a mythology: in real life it is only a question of *strong* and *weak* wills . . . one will at no price give up his 'responsibility', his belief in *himself*, the personal right to *his* deserts (the vain races belong here), the other, on the contrary, will not be responsible for anything, to blame for anything, and out of an inner self-contempt wants to be able to *shift-off* his responsibility for himself somewhere else. This latter, when he writes books, tends to espouse the cause of the criminal; his most pleasing disguise is a kind of socialist sympathy. (Nietzsche [1886] 1973: §21)

His more radical followers of 'the will' were largely influenced by the editorial corruption of Elisabeth Förster Nietzsche, his Nazi-supporting sister whose own hunger for power resembled that of Powell's 'agents'.[12] It has been remarked that Powell turns a blind eye to Mosley and British Fascism in *Dance* (Barber 2004: 111–12). Be that as it may, he certainly gives us a comic taste of the philosophy that inspired it, without throwing the Nietzschean baby out with the fascist bathwater.[13] In this he compares favourably to writers who either keep or reject both, and to those who simply get the balance wrong.[14]

3. Exercises of the will

The very forces that move us threaten to steal our liberty of choice unless we become their master. Given the choice, it may seem obviously preferable to be a member of the set of people who impose their will upon the world as opposed to those whose lives are subordinate to the wills of others, sufferers who are mere products of their time and place. As Nicholas Birns points out, however, this is not the case in Powell's novels, including *Dance*:

> Usually we are taught to think that to act is better than not to act, but the narrative does not privilege the agents over the patients. In a dichotomy that is

anticipatory of the one between men of will and men of imagination in *Dance*, Powell leads us to sympathize more with the preyed-upon Blore-Smith. (Birns: 2004: 48)

What Powell thinks about those who see themselves as men of will and action is made clear in his notebooks:

> There is always a yearning in England for strong-willed buffoons, even intellectual ones will serve. (*WN*: 106)

> In spite of what is said to the contrary, men of action tend to be woolly-minded, and imaginative people clear-minded. (*WN*: 48)

> People with strong personalities often have weak characters. (*WN*: 122)

This last remark is key to understanding what we might call Powell's dual-aspect presentations of figures such as Zouch and Widmerpool. If Powell ever appears to take these woolly minded, strong-willed buffoons of action seriously, it is only in the mocking sense in which Pope treats the 'rape of the lock' as a matter most serious. This is most evident with the bearded[15] Nietzschean 'supermen'[16] who in the petty feud of *From a View to a Death* (published in the United States as, *Zouch, Superman*) farcically impose their will on nature by hunting:

> Zouch was a superman. A fair English equivalent of the Teutonic ideal of the Übermensch. No one knew this yet except himself. This was because he had not been one long enough for people to find out. They would learn all in good time; and to their cost. Meanwhile he went on his way, taking but not giving, treating life as a sort of quick-lunch counter where you helped yourself and all the snacks were free.(*FVD*: 15)

> (Mr Passenger) as Zouch had recognised at once, was an Übermensch. A pretty grim figure in fact. Indeed part of Zouch's uneasiness at that moment was due to an instantaneous fear that in Mr Passenger he might have met his match. (*FVD*: 38)

> (Zouch) remembered that he was a superman and he saw no reason why he should not learn to do things which were required of him with perfect sense. The will to power should teach him how to ride. (*FVD*: 180)

> He was conscious that a situation had arisen which called for the superman touch and he was satisfied that he was proving himself equal to it. (*FVD*: 184)[17]

At the moment of his bitter end, Zouch is transformed into a patient or 'underman':

> He had not risen to the situation. As a superman he had let himself down. In this moment of emergency he had been thrown back on the old props of tradition and education and when he might have enjoyed a substantial revenge he had behaved with all the restraint in the world. (*FVD*: 192)

As with Zouch, things do not end well for Widmerpool and his will:

> not quite the scene portrayed by Poussin, even if elements of the Seasons' dance were suggested in perverted form; not least by Widmerpool, perhaps naked ... a battle of wills seemed to be in progress ... it looked as if he were losing ground in rivalry with a younger man. (HSH: 173)[18]

It is in the light of this end that we must understand Jenkins's earlier description of Widmerpool as 'the sort of man likely to make an MP' (*CCR*: 85). By the end of *Dance* it is clear that the joke is on MPs and not those unsuited to the job. It is no accident that throughout the novel Widmerpool's will to power is overshadowed by his co-dependence with his mother:

> my mother agrees that my decision was for the best. (*LM*: 239)[19]

Describing what he perceives as 'the theoretical side of Widmerpool's life', Jenkins narrates:

> The severe rule of ambition that he had from the beginning imposed upon himself: the determination that existence must be governed by the will. (*LM*: 46)

> something impressive in his total lack of interest in the fate of all persons except himself. (SA: 192)

> determination to become a success in life. (BM: 30)

> had devoted so much energy to achieving his present position in the world that even golf had been discarded. (LM: 62–3)

> not at all interested in the lives of others. (LM: 96)

> devoid of all aesthetic or intellectual interests. (*LM*: 107–8)

In these passages Widmerpool still appears the strong individual, albeit one whose single-mindedness is not a virtue but takes on the form of the vice of selfishness. There is a moment, relatively early on in the novel, when Jenkins surprises himself by realizing this:

> Certain actions take place outside the normal course of things so unexpectedly that they seem to paralyse ordinary capacity for feeling surprise; and I watched Widmerpool seize hold of Barbara in this way – by force. . . . To begin with, his act was a vigorous and instantaneous assertion of the will, quite out of keeping with the picture then existing in my mind of his character. (BM: 69)

Jenkins is not quite sure what to make of the moral psychology of agents:

> Like so many men who have made a successful career through the will, it was hard to guess how much, or how little, Sir Magnus took in of what was going on

immediately round him. Did he know that his own sexual habits were a source of constant speculation and jocularity; that Moreland was tortured by the thought of Matilda's former status in the house; that Betty Templar made the party a very uncomfortable one; or was he indifferent to these things, and many others as well? It was impossible to say. Perhaps Sir Magnus, through his antennae, was even more keenly appraised of surrounding circumstances than the rest of us; perhaps, on the other hand, he was able to dismiss them completely from his consciousness as absolutely unessential elements in his own tranquil progress through life. (*KO*: 122–3)

Ever the anti-hero, it is Moreland who provides us with the intoxicated clue to relating the outer world of action to the inner life of the mind:

discussing the roots and aims of action. . . . Moreland had been talking incessantly – by then a trifle incoherently – on the theme that action, stemming from sluggish, invisible sources, moves towards destinations no less indefinable . . .

'If action is to be one's aim,' he was saying, 'then is it action to write a symphony satisfactory to oneself, which no one else wants to perform, or a comic song every errand-boy whistles? . . . We know it's bad art. That is not the point. Is it action? Or *is* that the point? Is art action, an alternative to action, the enemy of action, or nothing whatever to do with action? I have no objection to action. I merely find it impossible to locate'. . . . 'Does action consist in having or loving? In having – naturally – it might first appear. Loving is just emotion, not action at all. But is that correct? I'm not sure' . . . 'or is action only when you bring off both – loving and having – leaving your money on, so to speak, like a double-event in racing'. . . . 'Now, Sir Magnus Donners,' said Moreland. 'Is he a man of action? In the eyes of the world, certainly. But does he, in fact, live intensely?' (*KO*: 75–7; cf. *WN*, 116–18, 121)

Where does the truth lie? As Powell notes:

Everyone is at least three people, what they are, what they think they are, what the world thinks they are. (*WN*: 148)

On all three counts, the seeming impenetrability of Sir Magnus's psychology is nothing compared with the lethal determination of General Conyers:

I attempted to find some parallel, however far-fetched, to link Widmerpool with General Conyers. . . . Both were accustomed to live by the will: both had decided for a time to carve out a career unburdened by a wife: both were, in very different ways, fairly successful men. There the comparison seemed to break down. (*LM*: 66)

(Conyers) was a man who gave the impression, rightly or wrongly, that he would stop at nothing. If he decided to kill you, he would kill you. (*LM*: 71)

Such are the egoistic ethics of personal ambition. This is never more clear than in the realm of love:

> No woman who takes my mind off work is ever to play a part in my life in the future. (*BM*: 272)

> Marriage, as I have said, is a form of action, of violence almost: an assertion of the will. (*LM*: 203)

> Barnby might have found a place among . . . those power-conscious young men, anxious to achieve success with women without the banal expedient of 'falling in love': a state, of course, necessarily implying, on the part of the competitor, a depletion, if not entire abrogation, of 'the will' . . . he possessed a woman, seeking a relationship in which sensuality merged with power, rather than engaging in their habitual conflict. (*AW*: 30; see Birns 2004: 58)

> You can only control the situation if you are not really in love. (*WN*: 96)

If patients are victims then, ultimately, agents are culprits. But they are *pathetic* ones, and it is this irony that Powell captures so well:

> His role . . . was that of a man of the will . . . even here, in giving an opinion of the landscape, the will must be exercised. (*LM*: 107–8)

> [Miss Weedon] spoke sadly, almost as if she were deprecating her own powers of dominion, trying to minimise them because their very hugeness embarrassed her; like the dictator of some absolutist state who assures journalists that his most imperative decrees have to take an outwardly parliamentary form. (*CCR*: 184)

Powell's Nietzschean characters most resemble the bearded John Tanner from George Bernard Shaw's 1903 play *Man and Superman*:

> John Tanner . . . a big man with a beard . . . Olympian majesty . . . a sense of the importance of everything he does which leads him to make as much of paying a call as other men do of getting married or laying a foundation stone. (Shaw 1903: 47)

> I sing, not the arms and the hero, but the philosophic man: he who seeks to discover the inner will of the world . . . and in action to do that will. (Shaw 1903: 151)

> The cry for the Superman did not begin with Nietzsche nor did it end with his vogue . . . we shall find how to produce him by the old method of trial and error. (Shaw 1903: 216)

There is just one difference between the two writers: Shaw espoused a philosophy of will to power and meant every word (see Bloom 1987: 2, 5–6; Crompton 1974: 88–9; Valency 1987: 176; Vogt 1987).[20] Powell's dancing men of the will, by contrast, prove to be barely human, monstrous buffoons.

4

Reasoning to action

Prologue

Aristotle's suggestion that we can equally reason from our current beliefs to action as we can to a new belief (*EN*: 1147a26-31; *DMA*: 701a18-23) found support from a number of important philosophers during the second half of the twentieth century, most notably G. E. M. Anscombe (1965), Donald Davidson (1969a) and G. H. von Wright (1972). Their *actionalist* conceptions of practical reasoning have more recently been subjected to pushback in the form of *cognitivist* and *intentionalist* alternatives, according to which practical reasoning is respectively said to result in a belief about what one ought to do (Raz 2011: Ch. 7), or an intention to act in a certain way (Broome 2013: Ch. 14). In *Practical Shape*, Jonathan Dancy builds on some of his earlier work to mount an original and sophisticated defence of *actionalism* that is 'sensitive to current debates but still Aristotelian in spirit', as the description on the back cover puts it. (All page references in this essay refer to *Practical Shape* (Dancy 2018) unless otherwise specified.)

Nobody denies, of course, that we can reason about what to do just as easily as we can reason about what to believe (perhaps even more so). But one could allow that reasoning might be practical in its *subject* (action) while denying the actionalist claim that it is practical in its *issue* (belief), to use a distinction from Davidson to which I shall later return. On such a view, practical reasoning issues in *beliefs* about what one ought to do, and is thus no different to theoretical reasoning in terms of the kind of output it issues. A *prima facie* worry with this outlook is that it seems committed to holding that reasoning about what to believe is, by analogy, reasoning to a belief about what one ought to believe. Yet it is implausible to think that all theoretical reasoning results in meta-belief. We would do better, perhaps, to distinguish between what we are trying to figure out in reasoning (namely, what it is that we should think or do) from the end product of reasoning gone well (namely, our believing or acting accordingly). If these two things sound identical to you, read on.

I have managed, so far, to avoid using the term 'conclusion', even though the aforementioned debates are typically cast in terms of whether or not the conclusion of a practical syllogism is an action. Dancy argues, persuasively, that this is an unfortunate way of thinking about things, since conclusions are things that we can draw or infer, and it makes no sense to talk of drawing or inferring actions (34–5). What about belief? Dancy argues, inter alia, that when we reason to belief, our reasoning does not result in a thing believed (e.g. that your mother was a hamster) but, rather, in our *believing* it. We cannot draw or infer such believings any more than we can actions. If reasoning 'concludes' in action, intention, or belief, it does so merely in the sense of resulting in our doing, intending (to do), or believing something. Actions, intentions and beliefs are not so much the conclusions of reasoning as they are its *outputs*. By the same token, the beliefs (and, on some accounts, desires) with which we begin our reasoning are not syllogistic premises but the mental inputs of a process. It would be bizarre, after all, if reasoning could take us from things believed to believings.

Does this mean that reasoning is a purely causal process? Not at all. An equally valid description of what is going on is that we take various considerations into account and then try to figure out, on their basis, what it is that we should think or do. The point is simply that such considerations need to register with us if our reasoning is to be more than hypothetical. We should, accordingly, distinguish between the rational *grounds* of reasoning, which are the considerations we take into account when reasoning, and the rational *springs*, which are the related believings with which we begin our reasoning.[1]

1. The Prichard Point

Dancy roughly conceives of considerations as states of affairs (or purported states of affairs) that favour a range of responses to the world (or the world as we take it to be). The takeaway message here is that only *responses* can be favoured (35). What Dancy means by this is that considerations count in favour of one's doing or believing something, as opposed to the things that one has most reason to do or believe.[2] In his own words, '[a] thing believed, whatever we take such a thing to be [. . .] is not capable of being favoured by anything' (33). Likewise, he takes reasons to be able to count in favour of *one's doing* some action. It is tempting to here add 'as opposed to the action done' but, for reasons we shall return to later, Dancy does not think that we can sensibly distinguish what is done from the doing of it (19). He is thus happy to say that 'in a successful case, the action done will be of the sort most favoured by the considerations adduced in reasoning, taken as a whole' (30).

This all leads Dancy to a difficulty he dubs 'The Prichard Point'. In §2, I introduce the worry and proceed to argue that it can be avoided in two (not so easy) steps. The first involves allowing for a distinction between the things we do and our doings of them. The second distinguishes further between (i) our reasoning outputs or results, namely, what we reason *to* or *towards*, and (ii) what we are trying to figure out in or by reasoning, namely, the aim or *object* of our reasoning. While these steps are antithetical to some of the details of Dancy's view, I think they strengthen the force of his overall picture.

In his article 'Duty and Ignorance of Fact', H. A. Prichard worries that 'since the existence of an obligation to do some action cannot possibly depend on actual performance of the action, the obligation cannot itself be a property which the action would have, if it were done' (Prichard [1932] 2004: 99). The trouble, presumably, is not that of how we can be obligated to do an action before it has been done (we can hardly remain obligated to do it afterwards, unless we have been condemned *à la* Sisyphus to do the same thing over and over again). Rather, as Prichard conceives of things, the paradoxical point is that no *particular* action we do can have the property of having been obligatory (or, for that matter, being right or wrong), since our obligation to do 'it' cannot take its particularities into account. Dancy's version of the problem replaces obligations with reasons for action.

According to Dancy, it follows from the Prichard Point that 'a reason is never a reason for any particular act' (31). This is in prima facie tension with Prichard's own talk of 'the fact that you, or that I, ought or ought nor, to do a certain action' ([1932] 2004: 99). Whether or not the tension is real depends on whether we take 'particular act' to be synonymous with 'certain action'. Dancy clearly sees a contrast that allows him to talk of 'a reason to act in a certain way' (31) without this being a reason to do a particular action. Whether the point holds will ultimately depend on what it exactly takes for any given thing one does to count as a particular. Dancy doesn't provide us with an explicit account of this, but he seems to identify possible actions with acting in a certain way and actual actions with particularized ways of acting in a certain way (32; see also §3).

I can fulfil my obligation to renew my library card through all sorts of particular acts of renewing it: I can do it online or in person, this morning or this evening, cheerily or grumpily, and so on. Indeed, even in cases where I have most reason to do it in one or more of these ways, there is no single particular act (no exact range of bodily movements performed in the most precise spatio-temporal location possible) that needs to have occurred for my obligation to have been met. Any one of a range of very similar particulars will do. To this, Dancy adds that 'all the reason does is to count in favour of my doing [. . .] some action or other' of the right sort (31), for example, the 'renewing my library card' sort, which he equates with acting *in a certain way*, before adding:

> [I]t is not at all clear to me that it makes sense to talk of favouring acting in a way. I don't know what sort of thing this 'acting in a way' is, such that it can be favoured by anything. But that difficulty, which I take very seriously, is not one that this book needs to address. For whatever the answer to it, that answer will have to work equally well for what we might call 'believing in a way'. (33)[3]

Whether or not Dancy is right that the same answer will have to work equally well for both the belief and action cases depends on whether the answer requires a distinction between believing and thing believed and, if so, whether he is right to think that there is no parallel distinction to be made between the doing and the thing done. In what follows, I shall answer the first question positively and the second negatively. I then proceed to argue that dealing with Prichard's point *is* relevant to the concerns of Dancy's book, because the correct way of doing so enables us to distinguish between the aims and results of reasoning in a way that sheds light on the precise sense in which practical reasoning may conclude in action.

2. One way too many

Dancy writes that '[a]ll that reasons can do is favour responding in a certain way – and there are many ways of responding in that way, as one might say' (32). Just as I may fulfil my obligation to do something via any number of particular actions, so I can come to believe what I have most reason to believe at a particular spatio-temporal location, with varying degrees of enthusiasm, and so on. Dancy has no real trouble understanding what it would be for a reason to favour acting in a certain way. The problem is what it would be for a reason to favour any *particularized*[4] way of acting in a certain way. But reasons don't do that, since any way will do. It is not particular believings or actings that are favoured but only doing or believing a certain thing. Any particularized believing or acting that falls under the relevant type, for example, 'believing that p' or 'doing x', will do, barring other constraints; if you pay me back by shoving the money in my mouth you may have fulfilled your obligation to pay me back, but you haven't acted rightly.

What reasons favour is not any event or process of my acting or believing a certain way, but *that* I do or believe something. Similarly, I have an obligation to do x, then I may fulfil my obligation via any particular act of doing it, though some of these may go against my other obligations. So I agree with Dancy that all reasons favour responding in a certain way. But all that this means, I think, is that they favour doing or believing some specific thing. They do not need to favour specific responses in the more particularized sense that Dancy tries to capture by speaking of a certain way of responding in some specified way. That would be, for me, one way too many.

It is a category mistake to claim that reasoning concludes in a thing believed, intended or done. As Dancy points out, reasoning concludes in a particular believing, intending or acting. But it doesn't follow from this that in reasoning we are trying to figure out what this particular should be. What we are trying to figure out is what to believe, intend or do. So while we reason *to* a response, in doing so we hope to settle *what* that response should be.

Dancy claims that reasoning to action falls short of taking us to a particular act because '[a]ny act of that sort will serve equally well' (32). The problem is alleviated only, he thinks, by the fact that it applies equally to believing as it does to acting.[5] We have seen that it is not the job of reasoning to select a particular doing or believing. But if reasoning cannot tell us which one to go for, how do we ever get to a particularized action at all? How come we don't always end up in a mental and physical paralysis akin to that which afflicts Buridan's ass? The answer is that it is not up to us (or reason) to choose the particularized way in which we think, intend or do something as the direct result of reasoning. As our reasoning concludes, the details are down to nature.

Dancy is right to claim that we can reason to action, just as we reason to belief. But while the output of practical reasoning is an action in the sense of a particularized doing at a certain time and place, from a certain motive and so on,[6] our aim in practical reasoning is simply to figure out what to do. So, why not think of practical reasoning as reasoning about *what is to be done*, just as theoretical reasoning is about *what is to be thought*? Dancy seems to informally allow for this (27), but it is hard to know what this amounts to given that he rejects distinction between a doing and a thing done:

> [W]hat is done does not seem to be distinct from the doing of it. To check on this, ask yourself what properties the doing might have that the thing done does not

have. If the doing took a long time, the thing done took a long time. If the thing done was stupid, so was the doing of it. And so on. (19)[7]

This is much too fast.[8] For one, it would help to have specific examples. Moreover, the exact differences between the two will depend on further ontological commitments: just as one may distinguish between the believing and the thing believed while not agreeing on whether the first is a state or event, and the second a proposition or a fact. Some conceive of the doing as a process and the thing done as the particular change it results in (Macmurray 1938; Prichard 1945; von Wright 1963). Others think of the doing as a (particular) token of the (universal) type that is the thing done (Hornsby 1980; Hanser 2008). The first set fail to account for the sense in which the same thing may be done by different people at difference times. The second don't do justice to the thought, defended by Dancy in the past, that it is particular things done that are right and wrong, and not the types they fall under.[9]

Let me give some examples to illustrate my preferred way of distinguishing between particular doings and particular things done. Particular doings have spatio-temporal locations, but particular things done do not. Only the latter are repeatable. Two people may do the same thing, be it separately or together, but they can't do one another's doing of it. If I do something dangerous (e.g. drink petrol) it doesn't mean that I was acting dangerously (in drinking from the gin bottle when there was no good reason to think that the gin had been replaced with petrol). Most importantly, it is doings and not things done that are variously describable. If I do the right thing (help a person in pain), it doesn't follow that I was acting in a right way (for my helping them might also be describable as my showing off in front of my new boss, or whatever).

Dancy writes that deciding '*how* it would be right to act, or *how* we are obligated to act' is 'not the same as deciding about some particular act, that this act is the obligatory one' (31; emphasis in original).[10] But this is true only of particular doings and not of particular things done. The latter may be assigned 'the property of being obligatory for us' (31) without contradiction.

3. Belief-in-action

We may reason to action, just as we may reason to belief and intention. Dancy is right that when we do so, our reasoning can conclude in our act*ing*, in much the same way in which it can conclude in our believ*ing* or intend*ing*. It can do so directly, without passing through any intermediary stage of reaching a belief about what we ought to do. Be that as it may, what we are trying to figure out in our deliberations is *what* we should do, believe or intend. Deliberating about *what* one should think or do will, in the successful case, conclude in one's thinking or doing it.

In each case we reach conclusions about *what* to think and do. These conclusions are both beliefs. It doesn't follow, however, that practical reasoning is reasoning to a belief. It is reasoning directly geared towards action in exactly the same sense that theoretical reasoning is directly geared towards belief. The way to reconcile this tension between what we use reasoning for and what reasoning towards is, I think, to allow for such a thing as reasoning to a belief-in-action, analogous to intention-in-action (167–9).[11]

Such belief does not in any way precede or otherwise lead to the action. Nor is it contained in it as the first part of some kind of causal chain. Rather, the belief is implied by one's acting as one does. It is what Davidson means by 'unconditional judgement' when he writes:

> Reasoning that stops at conditional judgements [...] is practical only in its subject, not in its issue. Practical reasoning does however often arrive at unconditional judgements that one action is better than another – otherwise there would be no such thing as acting on a reason [...] Aristotle's remark that the conclusion (of a piece of practical reasoning) is an action remains cogent. (Davidson 1969a: 39)

This is not to hold that there is a logical connection between belief and action so strong that one could not possibly act against one's better judgement. But akratic action can no more emerge as an output of practical reasoning than akratic belief can emerge as an output of theoretical reasoning. Akrasia is possible only when our reasoning fails to conclude, despite our having figured out what we ought to do or believe.[12]

Theoretical reasoning doesn't typically conclude in a meta-belief about what we should believe, but in our believing it. Similarly, practical reasoning doesn't typically conclude in a belief about how we should act. Reasoning *can* be like this (thereby rendering akrasia possible), but Dancy has shown why it need not be theoretical in its issue when it is practical in its subject.

Epilogue

The object or aim of practical reasoning is to help us figure out *what* to do. Such reasoning, though practical in its subject, may remain theoretical in form, thereby issuing in a belief. But it can also take the form of reasoning *to* action. Dancy argues persuasively that such reasoning leads directly to particular doings, the Prichard problem notwithstanding. I agree with him that such doings should not be thought of as conclusions of our reasoning, even when our reasoning may paradoxically be said to conclude in them. But nor are they the object of our reasoning, for they are not what we are trying to figure out (or even decide) when we reason practically. Because of the logical connection between the aim and issue of practical reasoning, it cannot result in action without also resulting in some form of belief-in-action. But it is not reasoning *to* such belief, let alone to belief proper. The conclusion of my own reasoning, then, is that actionalism holds true.

5

How to act against your better judgement

Prologue

Aristotle defines the akratic agent as one who 'does wrong because he feels like it, although he knows that it is wrong' (Aristotle *NE*: 227 (Book 7, Part I)). He then moves on to suggest that 'it will make a difference whether a person does wrong while having but not reflecting upon his knowledge, or whether he does wrong while reflecting that he is doing wrong' (Aristotle *NE*: 228 (Book 7, Part II)). This leads him to distinguish between two forms of Akrasia: *propeteia* and *astheneia*. The former refers to actions performed by agents who 'are carried away by their feelings because they have failed to deliberate', and the latter refers to actions performed by agents who deliberate and then 'under the influence of their feelings fail to abide by their decision' (Aristotle *NE*: 244 (Book 7, Part VII)). While *astheneia* can be translated as weakness of will or character, *propeteia* is a vulnerability of reason best understood as rashness or impetuosity, suggesting that – strictly speaking – it is only acts of *astheneia* that are completely irrational. Acts of *propeteia*, by contrast, are characterized by the clouding that covers the agent's judgement (the agent acting against it by doing something that he would have judged to be wrong, were the clouding not there. It is the possibility of acts of *astheneia* (or clear-eyed *akrasia*) that is thought to be problematic. Indeed, according to some philosophers, there is no such possibility at all.

The most influential modern picture of the alleged paradox is that provided by Donald Davidson, in part because it is accompanied by a detailed attempt at a solution. While I defend Davidson against the common objection that he assigns contradictory judgements to the (so-called) akratic agent, I argue that what he has in fact given us is a picture of *propeteia* and not *astheneia*. In this he remains as Socratic as Aristotle was,[1] and tells us little about the truly interesting cases of *akrasia*. These appear paradoxical, I suggest, only if we commit ourselves to internalism in the theory of motivation. There is little point in introducing *astheneia* as a counterexample to internalism (a sizeable part of the debate focusing on whether or not such acts exist), yet it stubbornly remains the case that an agent's perception of his motivation will nonetheless relate to whether or not he considers any of his actions to be akratic in the clear-eyed sense.

1. Davidson's formulation

Davidson gives us three principles that he thinks are true but incompatible:

(P1) If an agent wants[2] to do x more than he wants to do y and he believes himself to be free to do either x or y, then he will intentionally do x if he does either x or y intentionally.
(P2) If an agent judges that it would be better to do x than to do y, then he wants to do x more than he wants to do y.
(P3) There are incontinent actions. (Davidson [1969a] 2001: 23)

Davidson then writes:

> For someone (like myself) to whom the principles expressed by P1–3 seem self-evident, the problem posed by the apparent contradiction is acute enough to be called a paradox [...] if your assumption leads to a contradiction, no doubt you have made a mistake, but since you can know you have made a mistake without knowing what the mistake is your problem is real. (Davidson [1969a] 2001: 23)

According to Davidson, none of the premises are mistaken. Rather, the mistake lies in thinking that they are incompatible. His account of why they are not involves a distinction between conditional and unconditional judgements. I begin with a fairly crude formulation, refining along the way (in the face of certain well-trodden objections).

Davidson holds that we can consistently hold P1–3 because:

(1) There is a distinction to be made between conditional and unconditional judgements and P2 is a statement about unconditional judgements.
(2) Incontinence arises only when we act against our all-things-considered (ATC) conditional judgements.

Most objections to Davidson's 'solution' are related to 1 earlier. So let me try to explain what this distinction is.

Davidson argues that by their very nature conditional judgements are prima facie and hence (unlike unconditional ones which are sans phrase) cannot tell us anything about what we should do. It is important to note here that Davidson uses the term 'prima facie' (from here onwards '*pf*') differently from the way in which Ross used it when he first introduced it in *The Right and the Good* (indeed, Ross's *pf* duties are now commonly understood in *pro tanto* terms.[3]) According to Ross, *pf* duties are more or less incumbent upon the case (whichever one is found to be more incumbent being our duty *sans phrase* in the situation).[4] The duties that form the objects of Davidson's *pf* judgements, by contrast, cannot be detached (not even after all of the agent's considerations have been weighed up). Hence they cannot actually tell us how we should act.

Ross's account, then, is concerned with what people should unconditionally do (*pf*) while Davidson's *pf* judgements are focused on the conditional reasons of practical rationality (on what reasons agents may be said to have if their beliefs are true).[5] Accordingly, once an agent realizes that his beliefs may be mistaken there is nothing problematic in his judging that perhaps he should not be doing what his ATC *pf* judgement favours. What is meant by this is that although we can get practical rationality out of such judgements, they can never be judgements about what it would be most rational for us to do (for what makes this the case will include things we cannot consider which we should have).[6] It is in this sense that modal conclusions cannot be detached from *pf* judgements: it simply does not follow that we should do whatever we think we should do. While a Rossian duty to do x entails that *pf* we ought to do x, a Davidsonian *pf* judgement can do no such thing (and not merely because we may weigh up duties but not judgements). This can be demonstrated formally. Let 'O' stand for 'ought', 'B' for a certain belief (or judgement) and 'A' for a certain action. The point is that we cannot move from:

(a) $Ox (Bpx \to Ax)$

to

(b) $Bpx \to Ox (Ax)$

This is so regardless of whether or not B is a conditional judgement. There are objective requirements on what, judging certain things, we should do, and these will hold even if we shouldn't be doing these things (whatever our beliefs).[7] There are also normative requirements on what believing certain things, we should judge that we should do:

(c) $Ox (Bpx \to BxOx (Ax))$

For the same reasons as earlier, the detachment of the following conclusion would also be invalid:

(d) $Bpx \to Ox (BxOx (Ax))$

Given that it could be the case that my ATC judgement is mistaken, it cannot be the case that I ought to judge that I ought to do A simply because ATC I judge that I ought to do A. Grice and Baker (1985) argue that once all the available evidence (E) has been considered ATC judgements amount to unconditional judgements. But this must be mistaken, for a person x may consistently hold both that 'Ox (ATCx & Ex, Bpx, $\to Ax$)' and that '$Ox (\sim Ax)$'. A Fideist, for example, might think that all evidence points against the existence of God, yet without contradiction still maintain that he ought to believe in God, perhaps even because all the evidence counts against this (for belief-based on evidence is not faith). There is also the case of Miss Violet de Merville who, in Sherlock

Holmes' *The Adventure of the Illustrious Client*, judges that, while she ought to believe the best about her fiancé (Baron Gruner), she – in context, with the available evidence all things considered – ought not to.[8] In 'The Paradoxes of Irrationality' Davidson claims that the akratic agent goes against their own second-order principle that they ought to act on what they ATC-E judge to be best.[9] Yet this conclusion is precisely what we cannot detach. For one, it may be the case that I ought not to do what ATC-E I judge I should (think of all the various ways in which my judgement may be failed even after I have considered all the available evidence), so this would a very bad principle to have.

It is now perhaps tempting to ask whether (and if so how) we can ever reach any unconditional judgements, but there is no real difficulty here. Davidson's second-order principle of continence ('Perform the action judged best on the basis of all available reasons'[10]) tells us that we have no choice but to judge that we should do whatever our conditional judgement tells us to, even if this judgement is mistaken (in which case we shouldn't be doing whatever our conditional judgement tell us to). In short, it is internally rational for agents to form their unconditional judgements according to their ATC *pf* judgements. And yet if it is possible that an agent should not be doing what ATC they judge they should, it must also be possible for them to believe this despite also believing that they ought to judge that they should.

Since acting against one's better judgement (so-called weakness of the will) is a failure of internal rationality, it would therefore appear that by showing how it is possible for agents not to be internally rational Davidson has shown us how so-called weakness of the will is possible. I shall eventually be arguing that this is not so, but would first like to defend Davidson against a common misreading of his work.

2. Objections to Davidson

One objection against the aforementioned distinction involves the idea that if an agent judges that ATC he ought to do x they must also take it that they ought to judge (unconditionally) that they ought to do x. This is because to make an ATC judgement in favour of something is to think that all the considerations favour it, and one cannot think that all the considerations favour an action without judging that one should judge that one ought to do it. We might even go as far as to say that the best way of understanding the concept of 'counting in favour of' is in relation to its role in answering questions about what we should judge. It won't do to object that since it is possible that one may be wrong about what reasons one has, it must also be possible for one to think that he ought judge differently from his ATC judgement since what one should judge one should do need not necessarily correspond to what one should do. For example, probability may play a role in what one should judge one should do, as well as in what reasons we have for acting, but while playing no role in determining what one should do *tout court* (which is determined by what reasons there are).

So, if Davidson is right, it must be possible to judge that one should judge that one ought to do x while also judging that one ought not to do x. And yet these judgements seem contradictory. Charlton writes:

It seems artificial to distinguish 'I ought to judge that I ought to Q' from 'I ought to Q' for the judgement about a practical judgement seems to collapse into the practical judgement itself for to judge that I ought to judge that I should refrain from drinking this wine is *eo ipso* to judge that I ought to refrain. (Charlton 1988: 126)

At first sight this might seem to be trivially true, yet if Davidson is right it must be false. The Davidsonian argument runs as follows:

It is logically possible that it might be better for an agent A to do action x even if all the relevant facts available to him right now favour that he does not do x (for his judgement might be wrong for a variety of reasons). Hence it must also be logically possible for A to believe or to judge that he ought to do x, even if ATC, he judges (*pf*) that the best thing for him to do is y. Such a judgement would be irrational, but since it could even turn out to be true (if his conditional judgement were a mistaken one), it can hardly be illogical.[11]

It may be objected here that G. E. Moore has shown that there are things we know might be true that we cannot believe. So, for example, it would be paradoxical for A to assert 'p, but I do not believe that p' even though his not believing that p is perfectly compatible with his recognizing that he could be wrong. Moore's paradox would indeed be an objection to the claim that although A believes he ought to do y he does x because he also believes of himself that 'I ought to do x but I believe I ought to do y' (something that is clearly possible but not possible for him to believe). But this is not what A's ATC judgement amounts to. When we say that A irrationally believes that he ought to do x we mean that he believes this in spite of the fact that he judges that he should not believe that he ought to do x. There is no contradiction in this. In adopting the following two beliefs A would be irrational but not logically inconsistent:

(i) believing p, I ought to judge that I should do y.
(ii) I should do x.

Similarly, there is also no contradiction in his irrationally thinking that he ought to do whatever 'p' is a reason for doing, even if he doesn't think that he ought to believe 'that p'.

Were the agent to realize that an irrational belief cannot rationalize an action,[12] his conditional judgement about what he should do would indeed collapse into an unconditional one. But it is possible for an agent not to see this, and, as a consequence, to keep the two judgements apart in his mind. Suppose, for example, that I have an irrational fear of flying and am aware of this. The following may very well be true:

(1) I believe that the plane will crash.
(2) I realize that I have no reason to believe this.
(3) Seeing that I have no reason to believe this, I judge that ATC I should take the plane.

(4) This involves believing that (having the ATC judgement that I have) I should judge unconditionally that I should take the plane.
(5) I judge that I should not take the plane.[13]

The reason I give for my unconditional judgement is that the plane will crash. So I must obviously think this is a good reason for not taking the plane. In so doing, I ignore the requirement noted in (4), for it must also be true of me that I think that I should judge that I have no good reason for not taking the plane, since I have judged that ATC I should take the plane. I have no good reason for thinking that the plane will crash. This means that I judge that I have no good reason for my unconditional judgement. In short, I judge against my better (ATC) judgement.

Even if we accept the distinction, it may still be that Davidson cannot reconcile his three principles. So, for example, C. C. W. Taylor argues that if Davidson is committed to P2, he must also be committed to P2*, which is inconsistent with his account of irrationality:

(P2*) If an agent judges that all things considered, it would be better to do x than to do y, then he wants to do x more than he wants to do y. (Taylor 1980: 500)

The reason for this claim is that Taylor takes it that whatever the connection in P2, it must also hold for an agent who makes a conditional judgement that something is the best thing to do. He writes:

> If practical judgements give expression to desires, then the judgement 'all things considered it is better to do x than y' is a paradigm instance of a judgement fitted for that role ... if that kind of judgement lacks the capacity to generate desire, how could any judgement have that capacity? (Taylor 1980: 500)

I don't actually want to defend the connection in P2, but let us for the time being assume that it stands. If the connection holds then it will be true that ATC judgements give rise to some desire but why should it be true that *pf* judgements give rise to anything other than *pf* desires? In which case if one's unconditional judgement clashes with ones ATC judgement then one will desire to do as one judges unconditionally more than one desires to follow their conditional judgement. So P2* may not be true even if P2 is.

Nevertheless, Taylor seems to have hit a weak spot in Davidson's own account. For, according to Davidson, *pf* judgements can never lead to action, or even desire, for they are not practical in nature. Davidson writes:

> Intentional action [. . .] is geared directly to unconditional judgements [. . .] reasoning that stops at conditional judgements is practical only in its subject, not its issue. (Davidson [1969a] 2001: 39)

In other words, all actions involve unconditional judgements and these are the only judgements we act in virtue of.

3. Astheneia, propeteia, and the principle of continence

Davidson claims that we never act against our unconditional judgements but only against conditional ones. Yet, by his own admission, a conditional judgement cannot tell us anything about how we ought to act, but only how we ought to judge that we ought to act. This is problematic, for it cannot be irrational to act against a judgement that does not tell us anything about how we should act. The second-order principle is of no help either, since, as we have seen, it too cannot tell us how we should act but only what it would be internally rational to judge. Indeed, the second-order principle cannot be formulated as a judgement at all. But even if it could, on Davidson's account it too would have to be conditional (since we may fail to abide by it) and hence it could not tell us how to act.

Davidson has shown us how 'incontinent belief' (or 'epistemic weakness') is possible but has said nothing that supports the idea that we can clearly act against our better judgement. It would therefore seem that although the case that Davidson has described is (under some description) possible, it is not a case of *astheneia* but rather of *propeteia*, for the agent does not really reach a rational judgement and then fail to abide by it. Rather, he reaches an unconditional judgement that he abides by that he knows (or at least believes) he ought not to have reached.

True enough, what Davidson has described is not quite the same thing as Aristotle's description of *propeteia*, since according to Aristotle acts of *propeteia* are done rashly and there need not be anything rash in the judgements and actions that Davidson has in mind here. Nonetheless, it is far removed from what Aristotle defines as *astheneia*. After all, the agent still does what he thinks he ought to do.[14] It would seem that, not unlike Aristotle, Davidson began by taking it for granted that we can act against our (clear-eyed) better judgement, only to give an account of something quite different.[15]

Having established that Davidson's 'solution' allows for *propeteia* but not *astheneia*, let us now revisit the principles said to threaten the possibility of *akrasia* in the first place:

(P1) If an agent wants[16] to do x more than he wants to do y and he believes himself to be free to do either x or y, then he will intentionally do x if he does either x or y intentionally.

(P2) If an agent judges that it would be better to do x than to do y, then he wants to do x more than he wants to do y.

It would seem that, since Davidson understands and uses the term 'want' in a philosophers' sense, which makes it analytic that agents always do what they want, P1 is perfectly innocent. But I am a little bit sceptical about P2, given that it too is a claim about 'wants' in this philosophers' sense. In order to understand why this is puzzling, it might help to take another look at Taylor's *pf* principle:

(P2*) If an agent judges that all things considered, it would be better to do x than to do y, then he wants to do x more than he wants to do y. (Taylor 1980: 500)

This surely makes sense only if we understand 'wants' in the far narrower sense which allows that we constantly do things we don't 'really' want to be doing, for example because we have to (using the key terms here as they are used ordinarily), for the other understanding makes sense only if there is an action and as we have already seen, *pf* judgements need not lead to action (indeed according to Davidson they cannot). But if we understand the principle this way, it amounts to nothing other than motivation internalism – the thesis that all normative judgements are necessarily motivating. In other words P2* is only true if internalism is true. Let us return to Davidson's original principle again:

(P2) If an agent judges that it would be better to do x than to do y, then he wants to do x more than he wants to do y.

Davidson explicitly states that P2 is not committed to internalism as it is normally understood (Davidson [1969a] 2001: 30). If this were so, then the 'want' in question must be understood in the wide 'philosopher's' sense. In such a case the judgement in question must be unconditional. But then P2 would have the same meaning as the following principle:

(P2**) If an agent judges unconditionally that it would be better to do x than y, then he will do x and not y.

We get P2** in part because the 'want' in question implies that there has been an action. But not only is P2 a manifestation of strong motivational internalism,[17] it is also an all-out denial that *astheneia* exists, for we have seen that *astheneia* involves acting against one's unconditional judgement. There is something deeply unsatisfactory about the notion (occasionally voiced by Taylor) that we can rebut internalism simply by stating that weakness of the will exists. Still, we should not be too surprised if non-internalist accounts of motivation face no difficulties in allowing for the possibility of *astheneia*. One prerequisite might be that while actions should not necessarily follow from conditional judgements, they can do so. Davidson has not shown such claims to be false, but merely assumes so in holding that the conclusion of a practical syllogism is not only an unconditional judgement but also (as Aristotle is said to have thought) an action. At best, he views the conclusion as a judgement in action, which makes it logically impossible for the agent to act against it.

Epilogue

Davidson's distinction between different kinds of judgement remains a key element in any picture of how *astheneia* is possible, enabling us to understand how it is possible for someone to knowingly ignore a normative requirement on a combination of action and belief. Doing so involves acting (or omitting to act) against the unconditional judgement that this requirement is incumbent upon us. While this remains closer to *propeteia* than *astheneia*, the agent will have knowingly ignored a normative requirement in judging that he is doing the right thing. And if we can allow for that, there can be no problem with more paradigmatic cases of akratic action.

Part II

Reasons

6

Dretske on the causation of behaviour

Prologue

The term 'behaviour' has been used to refer to an immense variety of observable movements ranging from the motion of automobiles to voluntary and intentional human action. It is perhaps best, then, to begin with a brief characterization of how Fred Dretske uses the term. His use is no less idiosyncratic than that of most, as illustrated by the following passage from his book *Explaining Behavior*:

> [We should not] confuse movements which are brought about by internal events with their being brought about by these events. The former is an event, a movement, something that happens [. . .] the second, I shall argue, is a piece of behavior, possibly an action, something the rat *does*. (Dretske 1988b: 15)

Behaviour, so understood, is not any kind of bodily movement but something that creatures *do* as opposed to something that *merely happens* to their bodies as a result of some external force: it is a causal process in which they partake and not the result or effect of such a thing. This view rules out the counter-intuitive corollaries of more traditional accounts of action individuation, according to which A's act of killing B occurs *either* before B dies *or* at a time at which A may be dead.[1]

Dretske remains neutral on whether *all* behaviour, so understood, would count as action, let alone action that is voluntary and intentional (a point I return to further later).[2] What does follow from his account, however, is that behaviour involves more than *mere* bodily movement. More precisely, it is to be identified with the causal process of a bodily movement's *being caused* by an internal event. The event in question thereby stands in the wrong kind of relation to this behaviour to count as its cause, in any normal sense of the term.

1. Triggering and structuring causes

Dretske uses the term 'cause' in two different (though related) senses, distinguishing between what he calls '*triggering* causes' and what he calls '*structuring* causes':

> In looking for the cause of a process, we are sometimes looking for the triggering event: what caused the event C which, in turn, caused the movement M. At

other times we are looking for the events that *shaped* or *structured* the process: what caused C *to* cause M rather than something else. The first type of cause, the triggering cause, causes the process to occur *now*. The second type of cause, the structuring cause, is responsible for its being *this process,* one having M as its product, that occurs now. The difference [. . .] is familiar enough in explanatory contexts. There is a clear difference between explaining why, on the one hand, Clyde stood up *then*, and explaining, on the other hand, why what he did then was stand up (why he *stood up* then). He stood up *then* because that was when the queen entered, or when he saw the queen enter the room. He *stood up* then as a gesture of respect. The difference between citing the triggering cause of a process (the cause of the C which causes M) and what I have been calling its structuring cause (the cause of C's causing M) reflects this difference. (Dretske 1988b: 42–5)

As with 'behaviour', philosophical uses of the term 'cause' can be shamefully slippery. While Dretske does not enter ontological or metaphysical debates about the nature of causes and causal relations, one can infer from his general account that – contra Skinnerian behaviourism – he takes *triggering* (namely, mechanical or automatic) causes of behaviour to be mental 'states', 'events' or 'processes', and *structuring* causes to be the 'representational contents' of the aforementioned 'states' – namely, things we believe, desire, fear, suspect, and/or representational *facts* about the world.[3]

It is important to note that *both* triggering and structuring causes are taken by Dretske to be capable of *explaining* something about an event or an occurrence. The opening line of the previous quotation suggests that we have *one* object of explanation (one *explanandum*) to which we can attribute two (different kinds of) causes. But the second half of the passage suggests that there are *two* objects of explanation here: why he stood up *then*, and why he *stood up* then. Dretske (2004: 170–1) explicitly states that there are two things to be explained, this time identifying one as an *event* (which is caused by the triggering cause) and the other as the *background conditions* in which the triggering cause causes the event in question (conditions which are caused by the structuring cause).

As Dretske maintains, so long as we are clear about what we are doing it is harmless to refer to both as the cause of one and the same thing. Indeed, this way of putting things may sometimes be preferable, for there are (at least) two different kinds of things we might ask about *any* one given process or event, and depending on what we are asking (i.e. what we are trying to explain) we will sometimes be looking for a triggering cause and at other times for a structuring cause of the event in question. Yet we must not lose sight of the fact that for any given event we have (at least) two *different* objects of event explanation (two different things we are trying to explain). In Dretske's example quoted earlier, these were why an event occurred *now* (we might have also asked why it occurred at this location, or at this speed) and why *that* event (rather than another one) occurred (here, now, slowly) at all. Thus we get two explananda (two objects of explanation), one of which requires a triggering cause as its explanans and another of which requires a structuring cause; hence the need for two different kinds of causal explanantia. Dretske suggests as much towards the end of his book when he makes the following connection:

A *structuring* cause [. . .] helps explain, not why [desire] D or [movement] M is occurring now, but why, now, D is causing M (rather than something else). Failure to appreciate the difference between bodily movements (or external changes) and the behavior having those movements and changes as a product – hence, failure to appreciate the difference between a triggering and a structuring cause of behavior – is, I suspect, partly responsible for the mistaken idea that whatever triggers the behavior, whatever causes the beliefs (B) and desires (D) that (by causing M) constitute the behavior, must be the ultimate (causal) explanation of that behavior. (Dretske 1988b: 114–15)

The idea here seems to be that the difference between triggering and structuring causes of behaviour relies on a distinction between behaviour and its products (or results). This implies that there are two *different events* to be explained, something which, in turn, requires two different causal explanantia:

The difference helps to explain why one can know what caused each event constituting a process without knowing what caused the process. One can know what caused C (some triggering stimulus S), know what caused M (namely C), and still wonder about the cause of C's causing M. In this case, already knowing the triggering cause, one is clearly looking for the structuring cause of the process – what brought about those conditions *in which* C causes M (rather than something else). (Dretske 1988b: 43)

This is also implicit in an earlier passage of the book:

Think of one animal's catching sight of another animal and running away. The approach of the second animal (let this be the stimulus S) causes certain events (C) to occur in the first animal's central nervous system: it *sees* S. Together with relevant motivational factors, these perceptual events in the animal bring about certain movements M: the animal *runs*. To oversimplify enormously, S causes C, and C in turn causes M. This much might be inferred from casual observation – the animal ran *when*, and presumably *because*, it saw the intruder. But why did the sight of the intruder (C) cause flight (M)? Why did the animal run away? The intruder, after all, was not a predator. It was in no way dangerous. It was, in fact, a familiar neighbor. So why did C cause M? This question is a question about the structuring, not the triggering, cause of the process C→M. (Dretske 1988b: 43)

Dretske has here distinguished between the triggering cause of event M and the structuring cause of process C→M. But what of the structuring cause of M and the triggering cause of C→M? We have not been told anything about these things. This is because Dretske's distinction between two different sorts of causal explanantia is really a disguised distinction between two different explananda, each of which has a different explanatory cause. It makes no sense to say of *each* of these explananda that they have both a structuring and a triggering cause. Rather, what we want is a causal explanation (provided by C) of why the (mere bodily) movements M (running) occurred and a separate causal explanation for why $C{\to}M$ (the entire process of C causing M) occurred. What we are looking for here are not two different causes of one and the same event (e.g. in the sense that we might ask two different things about it), but rather two different causes each of which explains the occurrence of a different event (or process).

Consider a further example of his:

> The bell rings (S), and this produces a certain auditory experience (C) in the dog. The dog *hears* the bell ring. These sensory events, *as a result of conditioning*, caused saliva to be excreted (M) in the dog's mouth. What, then, causes the dog to salivate? Well, in one sense, the ringing bell causes the dog to salivate. At least the bell, by causing the dog to have a certain auditory experience, triggers a process that results in saliva's being secreted into the dog's mouth. Yes, but that doesn't tell us why the dog is doing what it is doing – only why it is doing it *now*. What we want to know is why the dog is salivating. Why isn't it, say, jumping? Other (differently trained) dogs jump when they hear the bell. Some (not trained at all) don't do much of anything. So what causes the dog to salivate? This clearly, is a request, not for the triggering cause of the dog's behavior, but for the structuring cause. It is a request for the cause of one thing's causing another, the cause of the auditory experience causing salivary glands to secrete. And once again, it seems, the answer to this question lies in the past, in what learning theorists describe as the *contingencies* (correlations between the ringing bell and the arrival of food) to which the dog was exposed during training. If salivation is thought of as something the dog *does* (not simply as a glandular event occurring *to* the dog or *in* the dog) – if, in other words, it is thought of as *behavior* – then the causal explanation for it resides, not in the stimulus that elicits the behavior, but in facts about the dog's past experience. (Dretske 1988b: 43–4)

For Dretske's purposes, classical (Pavlovian) conditioning plays the same functional role as operant (Skinnerian) conditioning, genetic determination, upbringing, duress or any other cause that structures emitted behaviour (be it intentional or otherwise).[4] In the previous case, we are informed that the event of the dog's salivating has both a triggering cause (the ringing of the bell) and a structuring cause (that the dog was exposed to correlations between the bell's ringing and the arrival of food), but that the causal explanation of the dog's *act* of salivating is typically provided by the structuring cause *alone*. The fact that the dog was exposed to certain correlations does not explain (causally or otherwise) why saliva was excreted from the dog's mouth but, rather, why the ringing of the bell caused him to salivate. That is to say, it does not explain why M occurred, but why the process that was $C{\to}M$ – which Dretske identifies with the dog's behaviour – occurred. By the same token, the ringing of the bell cannot (alone) explain why the dog salivated. For that we need both the 'triggering' and the 'structuring' cause: the dog salivated because the bell rang and he had already been subjected to the aforementioned training. Both these facts form parts of *one and the same* causal explanation of why the dog salivated; however, only the second fact provides us with a full causal explanation of a different *explanandum*, namely why the dog salivated *when the bell* rang.[5]

2. Psychological and non-psychological explanations

In more recent work, Dretske (1993, 2004) appeals to his distinction between *triggering* and *structuring* causes with the aim of showing how it is that *psychological* explanations of behaviour differ from *non*-psychological ones such as, for example, *biological* explanations. He concludes that intentional human behaviour is triggered by electrochemical events but structured by so-called 'representational facts', facts about *how* we view the world.

When we seek an explanation of intentional action in terms of an agent's reasons, Dretske maintains, we are always looking for a *structuring* cause (2004: 174–6) that is *internal*, in other words, intrinsic to the system whose behaviour we are seeking to explain (2004: 172). Unlike plant behaviour, which is never intentional and whose structuring causes are always external, that is, extrinsic to their system (2004: 172–3), human behaviour is typically explained in terms of the agent's beliefs and desires (2004: 172).[6]

Dretske maintains that, in the sense in which an agent's beliefs and desires may be called reasons *for* his behaviour, they are not to be identified with psychological states or events. This is because explanatory reasons for action, on his view, are not reasons that cause the occurrence of a bodily movement but, rather, reasons for a person's bringing about a bodily movement. This leads him to maintain further that the reasons for which an agent acts are to be identified with his so-called 'mental contents' or (as he sometimes also puts it) 'what a creature knows and wants' (Dretske 1988b: 32; 1988a: 40–3).[7]

Reasons, for Dretske, are not mental states or events but rather *what* agents believe and desire (e.g. *that* something is or becomes the case), where these might occasionally be facts *about* their beliefs and desires (and those of others) – for example, when one seeks to see (or send a friend to) a psychiatrist because one has (or they have) some irrational belief or desire. According to his representational theory of mind, such possible facts are the *contents* of mental states (see Dretske 1988a).

Dretske tells us that reasons for action are *structuring* causes of *movements* [M]. *Triggering* causes, by contrast, cause 'states' of *desire* (D):

> [W]hat makes it true to say that the rat presses the bar *in order to get food*, that getting food was the rat's *purpose* or *reason for pressing the bar*, that the rat pressed the bar because it *wanted* food, is that the rat's movements (M) are being caused, in part at least, by an internal state D, having food as its goal; and the explanation of *why* D is causing M, and hence an explanation of the behavior, is the fact that D has this goal, the fact that D is, specifically, a receptivity to *food*. It is this fact that explains D's recruitment as a cause of M and, thus, helps explain the rat's current behavior.

> The fact that a hungry rat, furiously pressing a bar in order to get food, occupies state D, a state that was recruited as a cause of bar-pressing movements because, *in the past*, these movements led to food does not, obviously, explain why D *now* exists, why the rat is *now* hungry. Nor does it explain why M is now occurring.

D's having *R* as its goal, its being *for R*, is not a triggering cause of behavior. It is a *structuring* cause. It helps explain, not why *D* or *M* is occurring now, but why, now, *D* is causing *M* (rather than something else). Failure to appreciate the difference between bodily movements (or external changes) and the behavior having those movements and changes as a product – hence, failure to appreciate the difference between a triggering and a structuring cause of behavior – is, I suspect, partly responsible for the mistaken idea that whatever triggers the behavior, whatever causes the beliefs (*B*) and desires (*D*) that (by causing *M*) constitute the behavior, must be the ultimate (causal) explanation of that behavior. (Dretske 1988b: 114–15)

Triggering causes, Dretske maintains, are neither our reasons for, nor the causes of, our actions (roles which only the *structuring* causes of our behaviour can play). Rather, the *triggering* causes of our behaviour are those (neural or perceptual) events which trigger beliefs and desires and thereby cause our movements M. *Structuring* causes of behaviour, by contrast, are the reasons for which we act: things which we believe. Reasons *can* be causes – but only of the *structuring* kind. The *triggering* causes of our behaviour are not reasons for which we act. We might illustrate this with the following diagram (all arrows signify, and reveal the direction of, a causal relation).

We saw earlier that (on Dretske's account) behaviour – be it intentional or otherwise – is to be identified with the process that is the causing of *M* (see Dretske 1988b: 15 and Dretske 2009). In the case of intentional behaviour *M* will always be caused (triggered) by a belief (*B*) and desire (*D*). This is a necessary condition, but not a sufficient one unless the explanation provided by the related structuring cause is teleological in nature. For Dretske, teleological explanations are ones wherein the reason which structurally causes the behaviour does so in virtue of the meaning of the 'mental contents' in question. Accordingly, action is intentional if and only if its structuring cause explains why the combination of belief *B* and desire *D* caused movement *M* by virtue of B and D's meaning and not some other property.

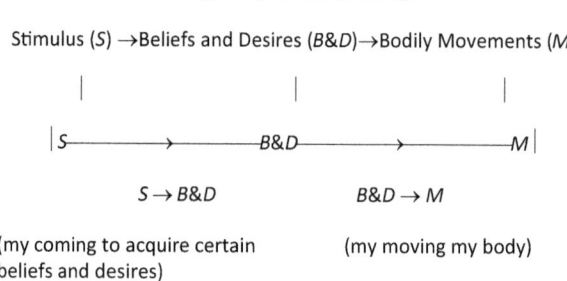

Triggering Causes (Events):

Stimulus (*S*) →Beliefs and Desires (*B&D*)→Bodily Movements (*M*)

|S————————B&D————————M|

S → B&D   B&D → M

(my coming to acquire certain   (my moving my body)
beliefs and desires)

Structuring Causes (Facts): Reasons which explain why *B* & *D* → *M* (why my moving of my body occurred/why I moved my body)

Figure 3 Moving my body © Constantine Sandis.

The structuring causal role played by meaning here enables Dretske to distinguish between explanations in which a belief–desire pair 'rationalizes' an action and ones where the same pair causes the same type of action in some non-rational manner (as in Davidson's examples of deviant causal chains).

This successful method meeting the challenge presented by so-called 'deviant causal chains' (in which belief–desire pairs cause the behaviour they rationalize in a non-rational manner) constitutes a serious theoretical advantage over other causalist theories (such as Davidson's), which cannot appeal to teleology here because they are in the business of providing a *reductive* account of what it is to act intentionally (a point nicely emphasized by Sehon 1997).[8]

In the next section, I raise an objection to Dretske's necessary and sufficient conditions for an action being intentional. I then consider and reject a possible response (in §5). I conclude that, while Dretske's account of action explanation is superior to other causalist accounts, it remains based on a picture which ultimately fails to distinguish between *intentional action* and instinctive *non-intentional* behaviour (of creatures) the explanation of which is still teleological in nature – namely, action that is neither intentional nor unintentional (e.g. reflex action).

3. Meaning in mind

According to Dretske, the difference between instinctive non-intentional behaviour and intentional action is that, in the case of the former, our beliefs and desires (though present) play no *relevant* role in the production of our behaviour:

> Meaning, though it is there, is not relevantly *engaged* in the production of output. The system doesn't do what it does, C doesn't cause M, *because* of what C (or anything else) means or indicates about external conditions. Though C has meaning of the relevant kind, that is not a meaning it has *to* or *for* the animal to which it occurs. That, basically, is why genetically determined behaviors are not explicable in terms of the actor's reasons. That is why they are not *actions*. (Dretske 1988b: 94–5)[9]

In other words, the structuring causes of reflex actions *are external*, and the explanation of instinctive behaviour is no different from the explanation of the behaviour of plants. This is surely right for *certain* non-intentional actions, but I believe that it is wrong for many others. Consider the following example, which aims to persuade that meaning may sometimes play a role in the explanation of non-intentional action.

Suppose I am walking down the street and somebody calls out 'Constantine'. Their doing so may cause me to turn my head towards the direction their voice is coming from. If asked why I turned my head that way, I shall reply (rightly) that I heard someone call out my name. This reason (the fact that someone called out my name) causally explains why the sound they made in doing so triggered the event that was my head turning around. The reason is the structuring cause of my behaviour. The triggering cause is the noise stimulus exerted by the person calling my name. We might illustrate what is going on here with the following diagram:

My hearing the noise causes me to turn my head because of the 'content' of the noise, because of what it *means* to me. It is because the word uttered ('Constantine') is my name that I turn my head. If what is being uttered is given a purely physical (rather than a linguistic) description, then we would not ordinarily *understand* why these noises caused me to turn my head.[10] This fact (the *reason why* I turned my head) is therefore of great *explanatory* value to us – but it does not *trigger* anything. It is *my hearing the noise* that triggers the turning of my head, not what the noise stands for, what it *means*, or, in Dretske's terminology, what it *represents* (1988b: Ch. 3).

Nevertheless, it is *by virtue of the meaning* of the sounds uttered (and not merely by virtue of the *physical properties* of the sound waves being transmitted) that *this* piece of causation occurs; the meaning of the sounds *structures* the (non-deviant) causation taking place. Moreover, it could have been sufficient (for my head to move) that I *thought* or *believed* that someone had called out my name (and that I had the relevant desire; see below). Say it turned out that what had actually been said was 'constant teen'. The fact that my hearing these words being uttered caused me to turn my head (because I *thought* I heard 'Constantine') does not render my behaviour any more intentional. Likewise, we may assume that I *wanted* to see who was calling my name. Had I been differently disposed (say that, for some reason, I wanted to be left alone), then my hearing my name (or my thinking that I heard my name) would *not* have caused me to turn my head (perhaps, instead, it would have caused me to hide). So it makes sense to think of my beliefs and desires as the structuring causes of my non-intentional behaviour. But what this means is that it is *the fact* that I have these beliefs and desires that is the structuring cause of my behaviour. There is a sense in which my beliefs and desires may be said to *cause* my head to move; however, what causally *explains* my moving my head (the reason *why* I moved it) is not a belief–desire pair itself but the *fact* that I have those beliefs and desires. Facts about our psychology may explain why we do certain things, and they may do so causally (in the sense that they point towards a cause), yet it would be ontologically perverse to identify them with any mental episodes that trigger bodily movements of any kind.

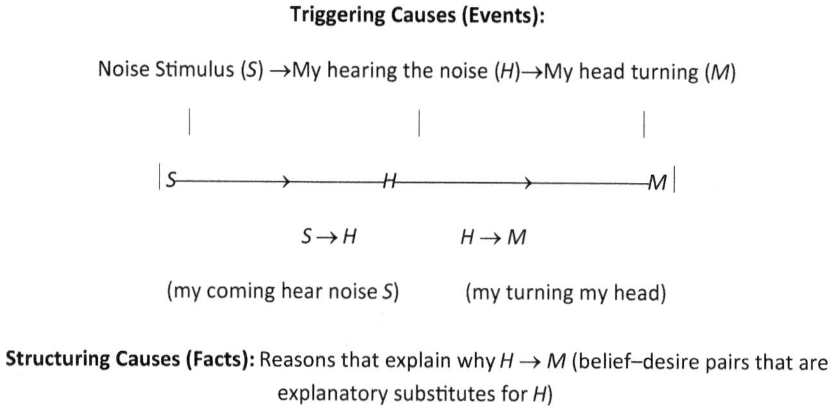

Triggering Causes (Events):

Noise Stimulus (S) →My hearing the noise (H)→My head turning (M)

| S————→————H————→————M |

S → H   H → M

(my coming hear noise S)   (my turning my head)

Structuring Causes (Facts): Reasons that explain why H → M (belief–desire pairs that are explanatory substitutes for H)

Figure 4 Turning my head © Constantine Sandis.

Now, according to Dretske, if *and only* if this is so, my behaviour *must* be intentional. Indeed, for Dretske, intentional behaviour just *is* a movement *being caused* (in the 'right way') by a belief–desire pair. But although my wants and thoughts causally explained why I turned my head, I did not turn my head *intentionally*. Nor was I motivated to do it (and I certainly did not turn my head in the light of any reasons). To say that you calling my name caused *me* to turn my head is just to say that my head turned when you called my name. I did not set out to turn it, nor did I turn it *for* a reason, though there is, of course, a reason which explains *why* I turned it. We should not, in such cases, conflate any teleological reasons we may give *after* the fact with *motivation* for the behaviour (which will have been entirely absent in cases of non-intentional action).[11] We can, no doubt, imagine someone who, in turning their head, acts upon the consideration that someone called their name, perhaps taking this to be a good reason for turning their head. The point here is only that this *need not* be so when a person turns their head because someone has called out their name (or something that sounds like it).

Anscombe (1957: §15) notes persuasively that the attempted contrast between having hung one's hat on a peg because one's host said, 'hang your hat on that peg' and turning around at hearing someone say 'Boo!' fails, because whether or not we should view either action as one performed for a reason is to be decided by facts such as that of 'how sudden one's reaction was'. Whether or not the triggering of any reaction is to be explained by a fact about what (if anything) the words meant to the person acting is neither here nor there. Mutatis mutandis, the question of whether one acted for a reason or was *merely* caused to behave remains open in certain cases of actions that have exactly the same structure as the one which Dretske provides for intentional action. In the case of turning my head described earlier, some internal events (namely, my hearing, or my believing I heard, someone call my name and my wanting to see who it was) in some way mediated between the initial triggering cause (calling my name) and the effect (my head turning), where this mediation played a causal role. Thus, the sound waves transmitted did *not directly* cause my head to turn (*that* would not have been a case of action at all – reflex or otherwise – but more like one's hair, or in the case of Mary Poppins one's whole body, being blown by the wind), yet we could not confidently describe a sudden action of this type as being intentional.

Of course, it remains possible that *some* cases of a movement's being produced by one's beliefs and desires are cases of intentional behaviour since, for all I have said, Dretske's analysis may have isolated *necessary* conditions on being an intentional action even if has failed to pick out *sufficient* ones. For my part, I remain content to have shown that Dretske's model fails to provide a criterion by which we can distinguish the explanation of intentional action from that of non-intentional behaviour. If I am right, then this would also help to explain Dretske's counter-intuitive description of the behaviour of a bird avoiding a noxious type of bug as *intentional* (2004: 174).[12]

Another possible response would be to narrow the Dretskean analysis of what it is for an action to be intentional by inserting the very concept of a reason for action straight into it. On such a revised view, an intentional action would be a bodily movement's being structurally caused by (only) those contents of a belief–desire pair which (further) constitute the *reason*(s) for which the agent acted.

One difficulty for this strategy is that some philosophers (e.g. Hursthouse 1991) have devised a number of counterexamples to the claim that all intentional actions are done for reasons (these include such actions as tearing one's hair or clothes in grief or clutching a picture or possession of a recently deceased loved one), while others (e.g. Knobe and Kelly 2009) question the parallel assumption that all actions performed for reasons are intentional. If their arguments convince, then reasons will not help to mark out intentional behaviour. Still, in what follows I shall not be relying on these controversial positions,[13] for I believe it can be demonstrated that the revised Dretskean analysis fails *even if* we should remain unpersuaded by the aforementioned challenges.

Suppose I raise my arm to wave to a friend. A Dretskean might illustrate this simple action with the following diagram:

Suppose further that stimulus S constitutes my seeing my friend across the road, and that S causes me to acquire the belief that my friend is across the road, and the desire to wave to her, and that this belief-desire pair further causes my arm to rise. According to Dretske, the *triggering* cause of my behaviour (my raising my arm) is *stimulus S*, and the *structuring* cause is made up of the *fact* that – as I believe – my friend is across the street, and the further fact that I want to wave to her. Dretske himself has illustrated such a point with the following kind of diagram (1988b: 88):

In Dretske's terminology, *B&D* come to *represent S* (the structuring cause of M) by *indicating S*, and because of this they come to be *recruited* as a triggering cause of M. As we have already seen, my reason for acting on this view is not *B&D*, nor (typically) the fact *B&D* are true of me, but rather the 'content' of *B&D*. But now a problem arises: if M is triggered by my belief(s) and desire(s) *proper*, then although it is causally relevant that these beliefs and desires have *a* (meaningful) content, I will have many other (competing) belief-desire pairs with meaningful content that may also be capable of rendering the same action intelligible. Content alone apparently cannot tell us *which* belief-desire pair triggered the action, for at any given time I may have several pairs

Triggering Causes (Events):

Stimulus (S) →Beliefs and Desires (B&D)→My arm's rising (M)

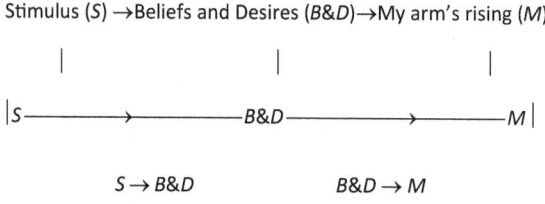

S → B&D	B&D → M
(my coming to acquire certain beliefs and desires)	(my raising my arm)

Structuring Causes (Facts): Reasons which explain why $B\&D \to M$ (why my beliefs and desires caused me to raise my arm).

Figure 5 Raising my arm © Constantine Sandis.

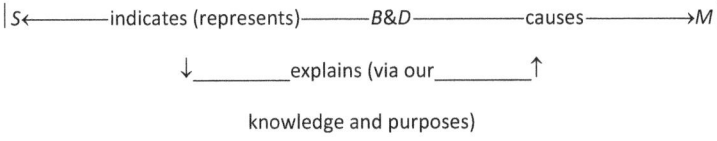

Figure 6 Indicating stimuli © Constantine Sandis.

whose content could render my action intelligible.[14] In sum, the purported explanation of action provided by Dretske's structuring causes does not say anything about why *one particular* belief–desire pair triggered the action rather than another (with an equally suitable 'content'), and *a fortiori* cannot (by Dretske's own lights) determine which reason(s) I acted upon.

It is no good to retort that the belief–desire pair that triggered my bodily movement was whichever one was (motivationally) 'strongest'. As it stands, this tired metaphor is next to meaningless, and the motivational information required to clarify things is not provided by a Dretskean structuring reason. While facts *about* my psychology may *indicate* a triggering cause, thereby explaining why certain features of my psychology caused me to move my body, so-called 'mental contents' cannot alone indicate such a thing.[15] The so-called contents of one or more of my belief–desire pairs may well explain (or at any rate, render intelligible) why I moved my arm in such a way so as to make a wave,[16] but (in so doing) they cannot explain why the *relevant* belief–desire pair (rather than some other one) triggered any movement at all – and yet this is precisely what a Dretskean account of action explanation requires. The problem is one of distinguishing between having a (motivating) reason and acting upon it (cf. von Wright 1988: 281).

Epilogue

On Dretske's account, the reasons one acts upon will just be the ones related to whichever belief–desire pair leads us to action, but 'mental contents' alone cannot inform us as to which one this is, for the mere existence of content that can render an action intelligible cannot explain which belief–desire pair triggered the bodily movement in question. Dretske's account offers no method of determining *which* 'mental contents' constituted the reason(s) for which the agent acted, leaving us with no demarcating criterion for intentional action.

Dretske's account of action and its explanation has been unjustifiably neglected in favour of that of Davidson. Yet the latter is far less plausible when it comes to accounting for the nature and individuation of action, the challenge of deviant causal chains, and the distinguishing mark of psychological explanation (namely, meaning). Despite the many insights relating to Dretske's account of agential reasons, we should reject his overall view that intentional human behaviour is triggered by electrochemical events but structured by representational facts. This is because it fails to capture what is distinctive about *intentional* action and its explanation.

7

The objects of action explanation

Prologue

Behaviour can, of course, be motionless. G. H. von Wright ([1988] 1998: 97) gives the example of pressing one's hand against a door to keep it closed. Other examples include standing still, refusing to answer a question by keeping quiet, reciting a poem to oneself or staring at something intensely. Motionless behaviour may – but need not – involve omissions.[1] In the same passage von Wright also notes that the term 'behaviour' has misleadingly been used to refer not only to macroscopic (molar) activity but also to microscopic (molecular) activity such as that of the neural processes that constitute the underlying physiology of bodily movement.[2]

Behavioural scientists invariably use the term 'behaviour' in all of the aforementioned senses. But even restricting ourselves to behaviour involving outward bodily movement, there remain at least three distinct candidates:

(a) The (mere) movement of the agent's body
(b) The event (b1) or process (b2) of the agent moving their body
(c) *What* the agent did (namely, move her body).

The precise individuation of (a–c) is, of course, a matter of much philosophical debate.[3] What follows is but a prima facie intuitive way of characterizing their interrelations.

What falls under (a) is a causal process or event, further specifiable (under a certain description) as a *movement* of the agent's body, in the intransitive sense of the term, according to which it doesn't take an intentional object. In Jennifer Hornsby's terminology, the movement in question refers to the agent's body's moving, and *not* to the agent's moving (of) her body.[4] We would not normally call such behaviour an *action*.

We may also think of (b1) as an event, but one not obviously identical to (a). We may describe (b1) as a movement in the transitive sense of the word – namely, the *agent's* moving (of) her body (intentionally or otherwise). Event (a) is arguably the bodily movement in which (b1) (the event of bringing the first event about) *results*.[5] The events featured in (a) and (b1) may thus be thought to be logically related, but not identical: a transitive movement event [T] is the event of bringing about an intransitive movement event [I].[6] Many philosophers are happy to call b1-events (but not a-events) 'action', for the sorts of reasons outlined by A. C. Ewing:

An action occurs in time, has a duration, however short, is a change, and is not universal or again a 'thing'. That being so I do not understand what is meant by denying that it is an event. (Ewing 1938: 91)[7]

Others prefer to view actions as (b2) *processes* of bringing a-events about, it being a moot point whether or not processes are *aspects* of events. Such processes are typically seen as being causal – that is, as processes of agents and/or their minds *causing* a-events.[8] On some Aristotelian views, however, actions are *non-causal* processes of people doing things.[9]

1. Actions, processes and events

While both processes and events *occur*, processes – causal or otherwise – cannot be said to *happen*. Processes differ from events in various additional ways: they do not *extend* in time or have essential temporal parts, though they may contain sub-processes which persist for part or all of their time.[10] More crucially, we can be *engaged* in a process as it *unfolds* over a period of time during which it may be interrupted (Anscombe 1957: 39 (§23)). One may, for example, be in the process of baking a cake without succeeding in baking one (without there ever being a cake-baking event).[11] So understood, the everyday action of tying one's shoelaces would not consist in a series of brief bodily movements, each followed by a tiny shoelace movement, but, rather, in a single process allowing no sharp distinction between the agent's own movements and those of the laces. Linguistic observations are here supplemented by phenomenological ones (try to imagine *teaching* someone how to tie their shoelaces without a shoe present). On such a conception, the non-causal bringing about of an a-event is *constitutive* of action. If, like me, you are always doing things but rarely get anything done, this view will be appealing to you.

The process view adheres to the *Oxford English Dictionary*'s first listed definition of 'action' as 'the *process* or *condition* of acting or doing (in the widest sense)'. This takes the preposition 'of' to be marking an identity as opposed to, say, a relation. So treated, the preposition is thought to function as it does in the phrase 'the city of Paris' in contrast to 'the hunchback of Notre Dame', 'the Pick of Destiny', 'the House of Lords' or – more contentiously – 'the property of being red'. If processes are different to events, then the *process of* my raising my arm cannot be identical to the *event of* my raising my arm. On the (b2) understanding of action, then, the 'of' in 'the event *of* my acting' does not mark an identity. On a (b1) understanding, by contrast, the event of my raising my arm *is* my raising my arm: an action (which may or may not be identical to the process of raising my arm, depending on whether the b1-theorist distinguishes processes from events.) It is also possible to hold a hybrid or disjunctivist view. For example Alexander Mourelatos (1978: 423) maintains that actions are occurrences which divide into activities (whose topic-neutral counterparts are processes) and performances (whose topic-neutral counterparts are events).

The *OED* distinguishes the process definition from that of action as '[a] thing done, a deed. Not always distinguished from act, but usually viewed as occupying some time in doing, and in *plural* referred to habitual or ordinary deeds, the sum of which constitutes *conduct*'. This brings us to (c), namely *what* the agent did: her deed (as opposed to her doing of it). We rightly talk of *acts* of doing things, but the *things* we do are not always actions. Kennett and Smith ([1996] 2004: 80) give the example of thinking. To perform an action, on the other hand, is by definition to do something. Even then, however, the things we do are neither bodily movements-I nor bodily movements-T. The latter are events of our bringing about movements-I. *What* we do is no more identical to what we bring about than it is to the event of our bringing it about. To do something just *is* to bring something about; we may also bring things about *by* and sometimes even *in* omitting to do them.¹²

In the aforementioned cases involving outward bodily behaviour the event of A's acting is an event of her bringing about a bodily movement-T. What she *brings about* (the movement) is the result of the former event. What she *does* is *to* bring it about. This is to be distinguished from the event, process or condition of her doing this in much the same way as *what* we believe is to be distinguished from the event, state or process of our believing it.¹³ John Macmurray has made a related point:

> The term 'action' is involved in the same ambiguity that recent philosophy has found it essential to resolve in the case of terms like 'perception' or 'conception'. It may refer either to what is done or to the doing of it. It may mean either 'doing' or 'deed'. When we talk of 'an action' we are normally referring to what is done [...] The analysis of the idea of action does not deal with the concomitants of action, but with action itself; and it yields only the distinction between the *doing* and the *deed*. It may be convenient to refer to these two aspects of action by the Latin words which distinguish them – *actio* and *actum*'. (Macmurray 1938: 74–6)

Strictly speaking, '*actio*' (like '*cogitatio*', which Macmurray contrasts it with) is not a verbal noun but a feminine third declension noun substantive, formed from the same past participle (of the verb '*ago*'), of which '*actum*' (which Macmurray contrasts with '*eventum*') is the neuter fourth declension version; Macmurray's translation most likely reflects English idiom arising from the legal context of the term '*actio*'. Grammatical quibbles aside, there is evident conceptual space for the sort of distinction he is making here and it is *at least* as natural to talk of actions as things we do, perform, undertake, execute, or carry out as it is to talk of them as our *doings* of such things. Similar semantic distinctions have been championed by Austin ([1954] 1961: 164), Brown (1968: 28–9), Thalberg (1977: 55), Hornsby (1980: Ch. 1) and Clark (1989). *Pace* Macmurray, who takes his distinction to demonstrate that actions are never events which happen but rather either activities we perform (in the sense in which acting contrasts with thinking) or deeds we do (1938: 79), I see no reason to deny that the term 'action' may legitimately be used to refer to either (i) *what* we do or (ii) the event and/or process and/or activity of our doing it. On the contrary, this arguably accounts for the practice of applying conflicting predicates to (i) an act performed and (ii) the performance of the act in question (cf. Clark 1989). For example:

- I do not object to *what you did* (e.g. hang a painting) but to *your doing it* (in the middle of the night, poorly, noisily, by yourself, and so on).

- *What she did* was not in the least scary but *her doing it* gave me a real fright at the time.
- He may have *done* what the rules required of him, but *his doing it* was completely accidental.
- I *did the same thing* as everyone else and yet *my doing it* was deemed irregular.

The general pattern may also be applied to utterances and beliefs:

- *What she said* may have been very clever but *her saying it* (to her employer) was less so.
- The fact that *what he believed* (e.g. that he would win the lottery) turned out to be true does not make *his believing it* (given the available evidence) any less irrational.
- Pascal thinks that *believing* in God is rational even if *what* is thereby believed is neither rational nor true.

The examples cast doubt on adverbial approaches to behavioural predication according to which 'she did a scary thing' is just another way of saying 'she acted scarily' (Dancy 2009: 404, 411). And while it is plausible to maintain that in the second clause of any evaluative proposition earlier, the true subject of the predicate is not an event but a person (Dancy 2009: 404, 411), the non-evaluative cases do fit this model as easily. None of this is being offered here as conclusive proof of anything other than the fact that – however one positions oneself in any of the previous debates – the terms 'behaviour' and 'action' have no obvious single referent, even when we restrict ourselves to acts involving visible bodily movements.[14] Given the openness of both terms to the distinctions laid out earlier, one cannot fix an *explanandum* by invoking them with no further comment.

2. Behavioural discoveries

Behaviour in any one of the senses described so far may correctly present itself to us in a multitude of different ways, thus rendering the explanation and evaluation of any given action relative to its mode of presentation, to use Husserl's expression for the way in which a thing may strike us. (Ever since the linguistic turn of modern 'analytic' philosophy, it has been more fashionable to express this idea in the considerably narrower terms of action *description* or *conceptualisation* (Anscombe 1957; Davidson [1963] 2001.)

But to identify an action under a certain description is not yet to identify *what it is about it* that is to be explained. After all, depending on our aims or objectives, we may ask different things about the occurrence of this event, each of which gives rise to a different *explanandum*, in turn requiring a different *explanans*: *how* it was done, *why* it occurred at time t_1 *rather than* at time t_2, why x was brought about *instead of y*, and so on. The point has been forcefully made by Peter Achinstein, who argues more generally that unless we specify what question we are asking of any given phenomenon, we will have failed to fix a specific *explanandum* or 'object of explanation', as he mischievously puts it (Achinstein 1975: 11–18).[15] Even if we restrict ourselves to events of people acting, it won't do to maintain – as Jon Elster, among many others, does – that to explain an event 'is to give an account of why it happened', let alone 'by citing an earlier *event* as its cause' (Elster 2007: 9).

Such concerns quickly lead to ontological questions regarding the general nature of both e*xplananda* and their *explanantia*. Thus, Hempel and Oppenheim (1948) famously conceive of *explananda* and *explanantia* as sentences and classes of sentences respectively, as opposed to the phenomena which these pick out. It may be preferable, however, to sympathize with 'ordered pair' and 'no product' propositional views, according to which 'we must begin with the concept of an illocutionary act of explaining and characterize explanations, by reference to this, rather than conversely' (Achinstein 1983: 102). So construed, *explanantia* are better understood as statements of fact whose explananda are neither sentences nor phenomena but *reperienda* or 'discoverables', namely, the things we seek to find out, for example, *why* the bridge exploded when it did, as opposed to the actual explosion of the bridge or a sentence describing it.

Let me now list three such *reperienda*, corresponding to the three conceptions of behaviour (a–c) outlined in §1 earlier:

(i) Why A's body moved
(ii) Why A's action of moving her body occurred
(iii) Why A moved her body.

In (i) we are searching for the *cause* of the event that was the movement of A's body. What is sought in (ii), by contrast, is the *cause* of the (related) event *of A's moving her body* to occur. Finally, to provide an explanation of (iii) is to explain neither (i) why A's body moved – after all it may have moved *because* she moved it – nor (ii) why an event of her moving her body occurred. Indeed, to explain why someone did something is not to explain why anything – including the event of her doing the thing in question – occurred. Nor is it to explain *the thing* she did. For an explanation of *what* she did is not necessarily an explanation of *why* she did it, although we may successfully explain why we do things by re-describing the things we do so as to make our aim or intention apparent.[16] Rather, it is to explain why A performed the action of moving her body. Here it is far less obvious that we are looking for a *cause*, and it may even be that she did what she did for *no reason* at all (which is not to say that the *event* of her doing so was uncaused); in certain contexts it may even be that she needs no reason to act as she does.

It is worth emphasizing that (i)–(iii) would remain distinct *even* on the implausible assumption that conceptions (a)–(c) are ultimately reducible to three different ways of characterizing one and the same phenomenon for – as we have just seen – there is a range of questions we may ask of any given phenomenon (even under a tightly specified description) and its name is legion.

But which of (i)–(iii) it is that they typically seek to explain? It seems to me that (i) is of purely *physiological* interest, (ii) is of far more interest to social and political scientists, historians, and economists than it is to the layperson, who is typically concerned with (iii). As laypeople (and academics are laypeople too, though we sometimes do our best to forget this), what we are normally interested in is why a person did something, or why they did it at a certain time, for a certain reason, instead of something else; so on, and not why the event of their doing it occurred.

Jennifer Hornsby helpfully relates the distinction between (ii) and (iii) to philosophical confusion over action explanation, observing that to request an explanation for why A did *x* is *not* to ask why the event of her doing it occurred, though both might legitimately be conceived of as behavioural *explanantia*:

> What a non-philosopher means when she accepts that there are actions is that the phenomenon of action is exemplified: people do things (for reasons). But she does not mean (even if it can be made obvious) that there are events each one of which is a person's doing something. The word 'action' is ambiguous. Where it has a plural: in ordinary usage what it denotes, nearly always, are *the things people do*; in philosophical usage, what it denotes, very often, are events, each one of them *some person's doing something*. We may find ourselves with views which we can readily express in the language of action, and then, finding it obvious that there are actions, we (as philosophers) assume that we have views which we can readily express in the language of events. Explanation of action is a case in point. *We may move from knowing that we have an instance of 'action explanation' straight to thinking that we have an explanation of an action (event)*. (Hornsby [1993b] 1997a: 142; my emphasis)

But the range of ambiguities discussed so far, it won't do to simply assume that the *explanandum* of behavioural explanation is some easily identifiable thing called 'action' or 'behaviour'. Indeed, this premature assumption is responsible for a serious amount of theoretical damage. In the following section I demonstrate how theorists regularly conflate two or more of the aforementioned senses of 'behaviour' and/or 'action' in ways that render their claims void, not least because – as we shall subsequently see – their initial conflation invariably leads to further ones relating to action explanation and motivation. I do so by spelling out a number of different 'conflating views' – namely, ways of approaching these matters that are steeped in both ontological and conceptual conflation.

3. Conflation in action

I claimed earlier that most theorists typically conflate three distinct conceptions of behaviour (a)–(c). That is to say, they write as if the term 'behaviour' simultaneously refers to at least two (if not all three) of these. Let us call the view which maintains that this is actually so the *Conflating View of Behaviour* (CVB):

(CVB) An agent's behaviour consists of the things she does: the movings of her body.

Here is a typical example of a psychologist committing himself to this:

> It should be anticipated that the answer of the trained motivational psychologist will be 'better' than that of the lay-person [. . .] For example, when a layperson

explains why an individual is drinking water, he or she may say that the person is thirsty. When the layperson accounts for why another individual is eating, he or she may infer that the person is hungry [. . .] the motivational psychologist, however, attempts to comprise these very disparate observations within the same theoretical network or explanatory system. Perhaps it is postulated that behaviour is determined by the amount of deprivation and the number of rewarded experiences. (Weiner 1992: 3–4)

The suggestion is that both the motivational psychologist and the layperson are trying to explain why a person is doing something (drinking water at time *t*). The answer 'because he is thirsty' we are told, is at best, incomplete: it doesn't tell us as much as the answers a scientist could give us would. Weiner calls the behaviour to be explained an 'action', and more tellingly, sees this action as a 'physical event' (Weiner 1992: 3–4). Yet, the explanation of why someone did something is *not* the explanation of why a physical event occurred. Weiner may be right to think that the explanation of all physical events must involve appeal to general laws from which the particular properties of the event in question may be derived, but this is not much help to someone trying to explain why a person did what he did.

Unlike psychologists, philosophers who talk about behaviour[17] usually offer some account of what kind of behaviour would count as action (which is not to say that they never revert to using the term 'behaviour' in an ambiguous fashion). Consequently, the *Conflating View of Behaviour* is a relatively rare occurrence in philosophy. Be that as it may, most philosophers writing about action and its explanation hold the related *Conflating View of Action*:

(CVA) An agent's actions consist of the things she does, for example, her movings of her body.

This is a sub-part of CVB, for it conflates questions (ii) and (iii) earlier. According to CVA, the things we do are things that can occur (and can be located spatio-temporally). To accept this is to inevitably also embrace the *Conflating View of Reasons* (CVR):

(CVR) The reasons for which we act are reasons *why* our actions occur.

Some even go as far as to claim that the reasons for which we act are reasons *for which* our actions occur. I call this the *Conflating View of Reasons for Action* (CVRA):

(CVRA) The reasons for which we act are reasons *for which* our actions occur.

Consider, for example, the following passage from G. F. Schueler:

The issue is whether reason explanations of actions are somehow reducible to, or explicable in terms of, explanations of the *same set of states or events* that use only the concepts available to physiology and neurophysiology. The suggestive reason for thinking that the answer is No here is that [. . .] the content of my belief [. . .] along with the content of my desire [...] plays an essential role in the reason explanation of why I am *running towards the bus stop*. (Schueler 2001: 254; my emphasis)

The trouble is that Schueler's clues lead in two opposing directions, for running towards the stop is not a state or event but rather, as Schueler himself describes it two paragraphs later, 'what I am doing' (Schueler 2001: 255). The *Conflating View of Action* arises from conflating what I am doing with my doing it and consequently concluding that my reason for the one must be a reason (indeed *my* reason, one would imagine) for the other.

The mistake occurs easily: because we call both (ii) and (iii) earlier 'actions', philosophers find themselves conflating – as Zeno Vendler does in the passages which follow – the action we do with the action (be it understood as a process or event) of our doing the action we do:

John broke the window. What he did, the breaking of the window, is clearly an event. Therefore, it seems, some actions are at least events. (Vendler 1984: 371)

What is an action is the *raising* of the arm: this is done by John [...] the raising of the arm is not caused by John but done by him. (Vendler 1984: 372)[18]

Likewise, in a paper whose aim is to answer the question, 'What explains an agent's actions?', Michael Smith repeatedly alternates between talk of action being 'an event' and action being 'what an agent does whenever he acts' (Smith [2003] 2004: 152). Jonathan Dancy, who is Smith's target in this piece, similarly identifies a 'moving of the body' with a 'thing done' when attempting to distinguish between the transitive and intransitive sense of 'bodily movement':

[W]e distinguish in the now standard way between two senses of 'bodily movement', the first being what we might call a 'moved-ness' of the body, something suitably preceded by and caused by some neural disturbances, and the second being a moving of the body, conceived as something done by an agent. (Dancy 2000: 172)

Dancy here conceives of 'moving of a body' as something done by the agent. But agents do not *do* bodily movements (in either of the two senses distinguished earlier). What they do is move their bodies, but not in the way in which they might move those of other people. Unlike a thing done, a moving of a body, by contrast, is an event that can occur at a particular place and time. This is why, after all, it makes sense to talk of such things (but not of the things we do) as bodily movements.

Both the *Conflating View of Reasons* and the *Conflating View of Reasons for Action* involve confused notions of reasons and their relation to action. Although we can, of course, give reasons that explain why an event (that was an action) occurred, it is deeply misleading to call such reasons 'reasons *for* action', for it makes no sense to talk of events having reasons *to* occur.[19] To put the point in a slightly different way: there are reasons *why* things occur, and these things are sometimes said to occur for reasons, for example, the reason why the process of sweating occurs is to cool the body down, but the process of sweating does not occur for a reason any more than the setting of the sun does. We may well imagine a situation in which we have reason to *make* ourselves sweat, but that would be a reason *for doing* something (namely causing ourselves to sweat), and not a reason for our sweating to occur. We do, of course, offer teleological explanations of certain natural occurrences but to say, for example, that the body's reason for sweating is to keep its temperature at a certain level (to cool it) is just a disguised way of saying that sweating causes the body to cool. The reason here is not the cause but the *effect* of sweating.[20]

Could this be the sort of thing philosophers are after when they treat explanations in terms of agential reasons as explanations of occurrences? Rowland Stout (1996) claims that there are 'things that happen because they should' and that we should count our intentional actions among them.[21] His argument for this view makes it clear that he subscribes to the *Conflating View of Reasons for Action*, and that he does so in virtue of also accepting the *Conflating View of Action*. Stout begins by telling the reader that he is going to argue for the view that:

> [T]here is a causal explanation of why I go for a walk in terms of the fact that going for a walk actually serves a purpose for me rather than in terms of its simply being represented as serving a purpose. (Stout 1996: 2)

And that:

> In the philosophy of action, this Aristotelian claim is located in a very strong externalism about *reasons* for action. According to this strong externalism, the reason for my going for a walk is the *fact* that walking is good for the health. (Stout 1996: 2)

Tellingly, although he begins by addressing the question of 'why I go for a walk', when it comes to citing *reasons for action*, Stout does not talk of 'my reasons for going for a walk' but rather about 'the reasons for my going for a walk', that is to say, reasons for why my going for a walk occurred. Soon after, he writes:

> My claim is that actions are the immediate results of causal processes which are sensitive to actual (external) means-ends considerations. [. . .] Like Davidson, I claim that an event constitutes an action in virtue of being explained in terms of a justification of it. (Stout 1996: 3–5)

In short, Stout assumes that the reasons why we do things are reasons for which our actions occur. Given this assumption (which is a form of the *Conflating View of Reasons for Action*) he takes the plausible view that the reasons for which we do things are facts to entail the considerably less intuitive view that:

> [I]ntentional actions are unique among natural phenomena in that they happen because they should. [. . .] there are ways of *evaluating* actions as rational or irrational, as justified or unjustified; and it is because they are rational or justified, according to such a way of evaluating things, that they happen. (Stout 1996: 1)

But to say that my action was justified is to say that I was justified in doing it, not that the event of my doing it is itself something that is justified. Nor can Stout be speaking merely figuratively when he says that actions are things that happen because they should, for it is a vital part of his account that 'teleological explanation is a species of causal explanation' and that 'an account of such explaining must make reference to causal determination' (Stout 1996: 40, 44).

There are, of course, many intelligent people who claim that 'everything happens for a reason'.[22] But all one can reasonably mean by this is that things happen according to 'God's plan' (or, in the case of animists, that of the universe). On such outlooks, to say that the dormant volcano exploded for a reason is not to say that what caused the volcano's eruption was its reason for exploding. Rather, it is to say that God had a reason for making a world in which this dormant volcano would erupt. Indeed, we might also note that on the theistic hypothesis, events in the natural world would still be 'acts of God' only in a metaphorical sense, for more literally, they would be either the *results* or the *consequences* of God's actions (depending on one's account of action individuation).[23] A slightly more powerful objection might be that, talk of God aside, historians legitimately use phrases such as 'the reasons for the fall of the Roman Empire'. But in doing so they do not imply that the Empire *had* reasons for falling (the way a person might do if people could fall intentionally[24]) but only that we can point to reasons (which explain) why it fell.[25] Our reasons for acting will be *related* to the reasons that explain why actions occur, but their relation cannot be one of identity (see Sandis 2012: Ch. 7).

What about the simpler *Conflating View of Reasons*? While it does not assume that events occur *for* reasons, it nonetheless equates the reasons for which we act with reasons why events occur. We saw earlier that to offer an explanation of why someone did something is not to offer an explanation of why the event of their doing it occurred (and vice versa). Mutatis Mutandis, the reasons for which we acted in a certain way cannot be reasons for the occurrence of the event of our so acting. To think otherwise is to subscribe to one or more of the Conflating views described earlier, views that ultimately fail to distinguish between the things we do and the events of our doing these things.[26]

Epilogue

I have tried to show that we would do well to opt for a pluralistic understanding of action and its explanation. I began by distinguishing between various different conceptions of behaviour and action, before exploring an accompanying variety of distinct things that 'action explanation' may plausibly amount to – namely, different objectives of action explanation. I then argued that numerous influential philosophers are guilty of conflating many of these and, consequently, offering inadequate accounts of the relation between 'actions' and 'reasons'. If this is right, we should reject such outlooks by emphasising the diversity of *explananda* which fall under the name 'action explanation'. Pari passu, there cannot be an informative discussion of the relation of reasons to causes unless we first settle on the precise relation between behaviour that may be said to be caused, and actions that are performed for reasons. But that is a topic for a different occasion (see Sandis 2012: Chs. 3 and 7).

8

Verbal reports and 'real' reasons

Confabulation and conflation

Prologue

This essay examines the relation between the various forces that underlie human action and our verbal reports about our reasons for acting as we did. I argue that much of the psychological literature on confabulations rests on a dangerous conflation of the reasons for which people act with a variety of distinct motivational factors. If this is right, then the most interesting aspect of the confabulation literature is that psychologists tend to confabulate in their accounts of why their subjects behaved as they did. I contend that subjects frequently give correct answers to questions about the considerations they acted upon, while remaining largely unaware of why they take themselves to have such reasons to act. Pari passu, experimental psychologists are wrong to think that they have shown our everyday reason talk to be systematically confused. This is significant because reason-ascriptions affect characterizations of action (in terms of intention, knowledge, foresight, etc.) that are morally and legally relevant. More positively, I conclude that far from rendering empirical research on confabulations invalid, my investigation helps to reveal its true insights into human nature.

1. Agential reasons

In deliberating about what to do we frequently weigh up various considerations for and against a certain course of action. In this essay, I shall call any consideration upon which one actually acts or refrains from doing so an *agential reason*. So defined, agential reasons are not psychological phenomena such as beliefs or desires but, rather, purported facts about the world: things that we believe.[1] I shall not concern myself here with whether or not so-called motivating reasons should be identified with agential reasons (as opposed to, say, mental states). All that matters, for my purposes, is that the very notion of a consideration one acts upon is a bona fide one. This is not to deny that we sometimes confabulate agential reasons when there are none, or that such reasons might not be fictional insofar as it remains meaningful to speak of a person acting upon the consideration that *p* when her belief that *p* is false.

Various features of our psychology, including repressed wishes, desires, and beliefs, may motivate our actions, but it would be a rookie mistake to identify them with agential reasons. In addition, facts about ourselves which we need not be aware of can explain why we mistakenly took something to be the case, or to favour a particular course of action. Agential reasons may be said to nest within such facts.[2] Once we have given an explanation in terms of a person's agential reasons, there will always be, as Jonathan Dancy puts it, 'a possible further question how it was that the agent was the sort of person to be influenced by such features' (Dancy 2000: 173).

To insist that the facts within which agential reasons are nested are reasons for which we acted is to hold what I have elsewhere (Sandis 2012: 86ff.) termed the *Conflating View of Nesting reasons*:

(CVNR) A reason why A took x to be a reason to φ is a reason for which A φ-ed (if she did so).[3]

The conflation is dangerous because it leads to the view that uncovering a nesting reason reveals the 'real' reason for an action, one that is in direct competition with the agent's own verbal reports about her reasons (cf. Stoutland 1998). To be sure, reason-nests serve to render actions intelligible, but they do not do so in virtue of being agential reasons.

Basic facts about human nature make possible all sorts of nesting relations. For example, it is common for incentive factors to awaken drive states, as when the aromatic fumes of the bakery stimulate one's hunger (see Cabanac 1979). Smelling the aroma may thus motivate me to enter the shop and buy a loaf of bread, but it is not my agential reason for doing so, regardless of whether or not I am conscious of the mechanisms at play. Likewise, I may be motivated to buy a bottle of a certain brand of rum by the advert portraying beautiful, happy, people on a yacht in some exotic location. My agential reason here will not be the thought that I could in some way be like them but, rather, the purported fact that the rum will be of good quality.

An explanation of why A took x to be a reason for performing a certain action may refer to nesting factors as diverse as her upbringing, a past trauma, or a fact about human nature. These may be further nested within neuro-scientific facts that 'explain why a person is more prone than normal to inhabit certain mental states – e.g. depression' which make them 'more liable to act for a certain kind of reason than someone with a different neuroscientific make-up' (Bennett and Hacker 2003: 29).

Consider Professor Moody, whose essay grading is easily affected by his emotional moods but who is labouring under the delusion that his grading is always done purely on grounds of actual merit: a certain essay is seen as being stylish and well-researched, another as lacking structure and so on. Moody thus takes himself to be guided by what he believes the merit of any given essay is and has the second-order belief that his beliefs are reliably based on stable criteria which he is sufficiently sensitive to. His moods cause him to think that the considerations of merit which he takes himself to be guided by dictate that it is appropriate for him to grade the papers as he does. Moody is clearly self-deceived, but it would be wrong to infer from this that his moods are the 'real reasons' for his actions. Rather, the moods explain why Moody took certain (seeming or actual) considerations to be reasons for grading the essays as he did – for example, why he perceived some reference to Julio Iglesias as being pedestrian, when in some different mood he might have found it imaginative. His agential reasons, by contrast, are not the moods themselves but the considerations which – given his moods – he came to focus on and be moved by. Accordingly, we should distinguish between:

(1) Moods that explain:

   (a) Why Moody had certain beliefs about the essays
   (b) Why he took the things he believed to be good reasons for giving a particular set of grades to the essays
   (c) Why he weighed his reasons as he did.

(2) Moody's agential reasons for grading the essays as he did.

Parallel distinctions ought to be made in explanatory narratives featuring the sorts of situational attributions described by Milgram (1963), Isen and Levin (1972), Doris (1998), Wilson (2002), and Ross and Nisbett (2011), or indeed a mix of psychological and situational attributions. One peculiarity about the situationist attack on virtue ethics (e.g. Doris 1998) is that virtue ethicists can agree that one may act for reasons that are situational features. So the debate is not really about whether we are 'motivated' by external factors or inner dispositions but, rather, whether external factors which we are not conscious of influence our behaviour more than 'internal' character traits. Yet the only way one can test for character traits in the first place is through behaviour. Such explanations work at a sub-rational level. By this I don't mean that personal or situational factors do not operate rationally (though this will frequently be the case, to varying degrees), but only that related explanations of what moves people to act as they do are not to be given purely in terms of agential reason. It is at best misleading to say that one's finding a dime in a phone booth is one's 'real reason' for helping a passer-by with directions. Personal and situational attributions explain why we take ourselves to have certain reasons for acting.

2. Purported confabulations

Timothy D. Wilson has claimed that 'our explanations are confabulations' and that 'people's reasons about their own responses are as much conjectures as their reasons for other people's responses' (Wilson 2002: 113). His main argument for this stems from earlier experiments he conducted with Nisbett in the 1970s:

> [P]assersby were invited to evaluate items of clothing – four different nightgowns in one study (378 subjects) and four identical pairs of nylon stockings in the other (52 subjects). Subjects were asked to say which article of clothing was the best quality and, when they announced a choice, were asked why they had chosen the article they had. There was a pronounced left-to-right effect, such that the rightmost object in the array was heavily chosen. For the stockings, the effect was quite large, with the right-most stockings being preferred over the left-most by a factor of

almost four to one. When asked about the reasons for their choices, no subject ever mentioned spontaneously the position of the article in the array. And, when asked directly about a possible effect of the position of the article, virtually all subjects denied it, usually with a worried glance at the interviewer suggesting that they felt either that they had misunderstood the question or were dealing with a madman. (Nisbett and Wilson 1977: 233)

Nisbett and Wilson had undertaken to show that we are largely ignorant of the 'cognitive processes underlying our choices, evaluations, judgments, and behavior' (Nisbett and Wilson 1977: 231) and that 'one has no more certain knowledge of the working of one's own mind than would an outsider with intimate knowledge of one's history and of the stimuli present at the time the cognitive process occurred' (Nisbett and Wilson 1977: 257). They argued further that the 'real reason' for this ignorance is not that we have 'no direct access to higher order mental processes' (Nisbett and Wilson 1977: 232) but that our mental reports are 'based on a priori, implicit causal theories, or judgments about the extent to which a particular stimulus is a plausible cause of a given response' (Nisbett and Wilson 1977: 231). From this they conclude:

[S]ubjects may have been making simple representativeness judgments when asked to introspect about their cognitive processes. Worry and concern seem to be representative, plausible reasons for insomnia while thoughts about the physiological effects of pills do not. Seeing weight tied to a string seems representative of the reasons for solving a problem that requires tying a weight to a cord, while simply seeing the cord put into motion does not. The plight of a victim and one's own ability to help him seem representative of reasons for intervening, while the sheer number of other people present does not. The familiarity of a detergent and one's experience with it seems representative of reasons for its coming to mind in a free association task, while word pairs memorized in a verbal learning experiment does not. The knit, sheerness, and weave of nylon stockings seem representative of reasons for liking them, while their position on a table does not. (Nisbett and Wilson 1977: 249)

A worry concerning this analysis is its lack of any distinction between the causes of bodily behaviour and agential reasons for action. Ironically, their argument unintentionally suggests that laypeople might be making just such a distinction. If so they would be right to do so: the position of a pair of stockings on a table is rarely, if ever, a reason for which one chooses them over another pair. It could, however, explain why we mistakenly come to think of them as being smoother, for example. What we are fabricating in such a case is not a tale about our agential reasons but one about the quality of the stockings. The subjects are quite right to intuitively distinguish between their agential reasons and the cognitive and conative nests that underlie them. Had they been explicitly asked about the latter rather than about 'reasons for their choices' they may have given significantly different answers.[4] It is not the subjects who are misled by theory, but the researchers analysing the data. The empirical evidence suggests that it is not laypeople who 'cannot correctly identify the stimuli that produced their response'

(Nisbett and Wilson 1977: 233), but those theorists who cannot correctly specify what they are asking their subjects to explain.

In a lesser-known paper, Wilson and Nisbett (1978: 124–5) speculated that the subjects in the stocking experiment did not have a right-to-left spatial position bias, but a temporal bias which led them to prefer the items they saw last (a bias which would favour late cinema releases at the Oscars). In this paper, they constantly switch between talk of 'reasons for their judgments and choices' (Wilson and Nisbett 1978: 118) and talk of 'what factors influenced their responses' (Wilson and Nisbett 1978: 118). For example, they write that '[n]ot a single subject mentioned the position of the stocking as a reason for their choice', furthering interpreting such responses as 'causal analyses' (Wilson and Nisbett 1978: 124).[5] Yet to ask a person 'why he performed a particular behaviour or chose a particular course of action' (Wilson and Nisbett 1978: 126) is at best ambiguous between a request for an agential reason and a causal/motivational factor. In addition, Wilson and Nisbett systematically conflate 'reported reasons for' (Wilson and Nisbett 1978: 122) with 'reports of influence', frequently switching between talk of 'reasons for', 'reasons why', 'influence', 'factors', 'explanations' and 'causal analysis'.

Nisbett and Wilson's theories work in the sense that they have been applied (e.g. in super-market product placement) with impressive results. But they do not work for the reasons which they give us. Writing with another collaborator, Nisbett would later conclude that 'when people are called upon to interpret the events that unfold around them, they tend to overlook or to make insufficient allowance for situational inferences' (Ross and Nisbett 2011: 90). Just so, but we must ask ourselves what exactly are subjects instructed to do before they give their verbal reports? Are they asked about motivational factors or agential reasons? As Ericsson and Simon (1980) have argued, it is crucial to explicate the mechanisms by which verbal report data are generated and the instructions they could be sensitive to.

In everyday parlance, the term 'reason for' is sometimes used to refer to the reasons why x happened and that it is consequently important to distinguish between a reason/ the reason for A's doing x and A's reason for doing x (see Haidt 2001; Wilson 2002). In light of this, consider the following pairs of propositions:

(i) The reason for her choosing product A was the colour of the packaging.
(ii) Her reason for choosing product A was the colour of the packaging.

(a) The reason for the cow's death was BSE.
(b) The cow's reason for dying was BSE.

In assuming that an agent's 'real reason(s)' for choosing x is identical to the reason(s) why she chose it, Nisbett and Wilson conflate (i) and (ii). Notice, however, that the difference between (i) and (ii) is identical to that between (a) and (b). Yet under ordinary circumstances (b) makes no sense. Similarly, (ii) makes little sense in the sorts of situations described in the experiments earlier, although one may well consciously choose to buy a product because they like the packaging. It is as fallacious, then, to infer (ii) from (i) as it is to infer (b) from (a).

Unlike propositions of the form shared by (i) and (a), propositions such as (ii) and (b) are about agential reasons. A person may hide their real agential reason from others, and we may even come to deceive ourselves about the real reasons behind our past actions not long after we have performed them[6] but, at the moment of action, it is our motives, needs, drives and associations that we are typically ignorant of, not the considerations we act upon. This is not to suggest that we are infallible about our agential reasons at the time of action, only that there is no empirical evidence to suggest that we are systematically deceived about them.[7]

The conflation of motivational facts with agential reasons amounts to the *Conflating View of Motivating Reasons*:

(CVMR) The reasons for which we act are identical to the things which motivate us to act (and vice versa).

The term 'real reason' is often used mischievously by researchers who claim that the discovery of nesting and/or motivating reasons trumps any beliefs we have about our agential reasons, as if the relation between them were that of actual truth versus mere appearance. The term thus actually serves to indicate a discrete shift of discourse, from issues pertaining to practical reasoning to questions of background psychology.

The experiments of Nisbett and Wilson were anticipated by air dealers such as the 1950s marketing and propaganda 'expert' Vance Packard. In his influential book *The Hidden Persuaders* (which claims to reveal 'what makes us buy, believe – and even vote – the way we do'), Packard writes:

> Psychologists at the McCann-Erickson advertising agency asked a sampling of people why they didn't buy one client's product – kippered herring. The main reason people gave under the direct questioning was that they just didn't like the taste of kippers. More persistent probing however uncovered the fact that forty percent of the people who said they didn't like the taste of kippers had never in their lives tasted kippers!
>
> The Color Research Institute [. . .] was testing to see if a woman is influenced more than she realizes, in her opinion of a product, by the package. It gave housewives three different boxes filled with detergent and requested that they try them all out for a few weeks and then report which was the best for delicate clothing. The wives were given the impression that they had been given three different types of detergent. Actually, only the boxes were different; the detergents inside were identical [. . .] In their reports the housewives stated that the detergent in the brilliant yellow box was too strong; it even allegedly ruined the clothes in some cases. As for the detergent in the predominantly blue box, the wives complained in many cases that it left their clothes dirty looking. The third box, which contained what the institute felt was an ideal balance of colors in the package design, overwhelmingly received favorable responses. The women used such words as 'fine' and 'wonderful' in describing the effect the detergent in that box had on their clothes. (Packard [1957] 2007: 39–40)

The most interesting thing such experiments reveal is just how deeply our agential reasons may be nested within psychological facts that we have absolutely no awareness of. So while we are indeed strangers to ourselves, as Wilson (2002) puts it in his book title, we've been given no reason to suppose that this is so when it comes to our agential reasons.

In the first example, people who have never tasted kippers claimed that their reason for not purchasing them is that they did not like their taste. Packard assumes that since they do not know – indeed it could even be false – that they don't like the taste of kippers, the purported fact that they do not like their taste cannot be their reason for not purchasing them. But this reasoning is fallacious. For although it might well be true that falsehoods cannot explain why people actually act as they do, it does not follow that a person can act only for the agential reason that p if they know (or at the very least if it is at least the case) that p.

The second example may be dealt with in a similar fashion. Subjects were indeed wrong to think that each of the detergents they tried had a distinct set of effects, and Packard offers a very plausible inference to the best explanation of why they perceived the effects as being distinct when they clearly were not so. But while it is both counterfactually true and psychologically interesting that people often choose to purchase detergents because of their packaging and nothing else, this fact is not in competition with their verbal reports concerning their agential reasons. Experimental manipulations may indeed lead subjects to act on reasons that they would have lacked without the manipulation, but the best explanation of why they would, in such cases, choose the fancier box is that they think it contains a better detergent, this supposed fact being the consideration they act upon, namely, their agential reason.[8]

Similar conflations may be found in the earlier work of Freud's nephew, Edward Bernays:

> A man buying a car may think he wants it for the purposes of locomotion, whereas the fact may be that he would really prefer not to be burdened with it, and would rather walk for the sake of his health. He may really want it because it is a symbol of social position, an evidence of his success in business, or a means of pleasing his wife. This general principle, that men are very largely actuated by motives which they conceal from themselves, is as true of mass as of individual psychology. It is evident that the successful propagandist must understand the true motives and not be content to accept the reasons which men give for what they do [. . .] what are the true reasons the purchaser is planning to spend his money on a new car instead of a new piano? Because he has decided that he wants the commodity called locomotion more than he wants the commodity called music? Not altogether. He buys a car, because it is at that moment the group custom to buy cars. (Bernays [1928] 2005: 75, 77)

Bernays's juxtaposition of true motives with agential reasons suggests that he embraces CVMR. His further identification of the question, 'Why did he buy a car?' with that of 'Why did he buy a car rather than a piano?' suggests a commitment to the more general *Conflating View of Reasons*:

(CVR)   The reasons for which we act are reasons why our actions occur.

Bernays is right to agree with 'the psychologists of the school of Freud who have pointed out that many of man's thoughts and actions are compensatory substitutes for desires which he has been obliged to suppress' (Bernays [1928] 2005: 75). The reasons in question, however, are not usually in competition with those offered by the layperson. Rather, they typically serve to explain why people have the agential reasons that they do. In what follows I argue that whether or not any explanatory factor is a real reason for action may be tested counterfactually, and that our everyday verbal reports about agential reasons typically pass such tests. The exceptions are cases such as hypnosis where the action performed is not obviously intentional.[9]

3. Consciousness and counterfactuals

It is tempting to think that the agential reasons of verbal reports are epiphenomenal, particularly if one adopts a counterfactual analysis of explanation and/or causation.[10] This temptation must be avoided. Consider the case of fancy packaging. This would not have the effect it does if it did not cause us to believe that the product it contains was good. Fancy packaging only 'causes' people to buy the product it contains in virtue of making them believe that the latter is of superior quality. But the reasons reported by laypeople would only be epiphenomenal in cases in which the quality of the packaging caused the subject to buy the product no matter what they took their reason to be. The empirical data, by contrast, confirm that features such as packaging and spatio-temporal location have the effects they do precisely because they alter our beliefs about our practical reasons.

This is not to say that there is no such thing as confabulation, only that we should not all-too-readily postulate the phenomenon without good counterfactual grounds. One such case is provided by Jonathan Haidt in relation to people whose disgust for incest and other taboo violations causes them to maintain related moral judgements after admitting that they cannot offer any good reasons for them:

> In these harmless-taboo scenarios, people generated far more reasons and discarded far more reasons than in any of the other scenarios. They seemed to be flailing around, throwing out reason after reason, and rarely changing their minds when Scott proved that their latest reason was not relevant.
>
> Subject: Um . . . well . . . oh, gosh. This is hard. I really – um, I mean there's no way I could change my mind but I just don't know how to – how to show what I'm feeling, what I feel about it. it's crazy! (Haidt 2012: 39–40)[11]

The reasons cited here really are epiphenomenal, but this doesn't entail that the subjects' feelings and emotions are their 'real reasons'. Rather, what is demonstrated is that such people hold certain beliefs for no reason at all. We can provide an emotional explanation of why they hold their beliefs, but it won't involve considerations of the form 'incest is bad because it is disgusting'. The subjects have no grounds for their beliefs, only causes. Of additional relevance to the main point of my paper is the fact that groundless belief is different from groundless action in that no belief is held intentionally in the sense in which an action may be performed intentionally. The question of whether beliefs held for no reason are nonetheless intentional does not arise the way in which it does for groundless actions.[12]

More recent empirical studies have yielded new insights into implicit associations that affect our daily actions in ways that we are unaware of, and which can only be controlled indirectly through calculated efforts over extended periods of time. These in turn lead to a range of prejudices or biases that affect our daily interaction with people.[13] Many claims made about implicit bias, however, rest on the sorts of conflations outlined earlier. Take, for example, the following remarks by Greenwald and Krieger:

> Theories of implicit bias contrast with the 'naïve' psychological conception of social behavior, which views human actors as being guided solely by their explicit beliefs and their conscious intentions to act. A belief is explicit if it is consciously endorsed. An intention to act is conscious if the actor is aware of taking an action for a particular reason [...] In contrast, the science of implicit cognition suggests that actors do not always have conscious, intentional control over the processes of social perception, impression formation, and judgment that motivate their actions. (Greenwald and Krieger 2006: 946)

In a footnote, they add that

> 'Naive psychology' refers to laypersons' intuitions about determinants and consequences of human thought and behavior, especially their own. Modern treatments were largely inspired by Fritz Heider's book, *The Psychology of Interpersonal Relations*, which initiated systematic investigation of how laypersons' intuitions differ from scientific understanding. (Greenwald and Krieger 2006: 967, n. 3)

What is naive, however, is the assumption that our implicit biases guide our actions in a way that is in tension with the layperson's reports on her agential reasons. If this were true, implicit associations would be far easier to detect and control. To have an implicit bias for or against *x* is to be disposed to view its features in a more positive or negative light than you otherwise would, but it is the features as we see them that guide our actions *qua* agential reasons.

Consider Frank, who gives a job to Arno instead of Maureen because he believes that, while they are both equally skilled and experienced in all other respects, Arno is a faster typist. Frank's being perfectly aware that this consideration was his agential reason for giving Arno the job is compatible with his being unaware that (i) Maureen is an equally fast – if not faster – typist, and/or more qualified for the job in other respects, and (ii) that his false belief is driven by an implicit gender bias.[14] The claim that Frank gave the job to Arno rather than Maureen, not because he is the better typist but because of Frank's implicit gender bias, is true but potentially misleading. It is true because (a) it is false that Arno is a better typist than Maureen and (b) Frank really does have a gender bias which affected his behaviour. But it is misleading insofar as it implies that Frank was not motivated by the thought that Arno is a better typist, and did not act upon the relevant agential reason.[15] This point is ethically significant, for the description under which Frank's act is intentional is not the description under which it is biased. From a legal and moral point of view, for instance, it is of vital importance that one does not conflate implicit association with unconscious reasons. Consider the question of whether discrimination based on implicit bias was performed for agential reasons relating to race. This could affect whether or not something counts as a hate crime.

Stronger examples of agent confabulation are cases of hypnosis or Korsakoff's syndrome (Sacks 1987; cf. Wilson 2002: 93ff.). These tellingly involve behaviour that is either obviously non-intentional or, at best, a borderline case (Schroeder 2010: 460). The experiments don't demonstrate that we fail to identify our agential reasons, only that we confabulate in cases where there is no reason whatsoever for our beliefs, preferences, or behaviour. The hypnotized person does what she does because she has been instructed to do so under hypnosis, but this explanation does not cite her agential reasons. Indeed, there are none, for the hypnotized person does not act upon considerations. To talk of 'real reasons' in such cases, then, is to once again conflate agential reasons for action with reasons why behaviour occurs.

A similar error may be found in the work of those who challenge our ordinary assumptions about free will. In his book *Who's In Charge*, for example, Michael Gazzaniga writes:

> I automatically jump back before I realize why. I did not make a conscious decision to jump, it happened without my conscious consent [. . .] If you were to have asked me why I had jumped, I would have replied that I thought I'd seen a snake. That answer certainly makes sense, but the truth is that I jumped before I was conscious of the snake: I had seen it, but I didn't know I had seen it. My explanation is from post hoc information I have in my conscious system [. . .] I jumped way before (in the world of milliseconds) I was conscious of the snake. I did not make a conscious decision to jump and then consciously execute it. When I answered that question I was, in a sense, confabulating: giving a fictitious account of a past event, believing it to be true. The real reason I jumped was an automatic nonconscious reaction to the fear response set into play by the amygdala. The reason I would have confabulated is that our human brains are driven to infer causality. They are driven to explain events that make sense out of scattered facts. The facts that my conscious brain had to work with were that I saw a snake, and I jumped. It did not register that I jumped before I was consciously aware of the snake. (Gazzaniga 2012: 77; see also McGilchrist 2009: 80–2)

As with the hypnosis and Korsakoff's syndrome cases, the situation described earlier is most plausibly one in which the subject doesn't act for a reason at all. He may be guilty of confabulation, but we cannot infer from this that he – let alone a part of his brain – is mistaken about his agential reasons, for there may not have even been any. The vignette certainly doesn't license us to conclude, as Gazzaniga does, that '[w]hen we set out to explain our actions, they are all post hoc explanations using post hoc observations with no access to nonconscious processing' or that 'the actions and the feelings happen before we are consciously aware of them' or that 'listening to people's explanations of their actions is [. . .] often a waste of time' (ibid.: 77–8). Gazzaniga 2012: 77–78.

It is also worth noting Gazzaniga's rhetorical over-use of the word 'conscious' here; as if I can only be in charge of my actions if there are such things as conscious brains and systems which enable me to give conscious consent to my behaviour by making conscious decisions which I consciously execute. Gazzaniga seems to assume that all thought and action is either completely conscious or hidden from us. But while it is true that one has to be conscious in the intransitive sense in order to act for agential reasons, it doesn't follow that one needs to be conscious of any particular thing (i.e. have consciousness in the transitive sense), let alone of one's agential reasons. To be conscious of something is to have your attention gripped by it (see White 1964), yet we normally act knowingly without thinking so much about things.

The mistake of drawing lessons concerning the explanation of everyday actions from experiments relating to behaviour that is not performed for reasons is also present in Gazzaniga's earlier work on confabulations and commissurotomy (Gazzaniga 1998) and by other work on direct brain stimulation (e.g. Hirstein 2009: 177). These are all extensions of the fallacy of assuming there is a common denominator between everyday cases and those involving error and illusion.[16]

A related worry is that of choice blindness, in which subjects are first asked to make a preference choice between two pictures and subsequently fail to detect that the picture they were looking at did not match the one they had chosen mere seconds before, offering reasons for preferring the wrong one that appear to be epiphenomenal (Johansson, Hall and Sikstrom 2008; Hall and Johansson 2009). Here the confabulation lies in attempting to justify – or at least explain – a choice that was never made, or a preference that was never had. Again, we must ask ourselves whether these experiments really demonstrate that we frequently fail to be conscious of our agential reasons, or whether we confabulate because we had no agential reason at all. If the latter, our failure to understand ourselves is not a failure of consciousness but of expectation. We simply presume, assume, or otherwise convince ourselves that we must have had an agential reason, and so confabulate it. It is highly plausible that we do so in order to make ourselves feel better. But this telos is not an agential reason, for we do not (unconsciously or otherwise) act upon the consideration that this will make us feel better. The drive to feel better acts as a (counterfactually robust) motive, not an agential reason.

It is worth stressing, at this point, that agential reasons are not the sorts of things that one may or may not be conscious of. This is because the things we consider are not to be found in our minds, be it via introspection or any other means. While we are often motivated by attitudes that we are unaware of, to the extent that it makes sense to talk of their propositional or representational content as agential reasons we acted upon – as opposed to considerations we may have failed to register – the question of consciousness simply doesn't arise. Pari passu, it is a mistake to talk here of an 'introspection illusion' as do both Emily Pronin (2009) and Peter Carruthers (2011: 326–33). Agential reasons – reasons *qua* considerations – are not mental states, although we may act upon considerations that are about our mental states (Dancy 2000). Consequently, when we are mistaken about our reasons this is not a case of failed introspection. *Pace* Nisbett and Wilson, then, mistakes about agential reasons cannot be introspective ones.

The faulty guesses that people make in trying to explain their thought processes have been termed 'causal theories' by some researchers. But when we talk of the considerations we acted upon we are not providing any kind of theory, let alone a causal one. A person who is not conscious of some taboo behavioural disposition of his may well be motivated to discriminate against others who manifest it because he is too ashamed to admit to himself that he shares the disposition, but this does not mean that his avowals are not things that he believes and acts upon. The mistake of thinking otherwise is even shared by critics of Wilson and others who hold similar views – critics such as Nielsen and Kaszniak (2007), who argue that people's causal explanations are not merely a matter of *a priori* theory but also frequently involve privileged information access.

Nisbett and Wilson originally distinguished between mental contents (thought to include feelings) and mental processes, arguing that while introspection gives us access to the former, the latter remain hidden. From this they concluded not only that people lack insight into the causes of their everyday responses,' but also that they consequently 'do not know reasons for their feelings, judgments, and actions' (Wilson 2002: 103–4). This was thought to be so on the grounds that:

> people have privileged access to a great deal of information about themselves, such as the content of their current thoughts and memories and the object of their attention [. . .] But these are mental contents, not mental processes', the former being thought of as 'results' of the latter. The view entails that while we may know what we think and do we don't know why this is so if we are ignorant of the causal processes that produced the 'contents' in question. (Wilson 2002: 105)

I have tried to show that is the very idea of agential reasons as 'contents' that misleads us into thinking that they are things which we might come to know via introspection.[17] Wilson allows (for reasons unrelated to the main thrust of this paper) that 'the distinction between mental content and process is not very tenable' (Wilson 2002: 105). This leads him to replace that distinction with one between the 'adaptive unconscious' and the 'conscious self', concluding that 'people do not have conscious access to the adaptive unconscious, their conscious selves confabulate reasons for why they responded the way they did' (Wilson 2002: 106). I have already noted some worries about overemphasizing consciousness. To this we might now add Richard Moran's concerns about first-person authority being based upon epistemic evidence (Moran 2001: 91; cf. Tanney [2002] 2013: 314–16). We don't discover what we think via self-directed mindreading. We don't know what our agential reasons are because we have better access to them (be it introspective or otherwise) but because it is our business to make up our minds about what to think and do and to do so is to weigh up considerations and settle.

Carruthers (2011: 325ff.) argues that 'our access to our own attitudes in general is interpretative rather than transparent'. But agential reasons are not attitudes and it makes no sense to talk of accessing them. Even if we assume (in my opinion, falsely) that beliefs and desires are mental states[18] and that Moran is wrong to say that we do not access these via introspection, the point about agential reasons still stands:

they are not bits of information which we may succeed or fail to be conscious of.[19] To realize that oneself or another has a reason to do *x* is not to make a mental discovery but to relate normative facts to some situation. A view that lies somewhere between Carruthers's and my own is that of Neil Levy. Like myself, Levy (2011: §V) argues against those who think we are systematically mistaken about the reasons on which we act, but he does so by appeal to a consciousness and awareness of our reasons, which he further maintains is important for moral responsibility (Levy 2013, 2014a, 2014b). A related difference between Levy's argument and my own is that he conceives of what I have been calling agential reasons as 'mental contents', whereas I am resistant to this metaphor. Indeed, it is this difference that enables him (and prevents me) from talking of consciousness and awareness.[20] So while we hold similar positions, we do so on radically different grounds.

Epilogue

There is much of great value that psychology and cognitive science can teach us about motivation. What these theories cannot do, however, is reveal our 'real' agential reasons. These rarely need uncovering, though we may come to misremember, or altogether forget them. Applications of flawed theories may – up to some point – nonetheless have the very results they predict, in deviant (but non-accidental) ways.[21]

The various conflations I have sought to outline cause researchers to misunderstand the way their own theories function, rendering psychological theories void of certain psychological insights. In misinterpreting their own discoveries, they pass over their true value. In light of all this, it is perhaps unsurprising then, that researchers like Gazzaniga proclaim that 'psychology itself is dead' and that 'everyone but its practitioners knows about the death of psychology' (Gazzaniga 1998: xi–xii). But psychology hasn't grown old, or useless, or reached the end of its lifespan. If it is dead it is because it has been murdered – or at the very least assisted in its suicide – by experimental science. This is a great loss, because while psychology without experimental data is empty, experimental data without psychology are blind.

9

Can action explanations ever be non-factive?

Prologue

Jonathan Dancy's book *Practical Reality* (2000) opens with the suggestion that the philosophical distinction between 'motivating' and 'normative' reasons as it is standardly conceived is in danger of leading to the awkward doctrine that one can never act for a normative reason.[1] In an earlier article (1995a), Dancy suggests that philosophers might be altogether better off without the very concept of a theory of motivation. If so, we should not talk of two distinct kinds of reasons, but of two overlapping sets of reasons that are motivationally and/or normatively operative upon us, it being an open question whether the former set is but a subset of the latter (cf. Moyar 2010). In *Practical Reality* Dancy takes a different route (2000: 6–7, 24), adopting a version of the motivating–normative distinction that allows normative reasons to meet the explanatory constraint of being 'capable of contributing to the explanation of an action that is done for that reason' (2000: 101) and motivating reasons to meet the converse 'normative constraint' of being 'capable of being among the reasons in favour of so acting' (2000: 103).

I here focus on the reasons for which we act, or 'agential reasons',[2] using this term as shorthand for the subset of motivationally operative reasons that are the reasons we act upon.[3] Given that normative reasons seem akin to facts or states of affairs, Dancy concludes that agential reasons must share a similar ontology: they are the things we believe and/or desire and not beliefs or desires themselves. Dancy inherits this distinction from Alan White and John McDowell, although its philosophical origins lie with Frege and Wittgenstein.[4] It is also explicit in Latin grammar (e.g. credo quod vs. *habeo fidem*). Dancy dubs his externalist view 'non-psychologism' because it denies that the reasons for which a person acts are psychological states of the agent. I shall presume that Dancy's cognitivist version of non-psychologism is by and large true, without quibbling about the differences between facts, truths and states of affairs.[5]

1. Thought and fact

Agential reasons, at least in so far as these are held to be motivating reasons, are commonly thought to be capable of explaining action (for a recent example of this assumption, see Setiya 2007: 23). This outlook, to which Dancy adheres, renders non-psychologism vulnerable to an objection from the possibility of false belief. The trouble is that things are not always as they appear to be to the agent. Dancy rejects the disjunctivist account of agential reasons as being external only when our beliefs about what is the case are true, suggesting instead that in cases where what the agent believes is false, her actions may be explained by a falsehood, namely, the agential reason in question.[6] In his own terminology, action explanations which cite agential reasons are non-factive in the sense that what the agent believes (the agent's reason, or AR) can explain her action (A) even if it (AR) is false. If this sort of non-factivism is true then we cannot infer both A and AR from a correct explanation of the form 'AR is the reason why it is the case that A occurred' (see Dancy 2000: 131).

It is more natural, however, to think that only truths are capable of genuinely explaining anything.[7] We do, of course, use the term 'explanation' in ways which do not imply that the explanation given is true, and accordingly speak of people offering 'poor explanations'.[8] However, such explanations are generally thought to be putative, not genuine: they do not actually explain anything but merely purport to. A poor explanation of action will at best correctly point to why someone might have done something, without offering any true information about why they actually did so: it can render action intelligible without genuinely explaining it (Strawson [1986] 2010: 30–1). Dancy's claim that AR can explain A even if AR is false thus stands in provocative contrast to the standard outlook.

If falsehoods were capable of providing real (one is tempted to say true) explanations, we would care a lot less about the truth of our beliefs than we actually do. The debate between creationists and evolutionists, for instance, would be inconsequential if we were happy to grant genuine explanatory power to falsehoods. This thought should not be confused with an argument from the metaphysical obscurity of 'how invoking a putative fact that does not obtain can do explanatory work' (Lenman 2009: §6). My complaint, rather, is that it is a basic truism that to have a genuine explanation of anything, the *explanandum* must in some sense, however loose, result because of the *explanans*; and this can happen only if the latter is actually the case.[9]

James Lenman frames the problem thus:

> The biggest headache for anti-psychologists such as Dancy however is furnished by cases where the agent's belief is false. The fact of Angus's being fired is naturally adduced to explain his punching his boss in cases where he has indeed been fired. But in cases where Angus punches his boss, believing mistakenly that he has been fired, it seems quite wrong to say he so acts because he has been fired. In such a case we surely must retreat to a psychologized explanation if we are to have a credible motivating reason explanation at all. (2009: §6)

I agree with Dancy's opponents that we should resist non-factivism. We would be throwing the baby out with the bathwater, however, if we took this to be a decisive objection against non-psychologism. Both Dancy and his critics have supposed that his accounts of non-factive explanation and agential reasons must stand or fall together. But it is not at all obvious that we must sacrifice non-psychologism in order to reject non-factivism.

The possibility of rejecting (a) non-factivism while holding on to (b) non-psychologism becomes apparent once we realize that (a) results from a conjunction of premises that include (b) but are not reducible to it:

(i) Agential reasons are considerations external to the mind (non-psychologism).
(ii) What we consider to be the case may be false (cognitivism).
(iii) Agential reasons are capable of explaining action (agentialism).

My own view is that we should hold on to (i) and (ii) but reject (iii). Indeed, the problem of false belief may itself be taken to confirm that (iii) is false, although I think that we also have independent grounds against this premise. None of this is to say that agential reasons may not feature in action explanations (regardless of the truth of our beliefs), but only that their role within them is not that of an explanans. Much of this essay is geared at developing the previous line of reasoning.

Dancy explains that in maintaining that reasons-explanation is non-factive he is simply denying the first premise of an 'apparently sound argument' that 'has a false conclusion' (Dancy 2003b: 469), conceding that this approach might lead one, as Aristotle warned, to say 'things that nobody would say unless defending a theory' (Dancy 2008: 267). While he admits that 'it is odd to suppose that on occasion a nothing (something that is not the case) can explain a something (an action that was done)', Dancy concludes that 'we can live with this oddity. Or rather that it is not as odd as people make out' (Dancy 2003a: 427). I suspect, however, that he would welcome less counter-intuitive ways of resisting the psychologistic conclusion.

Although critical of Dancy's account of action explanation, this essay is thus intended as a defence of his non-psychologistic view of agential reasons. The overall account that emerges is one that I take to cohere with Dancy's aforementioned paper 'Why There is Really No Such Thing as the Theory of Motivation' (1995a). I fear, however, that Dancy may see my gesture as a Greek gift harbouring all stripes of philosophical danger. With this in mind, in the final section I propose an alternative approach to which he may be more receptive, one that involves a deflationist attitude to the metaphysics of reasons that parallels his own deflationist approach to action theory (see Dancy 2009a).

2. As Dancy believes

Wayne Davis recommends an approach that is similar in spirit to that which I have been pursuing:

> We need to distinguish the claim that actions can be explained by reference to reasons from the claim that the reasons are what explain the actions. The former is true, the latter false. The statement that my reason for saving was that my son will need money for college does explain why I saved. But it does not follow, and is not true, that my reason explains my action. For my reason was that my son will need money for college. That something will be true in the future cannot explain the fact that I did something in the past. Moreover, my action would have the same

explanation even if I were wrong in thinking that my son will be going to college. (Davis 2003: 455)

Dancy (2003b: 480) has responded that Davis's 'nice distinction between saying that actions can be explained by reference to reasons and saying that the reasons are what explain the action' is not one of which he, Dancy, can make any use. The trouble, as Dancy sees it, is that statements of the form 'her reason for φ-ing was AR' cannot in their entirety be the *explanans* of her φ-ing, for they contain the *explanandum* (her φ-ing) as a part. Dancy continues, '[a]fter all, "his reason for φ-ing was that *p*" is equivalent to "he φ-ed for the reason that *p*", which contains his φ-ing as a part. If so, it appears that the *explanans* must be the reason for which he φ-ed and that alone' (481). Dancy takes it as obvious that the *explanandum* is the action itself. Yet it is as contentious to presuppose that the *explananda* in question are actions as it is to assert that their *explanantia* are agential reasons. In claiming that the statement 'he φ-ed for the reason that *p*' already contains the *explanandum*, Dancy in fact begs the question against some plausible accounts of the *relata* of explanations.

Hempel and Oppenheim (1948), for example, famously argue that we would do best to conceive of all *explananda* and *explanantia* as sentences and classes of sentences, respectively,[10] while Peter Achinstein builds a case for the superiority of 'ordered pair' and 'no product' views, according to which 'we must begin with the concept of an illocutionary act of explaining and characterize explanations, by reference to this, rather than conversely' (Achinstein 1983: 102). If we follow Achinstein's advice, *explanantia* are best understood as statements of fact whose *explananda* are neither sentences nor phenomena but rather *reperienda* or 'discoverables' – namely, the things we seek to find out (why the bridge exploded when it did, as opposed to the actual explosion of the bridge or a sentence describing it). The approach serves to highlight the proximity between *explanandum* and *explanans*, for in wishing to explain why the bridge exploded as and when it did we are after the reason it did so thus. This reason, which we seek to discover, informs us of the very thing we want to explain. The reason cannot be specified independently of any understanding of the thing to be explained, and vice versa,[11] which is not to say that either forms a part of the other.

Put another way, 'he φ-ed' is arguably not an *explanandum*, for to identify an action under a particular description is not yet to identify what it is about it that is to be explained. Depending on our interests, we may ask all sorts of different things about the occurrence of an action, each giving rise to a different *explanandum*: why or how he φ-ed, or perhaps why or how he φ-ed in such and such a way, at a certain time rather than another, for this or that reason, given his character or motivational set, and so on. As Achinstein has pointed out, unless we specify what question it is that we are asking of any given phenomenon we will have failed to fix a specific *explanandum* or 'object of explanation' (Achinstein 1975: 11–18).[12]

Explanantia are not contained in statements of the form 'he φ-ed for the reason that *p*' as these are statements about the agent's reason for acting. As such, they explicitly state what the agent's reason was, but they are not statements of the reason nor, *per impossibile*, of the action. This would explain why any implicatures relating to the truth of the agent's belief may be easily cancelled without loss of meaning.

Can Action Explanations Ever Be Non-Factive? 105

Dancy's non-factive view, by contrast, is that in sentences such as 'his reason for doing it was that, as he believed, *p*', the phrase 'he believed' should be taken appositionally:

> [T]he point of this rephrasing of things is that it removes any suggestion that the explainer is committed to its being the case that *p*. This helps with my second difficulty, which is how 'that *p*' can explain anything when it is not the case that *p*. A familiar form of argument threatens. Where the agent's belief is false, his reason must be that he believed that *p*. But he will not be acting for a different reason just because he is in the right on the matter. So even when he is right, his reason must still be that he believes that *p*, not just that *p*. I try to undercut this argument [. . .] by denying that explanation in terms of reasons is factive, i.e. that the *explanans* in such cases must itself be the case. First, it is not required for the purposes of the sort of light that reasons-explanations cast on action that things should be as the agent supposed. Second, it seems perfectly possible to continue at least some forms of reasons-explanation with a denial of the contained clause, thus: his reason for doing it was that *p*, a matter about which he was sadly mistaken. (Dancy 2003a: 427)

Dancy claims further that the explanatory statement 'his reason for doing it was that it would increase his pension' is not factive, because we can add that 'he was quite wrong' to think that it would do so, without this affecting the explanation in any way: 'If reasons-explanations were themselves factive, as causal explanations are supposed to be, such a continuation would lead to incoherence or contradiction. But no such result emerges' (Dancy 2003a).

What we infer from the aforementioned explanatory statement, however, is not 'that *p*', but that the agent thought or supposed that *p*.[13] Dancy claims that the whole statement can be true even if what he calls a 'contained part' might not be. But the phrase 'that it would increase . . . ' is not a part of what is being stated, let alone 'the thing that does the explaining' (2000: 134). After all, we may cancel any implicature that this is being stated with no explanatory loss. We do not deny its truth while still requiring its presence as a falsehood with explanatory work to do. Rather, when we say such things, we strictly imply that the agent took things to be a certain way and acted accordingly. This is central to our explanation of the action. Since the claim is not itself an agential reason, we must conclude that agential reasons do not explain our actions.

We are now in a position to resist the thought that 'a thing believed that is not the case can still explain action' (Dancy 2000: 137) without abandoning non-psychologism. What explains the action is the whole statement. More accurately, it is people who explain actions by citing one or more agential reasons, thereby implying strictly that (a) the agent took *p* and/or *q* to count in favour of her action and (b) acted accordingly. But the explanation is not done by the reason cited. What is stated (implicitly or otherwise) is not the thing that the agent believed but, rather, the purported fact that the person acted upon that belief. If this statement turns out to be false then it would fail to provide us with a genuine explanation. Even in cases where we mistakenly agree with the agent's belief at the time of acting and therefore (successfully) explain her action with a simple 'she did it because p' what does the explaining is not the falsehood 'that p' but the implied truth that she acted upon the belief that it was. The explanation is non-factive only in the weak sense that a falsehood can feature in an explanatory statement that is true. The reason cited does not itself even contribute to the explanation. Just as the statement 'this was her cat' can, if true, explain why the animal followed her without the cat being an *explanans*, so the statement 'this was her reason' can explain why she did something, without the reason functioning as an *explanans*.

3. Enabling to imply

In a more recent article, Dancy defines 'non-factive' explanations as ones whose correctness does not require 'that what is offered as an *explanans* in fact be the case' (2004c: 25). But the *explanans* on offer is not identical to the agential reason, only to a statement about it. The explanation does not require things to be as the agent took them to be because what the agent took to be the case (regardless of whether she was right or wrong to do so) does not explain her action. Dancy (2004c: 25) is right to say that 'the fact that he is wrong about whether *p* should not persuade us that his reason was something else, something that he was not wrong about', but this is compatible with the *explanans* not being an agential reason, but a fact about one.

Consider Dancy's own example of a 'perfectly correct explanation':

(a) His reason for doing it was that it would increase his pension (2004c: 26).

If all it took to make an explanation non-factive is the attribution of potentially false beliefs, then the previous explanation would certainly fit the bill. But (a) itself may well be a true statement about his reason. Consequently, it cannot be said to explain via a falsehood, the very property which Dancy identifies as the mark of non-factive explanations (2000: 132–7).

It is perhaps possible to distinguish between an explanation and an *explanans*, the latter being only a part of the former, namely the part that does the explaining. Dancy seems to suggest something like this in writing that 'the whole can be true as an explanation, though the contained part, the thing doing the explaining, is not' (2000: 134). I have already questioned the extent to which reasons cited may even count as explanatory parts of statements. To this we might add the worry that if only part of an explanation does the explaining, it is unclear what function the rest of it has.

There is an obvious objection to my line of argument so far, namely that when asked to explain our actions we tend to simply state the considerations we (take ourselves to have) acted upon. Similarly, when we explain the acts of others we frequently do so by directly stating their reasons, as follows:

(b) He did it because it would increase his pension.

Are these not instances of explaining an action by stating the reason itself and not through some further statement about what one's reasons are? Not if (b) is elliptical for (a) as John Hyman supposes when he writes: '[T]he canonical form of a sentence stating or giving a reason for doing or believing something is "A φ-ed because *p*" or B believes that *q* because *p*' (Hyman 1999: 443). Dancy (2011) acknowledges the 'factive pressure' of the word 'because', but denies that this factive way of giving a reasons-explanation exhausts the possibilities, rightly complaining that 'the selection of one rather than another way of giving a reasons-explanation as canonical seems [to be] arbitrary and tendentious'. But the fact that no one form is canonical does not entitle us simply to ignore the form given earlier, for it is not a question of favouring the factive form over the teleological (or vice versa). Rather, all reasons-statements must be translatable (without change of meaning) to any of the standard forms of explanation, on pain of failing to qualify as explanatory.

Explanatory statements that cite agential reasons, then, conventionally imply that the agent did indeed act upon the reason cited. This in turn implies (also strictly) that the agent had the relevant beliefs, all of which supports the view that agential explanation consists of statements citing our reasons (or facts related to such statements).

These statements form no part of our agential reasons, but are made implicitly whenever agential reasons are cited. To mention the consideration one acted upon, in response to a request for an explanation of one's action, is to strictly imply that it was the case; by contrast, to say that one acted for this or that reason, involves no more than a conversational implicature about what was the case, and conversational implicatures, it is commonly acknowledged, are easily cancellable without loss in meaning. The statement that this was his reason for doing it is altogether different from the statement that it would increase his pension and the truth of either one is independent of the truth of the other. Only the truth of the former is required for either statement (a) or (b) to explain his action.

I follow Dancy in allowing 'that someone's acting intentionally is always explained partly by her believing something, or that her believing as she does is always at least relevant to the explanation'; I also follow him in denying that we can infer from this that 'the agent's so believing was any part of the reason she had for acting as she did' (Dancy 2008: 274). Facts about the agent play a crucial explanatory role in statements which cite agential reasons without being identical to either the statements or the reasons cited. Dancy argues further that the phrase 'A's reason for φ-ing is that p' is not factive because 'A can act for the reason that *p* even where A is mistaken about whether *p*' (p. 270). But this is only true, it seems to me, if non-facticity amounts to no more than the truth of the explanatory statement as-a-whole being independent from whether or not it is the case that *p*.

It is worth undertaking some further Gricean litmus tests by way of comparison. Consider the following statement:

(c) I missed the lecture because I overslept, but this was not a consideration I acted upon.

In the aforementioned scenario, the explanation is non-contentiously factive: if it is false that I overslept, then the attempted explanation is not a genuine one. In stating that I missed the lecture because I overslept, I am implying that my sleeping is a reason that is explanatorily relevant. This implication is strict, it being far from clear what it would mean to state:

(d) I missed the lecture because I overslept, but my oversleeping was not a reason why I missed the lecture.

The reason in question is not an agential one, in that it is not a consideration I acted upon. Thus it can be perfectly true that:

(e) I missed the lecture because I overslept, although I had no idea that I had done so.

By contrast, we would need to tell a seriously complicated story in order for the following to make sense:

(f) I took an umbrella because it was raining, although I had no idea that it was raining.

This is because 'it was raining', in umbrella-taking contexts, typically functions as an agential reason. *Eo ipso*, the following statements also make little sense outside extraordinary explanatory contexts:

(g) I took an umbrella because it was raining, but this was not my reason for taking one.
(h) I took an umbrella because it was raining, but I did not believe that it was raining.

In so far as I am citing the consideration I acted upon, to cite it is to strictly imply that (i) I acted upon this consideration and therefore (ii) took it to be the case. Such examples stand in stark contrast to Dancy's illustrations of non-factive explanations, which have the following form:

(i) My reason for taking the umbrella was that (as I thought) it was raining, but it was not raining.

I have already conceded to Dancy that it can be true that 'that p' was my reason for acting even if it is not the case that p. Thus, we may say:

(j) She took the umbrella because it was raining, or so she supposed.

Statements such as (j) are factive in that what they assert is not to be identified with what the featured agent believes. They are statements about agential reasons and, *inter alia*, agential beliefs. To simply say (in looser language) that she took the umbrella because it was raining would only imply conversationally that she took it for the reason that it was raining. The wording in (j) transforms such (weak) implicatures into conventional ones. In mentioning a supposition of the agent, the statement conventionally implies, first, that she believed it was raining and, second, that she acted accordingly. The statement is factive insofar as it only works as an explanation if both first and second claims are true (see Davis 2003: 458; Smith 2010: 155–6).

For similar reasons (here echoing Moore's Paradox) statements such as the following make little sense:

(k) The (purported) rain motivated her to take an umbrella, but she did not take one for the reason that it was raining.
(l) Her reason for taking an umbrella was that it was raining, but she did not believe that it was raining.

Michael Smith ([1998] 2004: 158) has appealed to related counterfactuals with the aim of demonstrating that 'while an explanation in terms of a fact presupposes the availability of a Humean belief/desire explanation, the reverse is not true'. This must be right, but it would be an empty victory to infer that agential reasons are psychological states. Once we abandon the notion that agential reasons are capable of explaining action, the debate between Dancy and Smith evaporates, for neither side would any longer be entitled to place an explanatory constraint on the notion of an agential reason. Yet it is such constraints that lead to both Dancy's claim that falsehoods can explain and Smith's suggestion that agential reasons are more closely associated with psychological states that Dancy supposes.[14]

Smith's observations alone cannot persuade Dancy that psychological facts (including facts about our perceptions of where our reasons lie) form even part of action explanations in terms of agential reasons. This is because of Dancy's neat distinction between reasons and those conditions which enable certain considerations to count as reasons (namely, things without which reasons could not themselves do the explaining they do). In his own words:

> There is a difference between a consideration that is a proper part of an explanation, and a consideration that is required for the explanation to go through, but which is not itself a part of that explanation. I call the latter 'enabling conditions'. (Dancy 2000: 127)

With this distinction in place, Dancy can claim that what is required for an explanation to make sense cannot be part of the explanation itself. In the case in point, facts about the agent's psychology etc. need to be in place in order for the consideration(s) she acted upon to explain why she acted as she did, but these facts do not themselves form part of the explanation being provided (the one in terms of agential reasons):

> The suggestion is therefore that the believing, conceived traditionally as a psychological state, is an enabling condition for an explanation which explains the action in terms of the reasons for (that is in favor of—the good reasons for) doing it. This condition is required for that explanation to go through. That is, in the absence of the believing, what in fact explains the action would not then explain it, either because the action would not then have been done at all, or because, if it had, it would have been done for another reason and so have been explained in another way. But the believing does not contribute directly to the explanation. (Dancy 2000: 127)

While the distinction between enablers and reasons is a solid one, it is unclear that an analogous distinction is available between enablers and explanatory statements. This is because, as we have already seen, what is stated when one offers an explanation in terms of agential reasons is not the consideration that the agent acted upon (which, as Dancy concedes, the explainer need not commit herself to), but that she acted upon such a consideration. This is not merely an enabling condition of the statement being explanatory, but the core of the very statement itself. That it forms no part of the agent's reason lends further support to the view that agential reasons do not themselves explain action.

I agree with Dancy that we can 'explain action by laying out the considerations in the light of which an agent acted, without committing ourselves to things being as the agent conceived them to be' (2000: 131). The 'laying out', however, crucially involves numerous implicatures which the explanation is reliant upon. And while implicatures about what the agent believes are cancellable, statements that cite agential reasons conventionally imply that the agent acted upon certain beliefs. This implicature is no mere enabling condition but a core part of the explanation that cites agential reasons: cancel it and you have no such explanation at all.

To say that agential reasons do not explain action is not to say that we cannot explain action by citing such reasons. But conceiving that p is neither a necessary nor a sufficient condition for understanding why A acted as she did when she acted for the reason that p. Merely knowing that p is not sufficient: one must also know that she acted upon this reason. This brings us to the vexed question of the very nature of agential reasons. In the next and final section, I argue that Dancy's insistence that action explanation need not be factive is ultimately driven by the misguided idea that locutions of the form 'that p' refer to certain entities, specifically ones that can in certain contexts be termed 'reasons'.

Epilogue

Wayne Davis has objected that the suggestion that motivating reasons are things that explain actions is 'undermined by the fact that motivating reasons are intentional objects'. Davis argues that to think of reasons as explanatory is to treat instances of the locution 'that p' as referential – that is, as 'occupying the position of a quantificational variable' – when in truth such locutions are 'no more referential' than locutions of the form 'to φ':

> Motivating reasons are intentional objects. Instances of 'A's reason for φ-ing was that p' may be true, and we can explain their truth conditions. But it is misguided to ask 'What sort of thing is the referent of "that p"' therein. It does not have a referent [. . .] We get the same sort of false antimony if we wonder how someone thinking of the perfect husband can be thinking of anything, given that what she is thinking of does not exist. (Davis 2003: 454–5)

Dancy responded as follows:

Davis [. . .] appeals [. . .] to his view that in 'his reason for φ-ing was that p' the 'that p' is not referential. I allow this, taking it to mean that it need not be the case. But I still want to say that something that is the case can explain an action, by standing as the reason for which it was done. (Dancy 2003b: 481)

In a more recent publication, Dancy expands on this view, suggesting that '"that *p*" also names an "intentional object", namely, the sort of thing picked out by the expression "what we believe"' and could thereby qualify as a motivating reason (2009b: 289). Yet this is exactly what Davis is denying. His point is not simply that 'that *p*' is not referential in the sense of 'need not be the case' (as in the misleading analogy with the perfect husband). Davis's point is that when one states that *x* φ-ed for the reason that *p*, the that-clause no more refers to something that is not the case than to something that is. (This worry, that is, is not about the non-actuality of referents but about the actuality of non-referrers.) This is not to suggest that questions such as 'What am I thinking?' have no true answer, or to deny sense to phrases such as 'I am referring to the belief that *p*'; but merely to point out that the accusative here is a possible feature of people's psychology and not some mysterious entity 'that *p*' which may be variously described as a belief, a consideration one acts upon, a fact or a reason.

'That *p*' it is not the name of some object, actual or otherwise, about which it is possible to have various so-called attitudes or states, e.g. of accepting, considering, dreaming, fearing, forgetting, regretting, rejecting, supposing, wishing and so on. Nor is it a possible object we could be related to through processes or events such as those of acting upon one's thought, announcing, informing one, maintaining, signalling, writing, etc. If it were, there would be one thing (a type, if you like) called 'that *p*' which A suggests, B predicts, and C suspects. And yet it would not follow from the fact that A suggested that *p*, B predicted that *p* and C suspected that *p* that C suspected the thing that A suggested and B predicted, but only that he suspected that things would be as A suggested and B predicted. Likewise, if A says something silly – say, that fatty foods are healthier than fruit – what is silly is not that fatty foods are healthier than fruit. Nor can the account be that it is silly of A to say this, for in certain contexts it may be very clever of A to say such a silly thing. There is no end to the number of examples one could provide here. Suppose that A accepts that it will rain, B hopes that it will rain, C acts upon the consideration that it will rain. It would be a mistake to conclude from all this that A accepts what B hopes, namely the same consideration that C acts upon. For the meaning of 'that *p*' *qua* thing believed is different to that of 'that *p*' *qua* consideration (or indeed *qua* fact or *qua* reason). As Alan White has put it, what is said is not an object to which one does something called 'saying'; and what is translated, filled or interrupted is not an object to which one does something called 'translating', 'filling' or 'interrupting' (White 1970: 16).[15] Hans-Johann Glock (1997: 98) similarly argues that the word 'what' in the expression 'what I said' does not introduce the name of a thing but a propositional clause. Pari passu, what was said (e.g. that the cake was delicious) is not analogous to what was eaten (the cake).

White (1972) distinguishes between two different senses of the term 'belief': the believing and the thing believed, the former being something a person can be said to have and the latter something they believe: namely, that *p* (cf. Bennett and Hacker

2003: 172ff., 268). If what I have been suggesting is right, we should be distinguishing not between two but rather between three different things: the believing, the belief and the thing believed. More importantly, for our purposes, it would seem that 'that *p*' cannot be identified with the reason that *p* any more than it can with the reasoning that *p*. We may, of course, elucidate the concept of an agential reason by describing it as a consideration that we may wrongly take (a) to be the case and (b) to count in favour of an action, but we should not infer from this that agential reasons are at times identical to facts, truths or states of affairs.

It is helpful to look at Latin grammar here, since it highlights the clear distinction between the use of the word 'that' as a verbal clause (as in *vereor ut*) and as a noun clause (as in *vereor quod*). This is also true of ancient and modern Greek (e.g. 'πιστεύω πως' or 'πιστεύω ὅτι' versus 'πιστεύω αυτό') and French ('je pense que' versus 'ce que je pense'); the second construction in each pair is demonstrative in the sense that we could say 'I believe precisely that', whereas the first is not. By contrast, the English language does not explicitly discriminate between a conjunction in a verbal clause and a relative pronoun, thus making it all too easy to conflate the two through amphiboly. These and other translation exercises confirm that it is a mistake to think that clauses of the form 'that *p*' are typically nominal as opposed to verbal. *A fortiori*, such clauses do not necessarily pick out referents (be they existing or hypothetical), let alone name reasons in doing so. In philosophy, it has become commonplace to think of them as demonstratives. It is, for example, the assumed starting point of Davidson's highly influential paper 'On Saying That'.[16] But it is telling that the examples focused on are of locutions such as 'that *p*' as opposed to 'whether *p*' or 'to φ'.

Even if it were true that agential reasons can explain our actions, it would not follow that our actions are sometimes explained by falsehoods. The mischaracterization of reasons as being true or false is not aided here by the supposition that the clause in phrases such as 'my reason is that *p*' is a demonstrative one. No matter what the explanatory power of agential reasons, then, no genuine explanation in terms of agential reasons can be non-factive in the sense in which the *explanans* is 'something that may or may not be the case' (Dancy 2000: 147).

A corollary of this outcome is that we must reject Dancy's argument against causalist interpretations of explanations that cite agential reasons, for it relies on the thought that the former are factive but the latter are not (cf. Dancy 2003a: 427; Schroeder 2010: 559ff.). Ironically, philosophers on different sides of the reasons/causes dispute are united in their assumption that agential reasons are alone capable of explaining why we act.[17] Until this common assumption is abandoned, all progress in the theory of action explanation will be compromised.

10

Are reasons like shampoo?

Prologue

Interminable debates concerning the nature of reasons for action (RFAs) typically arise when philosophers, in the grip of specific pictures, enforce Procrustean uniformity onto their respective theories of what an RFA is. Accordingly, competing accounts will highlight features prevalent under one concept or conception of an RFA (a distinction I elaborate in §2 below) at the expense of those prevalent under other equally legitimate ones. For there is no such thing as *the* concept of an RFA – or so I shall try to show.

Four distinct pictures of an RFA have been particularly dominant in the literature, without exhausting it. One such outlook portrays RFAs as (i) *considerations* we act upon. Another views RFAs as (ii) *motivators* of our behaviour. A third conceives of them as (iii) providing *explanations* of occurrences of some kind, e.g. of the event or process of someone doing something. A final, teleological, picture takes reasons to be (iv) *ends* or goals. While not many philosophers identify (i) with (iv) (but see §3 below), they think that whatever the relation between them is, both (i) and (iv) can be further identified with (ii) and (iii). This conjunctive fact alone should raise our suspicions about how varying conceptions of RFAs are being grouped under a single concept. Conceptual analysts seeking to pin down *the* concept of an RFA tend to view two or more of (i)–(iv) as different aspects of one thing called a 'reason for action'.

Under the resulting pressure to provide an account of RFAs, which meet the constraints of all four pictures, theorists are forced to conceive of one or more of these in ways that are at best deeply awkward, on pain of abandoning them altogether.

We would do better to replace such 'shampoo accounts' with a conceptual pluralism according to which there is no coherent concept of a reason under which all three of these distinct features of reasons can be united. That is to say, there could be no single thing that performs the relevant triple function, or even some of the double-function combinations on offer. Reasons for action simply do not function like two-, three-, or four-in-one shampoos, capable of performing a number of traditionally distinct functions.

Conceptual pluralists should be purists about specific RFAs, employing different concepts of them for different purposes: normative, psychological and socio-historical. An added bonus of doing so is that the question of whether RFAs are *causes* of action dissolves as a result of a conceptual pluralism that allows us to point to the socio-historical causes of human action without conflating these with either psychological phenomena or the considerations we act upon (see Sandis 2006b). By contrast with the monist methods of conceptual analysis – which gave birth to such classics as Gilbert Ryle's *The Concept of Mind* (1949) and H. L. A. Hart's *The Concept of Law* (1961), and to the metaphysical theories (which replaced linguistic observations with modal intuitions) of later works such as David Chalmers's *The Conscious Mind: In Search of a Fundamental Theory* (1996) and Phillip Pettit's *A Theory of Freedom* (2001)[1] – the methodology behind my pluralistic approach is best viewed as a kind of analytic deconstruction.

1. Concepts and conceptions

It is quite natural to distinguish between concepts and conceptions, yet in recent years philosophers have by and large used the two terms interchangeably.[2] In his classic paper 'Essentially Contested Concepts', W. B. Gallie makes a throwaway comment distinguishing the concept of 'the way a game is to be played' from ' very different conceptions of how the game should be played' (Gallie 1956: 176). His suggestion is that a group might share the concept of *the* right way to play a game despite its members disagreeing what this way consists in. The distinction was subsequently taken up by Hart (1961), Rawls (1975), Dworkin (1972) and Lukes (1974). Hart considers the original *conception* of law as 'consisting of orders backed by threats' (1961: 37, see also 45) and Rawls famously argues for fairness as a *conception* of justice (1975: Chs: 1 & 3).[3] Dworkin (1972: §II) makes a similar move in relation to fairness itself, maintaining that the different members of a group may all share the same concept of fairness, yet differ in their conceptions of what would qualify as fair in certain cases (e.g. in terms of how utilitarian they are).

Briefly put – and remaining as neutral as possible with regard to various competing conceptions of the ontology of concepts[4] – two people may share the same concept of something to the extent that they agree on the relevant uses of the word(s) expressing it, and yet differ in their approaches to that which is being conceived. So understood, conceptions are ways of thinking of phenomena subsumed under concepts, the latter being expressible through (typically linguistic) behaviour. I am here largely in agreement with Peter Hacker, who takes the example of love:

> Possession of a concept is mastery of the use of an expression. A concept is an abstraction from the use of an expression. We have relatively little difficulty and, for the most part, little hesitation in translating l'amour, Liebe, amor, eros, and ahava (and their siblings and cousins) as 'love'. Whether the concepts expressed are the same or different depends upon the context of their use and on our fluid criteria for concept identity in this domain [. . .] There is no doubt that the ways in which thinkers, novelists, dramatists, and poets in different times or societies have conceived of love have been profoundly different. Some have thought of it as an ennobling emotion; others have conceived of it as a deplorable form of madness [. . .] Some have thought of it as a relationship between two human beings; others

conceived it as perfected only when directed at a non-human object, such as God or the Idea of the Good. (Hacker 2018: 268)

It is tempting to respond to Hacker's final suggestion by bringing up C. S. Lewis's distinction between four different *kinds* of love: storge, philia, eros and agape. Surely these are not different ways of conceiving the same thing but, rather, four different concepts *of* love.

One might here object that to share a concept of *x* just *is* to not differ in our approaches to it. But this seems wrong to me. For one, the approaches we may differ in, need not be conceptual. We might, for example, agree that anger is an emotion with certain qualities, but disagree on whether it is ever good or justified. This disagreement doesn't concern the concept of anger: we are not disagreeing about what anger *is*. It is just that one of us conceives of it as sometimes being justified and the other one doesn't. Similarly, we may both agree in what a diet soft drink is, even though one conceives of such drinks as an innocuous part of a healthy diet, and the other as a nutritionally void symbol of capitalism gone wrong.

Alternative conceptions need not be evaluative. To the extent that any given thing has properties that form no part of the concept of it, we may disagree in our conceptions of the nature of such properties without disagreeing about the concept itself. Thus, we may both share the concept of water, but disagree about its precise chemical constituents (of course those philosophers who think that being H_2O is part of the very *concept* of water do not share the same concept of water as those who deny it).[5] Or again, different people may conceive of God in radically different ways in relation to questions concerning time, emotion, interventionism, prayer, and so on, while nevertheless sharing the concept of God as an omniscient, omnipotent, omnibenevolent, and omnipresent being (for competing conceptions of omnipotence see Hart 1961: 149). The Ancient Greek concept of *a* god, by contrast, is an altogether different one, though not completely unrelated.[6] For any difference in conception, one can of course introduce a new technical concept to include it. I might, for example, explicitly state that I shall be using the term 'God' to just mean 'a being that shares the four qualities mentioned earlier but is, by *definition*, interventionist'. Such conceptual stipulation has its benefits, but the more we engage in it the less we can expect others to share our concepts and, pari passu, enter into meaningful exchanges with us.

Let me illustrate further by looking at different conceptions of reasons for action. Suppose we both share the concept of an RFA as (i) a consideration that one might act upon, irrespective of whether or not this is a good thing. We may nonetheless disagree about whether we should further conceive of such reasons as facts, states of affairs, propositions, or whatever else best fits our ontological scheme. Our dispute here is no longer conceptual but purely ontological,[7] but this is not to say that further conceptual explorations (e.g. ones related to facts or states of affairs) might not shed light on our disagreement. Which of these conceptions we end up favouring will at least partly depend on whether or not we are conceptual monists about RFAs. Those who assume that there is such a thing as *the* concept of a reason are likely to further identify RFAs with one or more of the following:

(i) considerations we act upon
(ii) *motivators* of our behaviour
(iii) *explanantia* of our actions.[8]

Accordingly, some conceive of RFAs as having the double or triple function of (a) serving as considerations that we might weigh in decision making, (b) motivating our behaviour and/or (c) explaining why our actions occurred as and when they did. This leads to attempts to conceive of reasons as having the kind of ontology that would enable them to perform functions (a), (b) and/or (c), despite the fact that each of these functions is increasingly more causal than the preceding one. Alternatively, one might insist that the concept of a reason for action covers only one of the above. But how are we to settle which one? Intuitively (i)–(iii) all seem central to what we take reasons for action to be. Ordinary language can only help us so much here. We ordinarily talk of reasons as considerations we act for, as things that motivate us (often invoking belief and desire talk), and as things that explain why we acted as we did. There is no doubt that (i)–(iii) are all associated with reasons for action in our everyday speech. The question we are trying to settle is whether there is one all-encompassing concept at play, or whether ordinary language allows us to switch between one and the other, with no explicit signalling.[9]

While what *in some sense* motivates an act can also explain it, and while the considerations we act for can *in some sense* be said to motivate us, these two senses are not the same. For example, I might be motivated by fear or jealousy but these are not considerations I act for, although the *fact* that I am afraid or jealous may act as a reason for me to seek help. In the sense in which my jealousy explains why I acted as I did, the explanation does not appeal to an agential reason for action, though the latter may be nested in the former (the same is true of character traits that aren't motives, e.g. shyness).[10] Similarly, a reason may rationalize an action without explaining it, and explain an action without rationalizing it. In the former case we can render an action intelligible by offering reasons for which it could have been done, while falling short of explaining why it actually was. In the latter case we may explain an action by reference to the physical or psychological state of the person performing it (e.g. she was exhausted, confused, angry, exhilarated), or to various features of the situation (e.g. it was dark, the handle was broken, time had run out), none of which necessarily rationalize the action when appealed to.

In the previous essay, I argued that the considerations *for which* we act do not, strictly speaking, explain *why* we so acted. This has important ramifications for the explanation of historical action, for it is one thing to try and render intelligible the thoughts and actions of a past figure, and quite another to explain why past historical events (including events of people acting) took place as and when they did (Sandis 2006, 2015).

Part of my aim of this current paper is to show that while this remains true in a sense, there may be other (equally legitimate) senses of 'explain' in which it would be unproblematic to think of considerations as explaining action (e.g. if by 'explanation' we simply mean any narrative, such as a myth or just-so story, that renders something intelligible).

A conceptual monist who has the consideration 'aspect' of RFA most clearly in sight, will quite naturally begin with an ontology best suited for such things and then attempt to stretch it to perform additional functions. Her philosophical task, then, is to place a 'consideration function' constraint on the motivating and explanatory 'aspects' of RFAs and only then proceed to explore how we might best conceive of considerations so that they might also perform additional functions. It is via such a process of reflective equilibrium, arguably, that Jonathan Dancy came to conceive of action explanation as non-factive, holding that to claim that something that is not the case may nonetheless motivate and thereby also explain one's actions (Dancy 2000).

By contrast, a conceptual monist, more focused on the 'motivator' aspect of RFA, will begin with a 'motivational function' constraint, as opposed to a consideration one. This initial conception of an RFA will thus be some kind of psychological state, and her philosophical task will be that of figuring out how a 'mental state' might also act as not only an *explanans* of action but also a consideration we act upon. It is through such reasoning that Michael Smith and Philip Pettit, for example, conceive of reasons for action as belief-desire pairs, which double as springs of action in light of their 'content', which serves as grounds (Smith and Pettit 1997). Or, again, one might begin with an 'explanatory function' constraint on RFAs and then try to figure out how something that explains the occurrence of an event (presumably causally rather than teleologically) can also double as a consideration we act upon and which might thereby be said to motivate us.

Having briefly distinguished between concepts and conceptions – and how these might play out for the conceptual monist working on RFAs – I now consider some specific arguments in more detail. If, as I shall be arguing, none of them succeed in providing a unified concept of an RFA that meets all three constraints then this gives us *prima facie* strong reason to accept conceptual pluralism,[11] thereby rejecting the promise of a shampoo account of RFAs. In what follows I confine myself to debates focusing on human action. The dogmas that already emerge here as a result of trying to make do with a one-size-fits-all conception of RFAs are bound to corrupt discussions of whether we can attribute RFAs to human animals and AI, but that is a topic for another occasion.

2. Four-in-one

Consider the category of a reason for action that one may be said to *have*. These may come in a variety of forms: *pro tanto*, prima facie, all things considered, overall, instrumental, substantive, and so on. Philosophers have conceived of various kinds of reasons that fall under such categories as moral reasons (Dancy 1993), normative reasons (Dancy 1993; Raz 2009), exclusionary reasons (Raz 1990), justifying reasons (Raz 2009), good reasons (Smith and Pettit 1997), grounds (Wittgenstein 1953), grounding reasons (Bond 1983), practical reasons (McNaughton and Rawling 2004), con-reasons (Ruben 2009), enticing reasons (Dancy 2004b), rationalizing reasons (Davidson 1963), reasons the agent has (Davidson 1963; Williams 1981), reasons *why one should* act (Sandis 2012; Skow 2016), reasons *for which* one *should* act (Sandis 2012), content-related and attitude-related reasons (Piller 2006), fact-type reasons

(Hornsby 2008), favouring considerations (Dancy 2000), and reasons from which one deliberates and/or acts (Hyman 2011).

Many philosophers take the above set to overlap with that of reasons *why* we act (Hornsby 2008: 249; Skow 2016: Ch.6), which are in turn often defined as motivating reasons (Falk 1948, 1963; Dancy 2000), explanatory reasons (Raz 2009), agential reasons (Davidson 1963; Hacker 2009; Sandis 2012), teleological reasons – including purposes, aims, goals and intentions (Sehon 1997; Bittner 2001; Schueler 2001; Skow 2016), considerations *upon* which one acted (Dancy 2000), facts by which a person can be guided (Hyman 2011), reasons that render action intelligible (Dray 1957), belief-type reasons (Hornsby 2008) and rational causes (Marcus 2012).

According to many philosophers, there are important connections between the two sets of reasons, not least because it had better be possible to act for the sorts of reasons that fall under the first set (Dancy 2000). We might then think that the second set of reasons is a subset of the first – that is, that one can act only for a reason that one in some sense *has*. We famously find this view in Donald Davidson's seminal paper 'Action, Reasons, and Causes' ([1963] 2001). Crucially, Davidson assumes that since it is possible to act for a reason that one has, the reasons we have *and* act for are indeed identical to the reasons *why* we act. He thus uses all of the following phrases interchangeably (page references given in each case):

(i) The agent's reason for doing what he did (3)
(ii) The reason that explains the action (3)
(iii) The reason why an agent did something (4)
(iv) The agent's reasons in acting (11).

For Davidson, these are typically all *sub-sets* of both of the following two co-extensive sets:

(v) The reason that rationalizes the action (3)
(vi) The reason the agent had (11).

The only exceptions are cases of (v) or (vi) that are reasons the agent did not act upon. In all other cases, Davidson maintains, the reason also doubles as a cause of the action in question. In the first published response in print to Davidson's article, V. C. Chappell writes that what is 'chiefly disturbing about Davidson's paper is that its central concepts – action, reason, cause, explanation – have not been delineated with sufficient clarity and detail' (Chappell 1963: 701). I have tried to show, earlier, that this is certainly the case with 'reason'.

It is easy to forget that Davidson was largely unconcerned with the nature of reasons for action after his initial 1963 paper. While he spent half his academic life delineating the concepts of action, cause and explanation, he felt no need to do this with reasons. Indeed, it is remarkable just how little Davidson engages with the notion of a reason for action throughout the remainder of his *Essays on Actions and Events*, with the brief exception of the clarificatory remarks in the opening pages of 'Intending' (Davidson [1978] 2001: 83–7). Even his famous discussion of so-called deviant causal chains ([1973] 2001: 78–80) is primarily concerned with 'the causal conditions of intentional action' (80), not the concept of a reason, which he frequently conflates with that of a motive (e.g. Davidson [1976] 2001: 264). It is part of his legacy that subsequent debates on the nature of 'reasons for action' took it for granted that there was no real distinction between (i)–(vi). Even Davidson's fiercest opponents, offering a radically different *ontology* of reasons, can only make sense of their opposition by assuming that all are agreed on the *concept* of a reason for action.[12]

Yet RFAs, on Davidson's conception, can explain and rationalize action. While Davidson himself doesn't talk of reasons *motivating*, his term 'primary reason' has effectively been replaced by 'motivating reason' with little comment. This is unsurprising given Davidson's aforementioned conflations of 'reason' with 'motive', coupled with his view that RFAs move us to action (a view that is, incidentally, endorsed by many anti-causalists, despite the fact that motivation is a causal notion).[13] An early analogue of Davidson's conflations may be found in W. D. Falk, who not only uses 'reason' interchangeably with 'motive', but further states that reasons are mental antecedents to the actions they move, rationalize, cause, and provide a *telos* for:

> A reason or motive is a moving or impelling thought, the thought of that for the sake, or in view, of which, some act is done [...] no intelligible alternative to saying that it 'moves' or 'impels' in the sense that it functions as a cause of actions [...] a *causa rationis*, a mental antecedent which [...] will terminate in the action itself. (Falk 1948: 25)

While Davidson does not mention teleology explicitly, he cites Ducasse's 1925 paper, 'Explanation, Mechanism, and Teleology', with approval (Davidson [1976] 2001: 261), and there is no doubt that he takes all talk of teleology to be reducible to belief/pro attitude pairs (see Sehon 2010). The philosophy of action has thus come to employ a shampoo model of RFAs, according to which they (i) motivate, (ii) rationalize, (iii) explain and/or (iv) serve as the purpose of any given action. I have purposefully not included the word 'cause' in this list, despite the fact that it is Davidson's claim that RFAs are causes of action that has received the most attention, both positive and negative. The chief debate between Davidsonians and their opponents has thus centred on the extent and sense (if any), to which reasons can achieve these four things *causally*.

Davidson was responding to anti-causalists about RFAs who frequently appealed to Wittgenstein's distinction between (i) the reason(s) for an action and (ii) its cause(s), to be further distinguished from (iii) the agent's motive(s) (e.g. Wittgenstein 1953: §§475–85). But by (i) Wittgenstein had in mind the grounds or justification for a belief or action (namely, what we now call 'good' or 'normative' reasons[14]), to be contrasted with the causes of a happening or event. In themselves, these distinctions tell us nothing about whether to group the reasons for which we act may ever be identical to *any* sort of cause or motive, or whether they form some fourth, *sui generis*, group. Whatever the merits of his own position, Davidson was right to be sceptical about many of the arguments he encountered in popular 'small red books', including the 'logical connection argument' that the relation between actions and causes is empirical, whereas that between actions and reasons is logical (for what we should still salvage from these books see Sandis 2015; D'Oro and Sandis 2013b: 13ff.).

My question, by contrast, is the preliminary one of whether we can expect RFAs to achieve all (as opposed to any given one) of these things at *all*. If they cannot do this, then we need to open ourselves up to the possibility that RFAs might be causes in some of these respects and not others. This is not the thought that there is one kind of thing called a 'reason for action' that performs some of its functions causally and some non-causally. Rather, we should be pluralists about the very sorts of things an RFA can be. We should abandon talk of *the* concept of a reason for action, replacing it with a conceptual pluralism that allows for different notions of RFAs that are closely related, but by no means identical.

A reason why an action *occurred* must be a cause of sorts. To this extent, the explanation of historical *events* is unavoidably causal, though it is a mistake to here downplay (as Hempel and Davidson do) the causal powers of humans. A reason one acts in the light of, by contrast, doesn't naturally double as a cause, though Anscombe (1957) was right to point out that 'we should often refuse to make any distinction at all between something's being a reason, and its being a cause' of a certain kind, for whether or not a cause is a reason (or vice versa) depends 'on what the action was or what the circumstances were' (§15) – although it doesn't follow from this that a cause is a 'mental event' (§10).

3. Real and apparent

In asking *why* someone did something, I may well be seeking to discover what her reason for acting was, in the sense of wanting to know the consideration or ground she acted upon. But, as already hinted in §1, it does not follow from this that grounds capable of rationalizing action may thereby also function as reasons *why*. Bradford Skow (2016: 142) argues persuasively that teleological answers to 'why' questions report *reasons why*. Thus, 'Lou went to Pusateri's in order to buy turmeric' is equivalent to 'the reason why Lou went to Pusateri's was [in order] to buy turmeric'. But while it is perfectly natural to refer to Lou's purpose (namely, to buy turmeric) as her reason, the consideration she acts upon here is not an end or purpose but, rather, the purported fact that Pusateri's stocks turmeric – that is, *what* she believes.[15] If it turns out that Lou was wrong about this, then it would not make her trip any less purposeful. She will have gone to Pusateri's in vain, but not without an end goal or purpose. Indeed, her failure to find what she was after requires the presence of a telos. But what about Lou's reason *for* going there? How does it relate to reasons *why*?

'She went to Pusateri's because they stock turmeric' is equivalent to 'the reason why she went to Pusateri's was that they stock turmeric'. The meanings of 'because' and 'reason why' are here ambiguous between reporting her reason for going, and reporting some unrelated reason why, as in 'the reason why she missed the lecture was that her alarm failed to work (cf. Sandis 2012: 50; Skow 2016: 175). Either way, the equivalence works only when Pusateri's does indeed have turmeric (see Skow 2016: 174).[16] So what of the case where Lou falsely believes that she will find turmeric at

Pusateri's? According to Maria Alvarez (2010), on such occasions the agent acts for *no reason at all*:

> When the reason why an agent acted is also a reason for which the agent acted, the explanation is what I have called a '*reason* explanation proper'. When an agent acts for an apparent reason, the explanation that cites this apparent reason is a Humean explanation: he ϕ-d because he believed that *p*. (Alvarez 2010: 197)

According to Alvarez, 'Pusateri's stock turmeric' is a reason for action only if it is true that they stock it. Otherwise it is merely an apparent reason and an apparent reason is no reason at all (it is no more of a reason than an apparent duck is a duck). On such an account, the reason *why* the agent acted is identical with her reason *for* acting as she did when (and only when) her relevant beliefs are veridical. When they fail to capture the truth, they are neither a reason why *nor* a reason for. In such cases, the agent acts for no reason at all, although there is a reason *why* she acts (which cites the apparent reason). A similar view is defended by Clayton Littlejohn:

> I agree that we can explain Leo's action by saying that he runs because he believes falsely that he is being chased. I agree that there are reasons why he acted as he did. I agree that when we see what these reasons are, we can see why Leo was perfectly reasonable in acting the way he did. What I deny is that Leo acted for a reason. There was nothing in the light of which he did what he did. We all know why Leo ran – he ran down the hall because he believed that the killer was after him. This does not explain his action in terms of motivating reasons because it does not tell us what his reasons were – it turned out that he had none. (Littlejohn 2012: 155)

But it is misleading, at best, to claim that the person who so acts under a false belief does not act for a reason, that is, acts for no reason at all. Suppose Lou is *certain* that Pusateri's will have turmeric when in actual fact it is merely *likely* that they will have it today. All else being equal, there is a (good) reason for her to go there, namely that it is likely they stock the ingredient she needs. But this cannot be her actual reason for going if probability formed no part of her reasoning. We might then say that Lou failed to act for a good reason, even though there *was* a perfectly good reason for her to act as she did, and one that was not too far removed from her own reasoning at that.[17] To infer from this that she is acting for no reason at all, however, is to falsely assume that all reasons we act for (i.e. all agential reasons) are *good* reasons.[18]

As Anscombe and Hursthouse have argued, people sometimes act intentionally for no (apparent) reason at all, such as when they perform the 'arational action' of throwing a plate in anger, or doodle during a lecture.[19] But my scenario earlier doesn't look like a case in point. After all, Lou is acting with a clear goal and intention and can explain why she acted as she did by citing the purported fact that Pusateri's will have turmeric. To say that someone acted *for no reason* is to imply that their action had no rational motivation at all. This is simply not the case when we are motivated by false beliefs. The difference between the Anscombe/Hursthouse and Alvarez/Littlejohn cases is that in the former agents do not even act for an apparent reason. We may capture the difference between Hursthouse cases and Alvarez cases with the thought that in the former people are said to act for *no apparent reason* whereas in the latter they act for *some apparent reason*. Yet, if Alvarez is right to think that an apparent reason is no reason at all, there would be no real difference between the two kinds of case, for neither would be acting for an *actual* reason at all. Yet, unlike the arational agents, who act intentionally for no reason and with no purpose whatsoever, Lou's trip to Pusateri's is purposeful and based on reasoning from various considerations, one or more of which are in some important sense *her reason* for going to the store (Sandis 2015).

We know what it is to act for a reason that is not a normative reason (a reason why one *ought* to act a certain way) but this is not to act for no reason of any kind at all. It is perhaps tempting to therefore say, instead, that Lou acts for a *real* 'motivating reason' that merely is an *apparent* normative reason. Whether this is right depends on what exactly is built into (and left out of) the technical notion of a 'motivating reason'. One highly misleading feature of the expression is that there is an important sense in which what motivates Lou here is the false believ*ing*, as opposed to the falsehood she believes. This may sound odd to the philosopher trained in reasonology, but it is standard psychology to talk of being motivated by drives, states and perceptions. Moreover, while it is perfectly grammatical to talk of being motivated by facts, in everyday language this is relatively uncommon compared to talk of being motivated by one's thoughts, fears, desires and beliefs, or indeed by motives such as jealousy, greed, money or love. Michael Smith (1987) is not making any kind of error, then, in claiming that the believing is what does the *motivating* in the veridical case too. The disjunctivist view of action explanations – as being provided by (i) the agent's reasons *for* action when they get things right and (ii) Humean belief/desire pairs (that are merely reasons *why*) when they get things wrong – thus fails.

The disjunctivist views of Alvarez and Littlejohn thus contrast with those of non-disjunctivists such as Michael Smith (1987), who claims that the agent's reason is always a psychological state, and Jonathan Dancy (2008), who claims that it is always a (purported) fact.[20] Dancy himself notes that 'both are awkward in the sort of way that is usually due to a bad theory. As Aristotle said, they leave one saying things that nobody would say unless they were defending a theory' (Dancy 2008: 267). Quite; he might have added: 'or in the grip of a picture'.

On Smith's picture, false beliefs pose no problem, but we lose the sense in which an agent's reason is a *consideration* she acted upon since considerations are *things believed* and not our so-called 'motivational states' of believing them. Dancy's view, by contrast, retains the latter at the cost of having to claim that either (a) falsehoods can motivate and explain action, or (b) reasons for action do not motivate or explain action (see Chapter 9). Dancy initially opted for (a) but has since abandoned this in favour of something closer to (b):

[T]he explanans is not identical with the reason for which the action was done [. . .] we can say that what explains the action is that it was done for the reason that *p*, without committing ourselves to saying that what explains the action is that *p*. It would remain true, however, that we explain an action by giving the reason for which it is done. All that we lose is the idea that the explanans is a proper part of the explanation as a whole [...] I said in *Practical Reality* that the explanans in a reasons-explanation does not have to be the case, and now I accept that this was wrong. (Dancy 2014: 90–1)

Dancy's U-turn reveals the benefits of abandoning the explanatory strand of a shampoo account of reasons, though he still wishes to hold on to the thought that 'the relevant explanations are non-factive, since they have a contained clause which does not have to be true if the whole is to be true' (Dancy 2014: 91). Nonetheless, we can now see the way out of several impasses. The mistake was to want to allow that one can act for a reason that is not a normative reason without having to deny that reasons can both motivate and explain action. All the claims in question can be fine *in themselves*, but not when accompanied by the firm persuasion that there is one thing called a 'motivating reason for action', which all these claims are about. Alvarez and Littlejohn are right to think that, in the case of false belief, we can truthfully state that what *motivates* and explains the action is not the agent's reasons for doing it, but a reason *why* she acts as she does. Smith and Dancy are both right to think that these cases still involve an agent acting *for* a reason, but wrong to maintain that the reason in question can either motivate or explain action *in the relevant sense* if it is to also serve as a consideration that the agent acts upon. Only by abandoning the shampoo picture of reasons can we find a way out of what otherwise appears as an impasse.

The desire to hold on to some unified conception of a reason has led philosophers on different sides of these debates to all make a suspiciously similar kind of distinction: between the apparent and the real. Thus, Dancy distinguishes between *apparent* and *actual* facts or states of affairs (Dancy 2000: 131ff.), Alvarez distinguishes between *apparent* and *proper* reasons (Alvarez 2010: 197ff.), and I have previously distinguished between *apparent* and *genuine* explanation (Sandis 2012: 105ff.). The parallels between these moves suggest a common problem in need of a general treatment. While I presented my own distinction in the midst of trying to argue that we should not conflate the considerations we act upon with either explanatory or motivating reasons, my distinction nonetheless looks suspicious when placed alongside those of Dancy and Alvarez. It would have been better, I now think, to distinguish between different senses of explanation, motivation and reason for action.[21]

Epilogue

Eric Wiland concludes his book *Reasons* with the following claim:

Reasons for action *explain* and *count in favor* of the actions for which they are reasons, and they *belong* to and are *spontaneously known* by the person whose reasons they are [...] our various criteria of what counts as a reason seem to struggle against each other – that is, in trying to meet some of the constraints, we make it more difficult to meet the others. This curious result suggests that we might not be able to fully understand the nature of reasons until we ourselves are fully reasonable [...] perhaps only the wise can do philosophy well. (Wiland 2012: 169)

Wiland and I agree on the aporetic symptoms of theorising about RFAs, but not the cause. I am consequently less optimistic than Wiland about the prospects of full wisdom enabling us to fully understand how a reason for action can fulfil the functional ranges mentioned by Wiland and others. This is not because I claim to have reached full reasonableness and wisdom and it has failed to produce a consistent overarching account of reasons. My conviction that the various competing functions that philosophers have desired cannot be combined by any single thing called an RFA is, rather, the result of observing the various dogmas that emerge as the result of Procrustean attempts to meet all constraints imposed by shampoo accounts of RFAs. We might summarize the most prominent ones as follows:

(1) **Non-Factivism**: The Explanation of action need not be factive.
(2) **Agentialism**: Agential reasons are capable of explaining action.
(3) **Apparentism**: We can act for apparent reasons that are *not* reasons.
(4) **Psychologism**: All RFAs are psychological states.
(5) **Anti-psychologism**: We are never motivated by features of our psychology.
(6) **Disjunctivism**: Whether or not someone acted for a reason could depend on something as trivial as whether there was a remaining jar of turmeric in the store when she got there.
(7) **Anti-disjunctivism**: There is a single explanatory schema in terms of which all actions are explained by RFAs.

If the main argument of the above essay is right, we have no reason to hold on to any of them, or others motivated by a similar concern. We should instead embrace a two-layered pluralism about both concepts and conceptions of RFAs. Such a pluralism facilitates the abandonment of the view that reasons resemble shampoo, with one caveat: insofar as a function (e.g. shampooing) is weakened or distorted to the extent that it is combined with additional functions (e.g. conditioning and body-washing), we might think that RFAs are not so different from shampoo after all.

Part III

Ethics

11

Gods and mental states

The causation of action in ancient tragedy and modern philosophy of mind

Ἐπεὶ κρεῖττον ἦν τῷ περὶ θεῶν μύθῳ κατακολουθεῖν ἢ τῇ τῶν φυσικῶν εἱμαρμένῃ δουλεύειν· ὁ μὲν γὰρ ἐλπίδα παραιτήσεως ὑπογράφει θεῶν διὰ τιμῆς, ἡ δὲ ἔχει τὴν ἀνάγκην.

Epicurus, Letter to Menoeceus 133–4

Prologue

R. P. Winnington-Ingram opens his famous study of causation in *Hippolytus* with the following words:

> Why did the events happen as they did? This is no problem to Aphrodite or to Artemis. Bitter enemies though they may be, on one point they agreed – that what takes place is the work of a god; and the responsibility which Aphrodite claims in the Prologue is endorsed by Artemis in the closing scene. Yet the human characters seem to choose their courses and to work out their disasters on the plane of human circumstance and motive, so that Wilamowitz could say: 'Aphrodite is not necessary for our understanding of the action'. (Winnington-Ingram 1960: 171)

The suggestion is that both gods *and* mortals are responsible for the thoughts and actions of the latter.[1] In the aforementioned example, Aphrodite causes the tragedy's events to unfold as they do, yet these are also said to include actions *chosen* by mortals:

> What does Aphrodite say? Her preparations, she tells us, are far advanced (22f.). If I may put it rather grotesquely, those preparations turn out to have been very elaborate indeed. She has caused Phaedra to fall in love with Hippolytus: well and good, that is within her province. But, if she is to be responsible for the whole action, she must also have placed Phaedra in the fatal environment of the palace and (more important still) provided her, through the wider social environment, with a set of moral ideas which proved inadequate to the situation. For all these

things played a part in her downfall. Aphrodite goes on to say that she will make the truth known to Theseus, and that Theseus will curse his son and kill him. But this involves the Nurse, *her* single-minded devotion to her mistress, and her moral limitations. It involves Theseus being what Theseus was – and a relationship (or rather a complete lack of relationship) between Theseus and Hippolytus, who himself has more aspects than the scorn of Aphrodite for which he is so cruelly punished. (Winnington-Ingram 1960: 183)

Double causation, for Winnington-Ingram, is a form of over-determination: while tragic actions are caused by both gods and mortals, either set of agents would have alone been sufficient not only for our *understanding* of all the behaviour involved but for its actual *production* too. He is here following a mainstream tradition championed by E. R. Dodds in *The Greeks and the Irrational* (Dodds 1951: 30ff). Dodds distinguishes between normal actions and actions performed in a state of *ate*, namely, from the 'experience of divine temptation or infatuation' (Dodds 1951: 2)), claiming that the latter are 'doubly determined, on the natural and on the supernatural plane'.[2] The origins of this view lie with Martin P. Nilsson, who claimed that an important characteristic of the Homeric hero was that his actions seemed alien to him once he had performed them, even if they did not seem so at the time of action (Nilsson 1921: 163–5).[3] For present purposes, however, what matters is not how the Greek notion of divine intervention originated but how it relates to various notions of double causation. For Dodds, this is essentially a question about agential control:

> When Theognis calls hope and fear 'dangerous daemons' [Theognis, 637f.], or when Sophocles speaks of Eros as a power that 'warps to wrong the righteous mind, for its destruction', [*Antigone* 791f.] we should not dismiss this as 'personification': behind it lies the old Homeric feeling that these things are not truly part of the self, since they are not within man's conscious control; they are endowed with a life and energy of their own, and so can force a man, as it were from the outside, into conduct foreign to him. (Dodds 1951: 41)

Aristotle would later rationalize tragic action as the result of a kind of error or fallibility (*hamartia*) brought about by *kakodaimonia*, the opposite of *eudaimonia* (literally 'good spirit' but typically translated as 'well-being', 'human flourishing', 'the good life' or even just 'happiness'). The word 'daimon' has been largely stripped of its previous supernatural status, still Aristotle understands the ultimate origins of good and bad fortune (including moral luck) to be external to the agent's control. Aristotle distinguishes between internal and external moving principles, but what is external to the agent's control need not literally lie outside the agent.[4] One need not be in bad faith (as is Nilsson's Homeric man) to experience such motivational forces as alien.[5]

Aristotle serves as a nice reminder of the fact that we need not take sides in the debate over whether gods are best characterized as psychological powers (Vernant 1962, 1965), persons (Burkert 1985: 3) or both (Bremmer 1999: 22–3) to agree with Dodds's suggestion that they serve as a constant reminder of 'man's helpless dependence on an arbitrary Power' (Dodds 1951: 30). Describing this state of affairs as a case of *over*-determination, however, is highly problematic. For how can we take seriously the idea that mortals are *dependent* on the gods if the latter are not required for either the occurrence or the explanation of human action?

As Dodds portrays things, the Greeks would seem to want to have their divine intervention and eat it too; it comes as no surprise, then, that he wished to attribute irrational modes of thought to them. The picture he offers is that of a form of *collective* – though by no means always congruous – action that would have still occurred had only one agent been involved. It is not dissimilar to that of one or more strangers joining a person in pushing a vehicle that she would have managed to move regardless: the strangers might be said to *interfere* (in the sense that they might be intruding) and perhaps, on occasion, to *help* (if the pushing consequently required less effort), but they cannot be said to *intervene* because they do not alter the natural course of human action in any way. Such agents would lack the kind of impact on human conduct that Nilsson's Homeric man attributes to the gods, their efforts are all but epiphenomenal.

It is tempting, in the light of all this, to abandon the notion that double causation necessarily implies *over*-determination. There are two obvious ways of doing this. One retains the *collective* model of tragic action but rejects the idea that a single agent would have been sufficient. The other rejects not only the *collective* model of tragic action but also the very idea that double causation requires two ontologically distinct causes. I begin with the latter.

1. Causation in ancient tragedy[6]

Using Sophocles as a study case, H. D. F. Kitto famously argued that divine causation is *reducible* or otherwise *identical* to human or otherwise natural causation:

> [T]he world of the gods and the world of men are not two worlds but one [. . .] the gods are not superior and remote powers who kick us around for our good or for their own amusement [. . .] the course of things in this human universe is not fixed by arbitrary decrees or a blind fate [. . .] the divine activity in the plays, provides them, so to speak, with a system of coordinates against which we can read off the permanent significance of the particular action. (Kitto 1958: 57)

On such a view the divine is nothing more than a *redescription* of the natural, the term 'double causation' indicating only that truths regarding the causation of tragic action may be captured in two strikingly different ways. Consequently, the question of sufficient *agency* does not properly arise, which is not to say that we cannot talk of sufficient *explanation* (the latter being sensitive to description). Kitto's interpretation promotes the notion (particularly popular among continental classicists such as Vernant (1962, 1965)), Zaidman and Pantel (1992: 177), and Oudemans, and Lardinois (1987: 94) that the gods are little more than representations of human powers or motivations. While happy to allow that gods 'really are implicated in the action' indeed '*are* active' (Kitto 1958: 31, 38) Kitto denies that divine occurrences exist *over and above* natural ones:

> [T]hese gods, collectively, *are* the natural order of events; they are not 'supernatural' at all, except that they are immortal and omnipresent [. . .] Sophocles could combine in one play human and divine drama, in such a way that each is a sufficient explanation of what happens, yet neither obscures the other. (Kitto 1958: 40–2)

Accordingly, the sole purpose of divine motivation is said to be that:

> it makes us see the particular action that we are watching not as an isolated, a causal, unique event; we see it rather in its relation to the moral and philosophical framework of the universe [. . .] the divine background [. . .] means ultimately that particular actions are at the same time unique and universal. (Kitto 1951: 57)[7]

This 'universalist' interpretation, which originates in Hegel,[8] allows Kitto to reject 'the grim old doctrine that human beings are only puppets in the hands of omnipotent and often malignant gods' and accept that ancient tragedy is 'full of entirely responsible and convincing human character and action' (Kitto 1958: 43). In an earlier book he portrays Homeric events in much the same way, arguing that the modern reader would be mistaken to think that mortals are being portrayed there as 'nothing but pawns pushed about on a chessboard by a set of capricious and irresponsible deities' and that Homer paints a 'picture of autonomous, responsible human agents' (Kitto 1951: 53).

The sentiment would later be echoed in Bernard Williams, who in *Shame and Necessity* declares that 'when the gods do intervene, they do not standardly do so by making people do things – winding them up, so to speak, and pointing them in a certain direction' (Williams 1993: 29). We must not forget, however, that Nilsson, Dodds, and Winnington-Ingram are all equally keen to reject the 'mere puppet' view of ancient tragedy as psychologically bankrupt. Kitto's particular achievement was to do so without invoking *over*-determination. But at what cost?

Kitto downplays the interventionist nature of the gods to a dangerous extent, effectively denying that there are any genuinely alien (or 'other') forces at play at all in ancient tragedy, a move that even Aristotle's agent-centred ethics takes care to avoid. He thus does away with what is perhaps the most central idea in ancient tragedy, namely that certain things which lie beyond human control may seriously affect the course of human lives. In so doing, he also rejects the corollary that mortals are not always entirely responsible for their actions.[9]

It is these precise ideas that motivate the other noted way of denying over-determination, namely, that which retains a robust sense of double causation as a particular form of collective action. This route results in the kind of picture presented by Adrian Poole (2005). Under the heading 'In league with the gods' he writes:

> Greek tragedies do not just expound upon beliefs about the gods; they debate them. And the most important aspects of this debate concern the points at which human beings and gods act *together*. This is the image used by Darius and his queen in *Persians*, when they try to explain how their son has committed this terrible *hamartia*: a god or daimon must have 'joined in' with him (724, 742). It takes two to make the tragic act happen, both the human agent and the divine or

non-human. This is a helpful clue to the treatment of blame in tragedy, that there is never a singular cause. Indeed, two agencies represent the absolute minimum; there may turn out to be far more, a whole complex chain or sequence of causation. (Poole 2005: 50)

The point about debate is an important one, for there is no reason to suppose that the tragic poets and their audiences all had firmly fixed common views about such things.[10] It is somewhat surprising, then, to find Poole limiting the scope of the debate to the *points* at which gods and mortals act together. *That* they act collectively and, to a certain extent, even the *way* in which they do so, is simply taken for granted.

As Poole presents things, a person whose behaviour is doubly caused is not unlike a vehicle that moves only if at least two agents are pushing it together (with or without shared goals and/or methods). Each agent participating in such collective action is thereby always open to partial – but never to complete – praise or blame. The truth is in the details which each tragedy, nowadays also each staging (and perhaps even each performance) of any given tragedy, disputes.

Pace Kitto, blame and responsibility do not, in ancient tragedy, rest absolutely with mortals any more than they do with the gods. But is this really because, as Poole puts it, these agencies perform each action *together*? Poole assumes this because, like Nilsson, Dodds, Kitto, Winnington-Ingram and many other commentators before him, he is working with a paradigm of double (or even multiple) causation of tragic action according to which double causation is the causation of *one* particular action (or *one* particular series of actions) by two or more agents. That is to say, there is one thing (or one set of things) with two (or more) causes.

But how true to ancient tragedy is this modern outlook? One of the aims of this essay is to argue that it seriously misinterprets the role of the divine: it is simply false that the gods of ancient tragedy typically, if ever, causally determine human action, or produce it by any other means. In thinking otherwise, I shall maintain, Dodds and the others are conflating the motivation and/or enablement of action with its actual production, an error shared by many modern philosophers of mind.

Indeed, the most popular current accounts of action causation are strikingly similar to those that classical scholars have mistakenly ascribed to the ancients, or so I shall argue in what follows. I replace this vision with a radically different interpretation of what is assumed and what is debated in ancient tragedy, one which ascribes to the ancients a considerably more plausible understanding of agency. Predictably, yet perhaps also provocatively, I suggest that modern philosophers would do well to adopt an analogous outlook.

2. Causation in modern philosophy of mind

In ancient tragedy it is simply false that the gods intervene in every single case,[11] whereas in modern philosophy of mind it is commonplace to hold that *all* our thoughts and actions (and not just those that are particularly tragic, heroic, deluded, akratic, etc.) are to be explained by both causally efficacious mental phenomena as well as the reasons in the light of which we perform actions and form beliefs and desires etc. Alvin I. Goldman, for instance, writes:

> If I ask you, for example, 'Why did Jones go to the concert tonight?' you might reply, 'Because Smith told him they were going to play the Trout Quintet'. The only event explicitly mentioned in this reply is Smith's telling Jones something. How does this explain Jone's [sic] act? Obviously, the reply implies that Smith's telling Jones that they were going to play the Trout Quintet caused Jones to believe that they were going to play the Trout Quintet. And this belief, presumably in conjunction with Jones' desire to hear the Trout Quintet, caused Jones to go to the concert. Thus, Jones' act is explained by implicitly indicating certain beliefs and desires and explicitly indicating the *cause* of the relevant belief. (Goldman 1970: 138)

This popular *causalist* view has been attributed to philosophers as diverse as Aristotle, Aquinas and Hume. It was revived in the mid-1960s by Donald Davidson, whose influential paper 'Actions, Reasons, and Causes' begins by setting an agenda that has ever since prevailed in modern philosophy of mind:

> What is the relation between a reason and an action when the reason explains the action by giving the agent's reason for doing what he did? We may call such explanations *rationalizations*, and say that the reason *rationalizes* the action. I want to defend the ancient – and common sense – position that rationalization is a species of causal explanation [. . .] Whenever someone does something for a reason [. . .] he can be characterized as (a) having some sort of pro attitude towards actions of a certain kind and (b) believing (or knowing, perceiving, noticing, remembering) that his action is of that kind. Under (a) are to be included desires, wantings, urges, promptings, and a great variety of moral views, aesthetic principles, economic prejudices, social conventions, and public and private goals and values in so far as these can be interpreted as attitudes of an agent directed toward actions of a certain kind [. . .] Giving the reason why an agent did something is often a matter of naming the pro attitude (a) or the related belief (b) or both. Let me call this pair the *primary reason* why the agent performed the action . . . rationalizations are causal explanations [. . .] the primary reason for an action is its cause. (Davidson [1963] 2001: 3)[12]

Yet if all of our actions are produced by our so-called 'mental states' (from here onwards simply 'mental states'[13]), it seems no more possible for us to perform voluntary and intentional actions *at will* than if they were caused by the gods.[14] For Davidson, the solution to such problems lies with a distinction between mental states causing *us* to act (problematic), and mental states causing our *actions* (unproblematic):

> There can be a great difference between 'The heat caused Samantha to return to Patma' and 'The heat caused Samantha's return to Patma'. The former implies, or strongly suggests, a limitation on Samantha's freedom of action; the latter does not. [. . .] An action may be caused without an agent being caused to perform it.

Even when the cause is internal, we sense a difference. 'Desire caused him to do it' suggests a lack of control that might be called on to excuse the action because it makes the act less than voluntary; 'Desire was the cause of his doing it' leaves the question of freedom open. (Davidson [1973] 2001: 65)[15]

The same solution had previously also been proposed by Wilfred Sellars:

> [T]here may be a sense of 'cause' which is stronger than that of mere predictability, and in which it is true to say that *actions are caused*, but not *that persons are caused to do them* [. . .] in this new sense volitions are, at least on occasion, the causes of action. (Sellars 1966: 144)

> For Sellars, there is no harm in saying that 'the volition is the *cause* of the action' *only* so long as one is sufficiently sensitive to the varieties of relationships that can be called causal, and avoids construing this case in terms of a paradigm that would lead one to say that volition *causes the person* to do the action. In voluntary action, we are not caused to act. (Sellars 1966: 156)

The Sellars–Davidson proposal has been largely ignored by causalist philosophers, perhaps with good reason, for the distinction between *X* causing an agent to act and *X* causing an action to occur is highly counter-intuitive. While we might easily agree with the claim that 'an action may be caused without an agent being caused to perform it' in cases where the action is caused (solely) by the agent, it is unclear why we should think this is so when the action is (also) caused by some other thing, be it internal or external to the agent.[16]

If anything, it is the latter kind of statement that places the greater emphasis on the limitations in question.[17] The phrase 'the heat caused Samantha to return to Patma', for example, seems to involve the agent in a way in which the phrase 'the heat caused Samantha's return to Patma' (ungrammatical as it may be) fails to. The former explicitly states that there was something Samantha *did* – namely, return to Patma (possibly even bring about the event of her returning to Patma) – even if she was caused to do it. The latter, by contrast, might be thought to downplay Samantha's agency by quantifying over an event caused by the heat without specifying whether the return was something Samantha did or merely something that happened to her.[18]

Either way, it is far from obvious how mental states might cause the occurrence of an intentional action without causing its agent to perform it. Consider the subject of Vermeer's *Woman Writing a Letter, with her Maid*. We might try to imagine her as composing the letter in a frantic or delirious state, with absolutely no control over her anxiety, nervousness, fear or depression, or any other psychological state that her action(s) might be a causal result of. On such a scenario the woman's mental states could easily be said to cause her action by causing her to perform it. But we may also imagine her as being more cool, calm and collected – to use the popular phrase that Michael Smith adopted as shorthand for those idealized conditions of reflection that form the naturalistic axis of his internalist realism, namely, a maximally informed, coherent and unified motivational set (Smith 1991: 399–410;

see also Smith 2000: 33ff.). It would be absurd to insist that in this case her mental states literally *made* or *caused* her to do it.

So what would it be for the woman's mental states to cause her action of writing the letter without making her to write it? Davidson's answer is that in the latter sort of case – but not the former – the protagonist acts 'in the light of some imagined good' (Davidson [1969] 2001: 22) in that 'the beliefs and attitudes in the light of which the action is reasonable' (Davidson [1963] 2001: 9) reflect 'the all-important process of weighing considerations', be it conscious or otherwise (Davidson [1969a] 2001: 35–6).

There are at least two distinct ways for the causalist to conceive of this process. According to the first, *rationalist* conception of human agency, we always intentionally do what we judge to be best, our actions caused by the reasons for which we judge it to be best (Davidson [1969a] 2001: 23). In its most popular form, this conception claims that:

1. We most desire to perform whichever action(s) we judge to be best.
2. We always intentionally do what we most desire to (and believe we can) do.
   (Davidson [1969a] 2001)[19]

On such a picture, all practical reasoning *inevitably* concludes in a corresponding action or omission; hence the age-old difficulty such theories face when it comes to providing an account of how it is that we can ever act against our better judgement. The rationalist conception also seems to render epiphenomenal the light through which reasons guide *agents*, as opposed to *states* and *events*.[20] Some follow Freud in biting the bullet and asserting that agents act in the darkness of their reasons and not in the light of them. Others follow the later Nietzsche in combining causalism with a physicalism that denies that there are any mental causes at all.[21] Either way, it would seem that a central aspect of human agency has been lost.

The aspect in question is the focus of what Joseph Raz calls the *classical* conception of human agency (because he holds that it may be found in Plato and Aristotle[22]), contrasting it with the *rationalist* conception, favoured by Davidson, Goldman and Sellars:

> In broad outline, the rationalist holds that paradigmatic human action is action taken because, of all the options open to the agent, it was, in the agent's view, supported by the strongest reason. The classical conception holds that the paradigmatic human action is one taken because, of all the options the agent considers rationally eligible, he chooses to perform it. (Raz 1999: 47)

On this model, we do not necessarily will to do what we take to have the most reason to do; practical reasoning never concludes in action or intention but in belief about 'the thing to do' or 'the thing to intend doing' (just as theoretical reasoning of an analogous nature might be said to conclude in a belief about 'the thing to believe'), which the agent may or may not decide to act upon.[23] At the very most, it might be allowed that it can conclude in (first-order) desire or volition, so long as the will is thought to include second-order desires about the first-order ones. Accordingly, weakness of will is said to occur when we do not sufficiently desire or intend to act upon a rational belief about what we ought to do and consequently fail to act upon it.

All this allows for greater agential space between practical reasoning and the action(s) it is sometimes said to conclude in, space filled by *the will* which plays a necessary role in the production of intentional action that is distinct from that of reason. It does so by insisting that it is one thing to have rational beliefs and desires, and another to act upon them: 'we can appropriately respond to reason *because* we have a will' (Raz 1999: 115, emphasis added)[24] but it is equally true that 'we follow our will when we act against our better judgement' (Raz 1999: 116).[25]

Philosophers who follow the classical conception frequently use the terms 'will', 'volition' and 'desire' interchangeably.[26] We should not let this mislead us into thinking that in their view the difference between action *within* and action *beyond* our control is *not* that between action caused by so-called 'volitions' and action caused in some other way, which bypasses the will. After all, such a stance may be easily attributed to rational causalists such as Goldman, Sellars and Peter Railton who all defend the 'standard' Davidsonian view that an action is intentional if it is caused (in a non-deviant way) by an intention that was in turn caused by the agent's beliefs and desires[27] while allowing conceptual space for volitions, so long as they are construed 'to include desires or intentions'.[28] Railton, for example, uses the term 'rational will' to describe the desire of a rational organism in which 'intentions spontaneously emerge [. . .] through the chemistry of belief and desire' (Railton 2004: 180, 199). Sellars similarly defines volitions as 'mental episodes that cause actions' (Sellars 1966: 156), specifying that they are 'one variety of occurrent intention (state)', that 'it is proper to think of the fact that a person has certain beliefs and/or desires which serve as *premises* in his drawing of a *conclusion*, as the *cause* of his accepting this conclusion' (Sellars 1976: 47, 53, 63)) and that 'practical conclusions, in the form of volitions, cause actions'. In so doing, he leaves no room for the agent to will to act either *upon* or *against* the conclusion(s) of his practical reason.

In taking mental states or episodes to play a *sufficient* role in the production of all intentional action, causalists such as Sellars and Railton fail to explain how it is that we can be in control of actions that are the causal product of our will any more than we would be in control of actions that were the causal products of divine will. While it is true that in the former case (but not the latter) the will in question is that of the human agent (who is an implicit part of any determinist story that refers to mental states[29]), it nevertheless remains a mere effect of other mental states and episodes whose force is ultimately alien to the agent.

Railton responds to such objections by stating that a human organism 'is no mere *bundle* of states. It is a structured, functional whole', it is a 'self-organised complex that exhibits the proper functioning of thoughts, beliefs, emotions, and desires' (Railton 2004: 200). Quite so, but the fact that the mental episodes in question are *parts* of human beings and may rightly be thought to belong to them *at the very most* establishes only that humans *cause* whatever their mental states cause.[30] While there are obvious differences between psychological determinism and external force (whose respective contrasts Hume named liberty of *spontaneity* and liberty of *indifference* (Hume [1739] 1978: 407–8)), the difficult question for causalism – which Railton bypasses – is not that of how we might identify ourselves as the *causes* of actions that can emerge spontaneously, but a question of identifying criteria for being *in control* of and/or *responsible* for the things which we undoubtedly cause.[31]

One way of approaching this issue, favoured by Hume as much as by Nilsson's Homeric man, is to make a distinction between those psychological causes that lie within our *character* and those that do not.[32] This raises the vexed question of what it is for volition to stem from one's character. In allowing that it is up to the will to choose whether or not to act upon the conclusions of our deliberations, the classical approach seems, at least prima facie, better equipped to answer this question. Indeed, they offer elaborate, often ingenious, accounts of what Harry Frankfurt has termed the 'identification' between agents and their motivation. These all view the will as the agent's representative,[33] appealing to various mechanisms thought to explain how it is that we can *identify* with actions that are the causal product of the will and the various alien (ultimately external) things that shape it. Examples of such mechanisms include reflexivity, decision, whole-heartedness, and second-order desires (Frankfurt), self-governing policies, self-reflection, and satisfied plans and intentions (Bratman), the semblance of responsiveness to reason (Raz), 'normative competence' or the capacity for critical evaluation (Watson), self-awareness and the desire to act in accordance with reasons (Velleman), and guidance control (Fischer).

Most of the aforementioned view the will as a mechanism or event that can cause behaviour. Michael Bratman, for example, thinks of the phenomena of planning, intending and valuing as kinds of willing that may act as causes of action (Bratman 2004: 29). Similarly, Frankfurt defines the will as 'an effective desire – one that moves (or will or would move) a person all the way to action' (Frankfurt [1971] 1988: 14–15). Such proposals may nonetheless be distinguished from those of rationalist causalism in virtue of their commitment to the claim that 'it is no part of the nature of an action to have a prior causal history of any particular kind' (Frankfurt [1978] 1988: 69). The negative emphasis here is on the words 'prior' and 'history' rather than 'causal'. Frankfurt writes:

> Explaining purposive behavior in terms of causal mechanisms is not tantamount to propounding a causal theory of action. For one thing, the pertinent activity of these mechanisms is not prior to but concurrent with the movements they guide. But in any case it is not essential to the purposiveness of a movement that it actually be causally affected by the mechanism under whose guidance the movement proceeds. [. . .] the causal movements which stand ready to affect the course of a bodily movement may never have occasion to do so; for no negative feedback of the sort that would trigger their compensatory activity may occur. The behavior is purposive not because it results from causes of a certain kind, but because it would be affected by certain causes if the accomplishment of its course were to be jeopardized. (Frankfurt [1978] 1988: 75)

While this is by no means the behaviour of what Frankfurt calls a 'wanton' (Frankfurt ([1971] 1988: 16), it remains true (on the above picture) that the will is itself caused by earlier, mental and/or neurological, events. Indeed, Frankfurt is responsible for introducing the notion of *volitional necessity* – namely, a constraint on the will that prevents agents from making use of their capacities to act (or refrain from acting) by making all apparent alternatives unthinkable.[34] Such thoughts awaken anxieties regarding accountability, responses to which cannot sensibly appeal to a hierarchy of volitions without bounding themselves to an infinite regress of the kind made famous by Gilbert Ryle. (1949: Ch. 3)

Frankfurt concedes that an agent 'will not be morally responsible for what he has done if he did it *only* because he could not have done otherwise, *even if* it was something he really wanted to do' (Frankfurt [1969] 1988: 10), emphasis added),[35] yet he also maintains that this does not mean that determinism necessarily constrains responsibility, on the grounds that determined actions may be performed wholeheartedly that is, for some reason other than the fact they were determined. This outlook seems to commit Frankfurt to the possibility of the kind of over-determination found in Winnington-Ingram's account of double causation. Yet volitional necessity surely implies not only that we have no choice but to do certain things but also that we have no choice but to do them *because* of certain reasons.[36] So what we should be asking when applying Frankfurt's revised principle of alternate possibility is not 'Why did A do x?' but 'Why did A do x for reason y?' (or, if one is interested in events, 'Why did the event of A's doing x for reason y occur?').[37]

On a determinist worldview, the answer sooner or later boils down to some aspect(s) of our facticity, some basic fact – or combination of facts – regarding the agent's psychology, history, current situation, or anything else that lies beyond her control.[38] By contrast, this need not be so on a libertarian understanding of intentional agency as a two-way causal power to decide (or refrain from deciding) as well as act (or refrain from acting) in accordance with *or* against not only one's better judgement but, more importantly, also one's will?[39]

Here, the argument reaches a new deadlock, but one need not take sides to appreciate (in light of all of the aforementioned) that the question of agency as understood in modern philosophy of mind and action is a question about how, if at all, we can be said to have agential control within a universe that appears to be highly deterministic (with certain micro-pockets of randomness). Even in its classical guise, this project remains the result of a highly mechanistic outlook not dissimilar to that projected onto ancient tragedy by Winnington-Ingram et al.[40]

In §3 I argue, *pace* these classical scholars, that the backdrop of ancient tragedy is the mirror opposite of that against which the modern search for agency is conducted. What is contested and debated there are not conditions for identification and control but rather the typically extraordinary conditions of alienation and constraint that present themselves in a world where agency and answerability are otherwise taken for granted. Accordingly, the difficult task of knowing thyself is not a matter of *identifying* oneself with one's mental states but of *disassociating* oneself from all alien forces. Deterministic threats are present, but only in a pre-theoretical sense not unlike that ascribed by McCann to modern-day undergraduates upon their first encounter with compatibilism (McCann 1998: 178): 'Most students fail to grasp compatibilism: they insist on taking it as a theory on which causal factors limit one's options but allow 'free will' to operate among those that remain.'[41]

From this 'naive' viewpoint, tragic or heroic decisions and actions are variously enabled, facilitated, motivated and constrained by alien forces, but *not* causally produced by them. Mortal and divine causation exist side by side, with no threat of reduction or elimination.

3. Divine intervention: Motivation vs causation

At the outset of the Odyssey, we find the following account of a divine assembly:

> [27] [T]he other gods were gathered together in the halls of Olympian Zeus. Among them the father of gods and men was first to speak, for in his heart he thought of noble Aegisthus [30] whom far-famed Orestes, Agamemnon's son, had slain. Thinking on him he spoke among the immortals, and said: 'Look you now, how ready mortals are to blame the gods. It is from us, they say, that evils come, but they even of themselves, through their own blind folly, have sorrows beyond that which is ordained. [35] Even as now Aegisthus beyond that which was ordained, took to himself the wedded wife of the son of Atreus, and slew him on his return, though well he knew of sheer destruction, seeing that we spake to him before, sending Hermes the keen-sighted Argeiphontes that he should neither slay the man nor woo his wife; [40] for from Orestes shall come vengeance for the son of Atreus when once he has come to manhood and longs for his own land. So Hermes spoke, but for all his good intent he prevailed not upon the heart of Aegisthus; and now he has paid the full price of all. (Homer, tr. Butler 1922)

Zeus is explaining that Aegisthus acted as he did in *full knowledge* of the consequences. We are not given sufficient information to determine whether or not the action is akratic but what is certain is that Aegisthus's choice is being described as a case of passion reigning over reason. It is only natural that a poet – or indeed anyone else seeking to explain action in an age predating modern psychology and neuroscience – would in such cases attribute the source of human motivation to gods. Among other things, they exhibit basic motivational forces such as desire (*Aphrodite*), lust (*Eros*, who in some myths is Aphrodite's son), ecstasy (*Dionysus*), memory (The Titan goddess *Mnemosyne*), fear (*Phobos*), dread (Phobos's twin brother *Deimos*), faith (*Pistis*), need (*Penia*), obsessive folly (*Ate*), modesty (*Aidos*), thoughtfulness (the Titan goddess *Metis*), mad rage (*Lyssa*) and battle fury (*Ares* and *Enyo*), as well as action-guiding values relating to justice (*Zeus*), wisdom (*Athena*), beauty and self-restraint (*Apollo*), protection (*Artemis*), marriage (*Hera*) and the home (*Hestia*), often in complicated scenarios involving divine greed, lust, jealousy and deceit.

This is well-trodden, comfortable, ground. A recent instance of this stance may be found in David West's treatment of Dido in his introduction to the *Aeneid*:

> The quarrel between the goddesses [Venus and Juno] can be seen as a dramatization of her emotions, the internal turmoil between love for Aeneas, longing for

marriage, loyalty to her dead husband and duty to the city of which she is queen. (West 2003: Book 4)

So far, so good. But a little later he then says of Aeneas that:

[t]he plan to attack an undefended city is not in origin his own: 'At that moment Aeneas' mother, loveliest of the goddesses, put it into his mind [. . .] to lead his army' (554–5) against the walls of the city. We have already seen double motivation in action. For example when Dido fell in love as a woman, while at the same time Venus and Cupid maneuvered her into the madness of love. There the double motivation made the event more complex and more profound. Here it is put to ingenious use. When the hero thinks of a course of action which does him little credit, any stain on his character is lessened by a narrative which attributes the motive force to a god, who by definition cannot be resisted. (West 2003: Book 11)

To the extent that we can talk about double motivation at all here, the two motivations in question are those of (i) the gods motivating the mortals and (ii) mental states motivating the mortals. There is no conflict here of the sort that Winnington-Ingram was trying to capture, at least not given the commonly accepted view (which, as we previously saw, West himself adheres to) that part of the gods dramatize the psychology of the mortals. And while human beings cannot directly resist being motivated (by either gods or mental states), we should not conclude from this, as West seems to, that the motivation *itself* cannot be resisted, that is, it inevitably leads to action because human beings are powerless before it. It is one thing to produce and/or explain motivation, and quite another for this motivation to produce and/or explain action. As far as human action is concerned, the gods are responsible only for its motivation, not its execution.[42] It is simply not true that gods cannot ever be resisted, let alone true by definition. Hence Zeus can truthfully claim that the mortals should not blame the gods so readily; this would be as absurd as attributing our actions to our beliefs and desires rather than to ourselves. Motivational states, like the ancient gods, can typically also be resisted.

In claiming that we always do what we are most motivated to do, causalists neglect to place a sufficiently large wedge between the *motivation* and the *causation* of action, thus leaving no space for a two-way agential power to either perform or refrain from performing that action which we find ourselves most motivated to perform.[43] It is only within such a closed framework that the presence of a motivating god (or mental state) leads to the puzzle of double causation.

The distinction between the motivation of action and the causation of action carries with it a parallel distinction between internal motivating forces and the (external) reasons for which we act (regardless of whether or not reasons are being thought of as causes here). The mere presence of motivation is insufficient to produce and/or explain voluntary and intentional action. This is not to say that gods never function (dramatically) as reasons but only that in so far as they do so their role is analogous to that of the so-called *contents* of mental states (e.g. the things believed, and indeed at times desired by mortals), rather than the psychological entities themselves (e.g. the beliefs and desires of mortals).[44] There is, after all, a difference between a god guiding someone towards (or away from) reason by affecting that person's psychology (thereby enabling them to see a reason, blinding them from doing so, or merely clouding their judgement) and doing so by appearing before them (typically in disguise) and simply *presenting* them with a reason. Indeed, the former kind of situation might even be used to explain why an agent behaved a certain way in the latter kind of situation (e.g. by offering an account of why she took something to be a reason for acting in a certain way).[45]

Either way, both gods and mental states merely motivate – rather than *produce* – actions that we perform for reasons. It is worth emphasizing here that the dramatizations of the agent's psychology may work, no matter what we (or indeed the poet in question) think about free will and determinism. They work as explanations not because gods and mental states causally produce human behaviour,[46] but because they can enable, structure, motivate or constrain it.

In Aeschylus's *The Libation Bearers*, for example, mortals such as Agamemnon and Aegisthus are *agents* of their own fates, even if their family history has ensured that certain outcomes are far more likely than others. Clytemnestra tries to justify her action as ordained by the gods (because it is a righteous retribution for the slaughter of her daughter), portraying herself as an instrument of divine causality and fate, but the Chorus will not hear of it and her guilt is announced with the appearance of Aegisthus, her lover. Likewise, Aegisthus himself may give revenge as his motive, but he is also motivated by power and ambition. More importantly, he does not *overcome* this motivation but *gives* in to it.

A different example of the limits of divine intervention may be found in Euripides's *Hippolytus*, where Phaedra's own perception of what is *happening* to her is focused on her motivation not her action:

> Where have I wandered from the path of good sense? I was mad, I fell by the stroke of some divinity. Oh, how unhappy I am. Nurse, cover my head up again. For I am ashamed of my words. Go on, cover it: the tears stream down from my eyes and my gaze is turned to shame. For to be right in my mind is grievous pain, while this madness is an ill thing. Best is to perish in unconsciousness. (Euripides, *Hippolytus*, 1996: 240-49)

And again, a little later (Euripides, *Hippolytus*, 1996: 319): 'A friend destroys me. Neither of us wills it.' Falling in love is not something we can do at will (voluntarily and intentionally, following deliberation, etc.), but something that happens to us, as with belief.[47] There will typically be reasons we respond to but we find ourselves *falling* in love, sometimes against our will, a picture affirmed by Phaedra's nurse (Euripides, *Hippolytus*, 1996: 473-5): 'So, my daughter, leave off these wicked thoughts, leave off this pride. It is pride, nothing else, to try to best the gods. Bear up under your love: it was a god that willed it.'

This is no cause for defeatism, however. Aphrodite may have clouded Phaedra's judgement by causing her to fall in love with Hippolytus (against her will), but there are also things that she can do to cure herself. Hence the nurse's advice (Euripides, *Hippolytus*, 1996: 476–80): 'And if you are ill with it, use some *good* measures to subdue it. There are incantations, and words that charm: something will turn up to cure this love. Men will be slow to invent such contrivances if we women do not find them.'

Gods and mental states *need not* win out every time, for while mortals may find themselves driven by the gods, they often also possess the ability to put an end to it. Tragedy strikes when, for whatever reason, we fail to overcome internal and external obstacles, and a god may succeed in manipulating us in much the same way that external factors and/or our drives and appetites may win out. Whether or not we should be held accountable is in part a matter of degree, and in part a matter of circumstance. Often we are excused rather than absolved:

> You have done dreadful deeds, but for all that it is still possible for you to win pardon for these things. Aphrodite willed that things should happen thus, sating her anger. Among the gods the custom is this: no god contrives to cross the will of another, but we all stand aside. For be in no doubt, if it were not that I feared Zeus, I would never have come to such a pitch of shame as to allow the death of the man I love most among mortals. Ignorance acquits your misdoings of baseness, and further the death of your wife made impossible the testing of her words, and thus she persuaded your mind. Chiefly upon you do these misfortunes break, but I too feel grief. For the gods do not rejoice at the death of the godly, but the wicked we destroy children, house, and all. (Euripides, *Hippolytus*, 1996: 328–40)[48]

But mitigating circumstances come by degrees, and are frequently too slight to excuse us from our 'dreadful deeds' (e.g. when they are the result of delusion and listlessness as opposed to disability or duress).[49] We may of course find ourselves in denial about this, or indeed deceived in any number of other self-induced ways.[50]

Like mortals, the gods do not always get what they want either (think of Artemis in *Hippolytus*, or for that matter Juno in the *Aeneid*). They may lose out to other gods (just as one drive or instinct may be overridden by another), or to mortal heroes who can and do succeed in their struggles against gods (just as it is possible for us to fight against our own instincts and overcome our moral weaknesses). The fact that this is always done with the *help* of another god or motivational drive does not entail that we play no (necessary) role in the production of our actions.

Gods and mental states cause mortals to be motivated to act in certain ways, but they do not produce the human actions themselves. Divine motivation typically occurs in the realm of mental antecedents (and the internal and external factors that give rise to them), not in the realm of bodily movement. Such intervention also remains compatible with Aristotelian insights regarding the ways in which we can train ourselves to develop certain habits and dispositions over time, not as an immediate result of volition but through a far slower and less conscious process.[51]

It is we humans – not gods or mental states – who produce both our dreadful and our heroic deeds; in the latter case we live up to our better selves by evaluating our own drives and instincts through second-order beliefs and desires as when a mortal favours one god over another thus setting off a chain of divine and human events, often tragic.⁵² Sometimes motivational power and rationality come hand in hand, other times it takes real effort; a powerful god is not necessarily wise, and a weak one not necessarily imprudent.⁵³

If the gods can be said to cause actions at all, it is only in a very indirect sense of meddling and interfering in their affairs. They might do this on both a psychological level (e.g. by endowing them with certain psychological attitudes, putting ideas in their heads, providing them with reasons, giving them courage, causing them to fall in love, lose their nerve) and a non-psychological level, for example, by causing natural events which may have the positive effect of enabling, facilitating or expediting action and – perhaps more typically – the negative effect of impeding, delaying, encumbering or otherwise hindering it (see §4 for examples of nature deities). Such 'acts of god(s)' do not determine behaviour but, at most, help to increase or decrease the likelihood of its occurrence.

As noted earlier a god may well, on occasion, cause certain human bodily movements to occur, but in such cases the behaviour in question is never portrayed as mortal action, let alone action that is intentional and/or voluntary. Divine causation may help to either foster or suppress human ability to initiate rational action at will (and for reasons), but it does not eliminate, supervene upon, join forces with *or* characterize it.

Epilogue

In being motivated by gods or mental states, mortals are not choosing to do (let alone doing) anything, be it voluntarily, intentionally or otherwise. Rather, they *find* themselves motivated. Simon Blackburn captures the truth of such situations as follows:

> What is true is that we 'find ourselves' with this or that concern, and if the experience is unpleasant, as when we find ourselves shamefully addicted to something, or obsessed by something or someone, or for that matter guilty of ceasing to care for things or people we once did care for, then it can feel as if we were assailed from outside, a victim of forces not of our own making. But, after all, it is *always* forces not of our own making that are responsible for who we are in the first place: in my case they have made me into a middle-aged white male of a certain education and class [. . .] nothing on this earth that makes deliberations is free of his or her natural and acquired dispositions as they do so. You, when you deliberate, are whatever you are: a person of tangled desires, conflicting attitudes to your parents, inchoate ambitions, preferences, and ideals, with an inherited ragbag of attitudes to different actions, situations, and characters. You do not manage, ever, to stand apart from all that. (Blackburn 1998: 252)⁵⁴

These truths may all be captured through accounts of divine intervention, the gods dramatizing not just features of our psychology but also environmental causes, be they man-related – such as our upbringing, education and particular situation (including the aforementioned values of home, marriage, etc., as well as the actions of other mortals)⁵⁵ – or purely natural as portrayed by nature deities such as the sun (Helios), the ocean (Okeanos), the moon (Selene), the night (Nyx), various winds (Boreas and Euros) and so on.[56] A boastful statement of such assorted meddling may be found in Aphrodite's prologue in *Hippolytus*:

> Yet for his sins against me I shall punish Hippolytus this day. I have already come a long way with my plans and I need little further effort. One day when he came from Pitheus' house to the land of Pandion to see and celebrate the holy mysteries of Demeter, his father's high-born wife Phaedra saw him, and her heart was seized with a dreadful longing by my design [. . .] But since Theseus has left the land of Cecrops fleeing the blood-guilt he incurred for the murder of the Pallantidae, and sailed with his wife to this land, consenting to a year-long exile from his home, from this point on the poor woman, groaning and struck senseless by the god of love, means to die in silence, and none of her household knows of her malady. But that is not the way this passion is fated to end. I shall reveal the matter to Theseus and it will come to light, and the young man who wars against me shall be killed by his father with the curses the sea-lord [. . .] Phaedra noble though she is, shall nonetheless die. I do not set such store by *her* misfortune as to let my enemies off from such penalty as will satisfy my heart. (Euripides, *Hippolytus*, 1996: 23–51)

We might, in an existentialist moment, say that Greek and Roman gods represent what Heidegger calls our *facticity*: the 'that it is' of human existence, into which we are 'thrown'[57] – or, according to existentialists such as Paul Tillich, have 'fallen' into (Tillich 1957: Part B). While we all share a common facticity, groups and individuals may also be said to have their own unique facticities, comprising facts regarding such things as their sex, genes, income, appearance, upbringing, neurology, socio-political surroundings and so on.

These and other aspects of our factual frameworks appear to place serious limitations upon all of our thoughts and actions. To misquote Wittgenstein, a dog may intend to greet its master, but it cannot intend to greet its master the day after tomorrow (it lacks the appropriate conceptual facticity).[58] Sartre appropriates Heidegger's term with the aim of distinguishing it from determinism.[59] To conflate the two, he tells us, is to be in *bad faith*, while to underestimate the constraints of facticity (as one does when attempting telekinesis) is to be in *good faith* (in the negative sense which this contrasts with the self-recovery that is authenticity).[60] The latter begins with the realization that without facticity of any kind, action is impossible. To put it more colloquially: we can choose to play only from the cards we are dealt, but we need to be dealt *some* cards in order to play at all, cards whose ultimate origins precede our existence.

Sartre famously describes this all-too-human desire to deal one's own cards from out of nothingness as 'the desire to be God' (Sartre 1943: 566), a characterization that owes much to Nietzsche's *causa sui* argument:

> [T]he desire for 'freedom of will' in that metaphysical superlative sense which is unfortunately still dominant in the minds of the half-educated, the desire to bear the whole and sole responsibility for one's actions oneself, and to absolve God,

world, ancestors, chance, society from responsibility for them, is nothing less than the desire to be precisely that *causa sui* and, with more than Münchhausen temerity, to pull oneself up into existence out of the swamp of nothingness by one's own hair. (Nietzsche [1886] 1973: §21)

Even ancient gods fall short of this ideal, with the possible exception of Zeus (who is not always clearly separable from fate). One would, however, be in bad faith to infer some kind of hard determinism from this (be it biological, psychological or any other kind). As Nietzsche proceeds to say: 'unfree will' too is a 'mythology' which 'amounts to an abuse of cause and effect' for 'in real life it is only a question of *strong* and *weak* wills' (Nietzsche [1886] 1973). While we may debate whether or not Nietzsche's paradoxical 'become what you are' outlook presumes the existence of necessitating constraints on the potential strength level of one's will, there is no doubt that he would have agreed with Sartre's claim that humans have the ability to transcend their facticity – of which freedom is the annihilation (Sartre [1943] 1956: 444).

Sartre warns further that there is no clear dividing line between facticity and its transcendence, each new situation we find ourselves in being the result of both. There are parallels here with the more radical Buddhist doctrine of *Paticca Samuppada* (usually translated as 'Dependent Arising') according to which all phenomena are causally – and therefore also ontologically – interdependent. The same thought arguably also motivated Nietzsche's *amour fati* and the desire for eternal recurrence that follows from it (cf. *The Gay Science*, §341) since, given such interdependence, the wish for any aspect of the past to be otherwise involves a desire for self-negation. Only *tragedy* could call for such regret.

This interdependence feeds our propensity to mistake effects for causes.[61] This adds to the complexity of the ancient debate on moral luck, it not always being clear to what extent any given factor – and the moral possibilities it may enable to or constrain – *results* from luck, let alone luck that is obviously either good or bad.[62] Such tension between what is in and what is out of our hands is a central theme of Sartre's own dramas, particularly *The Flies*, his version of the Elektra myth. In ancient tragedy the conflict is played out by Zeus in his two guises: as the head of a divine family and as Fate. We must not, however, fall into the trap of conflating fatalism with causalism. The necessity alluded to in the Greek claim that 'there is nothing here that is not Zeus' is that of facticity, not of scientific determinism. People's fates are typically *shaped* rather than *produced* by their facticity.[63]

Even in its *strongest* form, fatalism remains nothing more (or less) than a belief in extended forms of facticity, albeit of a kind no less mystical that the opposite belief of thinking that one can control external events through sheer volition. A person who takes astrological predictions seriously is no more committed to determinism than one who uses expressions such as 'it was meant to be', 'knowing my luck', 'he's a jinx' and the 'the devil made me do it'. This remains true even in cases where, for whatever reason, we choose to interpret fatalistic language literally instead of metaphorically, thus treating it as mystical rather than *merely* poetic (which is not to say that none of us are superstitious or religious).[64]

There is no obvious reason why we should judge the pronouncements of the ancients any differently.[65] Indeed, we have already seen that, despite its focus on tragic or otherwise abnormal circumstances, the divine theatre of the ancients is considerably less causalist than that of most current philosophy of mind, the latter marked by a tendency to conflate the motivation of action with its production. 'A people gets the gods which it deserves,' Bowra famously remarked (1957: 41), this is certainly true of the majority of modern scholars who model their philosophies of action on the natural sciences.

Motivated by the gods

Compartmentalized agency and responsibility

Prologue

Over half a century ago, Martin Nilsson wrote of the 'Homeric man' who distances himself from certain actions that he appears to have performed, laying the blame instead on a deity of one kind or another:

> Men turn to the gods [. . .] to lay upon them the blame for that which has happened contrary to desire or intention. Even in the divine apparatus this idea finds expression in the common phrase: 'Now this would have happened [. . .] had not a god [. . .] ' The Homeric man is absolutely under the dominion of the emotion of the moment. When passion has subsided and the unhappy consequences begin to appear he says: 'I did not desire this; hence I did not do it.' His own behaviour has become something foreign to him, it seems to be something which has penetrated into him from without. He lays the blame on some daimon or god or Até or on Zeus, Moira and the Erinyes, as Agamemnon does in regard to his treatment of Achilles. A kind of division of personality takes place within him, though not in the pathological sense of two different states of personality. Rarely do two contrary currents appear in the mental consciousness [. . .] The abrupt change from one state to the other cleaves the mind in two. The man becomes 'besides himself', and when he comes 'to himself' again his ordinary self refuses to recognise the effect of this derangement, and regards it as due to some force outside of him. The same cleavage takes place when man is overtaken by something unforeseen. An action may be disastrous in its results although it is undertaken not in the heat of passion but with calm self-control. Here too man says 'I did not intend this; hence it does not belong to me'. He regards it as something outside of him which has come into his life from without and crossed his designs. Here again he lays the blame on a higher divine power. (Nilsson 1952: 163–5)

What is it for an action to 'happen contrary to desire or intention'? One possibility is that the action was not desired or intended at all, but was some kind of reflex action lying completely outside the control of the person whose behaviour it nonetheless was. Such actions are neither intentional nor unintentional, voluntary or non-voluntary, but, rather, non-intentional and involuntary in the strict sense. Accordingly, there is a sense in which such things happen to people who might justly be seen as victims of alien impulses, be they divine or neurological. Yet the bodily movements in question are those of the person whose body it is, and so there is an obvious sense in which it is legitimate to speak of one's own reflex action even when one is disowning it through a refusal to identify with it. I am here in agreement with Jennifer Hornsby's contention that 'there is alienation of an unthinkable sort when an agent is portrayed as if she were merely an arena for events' (Hornsby 2008: §185).

A second possibility is that the action was not desired in that it was non-voluntary, performed under coercion or duress. Such actions remain intentional, though part of the responsibility shifts from the agent to the coercive power. A divine power may be thought to weaken a person's will so that she finds it difficult to resist for long. We might say of such actions that they are desired in the sense that they are intentional, but undesired in the sense that they are not voluntary.[1]

A final possibility is that of the agent who – under the influence of some tempting factor – changes his mind at the very last second, and sooner or later comes to regret this. The person who all-too-readily changes his intention might reasonably be called weak-willed (see Holton 1999). To the extent that Homeric man may be said to suffer from weakness of will, this suffering might in his eyes involve an alien interference which accounts for the fact that the resulting action appears to have been desired in the heat-of-the-moment, even though it did not accord with the agent's deeper, more long-term, desires.

Socrates, in some – but arguably not all – of Plato's relevant dialogues (see Barney 2010), appears to be suggesting that in such cases the first desire is informed by the false belief that the action will result in a genuine good (which is what is desired in the deeper sense).[2] Behind such claims lies the *Socratic Principle* that only ignorance (of that whose knowledge is alien to us) can explain foolish or evil acts. A contrasting way of demarcating the immediate desire one acts upon from one's true desires is to distinguish, as Harry Frankfurt does, between primary and secondary desires: I may have a (first-order) desire for x but a (second-order) desire to not desire x. Imagine a poisonous flower that releases a powerful scent so sweet that virtually no passer-by can resist the temptation to eat it. Anyone unfortunate to pass by the flower will desire to eat it, but most will not desire to have this desire. The difference between such a scenario and many people's daily subjection to advertising is one of degree rather than kind. I believe that this third kind of possibility is the one that best lends itself to the Homeric appeals to the divine focused on by Nilsson.[3]

What we might thereby call the *Homeric Principle* maintains that in acting against one's intention or desire one is momentarily possessed by something alien to oneself and is therefore a victim rather than a culprit. While most of us today do not attribute our thoughts and emotions to alien agents, the phenomenon of refusing to identify with certain drives and passions that one possesses remains as familiar as ever, and we do not need to restrict ourselves to clinical cases such as that of alien hand syndrome in order to encounter it.

Such scenarios bear some similarity to – but should not be confused with – ones in which I desire to do what I do alright, but do so against my own better judgement. These are not explicitly mentioned by Nilsson, and Plato notoriously denied their very possibility. Philosophers such as Frankfurt, by contrast, can in principle allow for even second-order desires that are akratic. The alien might once again be introduced to account for such actions.[4] But the ancients recognized that it can also be introduced to account for actions which, regardless of our ethical evaluation of them, may be thought to require enormous willpower. The *Homeric Principle* may thus be contrasted to the *Medea Principle*, according to which a person can only overcome akrasia in order to act *upon* their better judgement, when an alien force overwhelms their will. Medea begs her hand (arguably a bodily manifestation of the passion of revenge) to murder her children, because she can't muster her own willpower to do it:

> Oh, come, my hand, poor wretched hand, and take the sword,
> Take it, step forward to this bitter starting point,
> And do not be a coward, do not think of them,
> How sweet they are, and how you are their mother. Just for
> This one short day be forgetful of your children [σέθεν],
> Afterward weep; for even though you will kill them,
> They were very dear – Oh, I am an unhappy woman! (Euripides, *Medea*, 1944: lines 1244–50)

Or so she convinces herself.

1. Shadowy presentations

Consider now the explanation offered by Atossa to Darius in Aeschylus's *Persians*, as she conveys the news that his son, 'impetuous Xerxes', has recklessly brought the Persian and Batrician armies to ruin by leading it to the Greek continent:

> Darius: What! Did he succeed in closing the mighty Bosporus?
> Atossa: Yes indeed. One of the divine powers must have assisted him in his purpose [γνώμης δέ πού τις δαιμόνων ξυνήψατο].
> Darius: Alas! Some mighty power came upon him [μέγας τις ἦλθε δαίμων] so that he was not able to think clearly [φρονεῖν καλῶς].
> Atossa: Yes, since we can see the outcome, what ruin [κακόν] he wrought
> (Aeschylus, *Persians*, 1922: lines 723–6)

'Divine power' is here a translation of the Greek word 'daimon', used by Homer to signify any kind of god, but by the time of Aeschylus reserved for inferior supernatural beings, lesser than the gods but mightier than mortals. The daimon in question does not here act against the purpose of Xerxes, but rather assists him in it: it is an eu-daimon. A century and a half later, Aristotle would distinguish between internal and external forces of movement, but, stripped of any ontological connotations, what is external to the agent's control need not literally reside outside her (see Gill 1986: 270).

This serves as a nice reminder of the fact that we need not take sides in the debate over whether gods are best characterized as psychological powers (Vernant 1962, 1965), persons (Burkert 1985: Ch. 3) or both (cf. Bremmer 1999: 22–3) to agree with E. R. Dodds's suggestion that they serve as a constant reminder of 'man's helpless dependence on an arbitrary Power' that can 'force a man, as it were from the outside, into conduct foreign to him' (Dodds 1951: 30, 41).[5]

Dodds, like Aristotle, treats 'the outside' as a metaphorical device and not a literal location, implying that what is foreign to us as self-conscious persons may nonetheless lie within us, as true a part of our psychology and physiology as any other. What is hidden from our view need not be dark, but in contemporary culture it is those parts of us that we are most ashamed of that we so readily call alien (cf. Mulhall 2002; Trigg 2014), being all-too-happy to take the credit for any thought or behaviour that seems praiseworthy.[6] Nietzsche offers a wonderful putdown of both tendencies:

> [T]he desire to bear the whole and sole responsibility for one's actions and to absolve God, world, ancestors, chance, society from responsibility for them, is nothing less than the desire to be precisely that *causa sui* [self-cause] and, with more than Münchhausen temerity, to pull oneself into existence out of the swamp of nothingness by one's own hair [. . .] one will at no price give up his 'responsibility', his belief in himself, the personal right to his deserts [. . .] the other, on the contrary, will not be responsible for anything, to blame for anything, and out of an inner self-contempt wants to be able to shift-off his responsibility for himself somewhere else. (Nietzsche BGE: §21)

Prior to the aforementioned passage, Nietzsche questions the very notion of a self that thinks and acts as and when it wants:

> [A] thought comes when 'it' wants, not when 'I' want. (BGE: §17)
> and do not imagine that this thought can be separated from the 'willing'. (BGE: §19)

We need not agree with this generalized scepticism to appreciate the force of his claims about the fragile vanity of human nature. Complete knowledge and understanding of oneself involves the near-impossible task of appreciating the limits and extent of one's own agency and the varied ways in which we are in constant league with alien forces, be it consciously or otherwise. And while our interactions with the other do not of themselves render us guilty, disassociating ourselves completely from those parts of ourselves that we are not ostensibly responsible for is but another form of self-deception.

John Cottingham puts the case well:

> One of the great contributions of psychoanalytic theory to the moral life is the idea that splitting off one part of the self for contempt and disapproval by another part, although it may sound very morally impressive ('That was disgraceful! How could I have done it!') may actually be a ritualistic strategy of evasion, much easier

to perform than the long and painful task of coming to understand what truly motivated such lapses [...] there is all the difference between dramatic expressions of self-contempt and the contrite acknowledgment of failing that comes from serious self-examination. Contempt is here nowhere to be seen; but integrity, or the struggle to achieve it, is the guiding light of the whole project. (Cottingham 2008: 243)

This is an unsettling thought because psychoanalysis is often – and not entirely mistakenly – associated with the encouragement of the general outlook that Cottingham is criticizing in this passage. In particular, it is typically credited with compartmentalizing the mind with the aim of ascribing causal responsibility to a particular sub-part (such as the ego or the id) as if it were a homunculus agent capable of making intentional decisions behind the back, so to speak, of the subject and/or the other sub-parts of her mind. In making the point that he does, Cottingham downplays this partitionist aspect of Freud's approach in favour of a more holistic understanding of unconscious motivation, quoting the following passage from Jung with approval:

The psychoanalytic aim is to observe the shadowy presentations – whether in the form of images or feelings – that are spontaneously evolved in the psyche and appear –, without his bidding, to the man who looks within. In this way we find once more what we have repressed or forgotten. Painful though it may be, this is itself a gain – for what is inferior or even worthless belongs to me as my shadow, and gives me a substance and mass. How can I be substantial if I fail to cast a shadow? I must have a dark side if I am to be whole; and inasmuch as I become conscious of my own shadow, I also remember that I am a human being like any other. (Jung 1933: 40)[7]

On such an outlook – let's call it the *Jungian Principle* (in contrast with the Homeric one presented in §1) – the acceptance of who we really are involves identifying with darkness, regardless of whether or not we are responsible for – or approve of – it. We leave marks or traces upon the world, regardless of intention.[8]

2. Tragic descriptions

Donald Davidson provocatively suggests that the real tragedy of Oedipus was that he insisted on the validity of a certain kind of inference from true premises to a false conclusion:

Eleanore of Aquitaine intended (we may suppose) to marry Henri Plantagenet; she may not have intended to marry the man about to become King Henry II of England. If being intentional is a property of actions, we have an inference from true premises to a false conclusion. The tragedy of Oedipus was that he insisted on such invalid inferences: because he intentionally struck an old man and married Jocasta, he felt guilty as if he had intentionally married his mother and killed his father [. . .] similar considerations encourage a similar treatment of 'allegedly'. Alleged acts, like intended acts, may or may not exist; so they are not, of course, a kind of action. And while Oedipus may have been alleged to have married his mother, he may not have been alleged to have married Jocasta. It comes to this: either we give up simple inferences like the one that takes us from 'Oedipus married Jocasta and Jocasta was his mother' to 'Oedipus married his mother', or we recognise that being intended, alleged, or inadvertent are not properties of actions, and so cannot serve to individuate [. . .] Oedipus' marriage to Jocasta was identical to his marriage to his mother. We have seen why adverbs like 'intentionally' and 'surprisingly' do not require a multiplication in the number of events: they do not represent properties of events. (Davidson [1985a] 2001: 297–8)

The inference is invalid, Davidson maintains, because being intentional is not a property of actions per se, for the same action may be intentional under one description, and unintentional under another. What the myth of Oedipus anticipates, on this view, is not a Freudian or Jungian theory of motivation (which Greeks would have found at best obscure) but rather the idea, which Davidson inherited from Ross and Anscombe, that actions are only intentional under certain descriptions:[9]

[T]o describe an action as intentional is to describe the action in the light of certain attitudes and beliefs of a particular person; it may be necessary in order to illuminate what goes on in those cases in which the agent makes a mistake about who he is. It was intentional of Oedipus, and hence of the slayer of Laius, that Oedipus sought the slayer of Laius, but it was not intentional of Oedipus (the slayer of Laius) that the slayer of Laius sought the slayer of Laius [. . .] Oedipus struck the rude old man intentionally, but he did not strike his father intentionally. But [. . .] these strikings were one, since the rude old man was Oedipus' father. The obvious solution [. . .] is to take 'intentionally' as creating a semantically opaque context in which one would expect substitutivity of identity to seem to fail [. . .] One and the same action may be correctly said to be intentional (when described in one way) and not intentional (when described in another) [. . .] It is harder to avoid taking this position than one might think. I suppose no one wants to deny that if the rude old man was Oedipus' father, then 'Oedipus struck the rude old man' and 'Oedipus struck his father' entail one another [. . .] one will also presumably want to infer 'The striking of the rude old man by Oedipus occurred at the crossroads' from 'The striking of Oedipus' father by Oedipus occurred at the crossroads' and vice versa. But how can these entailments be shown (by a semantical theory) to be valid without also proving the following to be true: 'The striking of the rude old man by Oedipus was identical with the striking of Oedipus' father by Oedipus? Yet one of these actions was intentional and the other not. (Davidson [1967] 2001: 147–8)

Oedipus's action is not intentional under the description in which it is a killing of his father. On Davidson's view, this is not because his reason for killing his father was unconscious, but, rather, because he did not kill him for a reason that had anything to do with his being his father:[10]

> A man may have good reasons for killing his father, and he might do it, and yet the reasons not be his reasons for doing it (think of Oedipus) [. . .]. Suppose, contrary to legend, that Oedipus, for some dark oedipal reason, was hurrying along the road intent on killing his father, and, finding a surly old man blocking his way, killed him so he could (as he thought) get on with the main job [. . .] we could not say that in killing the old man he intentionally killed his father, nor that his reason in killing the old man was to kill his father. (Davidson [1974] 2001: 232)

We need not accept Davidson's analysis of intentional action to agree that Oedipus does not know (consciously or otherwise) the true identities of Jocasta and the old man and that he consequently does not act on such knowledge. A far simpler way, for example, would be to distinguish between *de re* and *de dicto* intentions. Oedipus may be said to have a *de re* intention to kill his father in that the person he intends to kill is indeed his father, but not a *de dicto* one, insofar as he does not conceive of him as such. On such a view, the event of his intentionally killing the old man is the same as the event of his unintentionally killing his father, for while Oedipus intends to kill the old man who is his father, he does not intend to kill the old man qua his father.[11] Indeed, the most standard versions of the story rely on his being motivated by false beliefs, blind not to truths about some kind of secret desire but to a dark fact about the sort of person he is: namely, one who non-secretly desires to do certain things to people who, unbeknownst to him, are his parents. For Oedipus really does desire and intend to kill a man who is in actual fact his father and (once again unbeknownst to him) marry a person who is his mother, and acts accordingly. The desires, aims and actions are all his regardless of whether or not he had some repressed Oedipal motive. Indeed, attributing such motives to him deflects attention from the true tragedy about the sort of person one can be even when one has the very best of intentions.[12]

Let us nonetheless suppose for the sake of argument that Davidson's account of intentional action is correct and that Oedipus is indeed guilty of a logical fallacy.[13] Why should we think, as Davidson does, that the mistake is a tragic one? The answer, presumably, is that it leads Oedipus to think that he is guilty of shameful acts that he does not intentionally perform and to consequently punish himself for this. This diagnosis of Oedipus's mistake is effectively Hegelian in nature (see Hegel PR: §117–8, quoted in Chapter 13).

On such a view, Oedipus feels guilty for his deed as if it were part of his purposed action.[14] Both Hegel and Davidson presuppose the truth of a *Description Principle* according to which we are only guilty if our action is a crime under the same description in which it is intentional. The trouble with this principle is that it completely misses the psychological importance of the Oedipus myth revealed by the *Jungian Principle* introduced in §2. For, whatever it is that Sophocles's Oedipus is plagued by, it is not moral guilt:

> The man I murdered – he'd have murdered me! I am innocent! Pure in the eyes of the law, blind unknowing I, came to this! (Sophocles, *Oedipus at Colonus*, 1982: lines 545ff)[15]

It is wrong, then, to think that Oedipus blinds himself out of guilt for a bad action as opposed to shame for a regrettable deed.[16] The 'dark side' of Oedipus (to use the term that George Lucas would famously appropriate from Jung) is revealed through the fact that, at the end of the day, the person he desired to sleep with really was his mother and the person he desired to kill his father, and that he did in fact act upon these desires. Indeed, there is no resisting the fact that in acting he brings it about that he kills his father and sleeps with his mother (as prophesied). It is thus plausible to re-describe his acts as ones of making it true that these things happen.[17] The tragedy is that there exists a darkness that is his and nobody else's, regardless of intention:

> My destiny, my dark power, what a leap you made [. . .] Dark, horror of darkness my darkness, drowning, swirling around me [. . .] Apollo – he ordained my agonies [. . .] but the hand that struck my eyes was mine, mine alone – no one else (Sophocles, *Oedipus Rex*, 1982: line 1313ff.)

Oedipus's acceptance is self-same with that which Prospero will later come to terms with in Shakespeare's *The Tempest* (V.i. 275–6):

> This thing of darkness I acknowledge mine.

Milan Kundera notes that Oedipus's self-blinding is not an act of punishment but a cry of despair:

> Is this an act he wants to impose on himself? The will of self-punishment? Or is it not rather a cry of despair? The wish to see no more of the horrors of which he is both cause and target? Therefore a desire not for justice but for nothingness? (Kundera 2007: 113)

And yet his choice of self-mutilation retains the formal marks of punishment in that it is a poetically fitting one, given that the darkness of his acts lay in the blindness of ignorance, as opposed to some unconscious vision (see Chapter 13). The thought that Oedipus's actions have polluted him, even though he is not morally responsible for them, has been voiced by Maurice Bowra, E. R. Dodds and Bernard Williams (the last of whom is often credited with the distinction, even though he was clearly influenced by the work of the other two):

> Oedipus is not legally or morally guilty of murder or of incest since he acted in ignorance. But he is something no less horrible; he is a polluted being, a man to be shunned as if he literally had some revolting and infectious plague [. . .] he himself feels intensely the horror of his position, and others feel it hardly less. Above all the gods feel it [. . .] it is wrong to think that the pollution exists only in the human mind. (Bowra 1944: 168–70)

> [N]o human court could acquit him of pollution; for pollution inherited in the act itself, irrespective of motive [. . .] and least of all could the bearer acquit

himself [. . .] Morally innocent though he is and knows himself to be, the objective horror of his actions remains with him and he feels that he has no longer any place in human society. Is that simply archaic superstition? I think it is something more. Suppose a motorist runs down a man and kills him, I think he ought to feel that he has done a terrible thing, even if the accident is no fault of his: he has destroyed a human life, which nothing can restore. In the objective order it is his acts that count, not intentions. A man who has violated that order may well feel a sense of guilt, however blameless his driving. (Dodds [1966: 43ff.)

There are two sides to action, that of deliberation and that of result, and there is a necessary gap between them. Regret must be governed, in good part, by results that go beyond intention. Sometimes regret can focus simply on the outside circumstances that made the action go wrong [. . .] you may have deliberated as well as you could, but you still deeply regret that that was how the deliberation went, and that this was what you did. This is not just a regret about what happened, such as a spectator might have. It is an agent's regret, and it is in the nature of action that such regrets cannot be eliminated, that one's life cannot be partitioned into some things that one does intentionally and other things that merely happen to one [. . .] That is the point of Oedipus's words at Colonus. The terrible thing that happened to him, through no fault of his own, was that he did those things. (Williams 1993: 69–70)

The acceptance of one's shadowy presentations is an acceptance of agency that bravely resists the ancient temptation to think that one was momentarily possessed by something alien to oneself – be it a desire or a demon that caused one to act against one's rational will and/or natural inclination – and therefore a victim rather than a culprit. Without such processes, questions of responsibility do not even arise since the person in question has failed to see herself as the agent of her actions: something 'other' has caused them.

3. Loving the alien

Accepting something as one's own need not involve endorsement or approval. This is equally true in the case of psychological properties as it is in the case of one's possessions, one's body, one's writing or one's relatives. We may choose to let such things define us, but we may also refuse to do so, distancing ourselves from them. Unlike our relatives, our personal possessions may often be acquired and disposed of intentionally, in ways that are both pragmatically and morally unproblematic.

What about features of our psychology? As with our own faces, clothes, work, actions and parents, we may simultaneously – and to varying degrees – experience aspects of our minds as both alien to us in one (perfectly ordinary) sense, and a close, perhaps even integral, part of us in another (equally legitimate) one. The acceptance of a desire as my own does not require a second-order desire to have it. On the contrary, a second-order desire to not have a certain (first-order) desire may be sparked by the very realization that I am the sort of person which has, or could come to have, desires that I (as a whole being) do not approve of.[18]

It is also possible, if not advisable, to identify much more strongly with one's favourite artist, brand, or uncle than with one's own self, whom one might come to hate. There is an important sense, then, in which it is wrong to reject what one doesn't approve of as alien, and accept what one endorses as one's own. Be that as may be, we rarely express ourselves more effectively than when we either distance or associate ourselves from something, regardless of whether it might be said to be our own. Indeed, we can even distance ourselves from the very person we have become. In the British television drama *Downton Abbey*, lady's maid Sarah O'Brien looks deep into her reflection in the mirror after having laid a cruel physical trap for her mistress, tells herself 'Sarah O'Brien this is not who you are', then hears the bodily crash that is the consequence of her action, just as she is setting out to undo it.[19]

In Theodore Dreiser's *An American Tragedy*, protagonist Clyde Griffiths falls under the spell of the wealthy Sondra Finchley and subsequently devises a plan to murder his working-class pregnant girlfriend, Roberta Alden, by pushing her off a boat. Once they are on the lake Roberta seeks to take his hand, at which point he lashes out at her 'but not even then with any intention to do other than free himself of her' (Dreiser [1925] 1964: 513), accidentally striking her with his camera and subsequently capsizing the boat in an attempt 'half to assist or recapture her and half to apologize for the unintended blow' (Dreiser [1925] 1964), after which he swims to shore but she (not knowing how to swim) drowns. As she cries for help, 'the voice at his ear' tells Clyde:

> is not this that which you have been thinking and wishing [. . .] despite your fear, your cowardice [. . .] this – has been done for you. An accident [. . .] an unintentional blow on your part is now saving you the labor of what you sought, and yet did not have the courage to do! But will you now, and when you need not, since it is an accident, by going to her rescue, once more plunge yourself in the horror of that defeat and failure which has so tortured you and from which this now releases you? [. . .] She herself is unable to save herself and by her erratic error, if you draw near her now, may bring about your own death also. (Dreiser [1925] 1964: 514)

In the ensuing court case, Clyde is asked to swear that the incident was an unpremeditated accident. In doing so we are told that he convinces himself – in bad faith – of a relevant distinction between the details of the intended act and the one that materialized:

> 'I do,' lied Clyde, who felt that in fighting for his life he was telling part of the truth, for that accident was unpremeditated and designed. It had not been as he had planned and he could swear to that. (Dreiser [1925] 1964: 738)[20]

Clyde is found guilty of murder owing to 'his whole manner' (Dreiser [1925] 1964: 749), which gives away his guilt. But what exactly is he guilty of? As he awaits the death penalty, Clyde's conversations with the Rev. Duncan McMillan reveal that there is a morally important sense in which he doesn't quite know – let alone understand – what he has done. Here are – in ultra-condensed form   some of the turns his mind makes in an attempt to capture the various incongruous facets of his action (page references in parentheses):

> [T]hose very strong impulses and desires within himself that were so very, very hard to overcome (825) [. . .] there was no doubt that he had plotted to kill Roberta [. . .] in spite of himself [. . .] never, under any other circumstances, would he have succumbed to any such terrible thought [. . .] unless he had been so infatuated – lunatic, even (827) [. . .] There were phases of this thing [. . .] which were not so easily to be disposed of [. . .] .in bringing Roberta there [. . .] and then growing so weak and furious with himself because of his own incapacity to do evil, he had frightened her into rising and trying to come to him. And that in the first instance made it possible for her to be thus accidentally struck by him and so made him, in part at least, guilty of that blow – or did it? [. . .] And since because of that she had fallen into the water, was he not guilty of her falling? [. . .] God already knew what the truth was (828–9) [. . .] That unintentional blow [. . .] there was more to it than he had been able yet to make clear, even to himself [. . .] there was much that was evasive and even insoluble about it [. . .] there had been no change of heart (834) [. . .] the accidental blow that had followed upon her rising and attempting to come to him, had been some anger against her for wanting to come near him at all. And that it was perhaps – he was truly not sure, even now, that had given him that blow its so destructive force [. . .] yet there was also the truth that in rising he was seeking to save her – even in spite of his hate [. . .]. Again, though [. . .]when she was drowning, he had been moved by the thought: 'Do nothing.' [. . .] all through, he had been swayed by his obsession for Miss X, the super motivating force in connection with all this (834).

The reverend's reaction to all this is initially marked by incomprehension ('So strange! So evasive! So evil! And yet –' (Dreiser [1925] 1964: 835)), but soon enough settles into an unequivocal verdict: 'In your heart was murder then' (Dreiser [1925] 1964: 836). We post-Davidsonians have been trained to ask whether the causal chain between the anger and the blow is a deviant one, in which case Clyde's action would not be intentional under the relevant description. But this is not what Clyde and Duncan are trying to figure out. The connection they are interested in bypasses intentionality, and yet it would be misleading to call it deviant insofar as this implies a morally crucial gap between the doer and the deed. This is Clyde's insight, but it remains clouded by a parallel fixation to reach some kind of verdict about both. What is this truth that Clyde and Duncan are both searching for, this truth that at least God would know? Perhaps Greek tragedies were attempting to describe an impossibility, and there is in fact no such thing as the realization in one's own will of the necessities from without. If so, then Clyde – like Eteocles before him – is unnaturally resigned to his lunatic fate (cf. Denham 2014: 157–8). Part of the trouble is that Dreiser's sustained efforts to maintain ambiguity are operating in the shadow of the Freudian view that there exists a realm of the subconscious about which there are discrete psychological facts to be uncovered.[21]

Epilogue

The *Homeric* and *Jungian* principles combine to reveal that coming to terms with the fact that the shadowy presentations are aspects of oneself and not some other is not to necessarily identify with them, at least not in any Frankfurtian sense requiring approval of some kind (Frankfurt [1969] 1988).[22] Over the years, different mechanisms of identification have been suggested. These embellishment theories[23] include whole-heartedness and second-order desires (Frankfurt [1969] 1988, [1971] 1988), self-reflection and satisfied plans and intentions (Bratman 2004), the semblance of responsiveness to reason (Raz 1999), the capacity for critical evaluation (Watson 2004), self-awareness and the desire to act in accordance with reasons (Velleman 1989), guidance control (Fischer 2006), and reflective endorsement (Korsgaard 2009). Such models all share a commitment to an *Identification Principle*, which states that we are responsible only for those beliefs and feelings that we consciously identify with, those that we reflectively want to be moved by, for only these are a mark of our 'true self'.

But while we may not be responsible for other aspects of our personality and behaviour, it would be in bad faith to treat these as merely alien, as if they had absolutely nothing to do with us, just as we would be in mistaken good faith to accept full responsibility for them. To think otherwise is to fall into the trap that Nietzsche warned us about in §2. Whether one sees oneself as a Homeric hero motivated by the gods, an evolutionary victim moved by selfish genes, or a divine creation born fallen, the fragility of both personal identity and responsibility[24] demands that we de-compartmentalize ourselves, whatever our attitudes towards the motivational powers that be.

13

The man who mistook his *Handlung* for a *Tat*

Hegel on Oedipus and other tragic Thebans

Prologue

Throughout his work, Hegel distinguishes between the notion of an act (*Tun*) from the standpoint of the agent (behaviour in so far as it relates to one's own foreknowledge, purpose, intention, and knowledge) and that of all other standpoints (e.g. legal, scientific, cultural)[1]. He terms the former *Handlung* (action) and the latter *Tat* (deed). This distinction should not be confused with the contemporary one between action and *mere* bodily movement. For one, both *Handlung* and *Tat* are aspects of conduct that results from the will, namely, T*un* (LA 1160ff.). Moreover, Hegel's taxonomy is motivated purely by concerns relating to modes of perception.[2] So, whereas theorists such as Donald Davidson assert that *all* actions are events that are intentional under some description, Hegel reserves the term 'action' for those aspects of behaviour that are highlighted by a specific (albeit contested) set of agent-related descriptions. This is not an ontological category, since there are no such objects as actions-under-specific-descriptions (see Anscombe [1979] 1981).

Sophocles's *Theban Trilogy*[3] reveals the central role that these notions must play in *any* Hegelian understanding of tragic drama. Indeed, the contrasts that matter most to Hegel's general take on both epic and tragic poetry are more closely related to the study of action than the standard theory attributed to Hegel would seem to allow.[4] It is more fruitful, then, to incorporate Hegel's insights into such tragedies into the model of action employed by him than it is to try to make them fit whatever 'theory' of tragedy might appear to be hinted at in his *Aesthetics*. Hegel perceives more clearly than any other philosopher of his time that ethics without action theory is blind, just as action theory without ethics is empty. In this, as I shall try to show, he anticipates the work of Prichard, Ross, Anscombe and Davidson.[5]

1. Tragic theorizing

Scholars frequently talk of Hegel's *theory* of tragedy, and textbook chapters invariably sandwich the suggested outlines of Hegel's poetics between those of Aristotle and Nietzsche (see, for example, Bushnell 2005 and Wallace 2007). Interpretations differ on details, but by and large commentators agree that, according to Hegel, tragedy results from a conflict of ethical claims that the Greeks took to be *absolute*.

The stock example and Hegel's own alleged favourite (Hegel LA: 1218; but see Paolucci and Paolucci 1962: xxv) is Sophocles's *Antigone* (cited as *A* herein; see n. 3 for details of abbreviations), in which the play's heroine rigorously adheres to familial claims at the expense of those of the city-state. She does so against the will of her uncle Creon, whose actions reflect the precise reverse priorities, with devastating results for both. Most tragedies seem to fit this Hegelian theory equally well. For instance, Aeschylus depicts a parallel tension between tribal and urban ethical outlooks in his *Oresteia*, and pits family love against military duty in both *Agamemnon* and *Seven against Thebes*. The clash between military and familial standpoints also forms the background to Euripides's *Iphigenia at Aulis*, and in *The Bacchae*, he similarly contrasts emotional values with rationalist ones.

It is usually further suggested that, on this model, tragic *awareness* has something to do with the dawning of a concept of individual morality held over and above collective ethics. The ancients are accordingly perceived to lack the self-consciousness required for what moderns would come to hold as the proper arbitration of competing sources of duty; it is only on the aftermath soil of each tragic event that the seeds of reconciliation start to grow. Are actions to be judged in accordance with personal motives, intrinsic features or objective consequences? The tensions between virtue ethics, deontology and consequentialism are all present in Hegel's reading of tragedy. Hegelian conflict arises when the absoluteness of the rights they feel bound by is under threat of being rendered partial by equally justified competing authorities, which they fail to recognize as such until after the event.[6]

The tragedy that Hegel discusses the most after *Antigone* is that of *Oedipus Rex*. And yet the drama here makes an uneasy fit for the aforementioned theory (see Houlgate 2007: 157). Hegel himself distinguishes between collisions of 'individuals who act and come into conflict' (such as that between Antigone and Creon) and the 'less concrete' collision of the right of 'wide awake consciousness' with the right of the deed done unconsciously[7] (as exemplified in Oedipus). To this he adds that 'there are other collisions depending partly on special circumstances and partly on the general relation between an individual's action and the Greek μοῖρα [fate]', though these are 'of less importance' for his purposes (*LA*: 1212–14; cf. *LPR*: 666).

How are these different types of collision related? The theory of tragedy typically attributed to Hegel models all possible collisions on the first type. As Anne and Henry Paolucci put it, 'in popular criticism of Hegel, attention is often focused on the first type of situation ... and then illustrations are drawn from plays involving the second' (Paolucci and Paolucci 1962: xxv–xxvi). This is a challenging, but not necessarily impossible, task. Stephen Houlgate, for example, accurately represents instances of this clash in terms that are more congenial to the theory of tragedy typically attributed to Hegel (e.g. Oedipus's violation of social taboos relating to family ties). Against the grain of Hegelian Aesthetics, I shall try to demonstrate that the importance of such characterizations is peripheral to Hegel's chief concern, neatly captured in Paul Ricoeur's remark that 'tragedy is the work of those who act and of their individuality' (Ricoeur 1992: 241).[8] Given this centrality of agency, it is more illuminating as well as truer to Hegel's vision — to subsume all three types of tragic collision (right vs. right; consciousness vs. objectivity; freedom vs. fate) under a philosophy of action.

2. Both sides now

The precise roles played by the aforementioned rights distinguished in Hegel's moral thought are a subject of much controversy.[9] The reception of Hegel's discussion of these rights as manifested in Greek tragedy, by contrast, has been considerably more unified. Yet, curiously, Hegel's language here is extremely ambiguous:[10]

> The original essence of tragedy consists then in the fact that within such a conflict each of the opposed sides, *if taken by itself*, has justification; while each can establish the true and positive content only by denying and infringing the equally justified power of the other. (*LA*: 1196)

> Creon's commandment is justified, *insofar* as the brother came as the enemy of the fatherland and sought to destroy it . . . Antigone has *a worthy reason* for action. (*LPA*: 95)

> Both are in the wrong because they are one-sided, but both . . . are *also in the right*. (*LPR*: 665)

> An individual's decision, justified by the object he aims at, is carried out in a one-sided and particular way, and therefore in specific circumstances, which already carry within themselves the real possibility of conflicts, he injures another and equally moral sphere of the human will. To this sphere another person clings as his own actual 'pathos' and in carrying out his aim opposes and reacts against the former individual. In this way the collision of equally justified powers and individuals is completely set afoot. (*LA*: 1213)

Commentators by and large retain the ambiguity of Hegel's qualifications:

> Creon is within custom and justified (ignoring for the moment his family tie) *insofar* as he shows dishonor to the corpse and forbids it burial in or near the city. (Nussbaum 2001: 438)

> Since Creon's decree is legitimate and such decrees constitute laws of the state that command respect, Antigone — *at least from the city's point of view* — must be wrong to violate it . . . *Insofar as* it prohibits the burial of a traitor in or near the city, it is right and justified; but *insofar as* it prohibits a sister from burying her brother at all, it violates the law of family piety and is wrong. One and the same edict is thus justified *in one respect* and unjustified in *another*. (Houlgate 2007: 153–4)

> For Hegel tragedy is the conflict of two substantive positions, each of which is justified, yet each of which is wrong *to the extent that* it fails either to recognise the validity of the other position or to grant it its moment of truth; the conflict can be resolved only with the fall of the hero. . . . The hero is both innocent and guilty insofar

as she adheres to the good by acting on behalf of a just principle; guilty insofar as she violates a good and wills to identify with that violation. (Roche 2006: 12–13)

What are we to make of all this talk of limited extents, respects, points of view and insofarness? Little effort has been made to clarify what it means to say that each person is absolutely right from their viewpoint. Does it amount to anything more than being partially right from an absolute standpoint? Can the rights in question be trumped? What does being *absolutely* justified in one respect, but not in another, amount to? And how literally are we to take the Dialectical Synthesis that dictates that if both a thesis and its antithesis are true then they are also false (and vice versa)?

As each new generation of commentary reminds us (Bradley [1909] 1950: 74; Kaufmann 1968: 280; Roche 2006: 15), tragic collisions need not contain claims of *equal* value, although such cases may magnify tragic intensity with greater aesthetic results. A. C. Bradley ([1909] 1950: 74–5) helpfully maintains that what Hegel takes to be equally justified [*Gleichberechtigt*] is not the claims of, say, Antigone and Creon, but their earthly *source*, namely the family and the state. His and Sophocles's own clear sympathy towards Antigone's cause, then, need not be at odds with the notion that Creon's 'side' is equally justified.

There is no hierarchy according to which familial concerns always trump state ones, or vice versa, but this is not to say that every particular *claim* made in the name of either one is ethically on a par with each and every claim made in the name of the other.[11] This fact alone is certainly sufficient for a very real kind of tragedy, for it may well turn out that in doing what is right *overall* one has to wrong certain people in certain respects. As Bradley puts it, 'it is tragic that observance of one [allegiance] should involve violation of the other ... no light matter to disobey the law or to murder a mother' (Bradley [1909] 1950: 75).

On such a conception, tragedy comes hand in hand with a kind of *fall* from absoluteness to particularity. We find it in the following passage in which Hegel follows the Greeks in associating justificatory power with deities:

> Only from this point of view can we be really serious about those gods who dwell in their peaceful tranquility and unity solely on Olympus and in the heaven of imagination and religious ideas, but who, when they now actually come to life as a specific 'pathos' in a human individual, lead, despite all their justification, to guilt and wrong owing to their particular specification and the opposition to which this leads. (*LA*: 1196; cf. 1218)

Dialectical Synthesis is thereby achieved via a *conceptual shift* in the notion of justification (cf. von Wright 1986: 13). There is an uncanny parallel between Hegel's portrayal of competing rights here and the account of duty that David Ross would develop in the early twentieth century.[12] Ross distinguishes between prima facie (or 'conditional') duties or obligations and overall *actual* (or 'proper') ones, which are absolute. Prima facie duties, for Ross, are tied to certain universally positive or negative characteristics shared by actions (e.g. he takes the keeping of a promise to always be a prima facie good):

I suggest 'prima facie duty' or 'conditional duty' as a brief way of referring to the characteristic which an action has (quite distinct from that of a duty proper) which an act has, in virtue of being of a certain kind (e.g. the keeping of a promise), of being an act which would be a duty proper if it were not at the same time of another kind which is morally significant. Whether an act is a duty proper or actual duty depends on *all* the morally significant kinds it is an instance of. (Ross [1930] 2002: 20–1)

Ross maintains that prima facie duties are *universal* but not a*bsolute:* keeping a promise always counted in favour of an action, but in any given case this feature could be outweighed. Conversely, actual duties are *absolute* but not *universal*: if in this particular case I have overall reason to keep my promise, then my duty to do so is *sans phrase*, but this does not entail that I always have an actual duty to keep my promises. In the perfect absence of competing duties, each prima facie duty is *identical* to a proper, absolute, duty. This identity is fractured, however, by the competing considerations of particular situations in everyday life, situations which create conflict that results in *wronging* people (by acting against one's prima facie duty not to harm them) for the sake of one's obligation overall.

We could say, then, that Antigone and Creon share prima facie duties towards both family and state. But, *pace* Bradley, their tragedy is not simply that of being in a position in which one of these must be violated if the other is to be upheld, nor is it 'sufficient for Hegel's principle that the violation should take place, and that we should feel its weight' (Bradley [1909] 1950: 75), although it is perhaps necessary. Rather, the protagonists mistake their conditional duties for ones that are absolute:

> Creon: These are my principles. Never at my hands
>   Will the traitor be honored above the patriot.
>   But whoever proves his loyalty to the state:
>   I'll prize that man in death as well as life. (*A*: li 232–5 [208–11])
> Antigone: Nor did I think your edict had such force
>   That you, a mere mortal, could override the gods,
>   The great unwritten, unshakable traditions.(*A*: li 503–5 [451–3])[13]

In refusing to ever accept a principle from a different source, Antigone and Creon each view their own claims as absolutely binding. Even on the weakest of readings and translations each still comes across as at the very least believing in a hierarchy of authority according to which certain kinds of claims *always trump* others. It is not as though Antigone decides, upon considered deliberation that, while there is *equal* reason to ally oneself to both family and state, on this particular occasion family wins out at the tragic cost of violating state regulations, any more than Creon takes himself to have a prima facie duty to bury Polynices. They each take the traditions to which they ally themselves to be unshakeable in a far deeper sense, and it is there that the seeds of their tragic destruction are planted. Milan Kundera has described such scenarios as follows:

> Two antagonists face to face, each of them inseparably bound to a truth that is partial, relative, but considered in itself, entirely justified. Each is prepared to

sacrifice his life for it, but can only make it prevail at the price of total ruin for the adversary. Thus both are at once right and guilty. Being guilty is to the credit of great tragic characters, Hegel says. A profound sense of guilt can make possible an eventual reconciliation [. . .] it made clear the need to do justice to the enemy. But moral Manichaenism has an indestructible vitality: I remember an adaptation of *Antigone* that I saw in Prague shortly after the war; killing off the tragic in the tragedy, its author made Creon a wicked fascist confronted by a young heroine of liberty. (Kundera 2007: 110)

The clash between those who blindly devoted themselves to the communist party and hard-line intellectual dissenters such as Václav Havel (who had little patience for Kundera's reformist hopes) ironically parallels that of Creon and Antigone, each side failing to recognize the justified claims of the other. As with numerous political adaptations of ancient Greek theatre (the most famous of which is Jean Anouilh's *Antigone*), actual tragedy has here destroyed the very possibility of producing theatrical tragedy from the outset.[14] The very freedom coveted evaporates with it; without mutual recognition there can arguably be no free individual action.[15] Frank Ramsey once remarked that 'it is a heuristic maxim that the truth lies not in one of the two disputed views but in some third possibility which has not yet been thought of, which we can only discover by rejecting something assumed as obvious by both disputants' (Ramsey [1925] 1960: 115–16). In tragic scenarios, what is assumed by both disputants is the very thought that moral right must lie *solely* in one of the two disputed views. This is the dangerous law of the excluded ethical middle.

3. The Greeks had a word for it

Notwithstanding his own very close relationship to his sister Christiane (see Pinkard 2000: 315–16), Hegel places *Antigone* above all other tragedies not because the colliding claims depicted in it are equal but for the developmentally more crucial reason that in her final moments the heroine appears to *recognize* (and not merely acknowledge) the competing claims of the other, thus progressing towards a harmonious reconciliation through the realization that they need not pursue their purpose 'one-sidedly and so contradicting and infringing someone else's purpose' (*LA*: 1197).

For Hegel, 'the reconciliation in which the specific individuals and their aims work together harmoniously without opposition and without infringing on one another' (*LA*: 1197) is but an ideal that we can only approximate on earth. As our moral consciousness grows, ancient tragic dilemmas resulting from one-sided pursuits of purpose transform into modern tragic dilemmas in which prima facie duties are sacrificed for the sake of a multi-sided overall duty. At the dawn of moral consciousness 'eternal justice is exercised on individuals and their aims in the sense that it restores the substance and unity of ethical life with the downfall of the individual who has disturbed its peace' (*LA*: 1197). This tragic unfolding allows us to glimpse at the structure of the absolute in which 'the eternal substance of things emerges as victorious in a reconciling way, because it strips away from the conflicting individuals only their false one-sidedness, while the positive elements in what they willed displays it as what is to be retained, without discord but affirmatively harmonised' (*LA*: 1199). None of this entails, however, that every entanglement of contrary determinations will necessarily lead to resolution (see de Boer 2010: 1–29).

Dialectical advancement does not require the death of the particular, but only its transcendence: 'the tragic denouement need not every time require the downfall of the participating individuals in order to obliterate the one-sidedness of both sides in their equal need of honour' (*LA*: 1218ff.).[16] Creon does not injure himself, but is nonetheless a 'walking corpse'.[17] The *Oresteia* culminates in Orestes's placating the Furies, which puts an end to the blood feud as the conflict is brought to the judgement of Athena, representing the divine aspect of the people's wisdom (see de Beistegui 2000: 18).Until, however, the transition from Right to Morality is complete (see *PR*: §104), the tragic beast is tempered but not tamed.

We need not follow Hegel in his historicism any more than we need follow Ross in the details of his thought in order to appropriate his conceptual scheme to Greek conflict in this way. Even the moral particularist who denies that prima facie duties *generalize* (e.g. Dancy 2004a) can allow that:

> Every act [. . .] viewed in some aspects, will be *prima facie* right, and viewed in others, *prima facie* wrong, and right acts can be distinguished from wrong acts only as being those which, of all those possible to the agent in the circumstances, have the greatest balance of *prima facie* rightness, in those respects in which they are *prima facie* right, over their *prima facie* wrongness, in those respects in which they are *prima facie* wrong. (Ross [1930] 2002: 41)

In cashing out Hegel's qualifications of extent in Rossian coinage we emphasize the thought that Hegelian Greek tragedy results from an error [*hamartia*] of some kind and is in principle avoidable, though not without a significant paradigm shift (arguably one which no individual could undergo in isolation). Indeed, the recognition that the error is in some sense avoidable is central to the possibility of reconciliation. This is not to reject outright the Hegelian thought that tragic conflict ultimately arises out of a *necessary* developmental deficiency of the pre-modern world, but only to emphasize that the overcoming of such deficiencies requires us to recognize them as such. In an angry article, E. R. Dodds protests against those who think of Aristotelian *hamartia* as a moral fault, rather than 'an offence committed in ignorance of some material fact and therefore free from *ponēria* or *kakia*' (Dodds [1951] 1983: 179). Quite so. 'To err is human', as Hegel acknowledges, but wrong conviction is no mere error when made the basis of ethics and pronounced as supreme and sacrosanct (*PR*: §140). The Theban heroes that Hegel explores may well be exceptional in glimpsing into an ethical future which only begins in the later age of Sophocles, but they also remain centres of that single subjective conviction which Hegel describes as a 'monstrous self-conceit', an absolute self-complacency which 'fails to rest in a solitary worship of itself but builds up a sort of community' (Dodds [1951] 1983).

As she is led off to the burial chamber, Antigone considers the possibility of error, be it hers or Creon's:

Very well: if this is the pleasure of the gods, Once I suffer I will know that I was wrong, But if these men are wrong, let them suffer Nothing worse than they mete out to me — These masters of injustice! (*A*: li 1017–21 [914–20])

Allen Speight (2001: 55) has pointed out that Hegel's mistranslation of the second line as 'because we suffer we acknowledge that we err' even hints at regret, thus arguably attributing Antigone with the notion that her error could have been avoided. But how might such an error have arisen and why should we think that this was inevitable given the stage of the Spirit in Ancient Greece?

Numerous interpreters present Hegel as replacing the Aristotelian notion that tragedy is generated through erroneous wrongdoing with the suggestion that it results from the fact that both of the colliding parties are right, thus producing a genuinely contradictory situation. For example, Jennifer Wallace (2007: 122) maintains that Antigone and Creon 'are justified in their beliefs', which misleadingly suggests that they have made no cognitive error in dismissing all competing authorities. Likewise, Terry Pinkard maintains that 'tragic drama consists in the portrayal of individual agents being required to do something that is *right* that is also at the same time unequivocally *wrong* [. . .] both sides to the conflict are in the right and yet commit wrong' (Pinkard 2000: 210). M. S. Silk and J. P. Stern take this reading to its natural extreme, writing that in Hegelian tragedy:

> There is no blindness or ignorance. There is no crime. The absolute tragic conflict is the conflict of two all but fully informed consciousnesses, two agents who all but fully understand themselves and each other, and who oppose each other by the assertion and counter-assertion of valid but conflicting laws. (Silk and Stern 1983: 316–17; cf. Bushnell 2008: 75ff.)

Martha Nussbaum, by contrast, concedes that tragedy may result out of an error of some kind, yet insists that the mistakes of tragic agents are all but unavoidable, agents being *forced* to act as they did by circumstances, thus leaving little room for culpability:

> We pity Oedipus, because the appropriate action to which his character led him was not the terrible crime that he, out of ignorance, committed. We pity Agamemnon because circumstances forced him to kill his own child, something deeply repugnant to his own and our ethical commitments. (Nussbaum 2001: 385)

Stephen Houlgate moves much closer to the direction I am steering towards in allowing that (at least on Hegel's view) both Antigone and Creon may be charged with *avoidable* error. He maintains, however, that they are both *justified* in doing so:

> Creon might err precisely in doing what is right and justified [. . .] for Hegel, that is Creon's tragedy, as it is Antigone's. (Houlgate 2007: 153)

> Hegel implies [. . .] that tragedy is avoidable if individuals are prepared to let go of their own justified interests and give way to one another. (Houlgate 2007: 157)

For Houlgate's Hegel, 'Antigone and Creon are both justified in what they do, but each sees only the rightness of his or her own position, and so fails to recognize the legitimacy of the other' (Houlgate 2007: 154). This seems right to me, but only *insofar as* we conceive of their actions as only being prima facie justified, which is to say that their one-sidedness is not justified at all: it is *myopic* or *muted* at best, and often completely blind or deaf. It cannot be an accident that the Gods' disapproval of Creon's typhlotic decision is expressed through the blind seer Tiresias, the same who could also see what Oedipus was doing better than the man himself (see §4). Antigone's and Creon's mistake is not that of allowing their *sans phrase* judgements to contradict their overall conditional ones (as Donald Davidson argues is the case with akratic agents; Davidson [1969a] 2001: 36ff.), nor is it the case that they have no realization of one another's claims; they simply refuse to accept them as valid, given the sacrosanct origins of their own: it is attempted self-sufficiency that brings each of them down (*A*: li 960ff.) – knowingly, voluntarily and unhesitantly rendering their ears deaf to arguments stemming from one another's spheres of concern. Indeed, it would not have been an inappropriate ending for them to cut off their ears, living the rest of their lives in muted harmony.[18]

Lack of moral perception may not be an error as such, but it often results from it and, at any rate, most certainly *leads* to non-veridical judgement. So the contrast with Aristotle is one of emphasis rather than substance. For Aristotle, error is largely a matter of judgement being *clouded* by passion. For Hegel, it occurs when the very possibility of correct judgement is clouded by social structure. It is of course possible for even a fully virtuous person to be misled by an epistemic situation, but this is not the sort of scenario in which Theban agents such as Oedipus, Creon and Antigone find themselves. Their ethical misperceptions result from a moral mental block of monstrous certainty. Thus, Creon himself howls for the 'senseless', 'insane' and 'stubborn' crimes that resulted from his own stupidity, to which the chorus unhesitantly replies that at least he now sees 'what justice means' (*A*: li 1390ff [1260ff.])[19]

Creon's guilt is not the product of *mere* stubbornness or whim in the face of the otherwise obvious (as manifested in the modern 'character tragedy' that Hegel contrasts to ancient tragedy),[20] but a failure of ethical *sensitivity*. The resulting error is that of conflating objectivity and universality with *absoluteness*; the rights in question are neither subjective nor particular, they are *pro tanto*.

4. Oedipal under some description

The conflict in *Oedipus Rex* is considerably more complex than those occurring in the tragedies discussed so far and we should be prepared for the possibility that it does not neatly fit into any *theory* of tragedy. The most obvious difference is that his character's ethical pathos does not contrast with that of another. This is not to say that what we are dealing with here is a case of *internal* conflict or fragmented character – what Roche calls 'the possibility of a tragic collision within an individual's consciousness' (2006: 16).

The fact that Oedipus is *not conscious* of the fact that he is interacting with his parents (what Hegel terms his 'unconsciously committed crimes'; *LA*: 1219) does not entail that he has *subconscious* knowledge of it.[21] Without wishing to completely dismiss the possibility of a Freudian reading of the myth, the conflict in Sophocles's play – certainly as it is perceived by Hegel – is that between Oedipus and Reality, between subjective and objective rights. Unlike the conflicts between different moral values, each of the contrasting modes of presentation responsible for Oedipus's predicament is both equally *true* and equally *justified* (for Oedipus never held an occurrent belief that the old man was not his father, or Jocasta his mother). The task of consciousness is to identify which of them are *morally* (as opposed to merely socially) relevant.

In subsection 3 of the Morality section in *Philosophy of Right,* Hegel famously warns against those who make their conscience sacrosanct. But we might still worry, as Ross's friend and colleague H. A. Prichard did in his influential paper 'Duty and the Ignorance of Fact', whether a person's obligation to perform (or omit from performing) some action depends 'on certain characteristics of the situation in which he is, or on certain characteristics of his thought about the situation' (Prichard [1932] 2004: 84).

The difficulty is this: on the one hand, we want to leave room for the thought that we can be *wrong* about what we ought to do. The fact that what we *believe* we ought to do and what we *actually* ought to do can come apart in this way would seem to lend credence to the first (objectivist) answer to Prichard's question. One the other hand, however, there is the procedural obstacle of the impossibility of stepping out of one's own mind in order to compare reality with one's impressions of it (arguably a key factor behind David Hume's sceptical account of causal knowledge). Thus, the objective view would seem to imply that 'although we may have duties, we cannot know but only believe that we have; and therefore we are rendered uncertain whether we, or anyone else, has ever had, or will ever have a duty' (Prichard [1932] 2004: 100).

In his initial article, Prichard ultimately let practicality trump theory, concluding that 'we cannot but allow that the [second] subjective view is true, in spite of what at first seems its paradoxical character' (Prichard [1930] 2004: 100). More importantly, for our purposes, he infers from this that 'in order to defend any moral rule whatever, we must first modify its form accordingly'. He thereby also reasons that 'an obligation must be an obligation, not to *do* something, but to perform an activity of a totally different kind, that of setting ourselves to do something, i.e. to bring something about' (Prichard [1930] 2004: 97). The idea is that since we can never know for certain what the consequences of our setting out to do anything might be, all we can ever be responsible for is the initial setting out. Jonathan Dancy has objected to this argument by suggesting that there is no reason 'to allow that I can never know what the consequences of my actions will be' (Dancy 2002: 233). Dancy may well be right, but this is happily not the place to debate the concept of knowledge. Either way, however, Oedipus's story is a testament to how the indefinite number modes (characters) which actions past, present or future may fail to present to us make any claim to knowledge defeasible, if not always tragically so. Prichard's conclusions were a clear retreat to a view that Ross's first book (*The Right and the Good*) had explicitly sought to attack. As Dancy notes, 'Ross was so completely persuaded by Prichard that he included in [his second book] *The Foundations of Ethics* a ten-page summary of Prichard's [17 page] argument, word for word' (Dancy 2002: 229). Prichard himself later recanted, and in a note added to the original paper, suggested that his original contrast between the subjective and objective views may have been a false one (Prichard 2004: 100–1). While Prichard's reasons for thinking this are largely unconvincing,[22] I believe that Hegel has shown that a deconstruction of this problem is indeed the right approach.

Hegel's solution famously offers two aspects of any given act: *Tat* (deed) corresponding to the objective (which I am causally responsible for), and *Handlung* (action) corresponding to the subjective (which can be morally imputed to me); rights relating to the latter in turn dividing into one relating to various elements of the self, such as knowledge, intention and purpose:

> [T]he fact that I am [causally] responsible for something does not mean that the thing can be [morally] imputed to me. (*PR*: §115)

> It is, however, the right of the will to recognise as its *action,* and to accept *responsibility* for, only those aspects of its *deed* which it knew to be presupposed within its *end*, and which were present in its *purpose*. I can be made [morally] *accountable* [chargeable] for a deed only if my *will was responsible* for it – *the right of knowledge.* (*PR*: §117)

> [W]hat we may call the right of the *objectivity* of the action is the right of the action to assert itself as known and willed by the subject as a *thinking agent.* (*PR*: 120)

> The right of intention is that the universal quality of the action shall have being not only *in itself,* but shall be *known* by the agent and thus have been present all along in his subjective will; and conversely, what we may call the right of the *objectivity* of the action is the right of the action to assert itself as known and willed by the subject as a *thinking agent.* (*PR*: §120)

It may seem that this view collapses into subjectivism; however, Hegel adds the following crucial proviso:

> There are inevitable consequences linked with every action, even if I am only bringing about some single, immediate state of affairs. The consequences in such a case represent the universal implicit within that state of affairs. Of course I cannot foresee the consequences — they might be preventable — but I must be aware of the universal character of my isolated act. The important point here is not the isolated thing but the whole, and that depends not on the differentia of the particular action, but on its universal nature. Now the transition from purpose to intention lies in the fact that I ought to be aware not simply of my single action but also of the universal which is conjoined with it. The universal which comes on the scene here in this way is what I have willed, my intention. (*PR*: §118A)

In other words, we are not only responsible for *known* characterizations of our actions and their effects but also for those that we *ought* to be aware of (even if we are not):

> Hegel acknowledges, however, that our ignorance does not always relieve us of responsibility for things we have done, because others can claim that, as rational

beings we *should* have known what we were doing even if we did not. When we should be held responsible for things done in ignorance, is something which Hegel believes cannot be determined by philosophy, but must be decided in the given context by the people involved. (Houlgate 2005: 294)

This criterion also enables the Hegelian to isolate cases of luck which we must take responsibility for:

> It happens of course that circumstances may make an action miscarry to a greater or lesser degree. In a case of arson, for instance, the fire may not catch or alternatively it may take hold further than the incendiary intended. In spite of this, however, we must not make this a distinction between good and bad luck, since in acting a man must lay his account with externality. The old proverb is correct: 'A flung stone is the devil's.' To act is to expose oneself to bad luck. Thus bad luck has a right over me and is an embodiment of my own willing. (*PR*: 119A)

Returning to the case of Oedipus, we are now in a position to further investigate the details of whether he may be held (ethically) responsible for the unknown aspects of his actions. Hegel's answer is an unequivocal 'no':

> Oedipus, who unwittingly killed his father, cannot be accused of parricide, although the legal codes of antiquity attached less importance to the subjective element, to responsibility. (*PR*: 117)

He cannot be so accused because:

> Actuality [...] does not show itself to consciousness as it is in and for itself – it does not show the son the father in the one who offends him and whom he slays, or the mother in the queen whom he takes as his wife. (*PR* [i]: §469)

Allen Wood elaborates that as far as objective guilt is concerned:

> Oedipus, in Hegel's view, bears none for killing his father or conceiving children by his mother, which belonged to neither his intention nor his purpose. (Wood 1990: 127)

> To say that parricide was not included in Oedipus's *Vorsatz* (in killing the querulous old man at the crossroads) is to say that he did not realise (and could not have known) that he was killing his father, so that his act under the description 'parricide' was unintentional. To identify the *Absicht* of an action, the universal under which the agent brings it in acting, is to identify the agent's reasons for doing it, or the features of the action (or its results) that counted in favor of acting that way. (Wood 2010: 135, n. 3)

The duty to not commit patricide is seen as being *absolute* as well as *objective*, but its scope is not universal, restricted as it is by the rights of intention and knowledge.

Oedipus is not bound by any duty to perform (or omit to perform) certain actions *no matter what their mode of presentation*. The fragility of *goodness* does not entail that *morality* is a matter of luck.[23]

5. The king who would be man

The trouble, Hegel thinks, is that Oedipus could not see any of this:

> The Self-consciousness of heroes (like that of Oedipus and others in Greek tragedy) had not advanced out of its primitive simplicity either to reflection on the distinction between deed [*Tat*] and action [*Handlung*], between the external event and the purpose and knowledge of the circumstances, or to the subdivision of consequences. On the contrary, he accepted responsibility for the whole compass of the deed. (*PR*: §§117–18; see Houlgate 2005: 190)

A similar thought would later be echoed by Davidson.[24] Hegel and Davidson both claim that the Theban king's great error was to mistake his *Tat* for a *Handlung*. But Sophocles's narrative actually lends itself to the exact opposite reading: Oedipus first (and foremost) mistakes his *Handlung* for a *Tat*. Throughout his life as an agent, he arrogantly assumed that his Purposed actions encompassed the totality of his deeds, cognitively resisting the reality of any other aspects of his acts. Had he been cognitively humbler, Tiresias's warning that 'the very insults' that Oedipus has thrown at him (namely, that the truth has power but not for Tiresias whose eyes are 'blind as stone') will soon be flung back at him by 'each man here' (*OT*: li 423–4 [372–3]), would not have fallen on deaf ears.

Nevertheless, does not Oedipus come to accept responsibility for the whole deed and feel related guilt? A more plausible understanding of his changed psychology, as portrayed by Sophocles, would be that upon realizing his perceptual error he is temporarily overwhelmed by the irony that he 'has been made equal in one thing' to the 'stone-blind, stone-deaf' seer, whom he had falsely accused of having had a hand in the murder of his father, now vindicated in the revelation that it was actually *he* (Oedipus) who had done the deed?[25] He whose name means not only 'swollen foot' but also 'knowing foot' (of pride) and who frequently boasted of his own knowledge, having become *tyrannos* in both senses of the Greek by answering the Sphinx that *man* is the measure of all the things she mentions;[26] he realizes much too late that in actual fact it is *things* that are the measure of all men and that he wasn't even man enough to measure his own *erga*. When a stranger asks the blind old exile what is to be gained from a man who cannot see, the latter replies that there is 'great vision' in every word he says (*OC*: li 88–9 [73–4]). It is possible to view this reaction as neatly fitting into a pattern of speech which reflects the fact that, for all that has happened, Oedipus still fails to shake off any of his arrogance. But this would be to turn a blind eye to the more interesting possibility that he has finally completed his transformation into Tiresias.

There are places in Hegel's *Aesthetics* that reveal him to be at one with such interpretations. He compares Oedipus's extraction of knowledge with that of Adam after biting the apple (his exile from Thebes mirroring Adam's departure from the Garden of Eden) and states that *he* is 'the seer now [. . .] his blind eyes are transfigured and clear' (*LA*: 1219). It is unsettling, for this reason, to find him claiming, in the *Philosophy of Right*, that Oedipus did not possess the self-consciousness (namely, notion of subjectivity) required to distinguish between *Tat* and *Handlung*. The key to reconciling these two outlooks may be found in Hegel's suggestion that 'the transfiguration of Oedipus always still remains the Greek transfer of consciousness from the strife of ethical powers, and the violations involved, into the unity and harmony of the entire ethical order itself' (*LA*: 1220; cf. *PR* [*i*]: §§347–483). In other words, Oedipus initially lacks but comes to *acquire* self-consciousness as a result of his tragedy. He thereby represents the very moment of the Greek transition to self-consciousness, one which Hegel takes to pave the way for the comedy of Aristophanes, in which characters have a conception of their own individual goods that is in tension with that of communal goods (*LA*: 1220ff.; cf. White 2002: 156ff.).

Charles Segal follows many commentators in writing that Oedipus represents a 'dawning of moral and intellectual self-awareness [. . .] the emergence of an ethical sense and an acknowledgement of guilt after the lack of consciousness of committing a crime' (Segal 2001: 37). I propose that he more or less represents the exact opposite: namely, the slow awareness that what the state law sees as a crime may be no moral crime at all, for we are not responsible for every single aspect of our deeds. If Oedipus feels guilt about anything, it is guilt about not having realized this *previously*, thus making the mistake of thinking he was self-sufficient (the same mistake which, incidentally, informs the libertarian and individualist notion of a person who is completely 'self-made').

At Colonus, the now-blinded but self-conscious exile proclaims his innocence in Creon's presence:

> Bloodshed, incest, misery [. . .] I have suffered it all and all against my will [ακων]! Such was the pleasure of the gods [. . .] say my unwilling crimes against myself and against my own were payment from the gods for something criminal deep inside of me [. . .] no, look hard, you'll find no guilt to accuse me of – I am innocent! [. . .] blind to what I was doing, blind to whom I killed – how could you condemn that involuntary [ακον] act with any sense of justice? [. . .] I knew nothing, she knew nothing [. . .] I made her my bride against my will. No, I'll not be branded guilty, not in that marriage, not in the murder of my father. (*OC*: li 1097–1130 [960–90])

Earlier in the same play he goes as far as to suggest (not obviously wrongly) that even full knowledge that it was Laius that he was attacking would not render him guilty, certainly not in an Athenian court[27] (it is less clear whether Sophocles's Oedipus similarly thinks of love or honour as an absolving motive for incest):

> [M]*y* acts, at least, were acts of suffering more than actions outright [. . .] how could you call me guilty [. . .] I was attacked — I struck in self-defence. Why even if I had known what I was doing, how could that make me guilty? But in fact, knowing nothing, no I went [. . .] the way I went — but the ones who made me suffer, they knew full well, they wanted to destroy me. (*OC*: li 284–94 [266–74])

One may wish to account for such passages by claiming that the older Sophocles had himself witnessed a growth of moral consciousness which he subsequently projects onto the character of Oedipus. Arguably, however, Oedipus's full appreciation of the relation between the subjectivity of his actions and the objectivity of his deeds is crucial to the reconciliatory denouement of his tragedy (cf. Williams 1993: 68–9). He learns what he *has done* from the way things turn out, but in so having the world in better view he, quite rightly, does not take himself to have discovered his *intention* (see McDowell 2009: 180).[28]

Those who insist on viewing Oedipus's self-blinding as an action performed out of guilt overlook the possibility that he is moved by an understanding that 'in the story of one's life there is an authority exercised by what one has done, and not merely by what one has intentionally done' (Williams 1993: 69). The limits of related analyses (such as Davidson's) are marked by a common reluctance to apply a *de re/de dicto* distinction to pro-attitudes yet, when all is said and done, it remains the case that the person that Oedipus married *was* his mother and the person he killed his father. As Bernard Williams has put it, 'the terrible thing that happened to him, through no fault of his own, was that he did those things' (Williams 1993: 70). Oedipus himself need not consider himself *guilty* of a bad action in order to feel *shame* for a regrettable deed.[29]

Dodds and Kundera both propose that we view Oedipus's final act not as an act of self-punishment but as a cry of despair, suggesting that he wishes to 'cut himself off from all contact with humanity' (Dodds [1951] 1983: 183) and 'see no more of the horrors of which he is both cause and target' (Kundera 2007: 113[30]). It is more fruitful, I think, to imagine that Oedipus no longer wishes to see what is to come, because he has realized that the unavoidability of aspect perception is a form of blindness. *Pace* Kundera, Oedipus's desire is not for nothingness (he does not kill himself) but for a state in which things no longer *appear* to him as clearly as they once misguidedly did. Indeed, his act of blinding *himself* is the only act he may now perform whose consequences (including the identity of the victim) he can be certain of, and which he wishes to experience as a constant reminder of his former blindness. Evoking his feelings towards the god whose temple bore the inscription 'γνῶθι σεαυτόν', Oedipus proudly announces that he now knows the limits of himself:

> Apollo, friends, Apollo – he ordained my agonies – these, my pains on pains! but the hand that struck my eyes was mine, mine alone [αὐτόχειρ][31] – no one else – I did it all myself! What good were eyes to me? (*OT*: li 1467–72 [1329–35])

When the king asserts that the hand that blinded him was *his alone* he is not interested in mere *causal* responsibility (strictly speaking, it was his hand alone that killed his father too) but in the rights of *knowledge* and *intention*. This is because he has realized that, as Ross would influentially put it, 'any act may be correctly described in an indefinite, and in principle infinite, number of ways'.[32] An act, Ross tells us, is typically 'the production of a change in the state of affairs' (Ross 2002: 42). The more distant a state of affairs is from us, the greater the chances that it will fail to present itself to us in some ethically crucial way. But 'the only changes we can *directly* produce are changes in our own bodies or in our own minds' (Ross 2002: 42). Thus, Oedipus resolves to blind himself, not *despite* the fact that self-changes 'are not, as such, what as a rule we think it our duty to produce' (Ross 2002: 42), but *because* of it.

Anticipating Ross, Hegel claims that 'to judge an action as an external deed without yet determining its rightness or wrongness is simply to bestow on it a universal predicate, i.e. to describe it as burning, killing, etc.' (*PR*: 119). What truly appears to Oedipus as self-defence may be described with *equal* truth as patricide. The tragedy of Oedipus is not simply that he did not foresee the *consequences* of his actions[33] but that he did not anticipate that they could fall under universal categories other than those in which they presented themselves to him.

Epilogue

Oedipus Rex adheres to the Greek practice of appealing to *double causation* in its account of tragic action. Hegel rightly allows, however, that the causal role of Apollo – who, in any case evinces himself as a substantial part of Oedipus's own inner life (see *LA*: 225, 227)[34] – is not that of moving Oedipus's hand but, rather, of masking the full reality of what his movements amounted to:

> The gods [. . .] and the real universal powers in general, are indeed the moving force and stimulus, but, in the real world, individual action is not to be assigned to them; action belongs to men. Therefore we have two separate sides: on the one there stand those universal powers in their self-reposing and therefore most abstract substantiality; on the other the human individuals on whom devolve the resolution, the final decision on action, and its actual accomplishment. (*LA*: 225)[35]

Hegel's account of double causation in *tragedy* contrasts sharply with his understanding of it in *epic*:

> The business which is the object of these general exertions has two sides: the side of the self, by which the business is accomplished by a totality of actual nations and the individualities standing at their head; and the side of the universal, by which it is accomplished by their substantial powers.

> Formerly, however, the relation of the two bore the character of a synthetic combination of the universal and the individual [. . . On this specific character depends the appraisal of this [the Epic] world. The relation of the two is thus a mingling of them which inconsistently divides and apportions the unity of the action, and superfluously throws the action over from one side to the other. The Universal powers have the form of individuality and hence the principle of action in them; what they effect appears, therefore, to proceed entirely from them and to be as free as an action as that of men. Consequently, both gods and men have done one and the same thing. The earnestness of those divine powers is a ridiculous superfluity, since they are in fact the power or strength of the individuality performing the action; while the exertions and labour of the latter

is an equally useless effort, since it is rather the gods who manage everything. (*PR* [*i*]: §141–2)[36]

This difference is a key manifestation of the unfolding of moral consciousness from what he perceives as the deterministic age of *epic* poetry to the agent-centred age of *tragic* poetry, reached via the mixed genre of *lyric* (*LA*: 1062ff.). Oedipus stands at the blinding edge of the third period, tragically conscious of the distinction between his self-caused actions and the aspects of his deeds that only the divine (and prophets blind to earthly modes of presentation) could fully comprehend in advance. The double causation involving Apollo keeps Oedipus's conscience clear of immorality while enabling him to retain *paternal* responsibility for his deeds.[37] Antigone (the 'unbending' or 'that opposed to parenting'), Ismene (the 'knowledgeable'), Polynices (of 'manifold strife') and Eteocles (of 'true rumour' as much as 'truly glorious') are the offspring of this dual paternity, their own tragedies a miasmatic reminder of how far and wide the polluting shadows cast by the most justified of deeds can fall.

14

The doing and the deed

Action in normative ethics

Prologue

There exists a contested distinction within the philosophy of action that entails that the correct evaluation of what one does or creates may part ways with that of one's act of doing or creating it.[1] Drawn correctly, this distinction is of utmost importance to questions in ethical theory, and how we generally evaluate our actions and lives. Or so I shall be arguing.

Attempts to relate philosophy of action to ethics have tended to focus on agency, responsibility, free will and other questions in moral psychology, the last of these now treated as a separate and increasingly empirical branch of ethics. This is not that project. There are additional ethical questions that the philosophy of action is in a position to address, not least in debates in normative and practical ethics about the nature of right action.[2] A particular case in point is the interminable debate between consequentialists, deontologists and virtue-theorists on the potential relevance of person's motives and intentions to the rightness or wrongness of her acts.

The questions of action, intention and motive I shall focus on are usually identified as belonging to moral psychology. To this extent, it is regrettable that the latter has branched off in a way that has encouraged philosophers to think that such questions do not belong in normative ethics. This is one of two unintended and unforeseen consequences of Anscombe's revolutionary paper 'Modern Moral Philosophy', published in *Philosophy* almost sixty years ago (Anscombe 1958).[3] The second involves the creation of normative virtue ethics as a separate position within moral theory, one to be adopted by *all and only* those who think that questions of character matter to right action.[4]

In what follows, I resist both trends by relating conceptual and ontological questions about action to normative ethics. We may characterize this method as *applied* philosophy of action, so long as such a thing leaves space for a kind of analytic deconstruction of moral theory.

1. Ambiguity in action

Someone interested in action might wish to explore a number of distinct things such as how the word 'action' is used, our concept(s) of action, different conceptions of action, and empirical findings about actions themselves.[5] In each case there are numerous distinctions to be made and different ways of carving things up. I shall focus on just one of these, namely the conceptual distinction between *what* one does and one's *doing* (of) it. There are radically different ways of understanding this distinction. Indeed, those who appeal to it, myself included, express such a wide range of competing conceptions of each of the two things distinguished that it is legitimate to wonder whether they are really all making the same distinction. I begin by quoting from three influential approaches, in chronological order.

John Macmurray writes the following in an *Aristotelian Society* exchange with A. C. Ewing on the nature of actions:

> The term 'action' is involved in the same ambiguity [as] terms like 'perception' or 'conception'. It may refer either to what is done or to the doing of it [. . .] either 'doing' or 'deed'. When we talk of an action we are normally referring to what is done. (Macmurray 1938: 74–6)

Leaving aside the final claim about ordinary language, the idea here is that the word 'action' is not in any way special for being ambiguous in this regard. Macmurray's distinction is presented as a formal one that may presumably also be extended to additional psychological phenomena such as those of belief, desire, fear, suspicion, thought and so on. In effect, it is a basic logical distinction between a kind of process or activity on the one hand, and its product, content, or object on the other (things which should themselves resist conflation). We don't do our own doings any more than we fear our own fearings or suspect our own suspectings.[6]

Paul Ricoeur extends this scope of interest to speech and writing:

> What in effect does writing fix? Not the event of speaking [. . .] it is speech itself insofar as it is *said* [. . .] To what extent may we say that what is *done* is inscribed? [. . .] in a metaphorical way, some actions are events that imprint their mark on their time. (Ricoeur [1986] 2008: 142–9)

In the case of writing, the distinction comes closer to that between a *process* and its resulting *product*. Ricoeur is suggesting that we might, by extension, hold the same to be true of the speaking and the thing said and, *a forteriori*, the doing and the thing done.[7] He is aware that his suggestion contains the difficulty that, when all is said and done, these things do not remain in the world in the literal way that things written might; they are not carved in stone, or even paper. And yet, Ricoeur reminds us, our events of acting – a subset of which are speech-act events – may nonetheless leave imprints or traces of a biographical, psychological, historical, cultural, or empirical nature.[8]

This thought of actions as *events* connects with Jennifer Hornsby's way of framing the distinction as one between (i) the spatio-temporally located events of our doing things and (ii) the things we do, the second admitting to being done by different agents across more than one location or occasion, including the possible future as in Lenin's *What is to be Done?*:

> The word 'action' is ambiguous. Where it has a plural: in ordinary usage what it denotes, nearly always, are the things people do; in philosophical usage, what it denotes, very often, are events, each one of them some person's doing something. (Hornsby 1993b: 142)

Like Macmurray, Hornsby takes our ordinary talk of action to typically denote things done. My own view is that in everyday language the term 'thing done' is itself multiply ambiguous, much as we might use the expression 'soup' in any of the following assertions: 'the soup is always great at *Gino's*'; 'tonight's soup is very good'; and 'your soup looks nicer than mine (even though they presumably come from the same kitchen batch)'. Such ambiguities account for much conflation in the philosophy of action, if not that of Donald Davidson who, misled by the Quinean dream of desert landscapes, provides a systematic argument for why all action statements quantify over events (Davidson [1967] 2001: 105–22). The trouble is that there exists conceptual space for a distinction that is only partially mirrored in our ordinary use of the terms 'doing' and 'thing done', the latter frequently being used rather liberally, as in 'the hardest thing I ever did'.

All analogies sooner or later come to an end, of course. What I do is neither the *product* nor the *content* of my doing. Nor is it an object in the way that the things I perceive, such as the records on the table, are. Deeds are not entities of any kind, be they type or token. Accordingly, we must take my soup comparisons with a pinch of salt: what I do is not the same sort of thing as what I ate or hope to eat,[9] not even in the Proustian sense in which I might lament that the rusty bicycle in the garden shed is not as bright or green as the one in my memory.[10] Moreover, it is at best contentious to assume that the 'of' in 'the event of my doing x' is one of identity (as in 'the county of Hertfordshire') as opposed to, say, relation (as in 'the University of Hertfordshire').[11]

Unsurprisingly, we find competing ontologies of doings and things done in the literature, with little consensus on whether the former are particulars, events, processes, instances of relations [. . .] , and the latter universals, types, results, products, and so on.[12] For now, however, I merely wish to highlight a more general agreement on the basic distinction between particular doings and repeatable things that you and I might both do.[13] We might, for example, both listen to Leonard Cohen's *You Want It Darker* again and again, with each of our singular, spatio-temporally located, acts of doing so differing in their properties: you play the MP3 as background on your iPod during your morning jogs and in the afternoons as you drive home from work; I listen to the LP attentively in the evenings by my fireplace at home, a glass of burgundy in hand.

2. Right and wrong action

Despite the relative prevalence of the previous distinction in the philosophy of action, it is all but completely ignored in normative theories concerned with right action. These are typically in the business of offering necessary and sufficient conditions of the form 'an action is right if (and only if) it . . . ' where the blank may be filled by statements such as 'promotes the greatest good', 'maximizes pleasure', 'stems from a good will', 'is what the virtuous agent would (advise you to) do', 'is prescribed by divine command' and so on.[14] But moral theorists rarely stop to ask conceptual questions about action, sticking to the bare minimum needed to deal with the act/omission distinction and the doctrine of double effect.[15] The unvoiced assumption is that one can simply plug in one's favoured account of action, the dominating consensus having largely been that actions are events. I maintain that this assumption lies at the core of what renders debates within normative ethics irresolvable.

To illustrate, I present some concise claims about right action, chosen randomly from across the normative spectrum. The first comes from Jesse Prinz's defence of sentimentalism about moral rightness and wrongness:

> An action has the property of being morally right (wrong) just in case it causes feelings of approbation (disapprobation) in normal observers under certain conditions. (Prinz 2007: 20)

Notice how actions are here understood as the sorts of things that can have moral properties, but there is no mention (and you will have to trust me that this is so throughout his book) about whether he is here thinking of a doing or a thing done. The sentence gives us some clues: it is the sort of thing that may be observed and 'cause feelings'; to this extent sound more like a *doing* than a thing done. Either way, the view is meant to be in competition with other accounts of right action which also fail to disambiguate.

Writing about moral obligation, H. A. Prichard claims that: 'An obligation is always an obligation *to do* some action' (1932: 95, emphasis added).[16] So long as I *do* the action in question, I have fulfilled my obligation, whatever my motive. This is why W. D. Ross, following Prichard, would ultimately claim that moral rightness should be distinguished from moral goodness.[17] The question remains, however, whether I can be said to be acting wrongly merely by virtue of doing the wrong thing. Jonathan Bennett seems to not only think that this is so but that it is a basic semantic truth:

> When we say that *what he did* was wrong we mean that *he acted wrongly.* (Bennett 1995: 46; emphasis added)

Yet *acting wrongly* is at best itself ambiguous between doing the wrong thing and doing something (right or wrong) for the wrong reasons or out of a wrong motive.[18] One might think that killing, lying, cheating and murder are all wrong. Such thoughts seem to be about act-types to the extent that it entails that all particular acts of killing, for example, are wrong. If Eevee kills Jolene and we think that *what she did* was wrong in the sense of 'thing done' delineated in §1 (namely, kill someone) then the wrong thing done is something that Ceddy could have also done. Indeed, Ceddy could have even killed the very same person (Jolene), although it is too late now that Eevee has done so.

If this is so, then it cannot matter what Eevee or Ceddy's motives are for it cannot be the case that 'kill someone' is a wrong thing done when Eevee does it but not when Ceddy does it, at least not systematically so according to any of the normative theories on offer.[19] By contrast, Eevee's killing of Jolene on Monday morning may be a vicious act motivated by jealousy, whereas Ceddy's possible killing of her on Monday evening (say after Simon's botched attempt) would have been an act of mercy.

Similarly, for right actions: Eevee and Ceddy may both give the same amount of money and/or the percentage of their income (two different things that may coincide) to the British Hen Welfare Trust. But suppose that Eevee's doing so *just is* her trying to impress Simon, whereas Ceddy does so in order to help rescue battery hens. In such a case, Eevee and Ceddy each do two things, only one of which is the same (give money to the British Hen Welfare Trust). Eevee's doing this one thing just *is* her showing off and, similarly, Ceddy's doing it is identical to his trying to help rescue battery hens. While the thing done may or may not be the right thing to do, it would seem that Ceddy is acting rightly (or at least well or justifiably) whereas Eevee is not.[20]

There seems, then, to be a huge difference between claims concerning a person's doing something, and claims about the rightness or wrongness of *what* they did. Once we become attuned to this, certain disputes within normative theory begin to dissolve. Recall the debate over whether or not intention matters to right action. If two or more people can do the same thing with different intentions, it is unclear how intention could possibly matter to the rightness or wrongness of the thing that they both do.[21] Conversely, it is highly implausible that intention doesn't matter to the moral evaluation of each individual's *doing* of this thing. It is hard not to conclude from this that the notion of right action most amenable to virtue ethics is different from that which is of interest to consequentialists. While I have chiefly been focusing on motive and intention, the moral appraisal of our doings will also depend upon biographical information relating to upbringing, ability, education, circumstance and more. Such facts may individually or collectively reveal that a person was acting rightly when they did the wrong thing, and wrongly when they did the right thing.

None of this is to say that there is no connection between descriptions of our doings and the things that we do. On the contrary, one can act with the best of intentions and still be acting wrongly, even if the action is not intentional under the negative description. An act intending to pay tribute to another culture, for example, may nonetheless be an instance of cultural appropriation. For everything one does unintentionally, there will be a relevant description of one's doing it. But there are no hard and fast rules by which we can decide which doings remain praiseworthy, permissible or excusable, and which do not.

Often, it can take years or centuries before we are in a position to fully understand what had been done. In such cases, we must be lenient on the doing without becoming relativists about the thing done. Consider the well-trodden debates on whether or not it would be anachronistic to judge nineteenth-century racism and slavery from a twenty-first-century standpoint. The answer, I contend, is that while *things done* centuries ago were as wrong then as they would be if done now, past *doings* may be more forgivable, and at times even justified (precise judgements of past *doing*s would need to be formed on a case-by-case basis).[22]

3. Inner and outer lives

I have been arguing that there is an important but neglected difference between what it is for *a thing one does* to be right or wrong and for *one's doing* it to be right or wrong. This lends itself to the response, alluded to in my Prologue, that those interested in the doing, motive, intention, etc subscribe to virtue theory, thereby embracing just one normative position among many, and that other views – in competition with it – simply deny the importance of such things to right action, if not to morality altogether.[23] Such points are sometimes put forward as criticisms of virtue ethics being *agent*-centred (as opposed to *action*-centred) and thereby either failing to provide a theory of right action or offering one whose focus is misplaced. Thus, even someone as sympathetic to the concerns of virtue ethics as Martha Nussbaum criticizes Iris Murdoch for being too obsessed with the agent's psychology to care about action:

> Murdoch is so preoccupied with the goings-on of the inner world that she seems almost to have forgotten about the difference that action can make [. . .] commitment to action can make the difference to people who are suffering, no matter whether the agents' intentions are pure. (Nussbaum 2011: 269)

Nussbaum is here completely separating action from intention, thereby implicitly running with a 'thing done' notion of action. The move is akin to thinking that, since Eevee gave 20 per cent of her salary to the British Hen Welfare Trust, we should not be morally distracted by the fact that she only did it to show off in front of Simon. What matters, on this outlook, is *what* she did. In the case in question, the thing that Eevee did was right since, unlike her inner motives, it made a good difference in the world. Nussbaum's worry is that concerns with another's inner world are overly precious and, in the case of one's own actions, narcissistic. Virtue ethicists such as Christine Swanton have responded to such criticisms with the following reasoning:

> Rightness, it may be claimed, has nothing to do with an agent's motives or reasons, but has exactly to do with success in the external realm [. . .] on my view, an act which mimics the action of a virtuous agent may be wrong, because *in the hands of the actor* it is unvirtuous [. . .] uncaring or racist. (Swanton 2003: 245)

This response is on the right track, but unless we can enrich it with a suitable version of the doing/thing done distinction it shall remain as question-begging as Nussbaum's original objection. The correct thing to say, I believe, is that while *what* the vicious agent is doing can be no more (or less) uncaring than what the virtuous agent does, *her doing it* may well be. Indeed, things done are, in this technical sense the wrong sorts of thing to be caring or uncaring, rash or prudent, and so on for only an individual person's doings may be described adverbially.

There is, of course, an ordinary sense of 'what she did' in which we might say that she did a kind or unkind thing, but all this amounts to is that her doing of *x* was unkind, or that she was unkind to do it.[24] If we ignore the conceptual space for this distinction and simply talk of things done as if *they themselves* are re-describable as virtuous or vicious, we will have saved the truth of virtue ethics at the cost of masking the truth of consequence-based views and deontologies (such as some forms of divine-command theory) which appeal to the intrinsic goodness of act-types (as opposed to motives). The truth of these views is that the rightness of what is done does not (indeed *cannot*) depend on the psychology of the agent.

4. Ontologies of action

At this juncture, it might help to delve a little into some of the ontological questions I remained neutral upon earlier. Is there any sense in which an event can itself be deemed to be morally right or wrong? And what, if anything, would it be for a universal to be right?

One answer to the first question appeals to Donald Davidson's notion that an action is an event that is intentional under some description. I shall not critique this here, save to say that while it is innocuous to say that the event of someone's doing one thing (e.g. playing music) intentionally may be identical to the event of their doing something else (waking up the neighbours) unintentionally, this does not reduce to the far more baffling claim that it is the event *itself* that is intentional under some description(s).

In a rare paper attempting to relate action theory to normative ethics, Matthew Hanser resists Davidsonian simplicity as follows:

> We may think of the 'things people do', [...] as act – or behavior – types. A particular person's throwing of a particular baseball on a particular occasion, by contrast, is not an act – or behavior – type. It is a token action, an unrepeatable, particular instantiation of the act-type *throwing a baseball* [...] 'What he did was wrong' concerns some unspecified act-type instantiated by the agent, whereas 'He acted wrongly in doing what he did' concerns the agent's particular instantiation of that act-type. (Hanser 2008: 272–3)[25]

Hanser's metaphysics seem implausible to me for a number of related reasons: the things we do are not types of action but actions that fall under types. The relation between doings and things done is thus not one between types and tokens. A doing is not an instance of a thing done any more than a believing is an instance of a thing believed, and there are type and token doings (just as there are type and token events and processes[26]) as well as type and token things done. If A kills B this may or may not fall under the type 'killing an adolescent' or 'killing an innocent human'.

A different way of resisting Hanser's approach is to deny that there is any morally relevant distinction to be made between doings and things done. An explicit defence of it has been made by Jonathan Dancy, who writes:

> There should be less of action in our moral metaphysics, not more [...] 'he did the right thing for the wrong reason' [...] means something like 'he acted rightly, but for the wrong reasons' [...] 'he V-ed, and in the situation he was right to V, but the reasons why he V-ed were not the reasons why he was right to V' [...] rightness is not a way of acting [...] there is no room for the combination of

blameless agent and wrong action that might force us towards some notion of an action as a distinct bearer of evaluative properties. (Dancy 2009a: 396ff.)[27]

On Dancy's account, we so conduct all the theoretical work we need to do with one notion of action, coupled with a narrative about the agent's reasons. While there is much to agree with in the previous passage, it won't do to say that the person who does the right thing for the wrong reason(s) is acting *rightly*. After all, she isn't acting virtuously, for it is merely by chance that she is doing the right thing at all. This point is brought out well in the following passage by Rosalind Hursthouse:

> [A]ct honestly, charitably, generously; do not act dishonestly, etc. [. . .] the adverbs connote not only doing what the virtuous agent would do, but also doing it 'in the way' she would do it, which includes 'for the same sort(s) of reason(s)' [. . .] What is misleading about this phrase is that it obscures the fact that, in one way, the agent is not 'doing the right thing'. What she is doing is, say, trying to impress the onlookers, or hurting someone's feelings, or avoiding punishment. (Hursthouse 1999: 29, 125)

Hursthouse makes her point without appealing to any form of the doing/thing done distinction and, pari passu, concludes that *what* the vicious agent is doing is wrong. And indeed, *one* of the things that she has done is wrong (namely showing off), but she has also done something quite right (donating to the British Hen Welfare Trust), albeit for the wrong reason, as Dancy puts it. Yet the idea that the agent has done anything right has all but disappeared from Hursthouse's narrative. Assuming that two people can do the same thing for different reasons, it can be true that the person acting wrongly is still doing the right thing. When two or more people do the same thing for different reasons, there will be huge discrepancies in our evaluation of their doings. We need look no further than the 69,456,897 people who voted for Obama in 2008, and the plurality of reasons in the offing.

5. Moral appraisal

Consider the following claim by Thomas Nagel, which forms a crucial assumption behind his understanding of moral luck:

> We judge people for what they actually do or fail to do [. . .] a person can be morally responsible only for *what he does*. (Nagel 1979: 146; emphasis added)[28]

Implicit in this remark is the identification of all action with the things we do, as made explicit by Swann in Proust's *in Search of Lost Time*, a novel fixated with the relation of fleeting particulars to repeatable universals:

> 'It's not for nothing', he now assured himself, 'that whenever people pass judgements on their fellows, it's always for their *actions*. It's only *what we do* that counts, and not at all what we say or think'. (*Proust* [1913] 1992: 430; emphasis added)[29]

Here we encounter, once more, the idea that we judge others simply by being provided with a list of the things they did. We might call this the obituary view of moral appraisal. It is no wonder that actions so conceived – without mention of the doings that reveal our reasons, motives and intentions – are so readily susceptible to moral luck.[30]

Moving further back into the history of deontology, we find the following pronouncement in Kant's second *Critique*:

> Most lawful actions would be done from fear, only a few from hope, and none at all from duty; and the moral worth of actions – on which alone, after all, the worth of the person and even that of the world hinges in the eyes of the highest wisdom – would not exist at all. (Kant [1788] 1997: 5, 147)[31]

It is no surprise that all law, be it divine, social or moral should primarily focus on things done rather than doings, for it is the fact that one did something that we can provide evidence for in any kind of court.[32] So it is that in Romans 2:6 of the *New International Version* of the Bible, we are told in God 'will repay each person according to what they have done' (see also Matthew 16.27 and Corinthians 11.15).[33] Kant's insight is that one could do the right thing and yet one's action might still lack moral worth, if done from the wrong motive. Suppose we knew for certain that heaven and hell existed: many of us might then make sure that we did all the right (morally lawful) things, but we would do them from an unethical motive (fear or hope, but never duty).[34] This appreciation of the fact that the moral worth of actions is completely separable from the rightness or wrongness of the things they do, a view shared by his most famous opponent in moral philosophy, John Stuart Mill:

> He who saves a creature from drowning does what is morally right, whether his motive be duty or the hope of being paid for his trouble [. . .] A right action does not necessarily indicate a virtuous character and [. . .] actions which are blameable often proceed from qualities entitled to praise. (Mill [1861] 1979: 18–20)[35]

Kant and Mill form a sharp contrast to the view from Nagel, according to which we are to appraise people for *what* they do, and nothing else.[36] The clash cannot be resolved in either party's favour, for it stems from muddled conceptions of action. In the passages quoted here, Kant and Mill separate the worthiness of actions from their rightness and wrongness, whereas Nagel wishes to align the two.[37] A third solution, proposed by Robert Audi, is that we 'should distinguish the moral worth of an act from its creditworthiness' (Audi 2004: 133). But this just digs deeper into the same conceptual pit. The solution is not to pile on further distinctions but to understand that between the things we do and our acts of doing them.[38]

A neater way forward would be to map the distinction onto that between evaluative and deontic concepts and norms, the former being concerned with praise or blame (good and bad), the latter with duty and obligation (right and wrong).[39] On this approach, doings are the sole bearers of moral worth and things done of rightness and wrongness.[40] If so then Kantians such as Onora O'Neil are guilty of a kind of category mistake in thinking of a 'morally worthy act' as something that an agent 'does'

(O'Neil 2013: 211). Such a view seems to me to track something important, but it would be a Procrustean stretch, however, to take things even further by insisting that doings are ontologically incapable of being morally right or wrong and, conversely, that things done cannot be good or bad in virtue of falling under a certain type (e.g. acts of kindness of charity).

No discussion of the distinction between the right and good would be complete without mention of the pluralistic deontology of Ross, who brings out the extremely paradoxical nature of maintaining, alongside Kant, that the right action may be morally worthless:

> [N]othing that ought to be done is ever morally good [. . .] the only acts that are morally good are those that proceed from a good motive [. . .] If, then, we can show that action from a good motive is never morally obligatory, we shall have established that what is morally good is never right [. . .] That action from a good motive is never obligatory follows from the Kantian principle [. . .] that 'I ought' implies 'I can'. It is not the case that I can by choice produce a certain motive [. . .] if we contemplate a right act alone, it is seen to have no intrinsic *value* [. . .] however carelessly I pack or dispatch the book, if it comes to hand I have done my duty, and however carefully I acted, if the book does not come to hand I have not done my duty. Of course I should deserve more praise in the second case than in the first [. . .] we must not mix up the question of right and wrong with that of the morally good and the morally bad [. . .] if the carelessly dispatched book comes to hand, it is not my duty to send another copy, while if the carefully dispatched book does not come to hand I must send another to replace it. (Ross [1930] 2002: 132ff.)

This is all well and good, but the paradox of the first line occurs precisely because the evaluative and deontic properties are being applied to one kind of thing called 'action'. The same holds true of the added claim that 'what is morally good is never right'. How could it possibly be true that the right and the good can never coincide? Ross holds that motives belong in the world of evaluation and actions in that of obligation. But this distinction is ill equipped to do the work required from it. Ross's aims would have been better served by one between the doing and the thing done.

As noted earlier, the doing/thing done distinction is in some respects analogous to many others, including that between what one believes and one's believing it. Suppose I believe something that's true and which I ought to believe, but I do so for very bad reasons. You may wish to criticize my believing it without criticizing the belief I have (which you and I might, after all, share). Conversely, I may be perfectly justified in having a belief that turns out to be false. Hence the initial divide of intuitions about whether Edmund Gettier's famous examples were indeed ones of justified true belief, for what was justified was the thing believed, not the believing. Clayton Littlejohn's diagnosis of the situation offers the following trifecta of ascriptions:

> Ascriptions of personal justification tell us something about a believer – whether *she* is justified in believing. An ascription of doxastic justification tells us something about a belief – whether *the belief* is justifiably held. An ascription of propositional

justification tells us something about a proposition – whether the proposition is such that there is sufficient justification for someone to believe it. (Littlejohn 2012: 5)[41]

Gilbert Harman makes a parallel disambiguation in relation to action:

> I do want to distinguish between using the word 'wrong' to say that a particular situation or action is wrong from using the word to say that it is wrong of someone to do something. (Harman 2000: 6–7)

This is the idea that what a person did was right but it was wrong of them to do it or, conversely, that what they did was wrong but it was right of them to do it. But what is it for something to be right or wrong *of* someone? Nothing that is worryingly relativistic or subjective. It is simply the thought that a person may be right or wrong to do something given all the evidence available in some further specifiable sense. Helpful as Harman's distinction is, it doesn't get us all the way. The problem, to return to the charity example, is not that it was wrong of me to make a donation to the British Hen Welfare Trust in the case where my doing so is vicious. The difficulty is not that some people ought to give to the British Hen Welfare Trust, but not me, it is that my giving to them was unethical despite the fact that it *would have been* right of me to make a donation.[42] This should not be confused with those of blameless wrongdoing as understood by either Bernard Williams or Derek Parfit, both of whom fail to distinguish between doing and thing done, thereby rendering their examples hostage to unnecessary paradoxes concerning luck and belief, respectively.[43]

Acting rightly does not amount to doing the right thing, or vice versa. Philosophers who stop shy of making this distinction find themselves having to make up for it by concocting new distinctions elsewhere. And yet these never seem quite capable of doing the work required. Without losing track of the fact that even Oedipus's tragic deeds are imputable to him,[44] we should not praise or blame people solely on the ground of *what* they did or didn't do.

In an obituary what one typically finds is a list of achievements and failures. The sorts of things listed here are *things done*; for example, she founded a charity, fought in the Second World War, directed two Oscar-winning films or wrote an influential book. Indeed, the very chronology of a person's life is typically offered in the form of a list of things done: she went to school A, studied subject *x* at university B, took a job as *y* at firm C and so on. What is much rarer is an attempt to reveal the person's acts of doing these things, as a serious biography might. Without this crucial feature any attempt at praise and blame will be half-blind and paradoxical. This holds true across moral theory as a whole. Normative ethics must leave space for both our deeds *and* doings.

Epilogue

John Macmurray, whose distinction between doing and deed we began with, would some decades later complain that art 'is treated not as a form of reflective activity, but as a set of "works" to be apprehended and appreciated' (Macmurray 1961: 11). Around the same time, art critic Harold Rosenberg baptized a non-cohesive group of artists, the most famous of whom was Jackson Pollock, as 'action painters'. Rosenberg's central idea – later taken up by David Davies (2004)[45] – was that the real work of art is not the painting or building (noun) but the act of painting or building (verb). We might equally, if not entirely analogously, distinguish between the dancing and the dance, the composing of a song, and the song composed, the photographing and the photograph taken and subsequently developed. Thus, Bob Dylan's 'Girl from the North Country' may be a superior song to 'Scarborough Fair', even if the composition of the former involved stealing both melody and line from the latter.

Rosenberg's theory is coupled with the additional thought that the painting on the canvas represents the act of painting it, not the way in which one might draw a self-portrait of the artist at work but by being a residue of the act of painting which bears the gesture traces of the brush strokes that produced it:

> A canvas is [. . .] an arena in which to act [. . .] A painting is an action [. . .] that becomes its own representation [. . .] An act can be prolonged from a piece of paper to a canvas. (Rosenberg 1960: 26–8)[46]

This echoes Ricoeur's metaphor of acting as the thing done as a kind of trace (of the event of acting) left in the world; a mark in history or memory. The mark or imprint is a reminder or at best a kind of souvenir of the artistic event of painting (verb). Hence the famous videos of Pollock painting his massive canvasses; this was not intended to just be a portrayal of the artist at work but a document of the art itself unfolding, with or without performance. What is subsequently hung on the wall being nothing but the marks which have been left behind; the ashes of an event long-gone.[47]

Rosenberg undoubtedly took his own metaphor too seriously, thus prompting Mary McCarthy to quip 'you can't hang an event on the wall, only a picture'.[48] But while it may be nonsense to say that a painting is an action or that it represents itself, the movement teaches us that art presents us with two objects of aesthetic evaluation: the creating and the thing created. As with right action, I have no interest in offering any theory of art here (let alone one which highlights one of these things over the other). I merely wish to point out that it is the act of creating which expresses the author's motives or intentions. After all, the thing created could have been made by a different person with a different aim.[49]

We are now in a position to appreciate Nietzsche's intriguing conception of life as art:

> Art is the real task of life, art as life's metaphysical activity. (Nietzsche [1886] 1973: §853, IV)

Nietzsche does not have the life of an artist in mind here. Rather, the task of any life is the *creating* of the life lived. The art in question, here, is not the life one creates for oneself, but the lifelong activity of creating it: the living of the life and not the life lived. In his magisterial work *Nietzsche: Life as Literature*, Alexander Nehamas parses Nietzsche's motto in terms of things done instead of doings:

> Everything we have done actually constitutes who each one of us is. (Nehamas 1985: 188)[50]

This is no misinterpretation of Nietzsche but rather a reflection of the fact that our ordinary term 'thing done' is itself ambiguous in ways that can be philosophically troubling. A case in point is Sartre's existentialist retelling of Nietzsche's tale:

> Man is nothing other than his own projects. He exists only to the extent that he realizes himself, therefore he is nothing more than the sum of his actions, nothing more than his life. (Sartre [1945] 2007: 37)

If this view is to capture the roundedness of human life, the sum of our actions had better include the totality of both our deeds *and* doings. It is in this spirit that Ronald Dworkin writes:

> The final value of our lives is adverbial, not adjectival. It's the value of the performance, not anything that is left when the performance is subtracted. (Dworkin 2011: 197)[51]

Dworkin models his distinction between having a good life and living well to that between art products and artistic acts of creation. The argument runs parallel to that of Rosenberg and Davies who claim that artistic value is adverbial, although, like me, Dworkin is not committed to any views about what art *is*. For my own part, I have merely sought to show that there is value to be found in both the living and the life lived, the doing and the thing done, the creating and the thing created.[52] In sum, we should be dualists about the objects of both moral and aesthetic evaluation.[53]

There is much that normative ethics can learn from the once fashionable 'death of the author' view of art. Its insight is not that the author has no say *tout court* but only that, *pace* intentionalism about art products, our aesthetic evaluation of their creation must, unlike that of their creative acts, ultimately carry on without them.[54] As with creations, our deeds are but the ashes of our acts in time. To evaluate our lives solely by these would be a grave mistake.

15

Ethics and action theory

An unhappy divorce

Prologue

In her seminal 1958 paper 'Modern Moral Philosophy' (MMP), Elizabeth Anscombe complains, inter alia, about the lack of 'an adequate philosophy of psychology' within moral philosophy, at least as practised from Sidgwick onwards. While her complaint (which I review in detail in §2) was not without cause, it remains a striking fact that there was considerably more moral psychology within moral theory before 1957 than there has been ever since. Moreover, much of it was conducted by a number of Anscombe's explicit or implicit targets, particularly G. E. Moore (1903), W. D. Ross (1930) H. W. B. Joseph (1931), A. C. Ewing (1938), John Macmurray (1938) and H. A. Prichard (1949).[1] Anscombe presumably didn't find any of this work 'adequate' and I shall try to show why this was so. Prima facie, however, her moral psychology and philosophy of action has much in common with many of the aforementioned targets, not to mention Hegel. In order to allow for sufficient depth of comparison, I shall focus my discussion on Ross, who is one of the explicit targets of MMP, but I shall add comparisons to other philosophers along the way.

1. Moral philosophy until Anscombe

Ross defends the proto-Anscombean view that 'any act may be correctly described in an indefinite, and in principle infinite, number of ways' and that what I do could, for instance, be truthfully described as 'fulfilling my promise', 'putting the book into our friend's possession' *and* 'the packing and posting of a book':

> [A]ny of the acts we do has countless effects [. . .] Every act therefore, viewed in some aspects, will be prima facie right, and viewed in others prima facie wrong. [. . .any act may be correctly described in an indefinite, and in principle infinite, number of ways. An act is the production of a change in the state of affairs [. . .]I may have promised, for instance, to return a book to a friend [. . .] to send it by a messenger or to hand it to his servant or to send it by post [. . .] in each of these cases what I *do* directly is worthless in itself [. . .] this is *not* what we should

describe, strictly, as our duty; our duty is to fulfil our promise, i.e. to put the book into our friend's possession [...What I do is as truly describable in this way as by saying that it is the packing and posting of a book [...] And if we ask ourselves whether it is right *qua* the packing or posting of a book, or *qua* the securing of my friend's getting what I have promised to return to him, it is clear that it is in the second capacity that it is right [...] by its own nature and not because of its consequences. (Ross 1930: 41–4)

There is much here that anticipates Anscombe. She would later even apply the same preposition ('qua') to distinguish her view that actions may be intentional under a description from the nonsensical claim that actions-under-a-description are intentional ([1979] 1981).[2]

So why did Anscombe dismiss Ross's work in such strong terms? His 'objectivism' may have lapsed into a form of 'consequentialism' so anathematic to Christian morality (see §2) that she didn't want to debate its details under the guise of doing 'moral philosophy',[3] but this is not in itself a reason to dismiss an entire method of doing moral philosophy that is uncannily similar to her own. A clue to our answer may be found in an earlier passage of *The Right and the Good*. Ross writes:

[G]reat confusion [...] has been introduced into ethics by the phrase 'a right action' being used sometimes of the initiation of a certain change in the state of affairs irrespective of motive, and at other times of such initiation from some particular motive, such as sense of duty or benevolence. I would further suggest that additional clearness would be gained if we used 'act' of the thing done, the initiation of change, and 'action' of the doing of it, the initiating of change, from a certain motive. We should then talk of a right act but not of a right action, of a morally good action but not of a morally good act. And it may be added that the doing of a wrong act may be a morally good action; for 'right' and 'wrong' refer entirely to the thing done, 'morally good' and 'morally bad' entirely to the motive from which it is done. (Ross [1930] 2002: 6–7; cf. Sidgwick 1874: Book III, Ch. 12 and Macmurray 1938)

From all this he concludes, in a deliberately provocative and paradoxical manner:

[N]othing that ought to be done is ever morally good [...] the only acts that are morally good are those that proceed from a good motive [...] action from a good motive is never morally obligatory [...what is morally good is never right [...] That action from a good motive is never obligatory follows from the Kantian principle [...] that 'I ought' implies 'I can'. [...] however carelessly I pack or dispatch the book, if it comes to hand I have done my duty, and however carefully I acted, if the book does not come to hand I have not done my duty. Of course I should deserve more praise in the second case than in the first. (Ross [1930] 1992: 132)

Anscombe has little time for this sort of distinction between what is done and the doing of it from a certain motive. She is consequently disinclined to relate the former to the right and the latter to the good, a disposition strengthened by her independent suspicion of the very distinction between good and right action (see §2). It is worth recalling, at this juncture, that Anscombe's objection was not that moral philosophers lacked a philosophy of psychology or action per se, only that they were in desperate need of one that was 'sound', or at least 'adequate'. The problem, at least from Anscombe's point of view, is that Ross puts his multiple descriptions of action to the disingenuous use of swallowing up features that would normally be regarded as their consequences, thereby presenting them as intrinsic properties that are 'utterly independent of consequences':

> That which is right is right not because it is an act, one thing, which will produce another thing, an increase in general welfare, but because it is itself the producing of an increase in the general welfare [. . .] we have to recognise the *intrinsic* rightness of a certain type of act, not depending on its consequences but on its own nature. (Ross [1930] 2002: 47)

Anscombe may have additionally found Ross's argument to the conclusion that an action that is good can never be right (and vice versa) to be 'unsound' because it fails to capture the correct relation between motive, intention, action and duty. Whatever the explanation, she seems to have thrown the baby out with the bathwater. For there is a sound and morally important difference to be made between the things we do and our doings of them, especially in relation to questions concerning intention, foresight, consequences and intrinsic wrongness.[4]

Ross's point about the rightness of an action being divorceable from the goodness or badness of one's performing is a sensible and important one, sharing affinities with Mill's stance that 'a right action does not necessarily indicate a virtuous character' and that 'actions which are blameable often proceed from qualities entitled to praise' (Mill [1861] 1979: 18–20).[5] Yet Anscombe's view that the things we do are happenings or events (1957: §29; 1969: 10–11; [1979] 1981: 208–10; Anscombe and Morgenbesser 1963: 4) with morally pertinent descriptions seems to leave no space for it. This is because it rules out the possibility that two people can do the very same thing, even though only of them is acting from a good motive.[6] In this she goes against her teacher, Wittgenstein, who cites this very possibility as an explanation for why self-understanding can be so difficult to achieve at times:

> It is hard to understand yourself properly since something that you might be doing out of generosity & goodness is *the same as* you may be doing out of cowardice or indifference. To be sure, one may act in such & such a way from true love, but also from deceitfulness & from a cold heart too. (Wittgenstein [1977] 1998: p. 54 [MS 131 38: 14.8.1946]; emphasis added; cf. Wittgenstein [1953] 2009: §§253–4)

While Anscombe can allow that two people can do the same thing, she understands this as there being at least one description that is applicable to both deeds (e.g. 'drinking gin') though many may not be (e.g. acting cowardly or bravely). But while *some* descriptions of the things we do have our intention built into them (e.g. to lie is, at least typically, to say something untrue with the intention of deceiving), many do not. Moreover, motives – as opposed to intentions – lend themselves more naturally to descriptions of our doings and not our deeds.[7] To be sure, in speaking loosely we may say that someone did a cowardly thing, but all this means is that they acted in a cowardly fashion; the thing they did (drink gin) is itself neither cowardly nor brave.

A year after Ross's book was published, Joseph wrote the following by way of commentary:[8]

> The same act, an objector might say, may surely be done from very different motives; and therefore the act must be something, irrespective of the motive. But are they really the same act? Different acts, having different motives, may work themselves into the same movements of bodies; but these are not the acts. A man who was fond of oysters might eat a plateful put before him for the sake of their flavour; a man who loathed them might do so to avoid hurting his host's feelings; a man who loathed or was indifferent to them might do so to prevent his neighbour, whom he knew to be fond of them and he disliked, from having two portions. I think these are three different acts, one morally good or else kindly, one morally bad or spiteful, one indifferent. They are not three instances of one act, viz. eating a plateful of oysters [...] an act proper is not analysable into behaviour and motive; it is indivisible. (Joseph 1931/33: 45–6)[9]

Joseph's view anticipates Anscombe's insofar as they both target Ross by maintaining that 'no act exists except in the doing of it, and in the doing of it there is a motive' (Joseph 1931/33: 38). The Joseph-Anscombe thesis offers a persuasive account of our *doings*, but ignores the distinction (implicit in Wittgenstein and explicit in Ross) between the deeds we do and our doings of them from some particular motive. This is done at the cost of allowing that one may do the right thing from the wrong motive.

One might object that 'A did the same thing as B' simply amounts to there being *some* description of what A did which is also true of what B did (e.g. 'give money to X' or 'show off to his friends'). But it would be a category mistake to think that such descriptions apply to things done, as opposed to our doings of them. If A *murdered* X then we can indeed describe this very thing that A did by saying (with some loss in specificity) that A *killed* X, for the latter is a sub set of the former. But if A *gave money* to X, we cannot truthfully describe the thing done (give money) as showing off, since one can do this very same thing without even intending to showing off in the process.

A particular *instance* of giving money may be truthfully describable as showing off, but the things we do, in the sense in which two people can do the same thing, are not instances of anything. In the case of the person whose donating a large sum of money is a case of showing off, then, there is not one single thing done that is good under one description and bad under another but, rather, one event of someone acting badly in doing two distinct things (one right, the other wrong). Hursthouse writes:

> [A]ct honestly, charitably, generously; do not act dishonestly, etc. [...] the adverbs connote not only doing what the virtuous agent would do, but also doing it 'in the way' she would do it, which includes 'for the same sort(s) of reason(s)' [...] What

is misleading about this phrase is that it obscures the fact that, in one way, the agent is not 'doing the right thing'. What she is doing is, say, trying to impress the onlookers, or hurting someone's feelings, or avoiding punishment. (Hursthouse 1999: 29, n. 7; 125)

But while one's act of donating to charity may also be correctly described as one's trying to impress the onlookers, this doesn't give us a reason to deny that in so acting a person may do (at least) two things: donate to charity and impress the onlookers, one of which is right and the other wrong. Anscombe can, of course, allow that one can donate to charity with the (bad) intention of impressing the onlookers. On her view, however, this provides a true description of *what was done*, thereby leaving no space for the view that one can do the right thing with a bad intention. This forces us to say that what was done was right under one description and wrong under another. But this is to confuse acting rightly with doing what happens to be the right thing to do, despite one's nefarious motives.[10] In Ross's terminology, it is to confuse such things as 'doing what is just' with such things acting 'in the spirit of justice' (Ross [1930] 2002: 53).

Anscombe's underlying account of action as a happening contrasts with that of Prichard, according to whom to do something is to bring about a change:

> It is, no doubt, not easy to say what we mean by 'an action' or by 'doing something'. Yet we have in the end to allow that we mean by it originating, causing, or bringing about the existence of something viz. some new state of an existing thing or substance, or, more shortly, causing a change of state of some existing things [. . .] by 'moving our hand' we mean causing a change of place in our hand; by 'posting a letter' we mean bringing about that a letter is in a pillar-box. (Prichard [1932] 2004: 84–5)

The view outlined earlier anticipates those of G. H. von Wright (1963) and, more recently, Maria Alvarez and John Hyman (1998). However, Prichard later came to embrace a volitionist account of action as a form of mental activity ([1945] 2004: 272–4).[11] Contra Macmurray and Ross, he now claimed that the term 'action' was not ambiguous at all: it referred to our mental 'doings' and not to their effected changes, which constitute our 'deeds' (Prichard 1945] 2004: 275; cf. von Wright 1963: 37ff.).

Anscombe would have undoubtedly rejected Prichard's invalid inference from the thought that we might conceivably fail to achieve anything we set out to do, to the conclusion that all we ever have a duty to do is to set ourselves (namely, will) to bring something about. Indeed, no *adequate* philosophy of psychology could ever allow for such an inference. But if, in uttering 'I do what happens', Anscombe had been running a million miles from Prichard's volitionism, then she ended up too far in the other direction.

2. 'Modern moral philosophy'

MMP remains as divisive today as it was when it was first published sixty years ago. Some hail it to be of huge philosophical and historical importance, not least by effectively giving birth to neo-Aristotelian Virtue Ethics as exemplified by Philippa Foot, Rosalind Hursthouse, Alasdair MacIntyre and John McDowell (Richter 2011; Solomon 2008: 110–11). Others present it as a dated or otherwise irritating text containing baffling and unsubstantiated claims, the deciphering of which is not worth the candle (e.g. Blackburn 2005).

One recurring complaint has been that Anscombe is unfair in dismissing the ideas of dead white men with brief statements that contain more disrespect than they do argument. Bishop Butler is 'ignorant' (MMP: 27), Immanuel Kant 'useless' and 'absurd' (Blackburn 2005), David Hume 'sophistical' (MMP: 28), and J. S. Mill 'stupid' (MMP: 33). These are the philosophers she likes. The rest of them are something much worse: 'consequentialists'. Anscombe uses the term In MMP as a pejorative,[12] but it was quickly reclaimed as a badge of honour by all its major proponents.

It is fashionable nowadays to remark that Anscombe meant something rather different by 'consequentialism' than we do today.[13] Yet her own characterization of it as the view that the 'right' action is that which produces the best possible consequences (MMP: 33, quoted in the next paragraph) is one endorsed by most contemporary consequentialists.[14] The exegetical difficulty arises because Anscombe protects the utilitarian Mill from this particular charge yet includes 'objectivists' such as her near-contemporary W. D. Ross, best known for defending the view that actions can be wrong in virtue of their intrinsic value, regardless of their consequences:

> There is a startling change that seems to have taken place between Mill and Moore. Mill assumes [. . .] that there is no question of calculating the particular consequences of an action such as murder or theft [...] In Moore and in subsequent academic moralists of England we find it taken to be pretty obvious that 'the right action' is the action which produces the best possible consequences (reckoning among consequences the intrinsic values ascribed to certain kinds of act by some 'Objectivists'.) (MMP: 33)[15]

This double-move is key to understanding the last of three related theses that MMP famously sets out to defend. These have proven to be as hard to interpret as they are easy to state:

(T1) It is not profitable for us at present [1958] to do moral philosophy; that should be laid aside at any rate until we have an adequate philosophy of psychology, in which we are conspicuously lacking.
(T2) The concepts of obligation, and duty – *moral* obligation and *moral* duty, that is to say – and of what is *morally* right and wrong, and of the *moral* sense of 'ought', ought to be jettisoned if this is psychologically possible; because they are survivals, or derivatives from survivals, from an earlier conception of ethics which no longer survives, and are only harmful without it.
(T3) The differences between the well-known English writers on moral philosophy from Sidgwick to the present day are of little importance. (MMP: 26)[16]

What makes T3 true for Anscombe is that the philosophers in question are all 'consequentialists'. Henry Sidgwick's predecessor, Mill, is off the hook from this charge for two distinct reasons. First, he was careful (at least according to Anscombe) to distinguish *intended* from merely *foreseen* consequences of an action. To understand how this helps to avoid 'consequentialism', one needs the 'adequate philosophy of psychology' required to reveal the role played by intention in determining the nature of any given action.[17] Second, Mill explicitly states that utilitarianism can never conflict with justice, going out of his way to explain why his philosophy is compatible with Christian morality in particular (Mill [1861] 1979: 27). He thus allows that *utilitarianism* leads us to re-evaluate whether acts of stealing or kidnapping must always be unjust, while rejecting the *consequentialist* conviction that an unjust act could ever be permissible, let alone obligatory:

> Have mankind been under a delusion in thinking that justice is a more sacred thing than policy, and that the latter ought only to be listened to after the former has been satisfied? While I dispute the pretensions of any theory which sets up an imaginary standard of justice not grounded on utility, I account the justice which is grounded on utility to be the chief part, and incomparably the most sacred and binding part, of all morality. Justice is a name for certain classes of moral rules which concern the essentials of human well-being more nearly, and are therefore of more absolute obligation, than any other rules for the guidance of life [. . .] to save a life, it may not only be allowable, but a duty, to steal or take by force the necessary food or medicine, or to kidnap and compel to officiate the only qualified medical practitioner. In such cases, as we do not call anything justice which is not a virtue, we usually say, not that justice must give way to some other moral principle, but that what is just in ordinary cases is, by reason of that other principle, not just in the particular case. By this useful accommodation of language, the character of indefeasibility attributed to justice is kept up, and we are saved from the necessity of maintaining that there can be laudable injustice. (Mill 1861: 57–8, 62)

Is Mill paying mere lip service to justice here or does he take the thickness of the concept to entail that no plausible moral theory can be at odds with it? In not counting him as a 'consequentialist', Anscombe charitably opts for the latter understanding – that he would give no weight to unjust actions, no matter what their effects:

> Mill assumes, as we saw [27], that there is no question of calculating particular consequences of an action such as murder or theft. (MMP: 33)

Yet Mill's view ultimately seems to be that any action prescribed by utilitarianism must be just *by definition*. If so, Anscombe would be wrong in her assessment that 'it did not occur to him that acts of murder and theft could be otherwise described' (MMP: 27). Indeed, we may plausibly attribute to Mill the view that some thefts are just precisely because they can be described as the taking of *necessary* food or medicine. On this point, the difference between Mill and someone like Aquinas is more semantic than it is moral. Unlike Mill, Aquinas maintains that *all* theft is unjust, but he also asserts that in cases of dire emergency it is not theft to take from another's possessions:

> When a person is in extreme need of material things, and there is no way of emerging from his extremity but by taking what belongs to another, the *surplus* which another possesses becomes common property, and the taker is not guilty of theft. (*ST*, IaIIae.66.7)[18]

Anscombe's evaluation of Mill contrasts starkly with that of Ross, according to whom *any* 'intrinsic' property of action, including that of being unjust, may in principle be outweighed by sufficiently positive consequences:

> Oxford Objectivists of course distinguish between 'consequences' and 'intrinsic values' and so produce a misleading appearance of not being consequentialists. But they do not hold – and Ross explicitly denies – that the gravity of, e.g., procuring the condemnation of the innocent is such that it cannot be outweighed by, e.g., national interest. Hence their distinction is of no importance. (MMP: 33, n. 4)

So understood, Ross allows that there are times when, all things considered, we are not only permitted but morally *obliged* to commit acts of murder, adultery or whatever. Anscombe rejects his thesis that there is no value so sacred that it cannot in principle be trumped by the greater good as being 'consequentialist', despite the fact that Ross's ethic of prima facie duties explicitly allows that goods of beneficence and non-maleficence are often outweighed by concerns of fidelity, gratitude, justice (Ross [1930] 2002: 21ff.). As Christopher Coope has argued, she would have also rejected some of Hursthouse's views on the same grounds.[19] Despite her own definition, then, Anscombe cannot ultimately view 'consequentialism' as the simple equation of 'rightness' with producing the best consequences. As Mary Geach puts it, one might hold the 'consequentialist' view that 'there is no act so bad [that] it might on occasion be justified by its consequences' while rejecting the consequentialist view that 'the right action is always that which produces the best consequences' (Geach 2008: xvii).

In his 1956 article 'Good and Evil', Peter Geach denounces Ross's moral outlook for very similar reasons. I quote at some length:

> I am deliberately ignoring the supposed distinction between the Right and the Good [. . .] Aquinas [. . .] finds it sufficient to talk of good and bad human acts. When Ross would say that there is a morally good action but not a right act, Aquinas would say that a good human intention had issued in what was, in fact, a bad action; and when Ross would say that there was a right act but not a morally good action, Aquinas would say that there was a bad human act performed in circumstances in which a similar act with a different intention would have been a good one (e.g. giving money to a beggar for the praise of men rather than for the relief of his misery) [. . .] [P]eople who think that doing right is something other than doing good will regard virtuous behaviour as consisting, not just in doing good and eschewing evil, but in doing, on every occasion, *the right act for the occasion*. This speciously strict doctrine leads in fact to quite laxist consequences. A man [. . .] if he knows that adultery is an evil act, will decide that (as Aristotle says) there can be no deliberating when or how or with whom

to commit adultery. But a man who believes in discerning, on each occasion, the right act for the occasion, may well decide that on this occasion, all things considered, adultery is the right action. Sir David Ross explicitly tells us that on occasion the right act may be the judicial punishment of an innocent man 'that the whole nation perish not' for in this case 'the *prima facie* duty of consulting the general interest has proved more obligatory than the perfectly *distinct prima facie* duty of respecting the rights of those who have respected the rights of others.' (Geach 1956: 41–2)[20]

Geach's outing of Ross as a crypto-consequentialist is, of course, directly linked to T3.[21] His further rejection of Ross's distinction between goodness and rightness is closely tied to Anscombe's other two theses. In particular, his contention that we should make do without the concept of a 'right action' at all helps to explain why Anscombe keeps 'the right action' within scare quotes. It also sheds light on her middle thesis (T2) that we must try to jettison the concept of a distinctly moral obligation. Terms such as 'moral obligation' and 'morally right action' ought to be jettisoned because they are survivals of an earlier, quasi-legal conception of morality, and make no sense outside the related contexts and practices that originally gave them meaning. This is not a rejection of morality, nor even of a *moral ought*, but only of the distinctively secular and mesmeric 'moral ought' that has been detached from the aforementioned conceptions.[22]

James Doyle (2018) has recently offered a more radical reading of T2. According to Doyle, Anscombe's claim is that the term 'moral' as ordinarily used is literally meaningless, standing for an empty pseudo-concept that provokes a certain feeling in us but has no content whatsoever.[23] Divine commands, on this understanding, neither describe nor create distinctly *moral* obligations, but only religious ones. Whatever the merits of the view itself (Doyle finds it more plausible than I do), we should be wary of it as an interpretation of what is going on in MMP, not least because there are plenty of later writings in which Anscombe endorses law conceptions of morality with no sign of having had the slightest change of mind.

In 'Authority in Morals' ([1962] 1981), Anscombe speaks of 'moral conclusions', 'revelation of moral belief', of a 'moral truth' concerning 'what kinds of thing ought to be done and ought not to be done' as well as of 'the moral law' as a 'range' and of taking one's morality from someone else, concluding that 'the *content* of moral law, that is, the actions which are good and just, is not essentially a matter of revelation'. Similarly, in 'The Moral Environment of the Child', Anscombe states that 'Catholic Christianity teaches a strict moral code' and speaks, without scepticism, of 'truth in the moral code' and 'our morality' (2008b: 231). This Christian morality is contrasted with 'a morality which consisted solely of absolute prohibitions on fairly definitely described actions' (presumably Kant's).

The idea of two contrasting moralities forms the core of her short essay 'Morality'(1982), in which she explicitly rejects the thought that there is such a thing as morality, not because she is a sceptic about moral concepts – she writes that 'human beings have always had morality' and talks of 'that part of morality which is associated with duties to God' ([1982] 2008: 13) – but because she finds Christian morality *so* distinct from the consequentialist one that they amount to two entirely different moralit*ies*: one that prohibits murder, and one that not only permits – but can even demand – it.

As Mary Geach writes in a 2005 letter to the *Times Literary Supplement*,[24] Anscombe herself, of course, had no intention of jettisoning the concepts of moral obligation and duty, which are needed to frame her other principal claim, which is that certain things are forbidden, whatever the consequences. While Christian morality does indeed require us to embody certain virtues, the question of which virtues we *ought* to have may also be addressed from the point of view of what is *good* for us, *qua* human. In pointing this out, Anscombe is in no way abandoning deontic terminology in favour of the aretaic (see Coope 2006: 22). The deontic and the aretaic are simply two different frameworks for talking about the very same goodness. By returning to Aristotle's talk of human excellence and virtue, MMP thus seeks to find a common language through which religious and secular thinkers alike (including Anscombe and her friend Philippa Foot) may converse about morality, and perhaps even reach agreement.[25]

3. Contemporary normative ethics

Anscombe's first thesis in MMP is that '[i]t is not profitable for us at present [1958] to do moral philosophy; that should be laid aside at any rate until we have an adequate philosophy of psychology, in which we are conspicuously lacking' (MMP: 26). By 'philosophy of psychology', she is not referring to the philosophy of cognitive science that currently goes under that name today,[26] nor to the philosophy of mind that used to share it,[27] but to an investigation into the concepts of action, character, intention, motive, desire, pleasure, and the relations between them:

> In present-day philosophy an explanation is required how an unjust man is a bad man, or an unjust action a bad one [. . .] it cannot even be begun until we are equipped with a sound philosophy of psychology [. . .] This part of the subject matter of ethics is, however, completely closed to us until we[28] have an account of what *type of characteristic* a virtue is – a problem, not of ethics, but of conceptual analysis – and how it relates to the action in which it is instanced [. . .] For this we certainly need an account at least of what a human action is at all, and how its description as 'doing such-and-such' is affected by its motive and by the intention or intentions in it; and for this an account of such concepts is required. (MMP: 29)[29]

The blueprint for this philosophy of action had already been laid down by her the year before in her masterpiece *Intention*. This book had already made good on MMP's request for 'an account at least of what a human action is at all, and how its description as "doing such-and-such" is affected by its motive and by the intention or intentions in it' (MMP: 29).[30] Whether Anscombe herself thought she had already provided an adequate philosophy of psychology, or merely a sketch of one, is a moot point.

The term 'philosophy of psychology' has long since been hijacked by philosophers of cognitive science to describe what they do, leaving 'philosophical psychology' as the term of choice for those still interested in asking philosophical questions about human psychology, and 'moral psychology' and 'philosophy of action' for the areas covering the kinds of issues that Anscombe is referring to. Indeed, both these fields owe part of their existence as we know it to Anscombe. In the aftermath of *Intention* and MMP, the 'philosophy of action' developed into a subject in its own right, albeit more closely associated with the philosophy of mind than with ethics.[31] Such branching-off comes at a heavy price, for ethics without philosophy of action is blind, and philosophy of action without ethics empty.

The philosophy of mind and action during the past sixty years has thus developed alongside that of normative ethics, with very little interaction between them. This has enabled philosophers to defend theories of 'right action' while remaining conspicuously silent about what actions are, or how to best conceive of their relation to intentions (on the one hand) and consequences (on the other). As a result of all this, contemporary moral philosophy has been neatly divided into the following four branches, which had yet to properly separate in 1958:

(a) meta-ethics
(b) normative ethics ('moral theory')
(c) practical or 'applied' ethics
(d) moral psychology.

To be sure, theorists debate the extent to which views within (a)–(d) are interrelated, but they are generally content to teach them as separate 'modules' and have been known to profess expertise in any one of the aforementioned while claiming near-ignorance on the remaining three. People do, of course, defend philosophical positions according to which one cannot do (c) without (b) and/or (b) without (a), but even these are parasitic on the divisions in question. Most importantly, (d) is typically reserved for questions relating to agency, motivation, moral responsibility, akrasia, and so on that are thought to be largely independent of (a)–(c). In complete opposition to this, MMP's first thesis effectively tells us that one cannot do (a)–(c) *at all* without first doing (d). While Anscombe certainly cared for 'practical' issues relating to everyday life as well as to medical, military and legal policies, she did not see these issues as remotely separable from either moral philosophy or the philosophy of psychology.[32]

I shan't concern myself much with (a) and (c), save to recall that the contemporary obsession of engaging in (c) by comparing intuitions about increasingly absurd trolley-cases is an unintended consequence of an argument made by Foot in which she defends, against Hare's consequentialism, an original combination of the doctrine of double effect and the doctrine of doing and allowing (Foot [1967] 1978: 23 ff.).[33] Anscombe would have been much more horrified by much of what falls under either of these 'branches' today than anything she was objecting to in 1958. Hardly any of it can be attributed as an effect of MMP though. This is not the case with (b) and (d), so I shall focus on these. I begin with some paradigmatic mainstream positions within normative ethics or 'moral theory':

> *Act consequentialism* is the claim that an **act is morally right if and only if** that act maximizes the good (Sinnott-Armstrong 2015: §1)

An act is wrong if and only if it is forbidden by the code of rules whose internalization by the overwhelming majority of everyone everywhere in each new generation has maximum expected value in terms of well-being. (Hooker 2002: 32)

[A]n **act is wrong if** it would be disallowed by any *principle* that no one could reasonably reject. (Scanlon 1998: 197; see also 153)

An action is right iff it is what a virtuous agent would characteristically do in the circumstances. (Hursthouse 1999: 17; see also 28–9)

An act is wrong just when such acts are disallowed by the principles that are optimific, uniquely universally willable, and not reasonably rejectable. (Parfit 2011: 413)[34]

What **makes an action morally right is** that it originates in a person's good will. (Sullivan 1989: 117)

[D]eontologists think that **acts are wrong because** of the **sorts** of acts they are. (Davis 1991: 210)[35]

It's hardly news that Anscombe would be particularly hostile to consequentialist theories, whose current division into several sub-species (act and rule focusing on actual, probable, expected or intended consequences) has partly resulted as a response to some of Anscombe's arguments in MMP and elsewhere. But what about deontology and virtue ethics? Surely, as a believer in Divine Command Theory and the view that some actions are absolutely prohibited, Anscombe could have no problem with deontology? And was MMP not striving towards a kind of virtue ethics? My answer to both these questions is a negative one.

To begin with, the very issue of what all of the aforementioned theories are doing – namely, attempt to provide accounts of 'the right action' – is problematic, for two reasons. First, as we have already seen (§1), Anscombe follows Geach in being troubled by the very notion of an action being morally right or wrong, as opposed to good or bad. This worry relates to the larger question of what is meant by 'action' in the first place. Robert M. Adams expresses a commonplace certainty when he writes that '[w]hat every competent user of "wrong" must know about wrongness is, first of all, that wrongness is a property of actions (perhaps also of intentions and various attitudes, but certainly of actions)' (Adams 1979: 74). Accordingly, normative theorists feel licensed to remain silent on the question of what an action is. In fact, it is shocking quite how little they are prepared to say on this topic.

The optimistic assumption is that one can simply 'plug in' one's favourite account of action, without this affecting the plausibility of the theory in question, let alone what it would even mean for an action to be right.[36] One explanation for this might be that there is nothing to puzzle over here. As Prichard notes:

> The question 'What is acting or doing something?' seems at first unreal, i.e. a question to which we already know the answer. For it looks as though

everyone knows what doing something is and would be ready to offer instances. No one, for instance, would hesitate to say to another 'You ought to go to bed', on the ground that neither he nor the other knows the kind of thing meant by 'going to bed'. Yet, when we consider instances that would be offered, we do not find it easy to state the common character which we think they had which led us to call them actions. (Prichard [1945] 2004: 272)

Moral theorists might occasionally say something about whether they take actions to be events, or whether they are talking of act 'types' or 'tokens'.[37] By and large, however, one finds little conceptual exploration of the relation between motive, intention, action, and consequence, save perhaps on questions of merely adjacent interest to the main event, such as the 'doctrine of double effect' or 'the doctrine of doing and allowing'.

In the second half of the twentieth century, the prevailing view of actions was Davidson's (Anscombe-inspired) contention that they are a subset of events (Davidson 1963). Yet hardly anyone seems to care about what it might mean for an event to be right or wrong (morally or otherwise) or, for that matter, *morally* good or bad.[38] Proponents of all sides share a related tendency to draw a hard distinction between the deontic and the evaluative, focusing their interest in action on its rightness or wrongness, and reserving terms like 'good' and 'bad' for its motives and/or consequences. From this big leap, it is but a small step to the conclusion that normative ethics is in the business of providing deontic accounts, leaving evaluative concerns to the 'branch' that is moral psychology.[39] Anyone who insists otherwise is branded a virtue-ethicist.

Should we not at least rejoice in the post-MMP 'revival of virtue ethics'? For some the writing was on the wall from the outset:

[W]hen the phrase 'virtue ethics' first came on the scene a number of people, I suspect, must have had a certain sinking feeling – without perhaps quite realizing why. The thing, we supposed, was almost bound to go to the bad. This gloomy assessment has I think proved quite realistic. (Coope 2006: 20)

Anscombe argued that a philosophical concern with virtue should permeate moral philosophy. Instead, it has led to just one more theory, competing with deontology, consequentialism, and contractualism to provide the best account of *right and wrong action*.[40] Julia Annas laments:

Doing the right thing turns out not to be so central in an ethics in which virtue is central. A virtue ethical theory will be interested in *virtuous* action, but will not get much out of the notion of *right* action. (Annas 2011: 47)

No one has done more than Rosalind Hursthouse to put forward virtue ethics on the map as 'a genuine rival to utilitarianism and deontology' which can 'give an account of right action in such a way as to provide action guidance' (Hursthouse 1999: 26, 28; see also Hursthouse 1996). While she did well to emphasize the guiding power of being concerned with virtue, the offering of a normative theory of right action could not be further removed from what Anscombe was hoping to achieve with MMP.[41] This may serve to explain Hursthouse's ambivalence towards this aspect of her own work. She may boast that virtue ethics 'is at least a possible rival to deontological and utilitarian theories' – one that 'can come up with an account of' right action – but she tellingly adds that it only does this 'under pressure, only in order to maintain a fruitful dialogue with the overwhelming majority of modern philosophers for whom "*right* action" is the natural phrase' (Hursthouse 1999: 223, 269; cf. Swanton 2003: 245). It's as if the wimpy school nerd feels reassured to have finally been accepted by those big nasty bullies, experiencing just a shade of residual resentment.

Virtue ethics thus solidifies itself as just one more position *within* moral theory, offering an account of right action in terms of what the virtuous agent would characteristically do in the circumstances. Such theories allow one to ask whether virtue ethics and consequentialism might be compatible. It is, after all, conceivable that the virtuous person is one disposed to perform whichever actions are expected to promote the greatest amount of good.[42] If this is what constitutes moral philosophy then Anscombe is not making a move *within* it. Her morality is not in direct competition with other normative theories, because it isn't in the business of producing a theory of right action at all.

Epilogue

Sixty years after MMP, contemporary moral philosophy is replete with consequentialist thinking obsessed with trolley-cases, a re-branded 'philosophy of psychology' that replaces conceptual explorations with unrefined findings from cognitive science, an experimental form of 'moral psychology' that culminates in the situationist scepticism about character traits, and the espousal of virtue ethics as a theory of 'morally right action' that may even be compatible with utilitarianism. By Anscombe's lights, moral philosophy would seem to have been in far better shape between Moore and MMP than it is now.

Whatever one's assessment of the views of action that Anscombe sought to combat and the account that she put forward in their place, MMP seems to have inadvertently created a wedge between ethics and action theory. This has largely been the result of two consequences that Anscombe could not have easily foreseen, and most certainly didn't intend. The first is the establishment of 'virtue ethics' as one more position within normative ethics, theorizing that an action is right if (and only if) it is what the virtuous agent would (advise us to) do. The second is the development of 'moral psychology' as an independent and increasingly empirical 'branch' of ethics whose interest in questions of motivation, agency and responsibility have been largely sawn-off investigations into the good and the right.

Ironically, before these interventions British moral theorists were *less* inclined to separate their defence of any particular account of 'right action' from their views in moral and philosophical psychology. Within the work of Joseph, Ross and Prichard alone, we find a properly philosophical psychology (one that includes conceptual explorations of the relation of action to motive, intention, and the will) to be central to moral thought. To end with a ray of hope: the twenty-first century has seen a resurgence of philosophers producing in moral philosophy which takes action seriously; for example, Shapiro (2001, 2021), Coope (2006), Pink (2016), Solomon (2003, 2008), Thompson (2008), Brewer (2009), Vogler (2009), Teichmann (2011), Frey (2019a, 2019b) and Hain (2019). This welcome revival of interest in her work is an opportunity for moral philosophers to work well and finally put things right.

Appendix

Basic actions and individuation

1. Basic actions

While its theoretical roots can be traced at least as far back as Aristotle,[1] the phrase 'basic action' was only introduced in 1963, by A. C. Danto in his paper 'What We Can Do'. The notions employed there, he tells us, were 'defended in a companion paper, "Basic actions," to be published subsequently [1965]'.[2] The two papers quickly gave rise to a substantial body of critical commentary that would drastically influence the shape of Danto's own subsequent formulations and beget a host of related concepts – such as those of *primitive* actions (Davidson [1971] 2001) and *simple* actions (Martin 1972).[3]

Danto's overall aim throughout his writings on basic actions is to identify the point at which the regress of things we can do comes to an end and agency thereby begins (and arguably freedom and moral responsibility with it, too).[4] So employed, basic actions play a foundational role similar to that of basic beliefs in epistemology, atomic propositions in the philosophy of language, and sense data in the theory of perception.[5] As Annette Baier has sceptically put it, the search for basic action is a hunt for the most manageable and, through rash induction, also the most minimal cases of action (Baier 1971: 161).

That we can locate the most minimal kind of action is entailed by Danto's following claims, which form a central part of his programme:

(i) If there are any actions at all, there are basic actions.
(ii) There are basic actions.
(iii) Not every action is a basic action.[6]

As Frederick Stoutland remarks, (i) is true on pain of infinite regress (assuming the coherence of Danto's notion of a basic action) and (ii) is jointly entailed by (i) and the contingent fact that there are actions of one kind or another (Stoutland 1968: 467).[7] (iii) is defended in Danto's 'first' paper, of 1963, which argues that there are some things that we can do only non-basically. However, the truth of (iii), as well as that of any answer to the question of what the starting point of agency turns out to be, is crucially dependent upon which definition of 'basic action' we plug in; without an account of what it *is* for an action to be basic, we have no firm conception of what agency consists in.

The nature of basic actions is the focus of Danto's 'second' paper, of 1965. A person's basic actions, Danto tells us there, are those that she 'cannot be said to have caused to happen' (Danto 1965: 141–2). Not, at any rate, by doing anything *first*.[8] On these definitions, however, it is arguable that *almost all* actions count as basic. Stoutland (1968), for example, maintains that it is a mistake to think that we typically cause our *actions*, as opposed to their intrinsic results and/or consequences. He thus comes to deny that all non-basic actions are cases of someone causing the occurrence of an *action* (in any way). After all, if I cause my right arm to move by pushing it with my left hand, the movement of my right arm hardly qualifies as an action. Moreover, *some* non-basic actions, such as that of honouring someone, are arguably not cases of causing *anything* to happen (Stoutland 1968: 474).[9]

Danto's own example of a paradigmatic basic action is that of moving an arm 'without having to do anything to cause it to move' (Danto 1965: 144). Yet, as Alvin Goldman has remarked, this is to confuse *causation* with *causal generation*, which Goldman further distinguishes from conventional generation, simple generation and augmentation generation (Goldman 1970: 23–9). It doesn't help matters that Danto also conflates *what* one does with the *event* of one's doing it.[10]

On some views, moreover, my moving my arm – that is, Danto's example of a basic action – just *is* my directly (yet perhaps nonetheless causally) bringing about its movement.[11] John Locke, Thomas Reid, H. A. Prichard and Hugh J. McCann have all argued that such causation occurs indirectly, *through* (more basic) volitions, which we cause at will.[12] It has also been argued that one may *cause* one's causing one's arm to move *by* causing its movement, and even that we typically cause our own actions – conceived of this time as a bodily movements – without doing anything else.[13] If so, then almost all of our actions would match Danto's criteria for being basic. The relative merits and demerits of such competing conceptions of agent causation must naturally influence any account of basic action.[14]

Danto frequently defines basic actions in terms of a causal independence from other things we might *do*. Yet these include the *mental* acts of thinking, intending, deliberating, deciding and the like, which, on some accounts, are all prime candidates for being causes of simple actions such as that of moving an arm. Danto thus rejects the view that bodily actions are the results of more basic *mental acts* of will. Indeed, he takes this to vindicate Descartes:

> Among the things I take Descartes to have meant when he said that we are not in our bodies the way a pilot is in a ship, is that we do not always do things, as pilots must with ships, by causing them to happen. (Danto 1965: 148)

Danto thereby explicitly rebuts all theories which push action back into the mind through inner volitions or any other kind of purported mental acts or undertakings, whose presumed causality he rejects on the ground that this would constitute a form of telekinesis (Danto 1963: 438). In doing so, he purposely denies the force traditionally ascribed to arguments from error and/or illusion.[15] This tactfully leaves both dualism and causal theories of action unscathed, Danto consistently maintaining that (a) the basic/non-basic distinction is reproduced in the world of mental acts and (b) basic bodily actions may be caused by their mental antecedents so long as the latter do not qualify as acts of any kind (Danto 1965: 142, 148).

The aforementioned complications have led philosophers such as Chisholm and Stoutland to redefine basic action in a manner which circumvents questions of causality:

> In our terms, 'A is performed by the agent as a basic act' could be defined as: the agent succeeds in making A happen, and there is no B, other than A, which he undertook to make happen with an end to making A happen. (Chisholm 1964: 617, n. 7)

> [A] basic action of M is an action M does *not* perform *by* performing some other action. (Stoutland 1968: 467)

In later works, Danto came to mirror Stoutland's model (Chisholm's being too teleological for his purposes), explaining that, 'through a series of invitations to present my views, the idea has undergone, under the fire of criticisms, considerable modification'.[16] His resulting definitions replace all causal and temporal talk with the notion of *mediation,* thus eliminating some of the aforementioned difficulties:

> An action is a *basic action* of an agent *m* only if (i) *m* performs x; and (ii) there is no action, distinct from, and such that *m* performs by performing. (Danto 1969: 66)

> [I]n the theory of action are cases in which a man *m* does something *through* some other thing that he does. He moves a stone, say, by pushing against it, and the stone is thus moved by him through the application of mechanical force. [...] Actions we do but not *through* any distinct thing which will also do [...] I shall call basic, and mediated ones are accordingly non-basic. (Danto 1973: 3, 28)

The shift from 'no distinct action' (Danto 1969) to 'no other thing he does' (Danto 1973) is motivated by concerns about things we do (from trying to omitting) which would not obviously qualify as actions. In fact, Danto's 1973 set of basic actions is considerably smaller than his 1966 one, effectively limiting paradigm cases to simple bodily movements.[17] It is also noteworthy that, while Danto takes the 'by' and 'through' qualifications to be equivalent in all relevant instances, one may easily construct counterexamples that cut both ways: I might annoy you *by* citing Wittgenstein or merely *through* my citing him (for instance if *in* doing so I win the argument); cases which may, but need not, coincide.

The problem of specifying what we mean by 'basic' remains even after we have settled for a specific causal, teleological or mediational relation. Annette Baier illustrates in her list of several ways of doing one thing *by* doing another, thus dividing actions into at least eight kinds of basicness: causally basic, instrumentally basic, conventionally (or expressively) basic, ontologically (including spatially and/or temporally) basic, logically basic, genetically basic, ease basic, and isolation basic (Baier 1971: 168–9). She might have also added epistemically basic (What is the most basic action we *set out* to do?), and there are doubtlessly further kinds besides. Indeed, Baier later introduced culture-relative and agent-relative senses of basic competence (Baier 1972).[18]

Baier concludes that 'the intuitive concept of basic action depended on a failure to separate these questions, and will not survive the clear recognition of their variety and distinctness' (Baier 1971: 170). Complex disjunctive formulae that match our basic (and challenge our non-basic) intuitions, strengthened ad infinitum by ingenious responses to innovative counterexamples, could no doubt be provided. But what would we have gained? *Pace* Danto's claim that 'we all intuitively know which actions are basic ones',[19] there are multitudes of equally legitimate conceptions of what counts as basic. An important upshot of all this is that we are not entitled to reject Danto's definitions on the mere ground that they either include or exclude actions which we would intuitively wish to classify as either basic or non-basic (as indeed numerous critics have done).[20]

Even upon stipulating a definition of basic action, the multitude of competing theoretical stances on the nature of action, causation and volition outlined earlier ensures that no example is uncontroversial. Moreover, any search for basic actions requires a method of action individuation. This brings us to the vexed question of whether the difference between basic and non-basic action is one of *kind*, *degree* or mere *description*.

2. Action individuation

Whichever sort of basicness we have in mind, it is tempting to think of qualifying actions as token members of the class of appropriately basic actions.[21] Accordingly, the aforementioned definitions may be viewed as attempts to isolate, through the specification of necessary and sufficient conditions, a suitable *type* or *kind*, which they all instantiate, albeit one that cannot be identified through generic action descriptions.[22] So understood, basicness is an *absolute* property (such as that of being saturated), not a *relative* one (like tallness). Such a conception nonetheless allows for varying *degrees* of approximation: if I poison the inhabitants by replenishing the water supply, doing the latter by operating the pump, which, in turn, I do by moving my arm in a particular way, my act of operating the pump may be seen as less basic than that of moving my arm but more so than that of replenishing the water supply (which may seem less basic than my act of poisoning the inhabitants).

But now a question arises with regard to how many actions I have actually performed here. In Elizabeth Anscombe's words:

> Are we to say that the man who (intentionally) moves his arm, operates the pump, replenishes the water supply, poisons the inhabitants, is performing *four* actions? Or only one? [...] moving his arm up and down with his fingers round the pump handle *is*, in these circumstances, operating the pump; and, in these circumstances, it *is* replenishing the house water-supply; and, in these circumstances, it *is* poisoning the household. So there is one action with four descriptions, each dependent on wider circumstances, and each related to the next as description of means to end. (Anscombe 1957: 45–6 (§26))

Irving Thalberg has labelled those who side with Anscombe 'reductive unifiers' (Thalberg 1977: 85). According to these reductionists, being basic is a matter of description, not kind. The most influential of them, Donald Davidson, maintains that *all* actions are basic under some description, since, strictly speaking, all we ever do is move our bodies: the rest is up to nature (Davidson [1971] 2001). By contrast, 'pluralists' or 'multipliers' such as Goldman (1970) and Thomson (1971) claim that each of the aforementioned descriptions picks out a different action, and that only one of them (at most) is basic.

Thalberg's own position, non-reductive unification, rejects the very choice between identity and independence in favour of a part–whole relation. On this view (developed in collaboration with Vivien Weil), the event of my replenishing the water supply *includes* – but is not identical to – the event of my operating the pump,[23] and is consequently not basic under any description. Mutatis mutandis, basic actions may contain (ontologically more basic) elements that are not themselves actions.[24] Whether or not any two mereologically related events are *numerically* distinct is a moot point. Jennifer Hornsby, for example, rejects the labels 'unifiers' and 'multipliers' in favour of 'identifiers' and 'differentiators', on the grounds that the former pair serves to conflate identity criteria with enumerative criteria that do not obviously apply to action (Hornsby 1979: 195–6). On Hornsby's conception of what is under dispute, Weil and Thalberg side with the differentiators; however, their *reason* for differentiating as they do has as little to do with numerical distinctness as it does with ontological independence.

We should, on any of the aforementioned views, be wary of equating the question, 'How many events occurred?' with that of 'How many *things* did I do?'; for we may legitimately speak of one event of my doing several things. This is not to deny that we may offer multiple descriptions of one and the same action: Oedipus does not kill Laius *and* his father (though it is true that he strikes Laius and that he kills his father). In addition to such Rylean conjunction tests, we may also apply spatio-temporal criteria to individuation. Suppose that Bob Marley shot the sheriff at time t_1, but that the sheriff only died at a later time t_3, before which – at time t_2 – Marley recorded his famous song. Did Marley kill the sheriff before or after recording his song (he certainly didn't do it during it)? It would be as implausible to claim (with differentiators such as Goldman (1970) and Thomson (1971)) that Marley did not kill the sheriff until t_3 – after he had left the scene of the crime and was back in the recording studio – as it would be to follow identifiers such as Davidson ([1969b] 2001) and Hornsby (1979) in maintaining that he killed the sheriff at t_1 – that is, before the sheriff died.[25]

It is often objected, for instance by Bennett (1973), that the implausibility of the latter claim is not (genuinely) ontological but (merely) a linguistic oddity. We do not call someone a parent before they adopt or give birth to any children, yet there is nothing problematic about such a child subsequently speaking of their *parents'* life before that moment. Similarly (or so the argument goes), while we cannot at t_1 (while the sheriff was still alive) truthfully *say* that Marley killed the sheriff, at t_2 (when the sheriff is dead) it becomes perfectly acceptable to talk of Marley 'killing' him at t_1 (before he died). But, if anything, the analogy proves the opposite, for in the former case we do not at t_2 imply that she was already a mother at t_1 any more than we can plausibly state at t_2 that Marley killed the sheriff at t_1. Legitimate talk at t_2 of a killer's life before t_1 (when his first victim died) does not license the inference – no matter when one makes it – that the said person was already a killer then.[26]

All such difficulties vanish, however, once we distinguish between the *cause* of the sheriff's death, namely the shooting, and the logically related yet distinct *causing* of his death, namely the killing.[27] While it is, *pace* Weintraub, legitimate to call both these things 'events' of people acting, it would be absurd to think of the causing of an event as something which could itself be brought about.[28]

Causings, like all processes and events, have temporal locations. But to insist that every killing must have as fine-grained a temporal location as an instant shooting is as silly as insisting that it must have also had a spatial location that is smaller than, say, that of a bread tin.[29] If Marley shot the sheriff in March 1973 – before recording his song about it in April 1973 – and if the sheriff (unlike the deputy) did not die until November 1973 (after the hit record was released), then we can truthfully and informatively say that Marley killed the sheriff in 1973. Needless to say, the location of any given event at a certain minute, hour, day, week, month, season, year, decade, century or millennium does not imply that it must have been occurring continuously throughout that period (consider cricket matches, for example).

Notes

Chapter 1

1. See Ricoeur [2000] 2004: 13ff.; cf. Changeux and Ricoeur 2000: 427.
2. Ricoeur (1986: 142–9).
3. See Chapter 13.
4. Anscombe 1957: §45; cf. Powell 1967.
5. PR: §114, see also §119; cf. Williams 1993: 69–70.
6. See Chapter 13.
7. Emphasis in the original. The precedence of 'intentional' over 'voluntary' and 'purposeful' here is telling.
8. For the Aristotelian origins of Hegel's outlook, see Speight 2001: 46ff.
9. See Hornsby 2021.
10. Cf. Wittgenstein [1953] 2009 – referred to as *PI* in the sequel: §89.
11. See Laitinen and Sandis 2019; Laitinen, Mayr and Sandis 2019.
12. See Frey 2019b: 1128.
13. See Anscombe [1979] 1981.
14. English Standard Version, although I have replaced 'the Skull' with 'Calvary'. Some translations (e.g. the New Revised International Version) have 'what they are doing'. This present-continuous parsing of 'what they do' suggests a single action that has yet to be completed, as opposed to a series of ongoing actions that fall under the same kind (see Sandis 2016a).
15. Admittedly, this sort of line has a little more mileage if one's victim claims to be the son of God.
16. In John (19.16ff.), it is the Roman soldiers who take charge of Jesus, but the 'forgive them for . . .' line is absent, as it is from the parallel passages in Matthew and Mark (in which 'they' remains opaque).
17. Purpose is more complicated, insofar as one's purpose may include 'external' aspects of one's deed that go beyond intention or even foresight, for example, consequences that one ought to have foreseen (see Laitinen and Sandis 2019).
18. See Chapter 2.
19. See Chapter 7.
20. This is not to suggest that there were no earlier uses of the word 'trace' to denote an earlier event. The *Oxford English Dictionary* offers Cowley 1656: I.iii, Whiston 1696 and Pope 1713: 372 [mistakenly identified by the OED as '1710'], but the philosophical concept of a historiographical trace as we know it today is not yet quite at work in these texts. Hume mainly uses it as a verb (see the subsequent note), though in Vol. V of his *History of England*, he tells the reader that 'though parity may seem at first to have had place among Christian pastors, the period, during which it prevailed, was so short, that few undisputed traces of it remained in history' (Hume 1754: V.54.2).

21 Most of the authors mentioned earlier use 'trace' as both a noun [*Spur, la trace*] and a verb [*verfolgen, tracer*].
22 It's unclear whether he took such appointment by community (if not quite committee) to be equally capable of downgrading what was previously taken to be a historical fact into a more commonplace one.
23 Elton 1967: 76ff. and Elton 1991: 27 and 65. Cf. Evans 1997: 75ff. I return briefly to the relation of facts to events in this essay's Epilogue.
24 See also Lanzmann [1985] 1995: 13, 45–6.
25 See Crampton (1974).
26 Levinas insists that only living beings can leave traces, but his point is ultimately a semantic one: 'things . . . in themselves do not leave a trace but produce effects, that is to say, remain in the world. One stone scratched another. The scratch can of course be taken for a trace: in reality, without the man who held the stone, the scratch is nothing but an effect. It is no more a trace than a brush fire is the trace of thunder' (Levinas [1972] 2003: 43).
27 When online traces are removed – for example, under the 'right to be forgotten' act – what happens to the traces left by the removers? Should these be removed too? And then what? Ricoeur writes that 'when there are no formal "records" (like those which are kept by institutions like employment offices, schools, banks, and the police), there is still an informal analogue of these formal records which we call reputation and which constitutes a basis for blaming' (Ricoeur [1986] 2008: 154). This social imprint partly constitutes what Angela Merkel has called 'the currency of trust'. How does trust relate to data, and its traces and lack thereof? And what of the traces on search engines of those looking for traces that have been removed? Detectives leave fingerprints too.
28 Ricoeur has speech-act theory in his sights but is more interested in the things we say through action than in the things we do with words. For 'the disclosure of the agent in speech and action', see Arendt [1958] 1998: 175–81.
29 Cf. Arendt ([1958] 1998: 19, n. 19) who relates the contrast between these activities to that between works and deeds, the differentiation of which ultimately informs her own distinction between work and action.
30 See Chapter 14.
31 We don't do our own doings any more than we fear our own fearings or suspect our own suspectings (cf. White 1972). Matthew Hanser (2008) thinks of all such distinctions as type/token ones (cf. Clark 1989; Harman 2000), but there is good reason to be suspicious of this, because the things we do are *instances* of types and it accordingly makes sense to think of one's doing something as one's instantiating the type that their deed falls under (cf. Steward 1997: 120–34 and Dancy 2009a: 401). Davidson ([1967] 2001) tries to demonstrate that *all* sentences that mention things done are replaceable by ones that only quantify over events without loss of meaning. His position, however, cannot adequately deal with normative statements (see Sandis 2012: 145f.).
32 Cf. Charles 2018: 38.
33 The Egyptian pharaohs have arguably done better in terms of the intended marks their burial preparations have left on time, although they were ultimately aiming for an afterlife that didn't take the form of a Boris Karloff movie. The traces one leaves do not necessarily point to anything resembling truth, as illustrated by Timothy Garton Ash's description of what he found in his Stasi file, which he in turn uses to trace and confront the German friends and acquaintances who had informed on him (Ash 1997).

34. Laitinen and Sandis 2019.
35. See Nagel ([1976] 1979) and Williams ([1976] 1981). Constitutive luck is trickier, because who we are is determined only partly by our deeds and doings.
36. Williams ([1976] 1981: 21 and 36).
37. The example originates with Bowra (1944: 168–70), quoted in Chapter 12, §2.
38. If this approach to moral luck is broadly right, then it should also help us with the old debate between subjectivism and objectivism about our duties when acting under uncertainty (see Zimmerman 2008).
39. See also Dancy 2009a: 400ff.
40. Derek Parfit similarly writes that 'our acts are merely events in time' but proceeds to conflate these with things done (Parfit 2011: 270).
41. See Chapter 11. Cf. Mason (2019:96).
42. See Austin, Strawson and Cousin 1950. Cf. Vendler 1967: 31–2 and 122–46; White 1995; and Evans 1997: 78–90.
43. See Chapter 14.

Chapter 2

1. Homer (2003). The translators note: 'The Greek for "no one" is *me tis*, but run together as *metis* it means "wily scheme, resourcefulness"'. Even as a nobody, Odysseus remains an acting hero, as opposed to a suffering one. For Homer (as opposed to, say, Chaucer), the distinction between doing and suffering is, indeed, an active one (see Crampton 1974).
2. Borges 1942. Cf. Luria [1968] 1987 and Sacks [1973] 1990: 75–6, n. 54.
3. A related debate between Russell (1956: 211–15) and Wittgenstein ([1922] 1961: 4.0621) focuses on the existence of negative facts.
4. See the title story in Neuman 2014.
5. Bentham 1789: 72.
6. See D'Arcy 1963: 41.
7. Many cases of forgetting are also instances of neglecting, though the Tory MP mentioned in the Prologue is only being said to have 'forgotten' in a sarcastic sense.
8. For earnest applications of the transformed dictum, see Weisbord and Janoff 2007.
9. Cf. Samuel Richardson's *Clarissa* and Georgette Heyer's *Arabella*.
10. Elsewhere in the novel we are told of a divorcing husband who 'was the sole director and only employee of an enterprise that made or did nothing' (p. 62).
11. The number of discussions on the moral relevance (or lack thereof) of action and intention is legion. I don't wish to add to these but to instead ask preliminary questions about the very nature of negative doings.
12. Other advocates of this view are von Wright (1963: 45–8) and Lewis (2004). I don't concern myself here with detailing the differences between these four accounts, although it is worth remarking that von Wright is happy to stipulate the forbearances are 'actions' in a technical sense, which includes both acts and their 'negative counterparts'.
13. Sandis 2012: 7; Brand 1971; Davidson 1985b; Goldman 1970; and Thomson 2003.
14. Schopenhauer similarly distinguishes between not-willing and performing an act of not-willing ([1851] 1974, 'Additional Remarks': 312).

15 See Appendix. We might also add that there are some things we can be said to have done without there ever having been events of our doing them.
16 Bach (2010: 55).
17 Cf. Brand 1971; Thomson 2003.
18 Anscombe 1957: 38, 46; Davidson [1967] 2001: 110.
19 For worries about whether the preposition 'of' here marks identity, see Sandis 2012: 8–9.
20 Davidson [1967] 2001 and 1999.
21 See Sandis 2012: 151ff.
22 E.g. Hornsby 1980, 1993a, 1993b, 1997c; Macmurray 1938; Ricoeur [1986] 2008 and Sandis 2012.
23 See also Hornsby 1980: 3–5.
24 Macmurray 1938 uses it in the exactly opposite way.
25 Can one do the same thing more than once the way that one can say or think the same thing on more than one occasion? I can certainly keep reading the same book, cooking the same meal or, indeed, making the same mistake or telling the same lie time after time. By contrast, I cannot keep killing the same person or eating the exact same carrot each time in the same way in which I can keep reading the same copy of a book, although I may bake something more than once. We can certainly build unrepeatability into some fine-grained descriptions of what was done, but this has nothing to do with the logic or ontology of action: were my victim to rise from the dead, I could kill him again.
26 Neuman 2014: 31. Things we haven't done arguably include those that are impossible for us to do, across a range of modal senses. Personally, I have never spoken Russian, flown down the stairs, performed miracles, travelled back in time, or squared the circle.
27 See also Bennett 1981: 91. For cases in which the doing/allowing and action/inaction distinctions come apart, see Foot 1985: 177–85. Cf. Woollard 2015: 21–35; Woollard and Howard-Snyder 2016.
28 See Sher 2009 for why responsibility may require less than is commonly assumed.
29 I return to this theme in Chapters 12 and 13.
30 See, for example, Smith 2013. There is, for sure, a morally relevant difference between *not* being aware, *pretending* one is not aware, and *doing* not being aware. Similarly, the difference between acting recklessly and *doing* 'acting recklessly' is that in the latter case the recklessness is part of the intended purpose of what you are doing – for example because you're trying to be all rock 'n' roll. The point extends to omissions more generally.
31 Hegel [1820] 1991: §§105–41.
32 See Laitinen and Sandis 2019.
33 'A flung stone is the devil's. To act is to expose oneself to bad luck. Thus bad luck has a right over me and is an embodiment of my own willing.' (Hegel 1821: §119A).
34 Conversely, if I wanted to offend you, but failed, I am responsible for what I tried to do *qua* intention, but not objectivity. In either scenario, I am further responsible for not eating *qua* intention, knowledge and objectivity, but *not qua* purpose, which only has a right over the hunger-strike aspect of my action.
35 See Hirstein 2009.
36 H. M. Smith 2013: 3665ff.
37 In this it is not dissimilar to the most popular sense of 'doing nothing'. See Burkeman 2005.

38 Hirstein (2009) distinguishes between three different kinds of negligence, but their differences need not concern us here.
39 All four examples stand only as *paradigm* cases of the phenomena they illustrate.
40 For complications involving character, see Sher 2006 and Sandis 2019a.
41 For moral and legal enquiries into our responsibility for harms caused by negligence, see Raz 2010 and Green 2015.
42 Technically, 'karma' is action based on desire (for gratification) and 'akarma' 'without reaction to work' (actions without fruitive reactions). 'Freedom from the bondage of action' is thus only possible 'when one is doing everything for Krishna' (Bhaktivedanta Swami Prabhupada 1972: 207–8). This is a clear precursor to Kant's thought regarding acting only from the motive of duty, although Kant would have never allowed for the murderous duties invoked by Krishna.

Chapter 3

1 The same is here held true of the painter, a view that should not be ignored when contemplating the role of Poussin in *Dance*.
2 For the relation between actions and omissions, see Bach 2010.
3 Unlike Kierkegaard, Nietzsche is oddly omitted from Hilary Spurling's book index, despite Spurling's determination to include 'virtually every character, factual or fictional' (Spurling 1977: ix).
4 With few exceptions, such as that of the dominating Amy Foxe, they are indeed men.
5 Jenkins criticizes this outlook: 'I could see, however, that one of the fallacies that made him so vulnerable was the supposition that manners, good or bad, had anything to do with the will as such' (*VB*: 228). I return to the vulnerability of Powell's agents in Section 3.
6 Powell's knowledge of Nietzsche was deepened via his friendship with Alick Dru (*FIMT*: 137–42). His review in Punch of F. A. Lea's book on Nietzsche (*The Tragic Philosopher*, New York: Philosophical Library, 1957) reveals a cautious admiration for the 'man of such gifts' who would have been deeply opposed to Hitler's Germany yet ironically 'provided Hitler with some sort of flimsy intellectual background'.
7 Nietzsche steals this thought from Ralph W. Emerson and Alexander Bain: 'life is a search after power . . . I like not the man who is thinking how to be good . . . but the man thinking how to accomplish his work' (Emerson 1860: 45); 'The state named the feeling or emotion of Power expresses a first-class motive of the human mind' (Bain 1884: 77).
8 An in-between case is that of Sillery, who bears a Nietzsche-like walrus moustache, admires Stalin during the war years, interferes in other peoples' business, fosters undergraduates' connexions which might be of use to him and prefers power to sensual enjoyment (Spurling 1977: 147–9).
9 Poussin's first name, of course, is inherited by Jenkins (Spurling 1977: xi).
10 Burton himself believed that we are in possession of a 'moving faculty' that 'causeth all those inward and outward animal motions in the body' (Burton [1628] 2001: Part I, 160; and see 167 for its complex relation to the will). This faculty contains an appetite for external things that thereby move us indirectly. Inspired by Xenophontis, Burton takes the worst external force of all to be money 'to whom we daily offer sacrifice, which steers our hands, affections, all: that most powerful goddess, by whom we are

reared, depressed, elevated, esteemed, the sole commandress of our actions, for which we pray, run, ride, go, come, labour, and contend as fishes do for a crumb that falleth into the water' (Burton [1628] 2001: Part I, 65).

11 Powell would have appreciated Bernard Williams's work on moral luck (Williams [1976] 1981), inspired by Bowra and Dodds. For Uncle Giles's impoverished brand of egotism, see *AW*: 8.
12 See Diethe 2003.
13 Though an admirer of much of Nietzsche's thought, Powell writes that 'it is hard to see how, in practice, any attempt artificially to build up government of the kind Nietzsche outlines could result in anything but an approximation to the Third Reich' (*TSN*: 720).
14 I return to this theme in the final section.
15 One could write an entire essay on the beard in Powell's novels (see, for example, *Wheel*: 80, 87), but suffice it to say here that this attribution of facial hair is not arbitrary. Indeed, it is perhaps no accident that (as we shall see in the last section) George Bernard Shaw's 'superman' is also portrayed as bearded.
16 Nietzsche took the word 'Übermensch' (now usually translated as 'overman') from Goethe's Faust.
17 Jay calls Passenger the 'true Superman' of the piece.
18 Simon Russell Beale's take on Widmerpool's descent into madness in the ITV adaptation of *Dance* would be echoed in his 2014 performances of *King Lear* at the National Theatre. In his notebook, Powell imagines some 'alternate endings' for Widmerpool, all of which emphasize passivity in one way or another, for example, dying in a hijacked plane.
19 Powell toyed with the possibility of Widmerpool missing his mother's funeral owing to some affairs of state. This would have crystalized the fact that from the moment she dies his power begins to diminish.
20 In this, the socialist Shaw is an unlikely predecessor to that propagator of the American cult of the individual self-made man, Ayn Rand (1964).

Chapter 4

1 Cf. Smith and Pettit 1997: 73ff.
2 Dancy also allows for considerations to favour having a particular emotion.
3 In his Précis for the 2020 symposium on *Practical Shape*, Dancy writes: 'Until we solve this problem my whole story about practical reasoning is unstable [. . .] Until we do resolve the Prichard point, we have not yet managed even to understand the notion of a reason, since we do not know what it means to talk of a consideration favouring a type of response or favouring acting in a certain way. This is not a happy situation' (Dancy 2020: 132).
4 I use the word 'particularized' rather than 'particular' because I suspect that what the latter denotes, at least as I use it, is not particular enough for what Dancy has in mind. After all, you can instruct me to act in a particular way that is very precisely defined, and any number of a fixed range of particular doings would still fulfil the instruction.
5 Not least because, for Dancy and Raz alike, it is the case that 'in believing we are as active as we ever are' (144).
6 See Ross ([1930] 2002: 6–7).

7   While Dancy recognizes such a distinction in the case of belief, his defence of the primacy of the practical leaves no real role for things believed to play in the theoretical case.
8   But see Dancy 2009 for a detailed defence of his deflationary approach to actions.
9   Dancy 2009: 401. If we must apply the type/token distinction to actions at all, I see no reason why we can't apply it to both doings *and* things done. The one is not a token of the other.
10 In a footnote, Dancy quotes the following passage from Michael Stocker, without comment: 'We fulfil duties by performing [. . .] act tokens [. . .] Nonetheless it is not a duty to perform any act token. For we could have fulfilled our duty by performing another act token of the appropriate type. For example, even though that returning of the book fulfilled the promise, many other returnings of the book would have done so as well' (Stocker 1968: 54, as quoted in Dancy 2018: 31, n.3). Yet the 'act tokens' that Stocker has in mind are not acts we perform but our particular performings of them. The acts we perform, such that of returning of the book, are what Stocker (in my opinion, wrongly) conceives of as act-types.
11 We would do better, I think, to talk of believing-in-action and intending-in-action.
12 See Chapter 5.

Chapter 5

1   Indeed, Davidson's reasoning is arguably closer to that of Socrates than was Aristotle's. Happily, this is not the place for such exegesis.
2   In both P1 and P2 the word 'want' is used by Davidson in the sense that allows us to say that if A did *x* intentionally, then he must have, in some sense, wanted to do it (cf. Davidson [1969a] 2001: 27).
3   See Dancy 1993: 180.
4   Ross 1930: 19.
5   While it may be that an agent does not have them until she is given them (or they have at the very least been made available to her), this is not the distinction at play here, for an agent may have both conditional and unconditional reasons.
6   It is this distinction that is under attack in Williams 1980.
7   See Broome [1999] 2000 and Dancy 2000: 70–6.
8   Doyle 1924. Whether or not we have two different sense of 'ought' here is a contested point. Perhaps we do, but the issue is complicated further by the fact that what matters is whether the agent must have these senses present in her mind, and whether having them would free her from any charges of being akratic in the relevant sense. In the case in question, we might even say that *akrasia* would consist in Miss De Merville's following her all-out judgement (against her ATC one).
9   Davidson [1982] 2004: 177–8.
10 Davidson [1969a] 2001: 41. The term 'principle of continence' implies that whoever follows the principle cannot be akratic. Furthermore, herein I argue that Davidson is mistaken about this.
11 For reasons why 'inconsistency must involve a contradiction', see Hodges 1977: 14–15.
12 My own view is that no belief can rationalize actions but only a thing believed, but I avoid such phrasing here in a bid to remain neutral on the issue.

13. Scanlon gives us the example of thinking I can rely on Jones despite the fact that I know that he is an artful deceiver and that I should therefore judge that I ought not rely on him. See Scanlon 1998: 35. Another example might be that of someone who buys a lottery ticket because she irrationally believes that she is going to win.
14. This suggests conceptual space for a form of *akrasia* that cannot be accurately described as either *propeteia* or *astheneia*. Given that the latter terms are in any case tainted with certain unwanted implications relating to strength and self-control it might be thought preferable to replace them with David Pears's talk of 'last ditch' and 'clear-eyed' *akrasia* (cf. Pears 1984). However, the term *akrasia* itself misleadingly implies that the agent does what he most desires (the root of P1–2 and in many ways of the paradox itself). The terms 'incontinence' and 'weakness of will' fare no better, for reasons that have already been noted elsewhere (e.g. Rorty 1988; Holton 1999).
15. Of course, Davidson does not explicitly state that he is doing so, and it is debatable whether or not he believes that he is.
16. See n. 2 this chapter.
17. Compare it, for example, with Michael Smith's version, according to which an agent will act upon his better judgement unless he is weak-willed (1994: 61).

Chapter 6

1. See Dretske 1988b: 17–18 and Dretske 2009; Cf. Appendix §2.
2. Action, for Dretske, is any causal process that may be explained by the behaving animal's *reasons* for undergoing it (see Dretske 2009). His account thus lies closer to that provided by von Wright (1963), who identifies action with the process of an agent bringing about a bodily movement, than to that of Davidson ([1963] 2001), who takes actions to consist of the subset of bodily movements that are intentional under some description.
3. See Dretske 1988a for a defence of his representationalism. The identification of true beliefs with facts is persuasively challenged by Rundle (1993). Such conceptions of facts undermine the notion of a 'representational fact' employed by Dretske. There is nothing in Dretske's account of action explanation, however, which renders it hostage to this detail of his presentation.
4. A structuring cause need not be a reason for which an agent acts in order for it to be apt to explain why a stimulus elicited a particular piece of behaviour.
5. Dretske is wrong to imply that the answer to the question (A) 'Why did the dog salivate?' will be the same as the answer to the question (B) 'Why did the dog salivate *instead of* jump?', for these are two distinct inquiries (see Achinstein 1975). Still, he is not alone in thinking this (see Nagel 1986: 115–17).
6. There are some superficial similarities between Dretske's account and that made famous by Donald Davidson: both philosophers claim that reasons are *causes* of behaviour and that these are further identifiable with the agent's beliefs and desires (compare, for example, Davidson [1963] 2001 with Dretske 1988b: 44). Yet not only do their accounts of *action* differ (cf. note 2 this chapter), they also conceive of *causes* in radically different terms. According to Davidson ([1967] 2001) the term 'cause' refers to an entity which 'causally explains' the event that is its 'effect', whereas Dretske takes what he calls a 'structuring cause' to causally explain why something triggered the event that is the *result* of the entire triggering process.

7   In this respect Dretske's account of reasons for which we act is not dissimilar from those 'externalist accounts' offered (typically in opposition to Davidson) by, among others, Baier (1985b: 125), Tanney (1995), Collins (1997), Stoutland (1998), Dancy (2000), Bittner (2001), Schroeder (2001) and Schueler (2003). However, these philosophers all distance themselves from the suggestion (endorsed by Dretske) that reasons are *representational contents* and/or *causes* in any serious sense.
8   Davidson himself has confessed that the possibility of causal deviancy forms an 'insurmountable' challenge to his view and that he despairs of 'spelling out. [...] the way in which attitudes must cause actions if they are to rationalize the action' (Davidson [1973] 2001: 79).
9   Cf. Dretske 1988b: 80.
10 On some non-anomalous physicalist views, an *extra*ordinary (neurobiological) understanding may be possible given a considerable amount of knowledge about relevant correlations. Dretske explicitly rejects such a possibility, claiming that he 'doesn't share these advanced ideas' (1988a: 31–2).
11 This particular form of *rationalization* should be distinguished from (i) cases where we deceive ourselves about the *real* reasons for which we acted (as in the range of examples made famous by Nietzsche, Freud and Sartre) and (ii) cases where we *concoct* explanations after a fact whose occurrence may have been random (see Taleb 2007).
12 This objection can also be applied to Davidson. I leave it for another occasion to discuss whether or not it could also be applied to the various 'identification' mechanisms of the kind offered by offered by Frankfurt ([1978] 1988).
13 See Smith ([1998] 2004: 158–61) for examples of some of the controversy.
14 This kind of objection owes its origin to Smith and Pettit (1997).
15 There is something unashamedly Humean in this remark.
16 Dretske's account can – and in my opinion should – be adapted in a way that leaves room for structuring causes which explain why my moving my body in a certain way is a piece of *meaningful* behaviour.

Chapter 7

1   See Chapter 2.
2   See, for example, Watson 1919: 19ff. For an early history of the molar/molecular distinction, see Tolman 1932: Ch. 1.
3   See Appendix.
4   Hornsby 1980: Ch. 1 and Hornsby 1986: 93–4. *Pace* Hornsby, I do not take the preposition 'of' to here mark an important distinction.
5   See von Wright 1963.
6   Cf. Stoutland's distinction between (i) the event of the moving of M's hand and (ii) the action of M's moving his hand (Stoutland 1968: 473–4, n. 10).
7   For motivated resistance see Bach 1980 and Lowe 2010.
8   Dretske 1988b and 2009; Alvarez and Hyman 1998. See Chapter 6.
9   Aristotle's *Physics* (Book III, 201a10–11). For the claim that Aristotle has no ontology of action see Ackrill 1978). Cf. Stout 1996: 155–63, Stout 1996: Ch. 6, and Charles 1984.
10 For near-exhaustive catalogues see: O'Shaughnessy 1972: 222; McCann 1979; Steward, 1997: Ch. 3; Stout 1996: 46–62; Stout 1997.
11 Events, by contrast, are more akin to facts; hence the strong intuition that no particular event could have been otherwise than it was, without being a different

event. For the relation between events and facts (as well as states of affairs), see Strawson 1950, Austin [1954] 1961, and McCann 1979.
12 For the by/in distinction as applied to doings, see Appendix, §1.
13 For the Fregean application of this distinction to things we think, perceive, believe, think and mean, see: Frege [1918–19] 1984; White 1972; McDowell [1994] 1996: 27; and Hornsby 1997b, 1997c. I shall not concern myself with disanalogies here, for the general point is neutral with regard to specific ontologies of things done, believed, perceived and so on. We don't do our own doings any more than we desire our desirings, believe our believings, suspect our suspectings, perceive our perceivings and so on.
14 For the view that all actions are inner mental acts, see Hornsby 1980: Ch. 1.
15 For complications relating to emphasis and illocutionary force see Achinstein 1983: 76–81. The similar but much weaker thesis that an *explanandum* is only fixed under sentential representation is briefly discussed by Kim ([1989] 1997: 275–6), who attributes the view to Hempel (1965: 421–2), with reference to Dretske's related suggestion that we may refer to 'event allomorphs', akin to *aspects* of events (Dretske 1977).
16 A point famously brought home by Anscombe (1957).
17 For example, Taylor 1964, Harré and Secord 1972, Stoutland 1976 and Dretske 1988.
18 It should be obvious from this quotation that the *Conflating View of Action* also leads to a misguided view of the causal history of our doings.
19 Cf. Dancy 2000: 131.
20 See Collins 1987: 125–8.
21 Nagel similarly talks about 'a reason for something simply to occur' (1970: 120, n. 1).
22 Cf. MacMurray 1938: 80–1: 'But how can we disprove the contention of a theistic hypothesis that all events, in the last analysis are acts of God? At the most we could perhaps show that we have no grounds for supposing this; though in fact I believe that even that is not demonstrable. Our certainty about action is of a higher order than our knowledge of events.'
23 See Appendix. For a plausible analysis of divine action, see Ward 2007: 18ff. The more extreme view that 'everything we do is God's creative action' may be found in Rumi's poem 'Emptiness' (1995: 26).
24 Davidson ([1971] 2001: 43) rightly claims that stumbling can be deliberate under some description, for my stumbling may be identical to my going home. But I don't stumble *for* whatever reason explains by stumbling.
25 Broome (2004: 34) gives 'the reason for the cow's death was BSE' as an example and calls it a non-normative reason. The mistake of thinking otherwise when it comes to natural 'selection-for' is one of the things that Jerry Fodor and Massimo Piatteli-Palmarini (2010: 95–138) rightly argue Darwin got wrong.
26 Typically, these conflations are not made *explicitly*, for they involve a failure to see that there is a distinction to be made. One important exception is Donald Davidson, who consciously rejects the possibility of such an ontological distinction, for semi-Quinean reasons (cf. Millgram 2009: Chs. 8 and 9).

Chapter 8

1 For competing ways of understanding this commonplace distinction between what one believes and one's believing it, see White 1972, Hornsby 1997c and Dancy 2000: 121ff. My argument doesn't hang on the particular details of any such approach.

2 I'm thinking of explanatory nesting here; normative nesting would require appeal to further agential reasons.
3 See also Chapter 7.
4 Regarding the subjects' alleged denial of 'a possible effect of the position of the article', one would like to know more about the exact question they were asked: an effect on what exactly?
5 Carruthers (2011: 329ff.) rightly criticizes Nisbett and Wilson (1977) and Wegner (2002) for placing too much emphasis on causal attributions, as opposed to confabulations about the very existence of 'some suitable mental event to serve as the cause'. But we must tread very carefully if we are to maintain, as Carruthers does (ibid.: 336), that these can include judgements.
6 For confabulations relating to motivated misremembering, see Henkel and Mather 2007.
7 In Section 5, I maintain that any deception cannot be due to straightforward lack of transitive consciousness.
8 This is not a case of falsely attributing a judgement to oneself (Carruthers 2011: 336) but of making a false judgement.
9 Arguably, the reasons for which we act should never be understood as reasons why we act. This is because the considerations we act upon maybe false, whereas all genuine (as opposed to merely purported) explanation is, by definition, factive. When we explain action by citing agential reasons, the explanatory work is done by true propositions about the reasons the agent acted for, and not by the reasons themselves (see Chapters 9 and 10).
10 See Ruben 2003: Ch.6 for a counterfactual theory of explanation and Martin 2011: Ch.2 for an attack on counterfactual analyses of causality.
11 Cf. Aronson 1956 and Haidt 2001. Similar strategies by end-of-the-world cultists whose predictions were disproved are reported in Aronson 1956.
12 For more on the difference between belief-orientated and action-orientated confabulations, see Hindriks 2015. Hursthouse (1991) offers persuasive examples of intentional actions not performed for reasons (but out of habit, anger etc.) which do not involve confabulation.
13 See Beeghly and Madva 2020.
14 An alternative scenario is one in which Frank honestly avows that he believes Arno and Maureen are equally skilled in every respect and takes himself to 'randomly' offer the job to Arno when in actual fact an implicit bias (which can be measured statistically) is at play.
15 Similar conflations surround Festinger's notion of cognitive dissonance (Festinger 1957: 1) and Tamar Gendler's notion of alief (Gendler 2008a, 2008b).
16 For a critical assessment of the fallacy across various debates relating to perception, belief and action, see Dancy 1995b.
17 For this reason I cannot endorse the letter of Peter Goldie's claim that there are 'influencing factors' on a person's mind that 'are not themselves part of the content of his mind', though I wholeheartedly agree with his contention that 'he proposed marriage to her at the party because he was drunk' is an explanation that offers 'a cause but . . . not a reason for . . . not a consideration' (Goldie 2012: 20).
18 But see Collins 1987.
19 A former consideration may nonetheless leave motivational traces that influence us unconsciously. I owe this point to István Zárdai.

20 For a counterfactual attack on Levy's view – and by extension by own – see Vierkant and Hardt 2015. Their challenges can be sustained only if one refuses to distinguish between agential reasons and other motivational factors.
21 See Kuhn (1962). This much is unquestionably true of Bernays ([1928] 2005), Packard ([1957] 2007) and Thaler and Sunstein (2008). For the relation of rhetoric to motives see Burke (1950).

Chapter 9

1 For the original distinction, see Smith 1992: 329. It is worth noting that Smith has since distinguished between two different senses of 'good reason', contrasting rational grounds (facts), on the one hand, and rational springs (psychological states), on the other (see Smith and Pettit 1997: 297ff.). Dancy's normative constraint is concerned with the former sense. While Smith concedes that we may act upon reasons so conceived, he denies that they have any explanatory power, which he takes to be part of the notion of a 'motivating reason'.
2 I borrow the term from Hacker (2009). A subset of agential reasons so understood form what John Skorupski (2010: Ch. 3.1) describes as reasons that we act from, in a self-determining sense requiring the capacity to recognize and assess reasons as such.
3 The remaining subset is that of 'defeated motivators' (Dancy 2000: 4), also a subset of the reasons that we don't act upon ('con-reasons', to use David-Hillel Ruben's terminology (2009: 63–4)).
4 See Wittgenstein 1921: §1; Wittgenstein 1953: §95, §429; Frege 1956; White 1972; McDowell [1994] 1996: 27; Hornsby 1997b; and Dancy 2009b. The distinction is decent as far as it goes, but in the final section of this essay I call for further refinement.
5 As will become apparent, I also side with Dancy in rejecting the view that one can only act for the reason that p if it is indeed true that p. For the opposite view, that acting for the reason that p is the exercise of the ability that is knowledge that p, see Hyman (1999 and 2010; cf. Dancy 2011).
6 As Dancy notes, there is 'more than one way in which things can go wrong. The agent can be wrong about whether p, or wrong about whether if it were the case that p, that would be a reason for acting' (2008: 267; cf. Dancy 2000: 140 and Parfit 2011: Vol. 1, 150–64). I do not concern myself with the second way here, although my suggestions are compatible with its possibility. Mele (2007) argues that non-psychologists such as Dancy should take the possibility of agents performing actions that they mistakenly think of as being 'objectively favoured' to show that not all 'intentional, deliberate, purposeful' actions are performed for reasons, unless the concept of a reason geared towards action explanation is different from that geared towards evaluation (Mele's own view is that such conceptual matters should be experimentally informed).
7 This is not to side with realists such as Boghossian (2006) and Peacocke (2008) against pragmatists such as Rorty (1998) and Dummett (2006), but merely to note that we frequently use 'explanation' as shorthand for 'true explanation'. This is so whatever the precise relation of truth to justification, meaning and belief. Indeed, I am here agreeing with Rorty that 'the resolution of these debates will have no bearing on practice' (Rorty and Engel 2007: 34).

8 Ruben (2003: 185–6) points out that 'poor' may also be used as a relative term, both objectively and subjectively.
9 Mark Lance pointed out to me that Dancy is not committed to the view that theoretical explanation can be non-factive. This renders his stance less counter-intuitive than it might initially appear to be. Be that as it may, I see no reason to limit the thought that all genuine explanations are factive to the theoretical domain. If it is false that JD likes to shop for leather trousers, then the statement 'JD went to the Milan conference because he likes to shop for leather trousers' cannot explain why JD went to the Milan conference (even if he ended up buying several pairs of trousers during his visit). The same applies to teleological explanation: if it is false that he intended to purchase any leather trousers, then we cannot explain his going to Milan by stating that he went there in order to do so.
10 Dancy (2011: 350) claims that 'if we take the whole sentence to be the *explanans*, then of course all explanation is factive, but trivially so'. But we might equally complain that reasons-explanation is trivially non-factive if we take reasons to be the *explanantia*. In what follows, I argue that we should not even think they form a part of any given *explanans*.
11 Hence Anscombe's characterization of intentional actions as 'those to which a certain sense of the question "Why?" is given application' (1957: § 5).
12 See Chapter 7. For complications relating to emphasis and illocutionary force, see Achinstein 1983: 76–81. The similar, but considerably weaker, thesis that an *explanandum* is fixed only under sentential representation is briefly discussed by Kim ([1989] 1997: 275–6), who attributes the view to Hempel (1965: 421–2), with reference to Dretske's related suggestion that we may refer to 'alomorphs' that are akin to aspects of whatever it is we seek to explain (Dretske 1977).
13 This contrasts sharply with the knowledge case that Dancy claims is analogous. For, in the knowledge case, what is false is the very thing that is being put forth as a truth/knowledge/fact, whereas here the truth claim/assertion is not 'that p' but 'that his reason was that p' (Dancy 2000: 131–2).
14 See Sandis 2012: 71–81. According to Dancy, Smith's line of argument lends no support to psychologism, but only to the 'new theory' that motivating reasons are facts about our psychological states, and not the states themselves (Dancy 2000: 121ff.; cf. Dancy 2003b: 469). Smith, by contrast, sees no great tension, taking 'motivating reasons' to be explanatory (Smith 2004: 152) and arguing that all explanations of intentional action appeal to psychological states (Smith [1998] 2004: esp. 155–8; cf. Mele 2013).
15 Despite certain parallels in their conclusions, White's argument should be distinguished from W. V. O. Quine and A. N. Prior's suggestion (later also taken up by Davidson) that we should parse sentences of the form 'Arthur said that it was raining' as 'Arthur said that/it was raining' rather than 'Arthur said/that it was raining' (Quine 1960: 216; Prior 1963 and 1971: 16–22; cf. Davidson [1968] 2001). Anthony Kenny comes closer to White in responding to Prior with the added suggestion that expressions of the form 'it was raining' are not names either (Kenny 1963: 127). For objections to the Quine-Prior thesis, see White 1972: 80; Rundle 1979: 286–7; and Künne 2003: 68–9.
16 Davidson briefly looks into French usage but with an altogether different aim. In doing so, however, he tellingly misreads the 'que' in 'dit que' as a demonstrative (1968: 98–9).
17 A refreshing exception is Alfred Mele (2013: 167), who holds that 'even if all reasons for action are true propositions and true propositions can cause nothing, it cannot be inferred from this that causalism about action explanation is false'.

Chapter 10

1. Despite its name, John Rawls's *A Theory of Justice* (1975) is a transition work that falls between these two approaches. For evidence that it originally developed as a result of conceptual investigations and was only subsequently transformed (as the tide was changing against Wittgenstein) into something approaching a theory, see O'Neill 2014.
2. Some exceptions are Ezcurdia (1988), Baker (2004), Lalumera (2014) and Hacker (2018: 267–9). Only the last of these, however, uses the two terms to mark the precise distinction I am after. A comparison with the others would, alas, take us too far afield.
3. See also Rawls's Preface to the revised edition (1999: xi–xvi).
4. For example, whether they are mental representations, abilities or Fregean senses (see Margolis and Lawrence 2014: §I).
5. In this, water is disanalogous to something like justice, for there is no question about what justice *is* that isn't conceptual (see Hanfling 2000: 17ff.). Prima facie, reasons are more like justice than they are like water. And yet, I shall attempt to show that there remains an important sense in which two people can share the same concept of a reason but differ in the particulars of their conceptions. One explanation of how this is possible is that terms like 'motivating reason' are highly technical and can be defined in terms such as 'whatever it is that turns out to both motivate and rationalize action'.
6. See Wittgenstein (RPPII: §139; Z: 646). I leave aside here complications introduced by the Wittgensteinian notion of a family resemblance concept, save to say that this arguably does more damage than good in (i) supposing that it marks out a special subset of everyday concepts, and (ii) blurring the distinction between singularity and multiplicity of concepts of any one given thing (Beardsmore 1992; Sandis 2017c).
7. While the distinction between conceptual and ontological disputes is a popular one, there are good reasons for thinking that it is – in its most general form – spurious. Hanfling (2000) gives the example of petrol. It is of course part of the very concept of petrol that it is a certain kind if liquid. But its precise chemical composition is a further, non-conceptual, question. In the case of petrol, this latter question is chemical as opposed to ontological. But there is no reason to suppose that certain kinds of ontological questions can't also be bracketed from conceptual ones in the case of technical notions.
8. This third requirement is further complicated by competing conceptions if what an action is.
9. Hornsby (2008: 247ff.) distinguishes between two different 'everyday conceptions' of reasons as (a) fact-based and (b) belief-based. These are not meant to be in competition with one another and so in some ways more closely resemble two distinct concepts (one could ask one's interlocutor whether they were talking about f-based or b-based reasons; cf. Dancy 2008: 275). Indeed, Hornsby's b-based reasons are akin to my agential reasons, and her f-based ones to what I would call 'good grounds' (but see Hornsby 2008: 249–50).
10. See Chapter 7.
11. One need not be a monist or pluralist about the concept(s) expressed by *all* terms, though one could find evidence suggesting that *most* terms are best captured by one rather than the other.
12. See essays in D'Oro and Sandis 2013a.

13 To be motivated by something is to be *moved* by it to perform some action, or refrain from doing so. Not everything that moves us so is what we would ordinarily call a 'motive', the latter being a specific kind of motivator linked to character traits. While there is a conceptual connection between seeing something as valuable and being motivated to act accordingly (see Sandis 2015), we are often moved to act against our better judgement and can, equally, remain listless in spite of it. Although we can evaluate motives but not causes as being good and bad, all this entails is that it makes no sense to speak of a motive as being good or bad *qua* cause. One sort of pill may be better *at* causing drowsiness than another, but we don't thereby consider it to be a *better cause* of it. Likewise, greed may be a more efficient motivator of certain forms of behaviour than temperance.

14 But see Smith and Pettit 1997 for a proposed distinction between reasons that are normative and reasons that are (merely) good.

15 Dancy 2000: Ch. 6); Sandis 2012: Ch. 6). Skow (2016: 162) talks of purposes as (non-factive) reasons that are additional to (factive) agential ones, but enumerating them thus would seem to imply that they can be weighed or added, which cannot be the case.

16 Things would be different if Lou's reasoning was epistemically cagier, for example, 'Pusateri's *might* stock turmeric' or even 'they stock turmeric but it's possible that they have run out'. When modifying the example to discuss acting under false belief it is simplest to take the belief in question to be something like 'they will definitely have it' (see further discussion following).

17 Comesaña and McGrath (2014) argue that there are certain cases in which one can have a normative reason that *p*, even when it is not the case that *p*. I remain neutral on this question here, save to say that it is misleading to talk of 'false reasons' in such cases, as if it is the reason *itself* that is true or false. The mistake is to think of 'that *p*' as the name of some actual or imaginary entity (see Sandis 2012: 115–19).

18 Hornsby (2008: 249–50) maintains further that an agent may *have* a reason to do something even when here is *actually no reason* for them to do it (cf. Dancy 2008: 275).

19 See Hursthouse 1991; cf. Anscombe (1957: §§17ff.).

20 Dancy's anti-disjunctivism about RFAs leads to his trijunctive account of *acting for a reason* (Dancy 2000: 140), eventually paired down to a disjunctive one (Dancy 2008: 268ff.). For complications that contrast a conception of reasons as premises or assumptions with that of reasons as facts see Hyman 2011.

21 Things become even more complicated once we introduce different senses of the term 'action', which any given sense of RFAs may be better or worse suited to (see Sandis 2012a and 2012b). On the conception of actions as events of our doing things, it would just be wrong to claim that there are reasons *for* action (Sandis 2012: 29; cf. Stout 1996 and Skow 2016: 160).

Chapter 11

1 I shall use the terms 'mortal' and 'human' interchangeably, although mortal demi-gods are not purely human. I shall also use 'gods' to refer to gods, goddesses and daemons (be they nature deities or Olympians).

2 Ibid.: 31; cf. ibid. 7, 16, where he talks of such actions as over-determined events.

3 See Chapter 12. Cf. Nietzsche [1886] 1973: §68: '"I have done that" says my memory. "I cannot have done that" – says my pride, and remains adamant. At last – memory yields'.

4. Frankfurt (1988b) rightly further distinguishes the internal/external and the identification/alienation distinctions from the active/passive distinction, all of which he takes to somehow relate to the action/happening distinction.
5. See Chapter 12, §3.
6. I use 'ancient tragedy' to refer to both Greek *drama* and Greek and Roman *epic*. For the view that epic is not a proper form of tragedy, see Kitto 1951: 59f.
7. See also Kitto 1958: 53, 57.
8. Hegel 1835: 220ff. For related exegesis, see Westphal 2003: §5 and Inwood 1993: xxii, 103 [note 4 on XIV]). Cf. Nussbaum's anti-Hegelian (particularist) interpretation of *Antigone* (Nussbaum 2001: 67–79).
9. Kitto concedes that the divine may intervene in human affairs (e.g. he allows that Athena makes Ajax mad at the last moment) but claims that such intervention is 'confined to the plot' and 'does not affect the significance of the play, and is no part of Sophocles' philosophy or religion' (Kitto 1958: 56).
10. I am thinking here primarily of issues relating to action theory (agency, control, free will, responsibility, etc.) and to ethical conflicts such as that between individual and social good. Cf. White 2002. For a wonderfully informative examination of 'group identity' at drama festivals, see Hall 1997: 93–126.
11. Cf. Williams 1993: 29. See also Williams 2006.
12. Tanney (2008) neatly places the paper in its historical context, and urges for a resurrection of some of the views which Davidson rejected.
13. But see Collins 1987 for sensible reservations.
14. Since gods and mental states are frequently not only thought to be determinants of our behaviour, but also taken to be equally capable of explaining them, the worry operates at both a causal *and* an explanatory level.
15. See Davidson [1967] 2001: 129 for his related pessimism regarding the possibility of an analysis of the concept of agency in terms of other concepts.
16. Talk of 'what caused her to do *x*' need not imply determination of any kind (cf. Anscombe 1957: §§9–12).
17. Davidson unhelpfully oscillates between talk of what is free, what is voluntary, and what is in our control. My interest in this essay is confined to the last of these three (to what we can do *at will*), regardless of whether we do so voluntarily, under duress, and so on.
18. Linguistic nuances will vary, of course. The phrase 'X caused her to act', for example, typically seems to allow the agent more control over her action than the phrase 'X caused her to perform the action', presumably because in the former case the term 'cause' can be used in a figurative sense more readily. But the subtleties of ordinary speech should, in any case, be of no concern to causalists such as Davidson who are working with a fixed analysis of the logical form of singular causal statements such as 'the heat caused Samantha's return to Patma', according to which the term 'caused' means something like 'causally explains' where, crucially, the success of the explanation relies at the very least on its being true that 'if *A* causes *B*, there must be descriptions of *A* and *B* which show that *A* and *B* fall under a law' (Cf. Davidson [1967] 2001: 162, 262).
19. Davidson's claim that this states 'a mild form of internalism' (1969a: 26) is somewhat modest.
20. This is not to say that it renders epiphenomenal the reasons themselves for these could still structurally explain why an action was triggered by a certain event (see Dretske 1988).
21. Cf. Nietzsche's 'The Error of False Causality' ([1888] 1977: 64).

22 But see Price (2005). Cf. Stocker 2004: 303–4 and Railton 2004: 178–9.
23 See Chapter 4.
24 For Davidson's characterization of the classical conception, see Davidson 1969a: 35.
25 Here Raz also suggests that to follow one's will is to choose to act upon a reason (although not necessarily the one that you judge to be strongest).
26 Cf. Frankfurt 1988: 164 and Watson 1975: 218.
27 Goldman 1970: 72ff.
28 For example Goldman 1976: 81. See pp. 68–9 for his helpful overview of the philosophical history of the concept, as well as references to Sellars, herein.
29 Cf. Goldman 1970: 83.
30 Even this is contentious. If a part of me (say my heart) causes something (e.g. blood circulation) it does not obviously follow that *I* have caused my blood to circulate.
31 See Chapter 12.
32 See Baier 2008; Sandis 2019a: Ch.5.
33 Davidson [1969a] 2001: 36.
34 Frankfurt [1982] 1988: 86. For various interpretations, see Watson 2004: 100–22.
35 For the plausible view that Frankfurt's rejection of the weaker principle that 'a person is not morally responsible for what he has done if he did it because he could not have done otherwise' begs the question against libertarians and/or irreducible agent causation see Widerker 1995a: 247–261 and 1995b: 113–8, McCann 1998: 173–9, & O'Connor 2000: 81–4. Theoretically unmotivated criticisms may be found in Alvarez 2008.
36 It is tempting to write '*for* certain reasons' here, but it is unclear to me whether an agent whose will is both necessitated *and* necessitating could sensibly be said to act *in the light of* reasons.
37 See Sandis 2006.
38 See §4 this chapter.
39 Cf. Reid [1788] 1969: Ch. 1, Kenny 1975, Kane 1996: 33, McCann 1998. For the view that one can endorse a compatabilist interpretation of the principle of alternate possibilities see Watson 2004: 300–1.
40 For detailed criticism of the mechanistic aspect of causalist accounts see Malcolm 1968: 45–72.
41 One difference between the 'student' viewpoint and the one I shall be ascribing to the ancients is that the latter allow that alien forces may enable choice as much as they might prevent it.
42 Notwithstanding rare incidents of *single* divine causation in the heat of battle (where the lines between intentional action and non-intentional reaction begin to blur) such as that of Athene forcing a spear in Ares' belly in Book 5 of *The Iliad*.
43 This lack of space is variously understood by competing causalist views as being conceptual, metaphysical and/or physical.
44 For an account of the role of desire in reason-giving explanations of action, see Alvarez 2008.
45 See Williams 1993: 29–32 for examples and elaboration.
46 It is neither here nor there whether the causality in question here is determinist or indeterminist.
47 For Pre-Socratic interpretations of Aphrodite's role, see Barnes 1979: 117–18.
48 For the view that the category of 'the will' did not fully emerge until Aristotle, see Vernant 1988. My overall argument would not be affected if we chose to translate *boulesis* as 'wish' instead of 'will' (cf. André Rivier's work on necessity in Aeschylus).

49 See Williams 1993: Ch.3 for some interesting observations on the relation between responsibility and temporary losses of selfhood and/or control.
50 For a stock of examples from Euripides see Allan 2000: 246. I discuss issues relating to bad faith in §4, this chapter.
51 Baier (2008) gives a clear account of Hume's understanding of such processes.
52 Allan 2000: 239ff.
53 Ibid.: 265, n. 125.
54 Blackburn further embraces the view that attitudes have a standard motivational role. For a critique of this position, see Zangwill 2008.
55 Think, for example, of the impact of Agamemnon's actions at Aulis on Clytemnestra.
56 Cf. Burkert 1985: Ch. 3. As William Allan notes in relation to Euripides, they do so 'both as characters in the plays and as unseen, enigmatic agents shaping the action from outside' Allan 2000: 233. Allan also discusses Burkert and Vernant's contrasting approaches to how the gods are meant to be perceived before agreeing with Bremmer's suggestion that we should view them as both persons and powers, without characterizing their existence as being either 'fictive' or 'actual' (a point he takes from Sourvinou-Inwood): 'we might state that the gods, without necessarily being the gods that the audience believe in, are to be taken seriously as agents within the play, acting with both power and personality' (Allan 2000: 236).
57 Cf .Heidegger [1927] 1962, especially where 'Dasein's facticity' is defined in relation to, but also distinguished from 'factuality' (56) and where 'throwness' is defined in relation to 'facticity' (135).
58 Cf. Wittgenstein [1953] 2009: §174.
59 In Hazel E. Barnes' *key to special terminology*, which accompanies her landmark translation of Sartre's *Being and Nothingness*, facticity is defined as 'The For-itself's necessary connection with the In-Itself, hence with the world and its own past. It is what allows us to say that the For-itself is or exists. The facticity of freedom is the fact that freedom is not able to be free' (Sartre [1943] 1956: 631, cf. 439ff.).
60 Sartre [1943] 1956: 70: 'Good faith seeks to flee the inner disintegration of my being in the direction of the in-itself which it should be and is not. Bad faith seeks to flee the in-itself by means of the inner disintegration of my being [. . .] If it is indifferent whether one is in good or bad faith, because bad faith re-apprehends good faith and sides to the very origin of the project of good faith that does not mean that we cannot radically escape bad faith. But this supposes a self-recovery of being which was previously corrupted. This self-recovery we shall call authenticity. The description of which has no place here.' Catalano (1974: 89) captures Sartre's thought here well when he writes that 'bad faith is an attempt to flee from our freedom, whereas good faith is an attempt to face our freedom' (two pages earlier he explains how good and bad faith compare in their attitudes towards factual evidence).
61 Compare Nietzsche's 'error of false causality' ([1888] 1977: 64) with Sartre's own radical view was that motives were parts of actions rather than causes of them and that 'under no circumstances can the past in any way by itself produce an [intentional] act' (Sartre [1943] 1956: 436).
62 Cf. Nussbaum 2001 xii–xvi, 1–22, 378–94; Williams 1981: Ch. 2; Statman 1993a, 1993b; Athanassoulis 2005.
63 Heidegger relates facticity to what he calls 'fateful destiny', noting that 'our fates have already been guided in advance, in our Being with one another in the same world and in our resoluteness for definite possibilities' ([1927] 1962: 384).

64 Cf. Philips 2004: 175.
65 As William Allan writes (2000: 237): 'we simply do not know how far ordinary people thought in terms of gods rather than of human motives when interpreting the behaviour of others and of themselves'; a point he takes from Winnington-Ingram (1948).

Chapter 12

1 For the distinction between these two senses of desire, see Raz 1999: 50ff.
2 For exegesis and debate, see Tenenbaum 2007 and essays in Tenenbaum 2010.
3 Homeric man need not be in bad faith to experience the motivational forces of 'divine inspiration' as alien to oneself. The gods do not only interfere when there is a mismatch between action and intention. They are also present in actions that require great strength of will, typically identified with courage or heroism. Similarly, the inspired artist is said to have been visited by a Muse, the wise thinker by Athena, and so on. For an indication of the wide range of divine intervention, see Denham 2014: 142.
4 For a catalogue of differences between weakness of will and akrasia, see Holton 1999.
5 For the vexed question of double causation between the human and the divine, see Chapter 11.
6 There are, of course, individual exceptions, such as the artist who cites divine inspiration.
7 This passage is also quoted in Cottingham 1998: 147.
8 For related discussions of 'the trace', see Levinas ([1972] 2003: IX) and Ricoeur ([1986] 2008: II; [2000] 2004: Ch. 3).
9 For a comparison of the three philosophers on this point, see Sandis 2010. It is not inconceivable that Ross inherited this outlook from Collingwood, if not Bradley or Green.
10 Davidson was nonetheless a Freudian who maintained that weakness of will is often best explained by appeal to unconscious desire; see Davidson 1982.
11 See Sandis 2012: Ch. 2, §2. The issue might also be clarified this way: the object of the adverb 'intentionally' here is the verb 'marrying' and not the verbal phrase 'marrying his mother'.
12 Numerous tragic moments appear to hinge on the *Socratic Principle* that what we universally always most desire (*de dicto*) is 'the good' even if we do not always know what it is (see §1). What is tragic is that our deeds may be terrible even when the best of intentions are fulfilled.
13 But see Chapter 13.
14 See Jaeggi 2014 for an overarching account of alienation in the Hegelian-Marxist tradition, and Sandis 2010: V for a comparative analysis of Hegelian and Davidsonian approaches to Oedipus' actions.
15 See also lines 960ff., quoted in Chapter 13.
16 Cf. Williams 1993: 88–94, 219–23. For Williams this only requires that the behaviour was his in the broadest possible sense. On Hegel's view, by contrast, it must be an act (*Tun*) that ultimately stems from the person's will.
17 For the view that agents produce truths, see Melden 1961: 39ff. and Anscombe [1992] 2005: 156.

18 Denham (2014: 155–6) uses the example of a committed vegetarian, raised on a carnivorous diet she still craves, to neatly distinguish between repudiation and alienation.
19 Aristotle, Sartre and Gandhi have all proclaimed that 'we are the sum of our actions'. The lesson of §3 was that this had better include actions that we are not responsible for. But even taking this into account, this outlook seems to leave out both our motivations and our thoughts about them.
20 In George Stevens's loose film adaptation, *A Place in the Sun*, it's Roberta (renamed Alice Tripp) who capsizes the boat, by trying to stand up after Clyde (renamed George Eastman) has taken pity on her and clearly changed his mind. Eastman subsequently incriminates himself with testimony that reveals a mismatch between his confessed prior intention and the incident as he reports it: 'In the back of my mind was the thought of drowning her. But I didn't want to think such things! I couldn't help myself, I couldn't . . . I couldn't go through with it . . . I didn't kill her'.
21 This outlook is even more explicit in Stevens's film, in which the priest tells Eastman: 'They say only God and ourselves know what our sins and sorrows are. Perhaps in this case only God knows . . . perhaps you've hidden the full truth of this even from yourself.'
22 Frankfurt rightly distinguishes the internal/external and identification/alienation distinctions from the active/passive distinction, all of which he takes to relate to the action/happening distinction.
23 See Aguilar and Buckareff 2010: 13ff.
24 Cf. Nussbaum 2001, Williams 1976 and Nagel 1976.

Chapter 13

1 See Quante 1993: 16.
2 Gianfranco Soldati has convinced me that Husserl's talk of modes of presentation is preferable to that of descriptions (shared by both Hegel and contemporary Anglo-Saxon philosophers), for the application of the latter is limited to linguistic scenarios.
3 I use the following abbreviations: A: *Antigone*;
OT: *Oedipus the King*;
OC: *Oedipus at Colonus*. All references are to Sophocles 1982 (tr. R. Fagles). (Line numbers for the Greek text are given in square brackets.)
4 See, for example: Bradley [1909] 1950: 69ff.; Sheppard 1911: 114; Pinkard 2000: 210; Poole 2005: 58; Roche 2005, 2006; Houlgate 2007; and Wallace 2007: 123. Cf. Kaufmann 1968: 283, 286 for dissent from this thesis, with which I am in sympathy.
5 To my knowledge the parallels with Prichard and Ross have not been previously explored. Taylor (1979, [1983] 2010) and Quante ([1993] 2004) touch upon certain related affinities between Hegel and Anscombe; Quante also compares Hegel to Davidson, as does Knowles (2010), cf. Laitinen and Sandis 2010b.
6 In *After Virtue*, Alasdair MacIntyre similarly claims that moral conflict occurs when ethical disputants unknowingly inherit ethical fragments from conflicting social structures and traditions, their respective claims making relatively little sense outside of the practical contexts which gave rise to them. Hegel sees tragedy as arising solely from conflict between representative perspectives. For MacIntyre, by contrast, it

may equally result from conflict that is *internal* to the individual. Indeed, MacIntyre accuses Hegel of following Plato and Aristotle in holding that the Greek Polis was 'more harmonious than it actually was' (MacIntyre 1967: 199), when in actual fact 'the values of Greek tragedy express the conflicts of Greek society as much as the values of Plato and Aristotle express or attempt to depict Greek society as a unified structure' (ibid: 99; cf. MacIntyre 1988: Ch. 4).

7 The former side of this conflict amounts to what he elsewhere calls 'the will's right . . . to recognize as its action, and to accept responsibility for, only those presuppositions of the deed of which it was conscious in its aim and those aspects of the deed which were contained in its purpose' (*PR [i]*: §§ 117–18), as well as to the 'right of intention . . . that the universal quality of the action shall not merely be implicit but shall be known by the agent' (ibid. §120); the latter is more closely related – without being tantamount – to 'the right of the objectivity of action . . . to evince itself as known and willed by the subject as a *thinker*'(ibid.). See §4 for why none of this requires a conception of *the unconscious*.

8 Cf. *LA*: 1160 and Aristotle 1940: 1450a15–17.

9 See Laitinen and Sandis (2010a).

10 The emphasis in both sets of quotations that follow is my own.

11 In the same passage Bradley also asserts that we misunderstand Hegel if we take him to be discussing 'what we should generally call the moral quality of the acts and persons concerned, or, in the ordinary sense, what it was their duty to do'. He does not furnish the reader with a positive account of what sort of claims he thinks Hegel *was* discussing, but presumably takes them to relate to social and religious norms and expectations. Either way, the point about inference still stands.

12 This is no coincidence given their common inheritance of both Aristotelian and Kantian traditions.

13 Jean-Pierre Vernant (1988: 314–16) reminds us that the play begins with Antigone expressing loyalty to an *oikos* which 'she refuses to split between the brother who is loyal to the city and the one who died attacking it' but ends up becoming the 'immoderate defender' of an *oikos* that 'is the incestuous and monstrous family of Oedipus and the Labdacids'. Conversely, 'Creon, for his part, is not a legitimate city magistrate but one who his own son describes as "a tyrant, a woman, a child"'. For related insights, see Ricoeur 1992: 241–8 and Butler 2002.

14 For an investigation into the various political Antigones, see Steiner 1984: Ch. 2. A recent exception that avoids the flaw afflicting many political Antigones is Heaney's *Burial at Thebes*. Heaney has expressed his struggle to create a contemporary political adaptation as follows: 'Antigone is poetic drama, but commentary and analysis had turned it into political allegory. What I wanted to point up was the anthropological dimension of Sophocles's work: I didn't want the production to end up as just another opportunistic commentary on the Iraq adventure, and that was why I changed the title [. . .] it emphasizes [. . .] what Hegel emphasised about Antigone, those "Instinctive Powers of Feeling, Love and Kinship" which authority must honour and obey if it is not to turn callous' (Heaney 2005).

15 But contrast Westphal (1994, 2003: 60–4) to Markell (2003: 62–89).

16 See Gasché 2000: 47.

17 See Vernant 1988: 314.

18 For an in-depth analysis of Creon and Antigone's errors to which I am at greatly sympathetic, see Westphal 2003: Ch. 3. While I shall be concentrating on the *Philosophy of Right*, Westphal critiques the form of consciousness in the *Antigone* as

an illustration of Hegel's method in the *Phenomenology of Spirit*, demonstrating that contradictions do not only lie *between* the consciousnesses of individual characters but also *within* each of them then.
19   See Westphal 2003: 25.
20   See Wallace 2007: 122; but see too Easterling 1983: 141–2.
21   Freud, possibly inspired by Nietzsche ([1872] 1999: §9), attacks Sophocles for modifying the myth 'for theological purposes' (Freud 1900: 364; cf. Knox 1989: 46–7). For suspicions of psychoanalytic interpretations see Vernant 1988: IV and Sandis 2012.
22   See Dancy 2002: 246–7.
23   See Nussbaum (2001) for an in-depth survey of the Ancient notion of moral luck as it relates to tragedy.
24   See Chapter 12, §3.
25   Temporarily because in *OC* (li 481ff. [437ff.]) he describes his reaction as excessive.
26   For such Sophoclean allusions to knowledge see Knox 1979: 96–111. Dodds ([1951] 1983: 183) and Vernant (1983: 191) both maintain that it was Oedipus's stubborn pursuit of truth which pushed him towards his otherwise avoidable ruin (cf. Houlgate 2007: 173), to be distinguished from his (sealed) fate.
27   See Bowra 1944: 165.
28   In this passage, McDowell criticizes Robert Pippin's retrospective account of intention, according to which we can only know what we intended to do after the deed was done (cf. Pippin 2010).
29   For the distinction between guilt and shame as manifested in Greek epic and tragedy, see Williams 1993: 88–94, 219–23).
30   Quoted in Chapter 12.
31   See Chapter 12, §3. Williams (1993: 191, n. 37) notes that Oedipus had previously applied (the plural of) the same word to his murder of Laius at *OT*: li 303 [266].
32   Ross [1930] 2002: 42; see also Anscombe 1957 and Davidson [1985a] 2001: 298.
33   As suggested by Kundera (2007: 113) and Houlgate (2007: 158; 2010: 174).
34   It is worth noting that if we follow Taylor (1979, 1983) in reading Hegel's notion of Handlung as the *expression* (as opposed to causal effect) of the inner then deities so conceived cannot possibly be causes of action.
35   See Houlgate 2007: 148. Hegel proceeds to claim that the otherwise impotent humans procure 'an actual existence and an interest in acting' for the gods while, conversely, the godly parasites provide the 'ethical matter and the "pathos"' that distinguish actions from mere deeds (*PR*: §142).
36   Gasché (2000: 46–7) fails to observe that Hegel distinguishes these between two different understandings of double causation and as a result projects the epic interpretation onto the tragedy.
37   Cf. Dodds 1983: 182 and Kundera 2005: 114.

Chapter 14

1   One might additionally distinguish between acts and actions but this wouldn't affect anything I have to say here. For a puzzling attempt to map the act/action distinction onto that between doing and thing done, see Wiggins 2006: 97, n.8.
2   For complications that need not detain us here, see Hooker 2000: 1, n.2.

3 For Anscombe's refusal to distinguish between doings and things done, see Chapter 15.
4 See Hursthouse 1996: 19–33.
5 See Chapter 7.
6 See White 1972: 69–84.
7 For the philosophy of what we are doing when we say things, see Saul 2012.
8 For his development of Levinas and Derrida's theories of the trace, see Ricoeur [2000] 2004.
9 See Glock 1997: 98. I discuss the individuation of things done in Sandis 2012: 34, 150.
10 As the narrator of *In Search of Lost Time* puts it in in the closing passage of *Swann's Way*, '[t]he places we have known do not belong only to the world of space on which we map them for our own convenience. They were only a thin slice, held between the contiguous impressions that composed our life at the time [. . .] houses, roads, avenues are as fugitive, alas, as the years' (Proust [1913] 1992: 513).
11 Sandis 2012: 8, 33.
12 Just as there are different conceptions of the basic distinction between doings and things done, so there are different conceptions of each of the two things distinguished; the latter may differ even when there is agreement on the former.
13 Not everybody conceives of the doing/thing done distinction in even these general terms. For example, H. A. Prichard, G. H. von Wright and David Charles all think of the thing done as the bodily event that action results in; see Prichard 1932; von Wright 1963: 39; and Charles 2018.
14 Andreas Lind has convinced me that the employment of such biconditionals is often confused with regard to whether they are picking out meanings, right-makers, truth-conditions, or some other kind of thing.
15 Neglected exceptions include D'Arcy (1963) and Brown (1968).
16 Prichard's view of what sorts of things we are obliged to do would later change radically upon his embracing the conclusion that to act is to perform a mental activity of some kind (namely, to will something); see Prichard 1945.
17 In §5, I argue that Ross makes this point in a strikingly paradoxical manner precisely because he lacks the doing/thing done distinction.
18 Both are, of course, to be distinguished from doing something in the wrong way or manner, such as when one goes about doing something without the appropriate skill or know-how.
19 Moral particularism might be an exception here, at least if the particularist is willing to distinguish between type and token things done (see §4).
20 See also Audi (2021), published some years after I wrote this essay. I return to the evaluative/deontic distinction in §5.
21 The case of speech-acts in which two people utter the same words but with different meanings highlights a wider truth concerning the significance of *all* the things we do.
22 Hence Luke 22.33-4, which could be alluding to multiple actions, from killing the son of God to giving birth to the Christian religion: 'And when they came to the place that is called The Skull, there they crucified him, and the criminals, one on his right and one on his left. And Jesus said, "Father, forgive them, for they know not what they do".'
23 The latter view is implicitly endorsed in Parfit 2011.
24 Macmurray and Hornsby are right to claim that in everyday language we typically talk of things done, but, as noted in §1, this way of speaking is very loose.
25 Cf. Clark 1989: 199–210.

26 It should already be clear by now that I don't maintain that doings *are* processes and/or events.
27 Cf. Dancy 2009: 278–98).
28 As Hornsby ([1993b] 1997: 143–8) observes, Nagel (1986: 114) explicitly conflates things done with events.
29 The set of things we do, of course, includes speaking.
30 It is noteworthy that simple descriptions of things done (e.g. 'lying') may reveal the agent's intention but not their motive.
31 Yet it is events that have consequences (even if we might ordinarily speak of 'the things we do' having consequences).
32 A complication here is that we can of course find evidence for the occurrence of *events*, which J. L. Austin ([1954] 1961) famously views as closely allied to facts. Those who follow Austin in his critique of P. F. Strawson may prove more inclined to identify things done, and not doings, with events of some kind. While this temptation should be resisted, we would do equally well to avoid conflating one's doing *x* with the *event of* one's doing *x* (it only being sensible to apply moral properties to the former).
33 Other translations have variants of judge, reward or render to everyone according to their 'deeds' (*King James*) or 'works' (*English Standard Version*), the latter being the more accurate translation of the Greek 'ἔργα' and the Hebrew 'שׂחמע' found in many of the Old Testament Parallels (Job 34.11, Psalm 62.12, Proverbs 24.1, Ecclesiastes 3.17, Jeremiah 17.10 and Ezekiel 18.20 and 36.19; cf. Exodus 32.34).
34 For a deflationist interpretation of what Kant means by the motive of duty, see O'Neill 1991: 183.
35 This is in tension with those aspects of Mill's philosophy that seem to require actions to be events with causes and effects.
36 Hegel famously talks of the history's progress from the ancient ethical concern with pure objective deed (*Tat*) to the modern interest in the subjective element of action (*Handlung*). For how this relates to my concerns see Chapter 13, 'The Man Who Mistook His *Handlung* for a *Tat*'.
37 Cf .Scanlon 2008, esp. 122–7, 151–9.
38 I don't claim that this way of carving things up is the only one true to the facts, just that it does a better explanatory job than its competitors.
39 Cf. Mulligan 1988: 161–88 and Tappolet 2013.
40 Peter Geach (1956: 41ff.) argues that we should jettison the concept of right action and make do with talk of good and bad acts, which was good enough for Aquinas. His illustrations, however, betray a conflation of deeds with doings.
41 Cf. White 1972 and Lowy 1978: 105–8. A further question (an analogue of which appears in my discussion of Harman further) is whether the person's being justified to have the belief that *p* is identical to her believing that *p* being justified.
42 Perhaps it neither was nor wasn't right of me to do so.
43 Williams 1993: 68–70 and Parfit 1984: 34.
44 See §3 of Chapter 12, 'Motivated by the Gods'.
45 For insightful critical overviews of attempts to capture something similar by distinguishing the phenomenology of making art from that of spectating, see Crowell 2011: 31–53 and Kirkpatrick 2018.
46 In his Preface to the book, Rosenberg nonetheless talks of art in terms of 'things made', which he contrasts with 'deeds done'.

47 Marks which sell for grotesque amounts of money, but this arguably only serves to illustrate our fetishistic attachment to unique souvenirs such as the original reels of music or film. See Sandis 2017b.
48 As quoted in Rosenberg's Preface, referring to 'her generous review of this book'.
49 Victor Dura-Vila reminded me that aesthetics places no value in the artistic analogue of a 'pure will'. To this extent, all art theory is on Mill's side. There remains, nonetheless, the Collingwoodian understanding of art as the imaginative creation (Collingwood 1938: 128–34; Cf. Croce [1909] 1922).
50 See also Simpson 2012.
51 Note the allusion to Wittgenstein's famous rhetorical question, 'What is left over if I subtract the fact that my arm goes up from the fact that I raise my arm?' (Wittgenstein [1953] 2009: §621).
52 For a theological approach to the latter see Kirkpatrick 2017.
53 As with soup and things done, we can talk of things produced as either repeatables or particulars. P. F. Strawson ([1966] 2008: 202) writes: 'We should be able to speak of the same painting being seen by different people in different places at one time, in just the same way in which we now speak of the same sonata being heard by different people at different times in one place.' I concur, but leave it for another day to quibble over whether Pierre Menard's *Don Quixote* could have ever been an identical work to that of Cervantes.
54 This does not preclude the possibility of better understanding the things we do and create by situating them within the normative contexts of their production. For the convoluted question of what, if anything, it is to understand an act or artwork, see Sandis 2017a.

Chapter 15

1 It has also been present, not merely in Aristotle (*NE*) and Aquinas (*ST*: I–II,1–21), but across the entire history of modern moral philosophy from Suarez onwards (see essays in Sandis 2019b). The 'Morality' heading of Hegel's *Philosophy of Right* (*PR*: §§105–41) is of particular relevance to Anscombe's interests. For comparisons between Hegel and Anscombe see Taylor (1979, 1983), Quante (1993), and Laitinen and Sandis (2010b). For Aquinas and Anscombe, see Jensen (2010).
2 For the relation between Ross's use of the conjunction and his ethic of *prima facie* duties see Ross ([1930] 2002: 29).
3 Cf. Wiseman 2016b: 10–11.
4 See Hornsby 1993.
5 For contrast see Kant ([1788] 1997: 5, 147–8).
6 Strictly speaking, one could defend an identity theory between action event and thing done while still allowing for the subtler distinction between one's *doing* X and the event *of* one's doing X (see Sandis 2012: 33), but the stance seems eccentric.
7 It is perhaps no accident that Ross's discussion focuses much more on motives and Anscombe's on intention.
8 Earlier in the chapter, Joseph uses the locution 'it is said' before discussing views now associated with Ross's *The Right and the Good* (Joseph 1931: 37), which appeared in print only after Joseph's proofs had been corrected Joseph 1931: v).The revised 1933 edited adds a footnote to Ross's book on p. 19.

9 I owe this reference to Andreas Lind.
10 See Sandis 2017, 2021.
11 The general shape of Prichard's account is retained in the early work of Jennifer Hornsby, who replaces willing with trying (1980: 46 48, 60 63; retracted in Hornsby 2010).
12 For an earlier coinage by her see Berkman 2022.
13 See, for example, Diamond 1997, Teichmann 2008: 86, and Wiseman 2016a: 18.
14 Cf. M. Geach 2008: xvii.
15 Entire papers could be written about the degree to which this passage offers plausible interpretations of either Mill or Moore. There is room for disagreement, for example, on whether murder and theft could ever fall under Mill's 'knotty points' (Mill 1861: 25), the answer depending on whether he conceives of them as being unjust by definition (discussed further later).
16 In her 2022, Sophie Grace Chappell argues that Anscombe's main complaint is T3 and that T1 and T2 are 'little more than auxiliary theses'.
17 This is partly because Anscombe primarily conceives of 'consequentialism' as a view regarding the sphere of personal responsibility (see Frey 2019a: 10–12). For more on Mill's anti-consequentialist utilitarianism see Vogler 2001.
18 I owe this reference to Sophie Grace Chappell.
19 Coope 2006: 46ff. Although I agree with Coope on this point, I don't share the conception of justice he uses to frame it.
20 To this he sneeringly adds: 'We must charitably hope that for him the words of Caiaphas that he quotes just had the vaguely hallowed associations of a Bible text, and that he did not remember whose judicial murder was being counselled.'
21 Geach and Anscombe would presumably be equally hostile to the moral particularist claim that there are no principles concerning right action (e.g. Dancy 2004). But particularism at the level of *things done* may be combined with generalism at the level of character traits (Sandis 2020; 2021; cf. Swanton 2015). Were Anscombe open to a conceptual distinction between doings and things done (see §3) she could more easily allow for such a view, whose origins lie with Aristotle's thought that the mean is grasped through perception and not by reasoning (*EN*: 1109b; but see Price 2005).
22 Cf. Solomon 2008: 114 and Gremaschi 2017, the latter finding Anscombe's concerns much more parochial than the former.
23 Cf. Richter 2019. Doyle has since revised his view, but still maintains that Anscombe thought – and was right to think – that nothing could count as understanding the word 'moral' (Doyle 2019). This goes against the more natural reading of Anscombe's quasi-Nietzschean genealogy as having been at least partly motivated by Wittgenstein's thought that the meaning of any given term or expression is dependent upon the practices that give it life (see Sandis 2019a; cf. Frey 2018). Wittgenstein's influence on Anscombe's understanding of normativity is further made evident in her discussions of forcing and stopping modals (Anscombe 1969).
24 M. Geach 2005a; see also 2005b.
25 Anscombe became increasingly pessimistic about the latter happening on any kind of wide scale. Jennifer Frey informs me that Aquinas was far more sanguine on this front.
26 See, for example, Botterill and Caruthers 1999, Bermúdez 2005, Thagard 2007, and Weiskopf and Adams 2015.
27 For example, Block 1980.
28 See Sandis 2019b.

29 Anscombe's contention here remains unaffected by John Rawls's famous argument for the independence of moral theory from the sorts of issues he associates with epistemology and the philosophy of mind and language (Rawls 1975). But even if Rawls's argument could be extended to show that many issues in moral theory are independent from philosophical psychology, we should not expect a theory of right *action* to remain silent on the relation of action to motive, intention and consequence.
30 For an excellent account, see Wiseman 2016a: Ch. 2; 2016b: §3.
31 For a brief period, philosophy of mind was also called 'philosophy of psychology' (see, for example, Block 1980).
32 This is evident across all her work in ethics, but particularly so in Anscombe 1981 (for which, see Wiseman 2016b).
33 For more context see Hacker-Wright 2013: 107–9) and Coope 2015. Anscombe anticipates and rejects a crucial component of trolley reasoning in MMP (40). Sixty years later, philosophy's most prominent appearance in popular culture is in the trolley-obsessed *The Good Place*, in which one of central characters (Chidi Anagonye) is a 'Professor of Ethics *and* Moral Philosophy'. The droll conjunction reminds me of the first time I taught 'Ethics' for *Florida Institute of Technology*'s study abroad programme at Oxford. All of the other professors introduced themselves as teaching courses 'X' and 'Y' to great enthusiasm from the students. But when I introduced myself as the lecturer for 'Moral Philosophy', I was greeted with baffled silence, until one of the students hesitantly asked, 'Do you mean "Ethics"?', to all-round relief.
34 The word 'virtue' cannot be found in any of the three volumes of Parfit's *On What Matters*.
35 Andreas Lind has brought to my attention the fact that normative theories frequently conflate accounts of rightness *conditions* with accounts of right-/wrong-*making*.
36 See Sandis 2017. Schapiro (2001, 2021) and Hurley (2018) also argue that different *conceptions of action* render competing normative views plausible, but what they really have in mind are different *theories of agency*.
37 Cf. Wetzel 2006: §2.2 and Hanser 2008.
38 By contrast, we know what it is for an event to be considered non-morally good or bad for us or other creatures (e.g. for a drought to be a bad thing, and subsequent rain good).
39 Consequentialism and other mainstream normative theories involve the *promotion* of goodness (see Korsgaard 1993), while virtue ethics sees goodness as a (not necessarily causal) *mark* of right action, but neither approach offers accounts *of* good action.
40 Cf. Solomon 1988 and 2003; and Coope 2015.
41 The point is put forth with a panoply of arguments by Coope (2006: 26–39).
42 See Geach 2008: xvii-xviii. Roger Crisp has argued for a 'Utilitarianism of the Virtues' according to which the virtuous agent lives 'in such a way that the total amount of utility in the history of the world is brought as close as possible to the maximum' (Crisp 1992: 154; cf. Hursthouse 1999: 5, 7–8). More recently, Crisp has defended the additional view that if we understand virtue ethics as providing an account of right and wrong action (as Hursthouse does), then it collapses into a form of deontology. He suggests, further, that this can be avoided by focusing on the question of the *value* of virtue, as opposed to the notion of right action (Crisp 2015, 2019: 142–5; cf. Baron 1997 and Singleton 2002). Anscombe's insight, by contrast, is that we cannot even begin to answer questions concerning *right* action without understanding what it is to act virtuously. It would be a mistake, however, to attempt to transform such an understanding into a normative theory.

Appendix

1. *Physics* 256a6–8; cf. *The Bhagavad Gītā*, Ch. IV, lines 16ff.
2. Danto 1963: 435.
3. Danto's much anthologized early papers continue to receive the greater degree of commentary despite the fact that much of the debate is superseded by his later work.
4. But contrast Prichard ([1945] 2004: 11) and Chisholm (1966) to Frankfurt (1969).
5. For complications, see Danto 1963: 436 and 1973: 1–27). Danto also takes his view to have certain theological consequences (1963: 438, 445 and 1965: 142).
6. Danto 1965: 142; cf. Danto 1963: 436.
7. Stoutland 1968: 467; cf. Baier 1971: 163.
8. Danto 1965: 142. Danto's phrasing suggests that he sees no conceptual space for the possibility of one's either (i) causing an action *directly* or (ii) causing an action by doing something that is simultaneous with it.
9. See Candlish 1984 for the view that an action is basic *if and only if* it has no result.
10. See Danto 1973: 39, for example.
11. Von Wright 1963: 35ff. and Alvarez and Hyman 1998.
12. Locke [1689] 1975: 2.21.5ff., Reid [1788] 1969: 50, Prichard [1945] 2004 and McCann 1972, 1974.
13. Chisholm 1979: 371–2 and Taylor 1966: 111–12), respectively.
14. See O'Connor 2000: 43–60.
15. Compare to Dancy 1995.
16. Danto 1973: xi; see also his 1969 and 1979.
17. Danto 1973: 78 and 1979: 484–5.
18. Developed further in Baier 1976, and subsequently discussed in Baier 1985: 4–5.
19. Danto 1965: 145; retracted in Danto 1979: 472.
20. For instance, Brand (1968) and Goldman (1970: 24).
21. See Danto 1973: 28.
22. Cf. Danto 1965: 146.
23. Weil and Thalberg 1981; cf. Lowe 2003.
24. Weil and Thalberg 1974.
25. For Cambridge actions see Ruben 2010.
26. See also Ginet 1982: 60 and Mackie 1997.
27. See Lowe 1981 and Weintraub 2003; cf. Hornsby 1982.
28. O'Connor 2000: 52–5, 61.
29. See Sorensen 1985, Dretske 1988: 20–1, Sandis 2006: 181; cf. Wittgenstein [1953] 2009: §71, Dennett (1978) commits the parallel fallacy of thinking that *spatial* imprecision with regard to the location of persons is philosophically problematic.

References

Achinstein, P. (1975), 'The Object of Explanation', in S. Körner (ed), *Explanation*, 1–45, Oxford: Blackwell.
Achinstein, P. (1983), *The Nature of Explanation*, New York, NY: Oxford University Press.
Ackrill, J. L. (1978), 'Aristotle on Action', *Mind*, 87 (348): 595–601.
Adams, R. M. (1979), 'Divine Command Metaethics Modified Again', *The Journal of Religious Ethics*, 7 (1): 66–79.
Aeschylus (1922), *Persians*, trans. H. W. Smyth, Portsmouth, NH: Heinemann.
Aguilar, J. H. and A. A. Buckareff, eds. (2010), *Causing Human Actions: New Perspectives on the Causal Theory of Action*, Cambridge, MA: MIT Press.
Allan, W. (2000), *The Andromache and Euripidean Tragedy*, Oxford: Oxford University Press.
Alvarez, M. (2008), 'Actions, Thought-Experiments, and the "Principle of Alternate Possibilities"', *The Australasian Journal of Philosophy*, 87 (1): 61–81.
Alvarez, M. (2010), *Kinds of Reasons: An Essay in the Philosophy of Action*, Oxford: Oxford University Press.
Alvarez, M. and J. Hyman (1998), 'Agents and their Actions', *Philosophy*, 73 (2): 218–45.
Annas, J. (2011), *Intelligent Virtue*, Oxford: Oxford University Press.
Anscombe, G. E. M. (1981), 'Mr. Truman's Degree (privately produced pamphlet)', as reprinted in her *Metaphysics and the Philosophy of Mind (The Collected Philosophical Papers of G. E. M. Anscombe, Volume 2)*, 62–71, Minneapolis, MN: University of Minnesota Press.
Anscombe, G. E. M. (1957), *Intention*, Oxford: Basil Blackwell.
Anscombe, G. E. M. (1958), 'Modern Moral Philosophy [MMP]', *Philosophy*, 33 (124): 1–9.
Anscombe, G. E. M. ([1962] 1981), 'Authority in Morals', in J. Todd (ed), *Problems of Authority*, London: Darton, Longman and Todd, 1962; reprinted in *Ethics, Religion and Politics (The Collected Philosophical Papers of G. E. M. Anscombe, Volume 3)*, 43–50, Minneapolis, MN: University of Minnesota Press.
Anscombe, G. E. M. (1965), 'Thought and Action in Aristotle: What Is Practical Truth?', in J. R. Bambrough (ed), *New Essays on Plato and Aristotle*, 143–58, London: Routledge and Kegan Paul.
Anscombe, G. E. M. (1969), 'On Promising and Its Justice, and Whether It Needs Be Respected in Foro Interno', *Critica*, 3 (7/8): 61–83.
Anscombe, G. E. M. ([1978] 1981), 'On the Source of the Authority of the State', *Ratio*, 20, as reprinted in her *Metaphysics and the Philosophy of Mind (The Collected Philosophical Papers of G. E. M. Anscombe, Volume 2)*, 130–55, Minneapolis, MN: University of Minnesota Press.
Anscombe, G. E. M. ([1979] 1981), 'Under a Description', as reprinted in her *Metaphysics and the Philosophy of Mind: Collected Philosophical Papers Volume II*, 208–19, Oxford: Blackwell.
Anscombe, G. E. M. ([1982] 2008), 'Morality', in C. Marneau (ed), *Pro Ecclesia et Pontifice*, 16–18; as reprinted in M. Geach and l. Gormally (eds), *Faith in a Hard Ground: Essays*

on Religion, Philosophy, and Ethics by G. E. M. Anscombe, 113–16, Exeter: Imprint, to which any page numbers given refer.
Anscombe, G. E. M. ([1992] 2005), 'Practical Truth', in J. M. Dolan (ed), *Working Papers in Law, Medicine and Philosophy*, Minneapolis, MN: University of Minnesota Press; as reprinted in M. Geach and l. Gormally (eds), *Human Life, Action and Ethics: Essays by G. E. M. Anscombe*, 149–58, Exeter: Imprint Academic, 2005, to which any page numbers given refer.
Anscombe, G. E. M. (2008a), 'Reasons and the Ambiguity of "Belief"', *Philosophical Explorations*, 11 (1): 53–65.
Anscombe, G. E. M. (2008b), 'The Moral Environment of the Child', undated manuscript first published in M. Geach and L. Gormally (eds), *Faith in a Hard Ground: Essays on Religion, Philosophy, and Ethics by G. E. M. Anscombe*, 224–33, Exeter: Imprint.
Anscombe, G. E. M. (2009), 'Reasons, Desires and Intentional Actions', in C. Sandis (ed), *New Essays on the Explanation of Action*, 203–19, Basingstoke: Palgrave Macmillan.
Anscombe, G. E. M. and S. Morgenbesser (1963), 'The Two Kinds of Error in Action', *Journal of Philosophy*, 60 (14): 393–401.
Arendt, H. ([1958] 1998), *The Human Condition*, 2nd edn, Chicago, IL: The University of Chicago Press.
Aristotle (1953), *[NE], Ἠθικὰ Νικομάχεια* [Nichomachean Ethics], trans. J. A. K. Thomson, London: Penguin.
Aristotle (1894), *[EN], Ethica Nicomachea*, ed. I. Bywater, Oxford: Clarendon Press.
Aristotle (1979), *[DMA], De Motu Animalium* [Movements of Animals], trans. M. Nussbaum, Princeton, NJ: Princeton University Press.
Aronson, E. (1956), *When Prophecy Fails*, New York, NY: Harper.
Ash, T.-G. (1997), *The File*, London: Random House.
Athanassoulis, A. (2005), *Morality, Moral Luck and Responsibility: Fortune's Web*, New York: Palgrave Macmillan.
Audi, R. (2004), *The Good in the Right: A Theory of Intuition and Intrinsic Value*, Princeton, NJ: Princeton University Press.
Audi, R. (2021), 'Acting Rightly: Three Dimensions of Moral Conduct', *Ratio*, 34 (1): 56–67.
Austin, J. L. ([1954] 1961), 'Unfair to Facts', *Proceedings of the Aristotelian Society*, Supplementary Volume XXIV, reprinted in his Philosophical Papers, 154–74, Oxford: Clarendon Press, 1961, to which any page numbers refer.
Austin, J. L., P. F. Strawson and D. R. Cousin (1950), 'Truth', *Aristotelian Society Supplementary*, 24: 111–72.
Bach, K. (1980), 'Actions Are Not Events', *Mind*, 89 (353): 114–20.
Bach, K. (2010), 'Refraining, Omitting, and Negative Acts', in T. O'Connor and C. Sandis (eds), *A Companion to the Philosophy of Action*, 50–7, Oxford: Wiley-Blackwell.
Baier, A. C. (1971), 'The Search for Basic Actions', *American Philosophical Quarterly*, 8 (2): 161–70.
Baier, A. C. (1972), 'Ways and Means', *Canadian Journal of Philosophy*, 1 (3): 275–93.
Baier, A. C. (1976), 'Mixing Memory and Desire', *American Philosophical Quarterly*, 13 (3): 213–20; as reprinted in Baier (1985: 8–21).
Baier, A. C. (1985a), *Postures of the Mind: Essays on Mind and Morals*, London: Methuen.
Baier, A. C. (1985b), 'Rhyme and Reason: Reflections on Davidson's Version of Having Reasons', in Lepore and McLaughlin (eds), *Actions and Events: Perspectives on the Philosophy of Donald Davidson*, 116–29, Oxford: Blackwell.

Baier, A. C. (2008), 'Acting in Character', in C. Sandis (ed), *New Essays on the Explanation of Action*, 241–56, Basingstoke: Palgrave Macmillan, 2009.
Bain, A. (1884), *Education as a Science*, New York: D. Appleton and Co.
Baker, G. (2004), 'Wittgenstein: Concepts or Conceptions?' in K. Morris (ed), *Wittgenstein's Method: Neglected Aspects*, Oxford: Blackwell.
Barber, M. (2004), *Anthony Powell: A Life*, London: Duckworth.
Barnes, J. (1979), *The Presocratic Philosophers*, London: Routledge.
Barney, R. (2010), 'Plato on the Desire for the Good', in S. Tenenbaum (ed), *Desire, Practical Reason and the Good*, 34–64, Oxford: University Press.
Baron, M. (1997), 'Kantian Ethics', in M. W. Baron, P. Pettit and M. Slote (eds), *Three Methods of Ethics*, 3–91, Oxford: Blackwell.
Beardsmore, R. W. (1992), 'The Theory of Family Resemblances', *Philosophical Investigations*, 15 (2): 131–46.
Beeghly, E. and A. Madva (2020), *An Introduction to Implicit Bias: Knowledge, Justice, and the Social Mind*, London: Routledge.
Bennett, J. (1973), 'Shooting, Killing and Dying', *Canadian Journal of Philosophy*, 2 (3): 315–23.
Bennett, J. (1981), *Morality and Consequences: The Tanner Lectures on Human Values*, Salt Lake City: University of Utah Press.
Bennett, J. (1995), *The Act Itself*, Oxford: Oxford University Press.
Bennett, M. R. and P. M. S. Hacker (2003), *Philosophical Foundations of Neuroscience*, Oxford: Blackwell.
Bentham, J. (1789), *An Introduction to the Principles of Morals and Legislation*, London: Payne and Son.
Berkman, J. (2022), 'Justice and Murder: The Backstory to Anscombe's "Modern Moral Philosophy"', in R. Teichmann (ed), *The Oxford Handbook of Elizabeth Anscombe*, 225–70, Oxford: Oxford University Press.
Bermúdez, J. L. (2005), *Philosophy of Psychology: A Contemporary Introduction*, London: Routledge.
Bernays, E. ([1928] 2005), *Propaganda*, New edn, Oxford: IG Publishing.
The Bhagavad Gītā [BG] (1994), trans. W. J. Johnson, Oxford: Oxford University Press.
Bhaktivedanta Swami Prabhupada, A. C. (1972), *Bhagavad Gītā - As It Is*, 2nd edn, Los Angeles, CA: The Bhaktivedanta Book Trust.
Birns, N. (2004), *Understanding Anthony Powell*, Columbia, SC: University of South Carolina Press.
Bittner, R. (2001), *Doing Things for Reasons*, Oxford: Oxford University Press.
Blackburn, S. (1998), *Ruling Passions*, Oxford: Clarendon Press.
Blackburn, S. (2005), 'Anscombe's Ethics', letter to *Times Literary Supplement*, 14 October.
Block, N., ed. (1980), *Readings in Philosophy of Psychology*, Vol. 1, Cambridge, MA: Harvard University Press.
Bloom, H., ed. (1987), *Modern Critical Views: George Bernard Shaw*, New York, NY: Chelsea House Publishers.
Boghossian, P. (2006), *Fear of Knowledge: Against Relativism and Constructivism*, Oxford: Oxford University Press.
Bond, E. J. (1983), *Reason and Value*, Cambridge: Cambridge University Press.
Borges, J. L. (1942), 'Funes el memorioso', *La Nación*, June.
Botteril, G. and P. Caruthers (1999), *The Philosophy of Psychology*, Cambridge: Cambridge University Press.
Bowra, C. M. (1944), *Sophoclean Tragedy*, Oxford: Clarendon Press.

Bowra, C M. (1957), *The Greek Experience*, London: Weidenfeld and Nicholson.
Bradley, A. C. ([1909] 1950), *Oxford Lectures on Poetry*, 2nd edn, London: Macmillan.
Brand, M. (1968), 'Danto on Basic Actions', *Noûs*, 2 (2): 187–90.
Brand, M. (1971), 'The Language of Not Doing', *American Philosophical Quarterly*, 8 (1): 45–53.
Brand, M. and W. Walton, eds. (1976), *Action Theory*, Dordrecht: Reidel Publishing.
Brandom, R. B. (2019), *A Spirit of Trust: A Reading of Hegel's Phenomenology*, Boston, MA: Harvard University Press.
Bratman, M. (2004), 'Shared Valuing and Frameworks for Practical Reasoning', in R. Wallace, P. Pettit, S. Scheffler and M. Smith (eds), *Reason and Value: Themes from the Moral Philosophy of Joseph Raz*, 1–27, Oxford: Clarendon Press.
Brecht, B. ([1936] 1964), 'Theatre for Pleasure or Theatre for Instruction', as published in (ed. & trans.) J. Willett, *Brecht on Theatre: The Development of an Aesthetic*, 131–8, London: Methuen.
Bremmer, J. N. (1999), *Greek Religion*, Cambridge: Cambridge University Press.
Brewer, T. (2009), *The Retrieval of Ethics*, Oxford: Oxford University Press.
Broome, J. (2004), 'Reasons', in R. Wallace, P. Pettit, S. Scheffler and M. Smith (eds), *Reason and Value: Themes from the Moral Philosophy of Joseph Raz*, 28–55, Oxford: Clarendon Press.
Broome, J. (2013), *Rationality Through Reasoning*, Oxford: Wiley-Blackwell.
Brown, D. G. (1968), *Action*, London: George Allen and Unwin.
Burke, K. (1950), *The Rhetoric of Motives*, New York, NY: Prentice-Hall.
Burkeman, O. (2005), 'Five Reasons Why We Should All Learn How to Do Nothing: The Do Something Guide to Doing Nothing', *The Guardian*, 9 January. Available online: https://www.theguardian.com/lifeandstyle/2015/jan/09/five-reasons-we-should-all-learn-to-do-nothing (accessed 31 January 2023).
Burkert, W. (1985), *Greek Religion*, Oxford: Blackwell.
Burton, R. ([1628] 2001), *The Anatomy of Melancholy*, 2001 edn, New York, NY: New York Review of Books.
Bushnell, R., ed. (2005), *A Companion to Tragedy*, Oxford: Wiley-Blackwell.
Bushnell, R. (2008), *Tragedy: A Short Introduction*, Oxford: Wiley-Blackwell.
Butler, J. (2002), *Antigone's Claim: Kinship Between Life and Death*, New edn, New York, NY: Columbia University Press.
Cabanac, M. (1979), 'Sensory Pleasure', *The Quarterly Review of Biology*, 54 (1): 1–29.
Candlish, S. (1984), 'Inner and Outer Basic Action'. *Proceedings of the Aristotelian Society*, 84 (1): 83–102.
Carr, E. H. (1961), *What Is History?* London: Macmillan.
Carroll, L. (1871), *Through the Looking Glass*, London: Macmillan.
Carruthers, P. (2011), *The Opacity of Mind: An Integrative Theory of Self-Knowledge*, Oxford: Oxford University Press.
Catalano, J. S. (1974), *A Commentary on Jean-Paul Sartre's Being and Nothingness*, Chicago, IL: University of Chicago Press.
Chalmers, D. (1996), *The Conscious Mind: In Search of a Fundamental Theory*, Oxford: Oxford University Press.
Changeux, J.-P. and P. Ricoeur (2000), *What Makes Us Think?: A Neuroscientist and a Philosopher Argue about Ethics, Human Nature, and the Brain*, Princeton, NJ: Princeton University Press.
Chappell, S. G. (2022), 'Anscombe's Three Theses After Sixty Years: Modern Moral Philosophy, Polemic, and "Modern Moral Philosophy"', in R. Teichmann (ed), *The Oxford Handbook of Elizabeth Anscombe*, 91–117, Oxford: Oxford University Press.

Chappell, V. C. (1963), 'Causation and the Identification of Actions: Comments', *The Journal of Philosophy*, 60 (23): 700–1.
Charles, D. (1984), *Aristotle's Philosophy of Action*, London: Duckworth.
Charles, D. (2018), 'Processes, Activities and Actions', in R. Stout (ed), *Process, Action and Experience*, 20–40, Oxford: Oxford University Press.
Charlton, W. (1988), *Weakness of Will – A Philosophical Introduction*, Oxford: Blackwell.
Chisholm, R. M. (1964), 'The Descriptive Element in the Concept of Action', *Journal of Philosophy*, 61 (20): 613–24.
Chisholm, R. M. (1966), 'Freedom and Action', in K. Lehrer (ed), *Freedom and Determinism*, 11–44, New York, NY: Random House.
Chisholm, R. M. (1979), 'Objects and Persons: Revisions and Replies', in E. Sosa (ed), *Essays on the Philosophy of Roderick Chisholm*, 317–88, Amsterdam: Rodopi.
Clark, R. (1989), 'Deeds, Doings and What Is Done: The Non-extensionality of Modifiers', *Noûs*, 23 (2): 199–210.
Collingwood, R. G. (1938), *Principles of Art*, Oxford: Clarendon Press.
Collins, A. W. (1997), 'The Psychological Reality of Reasons', *Ratio*, 10 (2): 108–23.
Collins, A. W. (1987), *The Nature of Mental Things*, Notre Dame, IA: University of Notre Dame Press.
Collins, J., N. Hall and L. A. Paul (2004), *Causation and Counterfactuals*, Cambridge, MA: MIT Press.
Comesaña, J. and M. McGrath (2014), 'Having False Reasons', in C. Littlejohn and J. Turi (eds), *Epistemic Norms: New Essays on Action, Belief, and Assertion*, 59–79, Oxford: Oxford University Press.
Coope, C. (2006), 'Modern Virtue Ethics', in T. Chappell (ed), *Values and Virtues: Aristotelianism in Contemporary Ethics*, 20–52, Oxford: Oxford University Press.
Coope, C. (2015), 'Review of David Edmonds' *Would You Kill the Fat Man?*', *The Philosophical Quarterly*, 65 (259): 275–313.
Cottingham, J. (1998), *Philosophy and the Good Life*, Cambridge: Cambridge University Press.
Cottingham, J. (2008), 'The Self, The Good Life and the Transcendent', in N. Athanassoulis and S. Vice (eds), *The Moral Life: Essays in Honour of John Cottingham*, 231–74, Basingstoke: Palgrave Macmillan.
Cowley, A. (1656), *Pindarique Odes*, London: Humphrey Moseley.
Crampton, G. R. (1974), *The Condition of Creatures: Suffering and Action in Chaucer and Spenser*, New Haven, CT: Yale University Press.
Crisp, R. (1992), 'Utilitarianism and the Life of Virtue', *The Philosophical Quarterly*, 42 (167): 139–60.
Crisp, R. (2015), 'A Third Method of Ethics?', *Philosophy and Phenomenological Research*, 90 (2): 257–73.
Crisp, R. (2019), *Sacrifice Regained: Morality and Self-Interest in British Moral Philosophy from Hobbes to Bentham*, Oxford: Oxford University Press.
Croce, B. ([1909] 1922), *Aesthetic: As Science of Expression and General Linguistic*, trans. D. Ainslee, London: Macmillan.
Crompton, L. (1987), 'Caesar and Cleopatra', in H. Bloom (ed), *Modern Critical Views: George Bernard Shaw*, 85–98, New York, NY: Chelsea House Publishers.
Crowell, S. (2011), 'Phenomenology and Aesthetics; or Why Art Matters', in J. Parry (ed), *Art and Phenomenology*, 31–53, London: Routledge.
Dancy, J. (1993), *Moral Reasons*, Oxford: Blackwell.

Dancy, J. (1995a), 'Why There Is Really No Such Thing as the Theory of Motivation', *Proceedings of the Aristotelian Society*, 95 (1): 1–18.
Dancy, J. (1995b), 'Arguments from Illusion', *Philosophical Quarterly*, 45 (181): 421–38.
Dancy, J. (2000), *Practical Reality*, Oxford: Oxford University Press.
Dancy, J. (2002), 'Prichard on Duty and Ignorance of Fact', in P. Stratton-Lake (ed), *Ethical Intuitionism: Re-evaluations*, 229–47, Oxford: Oxford University Press.
Dancy, J. (2003a), 'A Précis of *Practical Reality*', *Philosophy and Phenomenological Research*, 67 (2): 423–8.
Dancy, J. (2003b), 'Replies', *Philosophy and Phenomenological Research*, 67 (2): 468–90.
Dancy, J. (2004a), *Ethics Without Principles*, Oxford: Oxford University Press.
Dancy, J. (2004b), 'Enticing Reasons', in R. Wallace, P. Pettit, S. Scheffler and M. Smith (eds), *Reason and Value: Themes from the Moral Philosophy of Joseph Raz*, 91–118, Oxford: Clarendon Press.
Dancy, J. (2004c), 'Two Ways of Explaining Actions', in J. Hyman and H. Steward (eds), *Action and Agency*, 25–42, Oxford: Oxford University Press.
Dancy, J. (2008), 'On How to Act Disjunctively', in A. Haddock and F. Macpherson (eds), *Disjunctivism: Perception, Action, Knowledge*, 262–80, Oxford: Oxford University Press.
Dancy, J. (2009a), 'Action in Moral Metaphysics', in C. Sandis (ed), *New Essays on Action Explanation*, 396–415, London: Palgrave Macmillan.
Dancy, J. (2011), 'Acting in Ignorance', *Frontiers of Philosophy in China*, 6 (3): 345–57.
Dancy, J. (2014), 'On Knowing One's Reasons', in C. Littlejohn and J. Turi (eds), *Epistemic Norms: New Essays on Action, Belief, and Assertion*, 81–96, Oxford: Oxford University Press, 2014.
Dancy, J. (2018), *Practical Shape: A Theory of Practical Reasoning*, Oxford: Oxford University Press.
Dancy, J. (2020), 'Précis of *Practical Shape*', *Philosophical Explorations*, 23 (2): 130–4.
Danto, A. C. (1963), 'What We Can Do', in S. Morgenbesser (ed), *Symposium: Human Action (Journal of Philosophy)*, 60 (15): 435–45.
Danto, A. C. (1965), 'Basic Actions', *American Philosophical Quarterly*, 2 (2): 141–8.
Danto, A. C. (1966), 'Freedom and Forbearance', in K. Lehrer (ed), *Freedom and Determinism*, 45–63, New York, NY: Random House.
Danto, A. C. (1969), 'Complex Events', *Philosophy and Phenomenological Research*, 30 (1): 66–77.
Danto, A. C. (1973), *Analytic Philosophy of Action*, Cambridge: Cambridge University Press.
Danto, A. C. (1979), 'Basic Actions and Basic Concepts', *Review of Metaphysics*, 32 (3): 471–85.
D'Arcy, E. (1963), *Human Acts: An Essay in Their Moral Evaluation*, Oxford: Oxford University Press.
Davidson, D. ([1963] 2001), 'Actions, Reasons, and Causes', *Journal of Philosophy*, 60: 685–700; as reprinted in D. Davidson (2001: 3–19), to which any page references refer.
Davidson, D. ([1967] 2001), 'The Logical Form of Action Sentences', in N. Rescher (ed), *The Logic of Decision and Action*, Pittsburgh: University of Pittsburgh Press; as reprinted with 'Criticism, Comment, and Defence', in Davidson, D. (2001: 105–48), to which any page numbers given refer.
Davidson, D. ([1968] 2001), 'On Saying That', in his *Inquiries into Truth and Interpretation*, 2nd revised edn, 93–108, Oxford: Oxford University Press.

Davidson, D. ([1969a] 2001), 'How Is Weakness of the Will Possible?' in J. Feinberg (ed), *Moral Concepts*, Oxford: University Press; as reprinted in D. Davidson, *Essays on Actions and Events*, 2nd revised edn, 21–42, Oxford: Clarendon Press, 2001, to which any page references refer.

Davidson, D. ([1969b] 2001), 'The Individuation of Events', in N. Rescher (ed), *Essays in Honor of Carl G. Hempel*, 216–34, Dordrecht: D. Reidel; as reprinted in D. Davidson, *Essays on Actions and Events*, 2nd revised edn, 13–80, Oxford: Clarendon Press, 2001, to which any page numbers given refer.

Davidson, D. ([1971] 2001), 'Agency', in R. Binkley, R. Bronaugh and A. Marras (eds), *Agent, Action, and Reason*, Toronto: University of Toronto Press; as reprinted in D. Davidson, *Essays on Actions and Events*, 2nd revised edn, 43–62, Oxford: Clarendon Press, 2001, to which any page numbers given refer.

Davidson, D. ([1973] 2001), 'Freedom to Act', in T. Honderich (ed), *Essays on Freedom of Action*, London: Routledge and Kegan Paul; as reprinted in D. Davidson, *Essays on Actions and Events*, 2nd revised edn, 63–82, Oxford: Clarendon Press, 2001, to which any page numbers given refer.

Davidson, D. ([1974] 2001), 'Psychology as Philosophy', in S. C. Brown (ed), *Philosophy of Psychology*, London: Macmillan; as reprinted with 'Comments and Replies', in D. Davidson, *Essays on Actions and Events*, 2nd revised edn, 229–44, Oxford: Clarendon Press, 2001, to which any page numbers given refer.

Davidson, D. ([1976] 2001), 'Hempel on Explaining Action', as reprinted in D. Davidson, *Essays on Actions and Events*, 2nd revised edn, 261–76, Oxford: Clarendon Press, 2001, to which any page numbers given refer.

Davidson, D. ([1978] 2001), 'Intending', as reprinted in D. Davidson, *Essays on Actions and Events*, 2nd revised edn, 84–102, Oxford: Clarendon Press, 2001, to which any page numbers given refer.

Davidson, D. ([1982] 2004), 'Paradoxes of Irrationality', in R. Wollheim and J. Hopkins (eds), *Philosophical Essays on Freud*, 289–305, Cambridge: Cambridge University Press; as reprinted in D. Davidson, *Problems of Rationality*, 169–87, Oxford: Clarendon Press, 2004, to which all page references refer.

Davidson, D. ([1985a] 2001), 'Adverbs of Action', in B. Vermazen and M. B. Hintikka (eds), *Essays on Davidson: Actions and Events*, 230–41, Oxford: Oxford University Press; as reprinted in D. Davidson, *Essays on Actions and Events*, 2nd revised edn, 293–304, Oxford: Clarendon Press, 2001, to which any page numbers given refer.

Davidson, D. (1985b), 'Reply to Bruce Vermazen', in B. Vermazen and M. B. Hintikka (eds) *Essays on Davidson: Actions and Events*, 217–21, Oxford University Press.

Davidson, D. (1999), 'Reply to Jennifer Hornsby', in L. E. Hahn (ed), *The Philosophy of Donald Davidson*, Library of Living Philosophers, 636–40, Chicago and La Salle, IL: Open Court Publishing, 1999.

Davidson, D. (2001a), *Essays on Actions and Events*, 2nd revised edn, Oxford: Clarendon Press.

Davidson, D. (2001b), *Inquiries into Truth and Interpretation*, 2nd revised edn, Oxford University Press.

Davidson, D. (2004), *Problems of Rationality*, Oxford: Clarendon Press.

Davies, D. (2004), *Art as Performance*, Oxford: Blackwell.

Davis, N. (1991), 'Contemporary Deontology', in P. Singer (ed), *A Companion to Ethics*, 205–18, Oxford: Blackwell.

Davis, W. A. (2003), 'Psychologism and Humeanism', *Philosophy and Phenomenological Research*, 67 (2): 452–9.

de Beauvoir, S. (1985), 'Preface' to C. Lanzmann, *Shoah*, New York, NY: Da Capo Press.
de Beistegui, M. (2000), 'Hegel: Or the Tragedy of Thinking', in M. de Beistegui and S. Sparks (eds), *Philosophy and Tragedy*, 11–37, London: Routledge.
De Boer, K. (2010), *On Hegel: The Sway of the Negative*, Basingstoke: Palgrave Macmillan.
Denham, A. (2014), 'Tragedy Without the Gods: Autonomy, Necessity and the Real Self', *British Journal of Aesthetics*, 54 (2): 141–59.
Dennett, D. (1978), 'Where am I?', in his *Brainstorms: Philosophical Essays on Mind and Psychology*, 310–23, Cambridge, MA: MIT Press.
Derrida, J. (1967a), *L'écriture et la différence*, Paris: Éditions du Seuil.
Derrida, J. (1967b), *De la grammatologie*, Paris: Les Éditions de Minuit.
Diamond, C. (1997), 'Consequentialism in Modern Moral Philosophy and in "Modern Moral Philosophy"', in D. S. Oderberg and J. Laing (eds), *Human Lives: Critical Essays on Consequentialist Bioethics*, 13–38, London: Palgrave Macmillan.
Diethe, C. (2003), *Nietzsche's Sister and the Will to Power: A Biography of Elisabeth Förster-Nietzsche*, Chicago, IL: University of Illinois Press.
Dilthey, W. ([1860] 1996), 'Schleiermacher's Hermeneutical System in Relation to Earlier Protestant Hermeneutics', trans. T. Nordenhaug, in R. A. Makkreel and F. Rodi (eds), *Wilhelm Dilthey: Selected Works Vol. IV, Hermeneutics and the Study of History*, Princeton, NJ: Princeton University Press.
Dodds, E. R. (1951), *The Greeks and the Irrational*, Berkeley, CA: University of California Press.
Dodds, E. R. (1966), 'On Misunderstanding the Oedipus Rex', *Greece and Rome*, 13 (1): 37–49.
Doris, J. M. (1998), 'Persons, Situations, and Virtue Ethics', *Noûs*, 32: 504–30.
D'Oro, G. and C. Sandis, eds. (2013a), *Reasons and Causes: Causalism and Anti-Causalism in the Philosophy of Action*, 7–48, London: Palgrave Macmillan.
D'Oro, G. and C. Sandis (2013b), 'From Anti-Causalism to Causalism and Back: A History of the Reasons/Causes Debate', in G. D'Oro and C. Sandis (eds), *Reasons and Causes: Causalism and Anti-Causalism in the Philosophy of Action*, 7–48, London: Palgrave Macmillan.
Doyle, A. C. (1924), 'The Adventure of the Illustrious Client', collected in *The Case-Book of Sherlock Holmes*, London: John Murray, 1927.
Doyle, J. (2018), *No Morality, No Self: Anscombe's Radical Scepticism*, Cambridge, MA: Harvard University Press.
Doyle, J. (2019), 'How Should We Understand Anscombe's Claim That "Moral" Does Not Express a Concept?', unpublished.
Dray, W. H. (1957), *Laws and Explanation in History*, Oxford: Clarendon Press.
Dreiser, T. ([1925] 1964), *An American Tragedy*, New York, NY: Boni and Liveright, Signet Classics Printing.
Dretske, F. (1977), 'Referring to Events', in P. A. French, T. E. Uehling and H. K. Wettstein (eds), *Contemporary Perspectives in the Philosophy of Language, Midwest Studies in Philosophy 2*, 90–9, Minneapolis, MN: University of Minnesota Press.
Dretske, F. (1988a), 'The Explanatory Role of Content', in R. H. Grimm and D. D. Merrill (eds), *Contents of Thought*, 31–43, Tucson, AZ: University of Arizona Press.
Dretske, F. (1988b), *Explaining Behavior: Reasons in a World of Causes*, Cambridge, MA: MIT Press.
Dretske, F. (1993), 'Mental Events as Structuring Causes of Behavior', in J. Heil and A. R. Mele (eds), *Mental Causation*, 121–36, Oxford: Clarendon Press.

Dretske, F. (2004), 'Psychological vs. Biological Explanations of Behavior', *Behavior and Philosophy*, 32 (1): 167–77.
Dretske, F. (2006), *Thought and Reality*, Oxford: Oxford University Press.
Dretske, F. (2009), 'What Must Actions Be for Reasons to Explain Them?', in C. Sandis (ed), *New Essays on the Explanation of Action*, 13–21, Basingstoke: Palgrave Macmillan.
Ducasse, C. J. (1925), 'Explanation, Mechanism, and Teleology', *Journal of Philosophy*, 22 (6): 150–5.
Dummett, M. A. E. (2006), *Thought and Reality*, Oxford: Oxford University Press.
Dworkin, R. (1972), 'The Jurisprudence of Richard Nixon', *The New York Review of Books*, 18 (8): 27–35.
Dworkin, R. (2011), *Justice for Hedgehogs*, Cambridge, MA: Harvard University Press.
Easterling, P. E. (1983), 'Character in Sophocles', in E. Segal (ed), *Oxford Readings in Greek Tragedy*, 138–45, Oxford: Oxford University Press.
Edmunds, F. (1869), *Traces of History in the Names of Places*, London: Longmans, Green, and Co.
Egloff, B., A. Schwerdtfeger and S. C. Schmukle (2005), 'Temporal Stability of the Implicit Association Test-anxiety', *Journal of Personality Assessment*, 84 (1): 82–8.
Elster, J. (2007), *Explaining Social Behavior: More Nuts and Bolts for the Social Sciences*, Cambridge: Cambridge University Press.
Elton, G. R. (1967), *The Practice of History*, Sydney: University of Sydney Press.
Elton, G. R. (1991), *Return to Essentials: Some Reflections on the Present State of Historical Study*, Cambridge: Cambridge University Press.
Emerson, R. W. (1860), *The Conduct of Life*, Boston, MA: Ticknor and Fields.
Ericsson, K. A. and H. A. Simon (1980), 'Verbal Reports as Data', *Psychological Review*, 87 (3): 215–51.
Euripides (1944), *Medea*, trans. R. Warner, London: John Lane/The Bodley Head.
Euripides (1996), *Hippolytus*, trans. D. Kovacs, Cambridge, MA: Harvard University Press.
Evans, R. J. (1997), *In Defence of History*, London: Granta Books.
Ewing, A. C. (1938), 'What Is Action?' *Proceedings of the Aristotelian Society Supplementary Volume*, 17 (1): 86–101.
Ezcurdia, M. (1988), 'The Concept–Conception Distinction', *Philosophical Issues*, 9 (Concepts): 187–92.
Falk, W. D. ([1948] 1986), 'Ought and Motivation', *Proceedings of the Aristotelian Society*, 1947–8, 492–510; as reprinted in W. D. Falk, *Ought, Reasons, and Morality: The Collected Papers of W. D. Falk*, 21–41, Ithaca, NY: Cornell University Press, 1986, to which any page numbers given refer.
Falk, W. D. ([1963] 1986), 'Action-Guiding Reasons', *Journal of Philosophy*, 60: 702–18; as reprinted in W. D. Falk, *Ought, Reasons, and Morality: The Collected Papers of W. D. Falk*, 82–98, Ithaca, NY: Cornell University Press, 1986, to which any page numbers given refer.
Falk, W. D. (1986), *Ought, Reasons, and Morality: The Collected Papers of W. D. Falk*, Ithaca, NY: Cornell University Press.
Festinger, L. (1957), *A Theory of Cognitive Dissonance*, Stanford, CA: Stanford University Press.
Fischer, C. (1987), *Postcards from the Edge*, New York, NY: Simon and Schuster.
Fischer, J. M. (2006), *My Way: Essays on Moral Responsibility*, Oxford: Oxford University Press.
Fodor, J. and M. Piattelli-Palmarini (2010), *What Darwin Got Wrong*, London: Profile Books.

Foot, P. ([1967] 1978), 'The Problem of Abortion and the Doctrine of Double Effect', *Oxford Review*, 5: 5–15; as reprinted in her *Virtues and Vices*, 19–32, Oxford: Oxford University Press, 1978, to which any page numbers refer.
Foot, P. (1985), 'Killing and Letting Die', in J. Garfield (ed), *Abortion: Moral and Legal Perspectives*, 177–85, Amherst, MA: University of Massachusetts Press.
Frankfurt, H. G. ([1969] 1988), 'Alternate Possibilities and Moral Responsibility', *Journal of Philosophy*, 66: 829–39; reprinted in H. G. Frankfurt, *The Importance of What We Care About*, 1–10, Cambridge: Cambridge University Press, 1988, to which any page numbers given refer.
Frankfurt, H. G. ([1971] 1988), 'Freedom of the Will and Concept of a Person', *Journal of Philosophy*, 68; reprinted in H. G. Frankfurt, *The Importance of What We Care About*, 11–25, Cambridge: Cambridge University Press, 1988, to which any page numbers given refer.
Frankfurt, H. G. ([1978] 1988), 'The Problem of Action', *American Philosophical Quarterly*, 15; as reprinted in H. G. Frankfurt, *The Importance of What We Care About*, 69–79, Cambridge: Cambridge University Press, 1988, to which any page numbers given refer.
Frankfurt, H. G. ([1982] 1988), 'The Importance of What We Care About', *Synthese*, 53 (2): 257–72; as reprinted in H. G. Frankfurt, *The Importance of What We Care About*, 80–94, Cambridge: Cambridge University Press, 1988, to which any page numbers given refer.
Frankfurt, H. G. (1988a), *The Importance of What We Care About*, Cambridge: Cambridge University Press.
Frankfurt, H. G. (1988b), 'Identification and Externality', in H. G. Frankfurt, *The Importance of What We Care About*, 58–68, Cambridge: Cambridge University Press.
Frege, G. (1956), 'The Thought: A Logical Inquiry', *Mind*, 65 (1): 289–311.
Frege, G. ([1918–19] 1984), 'Der Gedanke' ('The Thought'), in *Eine logische Untersuchung, in Beiträge zur Philosophie des Deutschen Idealismus* I: 58–77. Published in an English trans. P. Geach and R. H. Stoothoff as 'Thoughts', in B. F. McGuinness (ed), *Frege's Collected Papers on Mathematics, Logic, and Philosophy*, 351–72, Oxford: Blackwell, 1984, to which any page numbers refer.
Freud, S. (1900), *Die Traumdeutung*, Leipzig and Vienna: Franz Deuticke.
Frey, J. A. (2018), 'Review of *No Morality, No Self*, *Notre Dame Book Reviews*. Available online: https://ndpr.nd.edu/news/no-morality-no-self-anscombes-radical-skepticism/ (accessed 31 January 2023).
Frey, J. A. (2019a), 'Revisiting Modern Moral Philosophy', *Royal Institute of Philosophy Supplement*, 87: 1–23.
Frey, J. A. (2019b), 'Anscombe on Practical Knowledge and the Good', *Ergo*, 6 (39): 1121–51.
Gallie, W. B. (1956), 'Essentially Contested Concepts', *Proceedings of the Aristotelian Society*, 56 (1): 167–98.
Gasché, R. (2000), 'Self-Dissolving Seriousness: On the Comic in the Hegelian Conception of Tragedy', in M. de Beistegui and S. Sparks (eds), *Philosophy and Tragedy*, 38–58, London: Routledge.
Gavanski, I. and C. Hoffman (1987), 'Awareness of Influences on One's Own Judgments: The Roles of Covariation Detection and Attention to the Judgment Process', *Journal of Personality and Social Psychology*, 52 (3): 453–63.
Gazzaniga, M. S. (1998), *The Mind's Past*, Berkeley, CA: University of California Press.
Gazzaniga, M. S. (2012), *Who's in Charge?* London: Constable and Robinson.

Geach, M. (2005a), 'Anscombe's Ethics' [Letter], *Times Literary Supplement*, 14 October, 5349.
Geach, M. (2005b), 'Anscombe's Ethics' [Letter Reply], *Times Literary Supplement*, 21 October, 5350.
Geach, M. (2008), 'Introduction', in M. Geach and L. Gormally (eds), *Faith in a Hard Ground: Essays on Religion, Philosophy and Ethics: Essays by G. E. M. Anscombe*, xiii–xxi, Exeter: Imprint Academic.
Geach, P. (1956), 'Good and Evil', *Analysis*, 17 (2): 33–42.
Gendler, T. S. (2008a), 'Alief and Belief', *Journal of Philosophy*, 105 (10): 634–63.
Gendler, T. S. (2008b), 'Alief in Action (and Reaction)', *Mind and Language*, 23 (5): 552–85.
Gill, C. (1986), 'The Question of Character and Personality in Greek Tragedy', *Poetics Today*, 7 (2): 251–73.
Ginet, C. (1982), *On Action*, Cambridge: Cambridge University Press.
Glock, H.-J. (1997), 'Truth Without People?', *Philosophy*, 72 (279): 85–104.
Goldie, P. (2012), *The Mess Inside: Narrative, Emotion, and the Mind*, Oxford: Oxford University Press.
Goldman, A. I. (1970), *A Theory of Human Action*, Princeton, NJ: Princeton University Press.
Goldman, A. I. (1976), 'The Volition Theory Revisited', in M. Brand and W. Walton (eds), *Action Theory*, 67–86, Dordrecht: Reidel Publishing.
Goldschmidt, T. (2016), 'A Demonstration of the Causal Power of Absences', *Dialectica*, 70 (1): 85.
Green, O. H. (1980), 'Killing and Letting Die', *American Philosophical Quarterly*, 17 (3): 195–204.
Green, S. (2015), *Causation in Negligence*, Oxford: Hart Publishing.
Greene, G. (1970), *Collected Essays*, London: Penguin.
Greenwald, A. G. and L. H. Krieger (2006), 'Implicit Bias: Scientific Foundations', *California Law Review*, 94 (4): 945–6.
Gremaschi, S. (2017), 'Anscombe on the Mesmeric Force of "Ought" and a Spurious Kind of Moral Realism', *Ethics and Politics*, 19 (2): 51–86.
Grice, P. and J. Baker (1985), 'Davidson on 'Weakness of the Will'', in B. Vermazen and M. B. Hintikka (eds), *Essays on Davidson: Actions and Events*, 27–49, Oxford: Clarendon Press.
Hacker, P. M. S. (2009), 'Agential Reasons and the Explanation of Human Behaviour', in C. Sandis (ed), *New Essays on the Explanation of Action*, 75–93, Basingstoke: Palgrave Macmillan.
Hacker, P. M. S. (2018), *The Passions: A Study of Human Nature*, Oxford: Wiley-Blackwell.
Hacker-Wright, J. (2013), *Philippa Foot's Moral Thought*, London: Bloomsbury.
Hahn, L. E., ed. (1999), *The Philosophy of Donald Davidson*, Library of Living Philosophers, Chicago and La Salle, IL: Open Court Publishing.
Haidt, J. (2001), 'The Emotional Dog and Its Rational Tail: A Social Intuitionist Approach to Moral Judgement', *Philosophical Review*, 108 (4): 814–34.
Haidt, J. (2012). *The Righteous Mind: Why Good People Are Divided by Politics and Religion*. New York, NY: Pantheon Books.
Hain, R., ed. (2019), *Beyond the Self: Virtue Ethics and the Problem of Culture*, Waco, TX: Baylor University Press.
Hall, E. (1997), 'The Sociology of Athenian Tragedy', in P. E. Easterling (ed), *The Cambridge Companion to Greek Tragedy*, 93–126, Cambridge: Cambridge University Press, 1997.

Hall, L. and P. Johansson (2009), 'Choice Blindness: You Don't Know What You Want', *New Scientist*, 2704: 26–7.

Hanfling, O. (2000), *Philosophy and Ordinary Language: The Bent and Genius of Our Tongue*, London: Routledge.

Hanser, M. (2008), 'Actions, Acting, and Acting Well', in R. Shafer-Landau (ed), *Oxford Studies in Metaethics*, 3: 171–98.

Harman, G. (2000), *Explaining Value and Other Essays in Moral Philosophy*, Oxford: Oxford University Press.

Harré, R. and P. F. Secord (1972), *The Explanation of Social Behaviour*, Oxford: Blackwell.

Hart, H. L. A. (1961), *The Concept of Law*, Oxford: Clarendon Press.

Heaney, S. (2005), 'Search for the Soul of Antigone', *The Guardian*, 2 November. Available online: https://www.theguardian.com/stage/2005/nov/02/theatre.classics (accessed 31 January 2023).

Heath, C. (2021), 'The Happiness Project: Finding Joy in Tough Times', *GQ*, 25 January. Available online: https://www.gq.com/story/the-happiness-project (accessed 31 January 2023).

Hegel, G. W. F. ([1820] 1991), *[PR], Elements of the Philosophy of Right [Grundlinien der Philosophie des Rechts]*, [i] ed. S. Houlgate, trans. T. M. Knox, Oxford: Oxford University Press, [1952] 2008; [ii] ed. A. W. Wood, trans. H. B. Nisbet, Cambridge: Cambridge University Press, 1991.

Hegel, G. W. F. ([1832] 1984–87), *[LPR], Lectures on the Philosophy of Religion* [Vorlesungen über die Philosophie der Religion], trans. P. C. Hodgson. 3 vols., Berkeley, CA: University of California Press, 1984–87.

Hegel, G. W. F. ([1835] 1993), *[LA], Aesthetics: Lectures on Fine Art* [Vorlesungen über die Ästhetik], trans. T. M. Knox. 2 vols., Oxford: Clarendon Press, 1975. Also published as *Introductory Lectures on Aesthetics*, trans. B. Bosanquet, London: Penguin, 1993.

Hegel, G. W. F. ([1837] 2011), *[LPH], Lectures on the Philosophy of World History* [Vorlesungen über die Philosophie der Weltgeschichte], Vol. I: Manuscripts of the Introduction and the Lectures of 1822-3, eds. and trans. R. F. Brown and P. C. Hodgson, Oxford: Clarendon Press, 2011.

Heidegger, M. ([1927] 1962), *[BT], Being and Time* [Sein und Zeit], trans. J. Macquarrie and E. Robinson, Oxford: Blackwell.

Heidegger, M. ([1929] 1977), 'What Is Metaphysics? [Was ist Metaphysik?]', trans. D. F. Krell, in D. F. Krell (ed), *Heidegger – Basic Writings*, 89–110, San Francisco, CA: Harper Collins.

Heil, J. and A. Mele, eds. (1993), *Mental Causation*, Oxford: Clarendon Press.

Hempel, C. G. (1965), *Aspects of Scientific Explanation and Other Essays in the Philosophy of Science*, New York, NY: Free Press.

Hempel, C. G. and P. Oppenheim (1948), 'Studies in the Logic of Explanation', *Philosophy of Science*, 15 (2): 135–75.

Henkel, L. A. and M. Mather (2007), 'Memory Attributions for Choices: How Beliefs Shape Our Memories', *Journal of Memory and Language*, 57 (2): 163–76.

Herstein, O. J. (2019), 'Nobody's Perfect: Moral Responsibility in Negligence', *Canadian Journal of Law and Jurisprudence*, 32 (1): 109–25.

Hindriks, F. (2015), 'How Does Reasoning (Fail to) Contribute to Moral Judgment?: Dumbfounding, and Disengagement', *Ethical Theory and Moral Practice*, 18 (2): 237–50.

Hirstein, B. (2009), 'Confabulation', in T. Bayne, A. Cleeremans and P. Wilken (eds), *The Oxford Companion to Consciousness*, 176 ff., Oxford: Oxford University Press.

Hodges, W. (1977), *Logic*, London: Penguin.
Holton, R. (1999), 'Intention and Weakness of Will', *The Journal of Philosophy*, 96 (5): 241–62.
Homer (1922), *Odyssey*, trans. S. Butler, London: Cape.
Homer (2003), *The Odyssey*, trans. E. V. Rieu, revised by D. C. H. Rieu and P. Jones, London: Penguin.
Hooker, B. (2002), *Ideal Code, Real World*, Oxford: Oxford University Press.
Hornsby, J. (1979), 'Actions and Identities', *Analysis*, 39 (4): 195–201.
Hornsby, J. (1980), *Action*, London: Routledge and Kegan Paul.
Hornsby, J. (1982), 'Reply to Lowe on Actions', *Analysis*, 42 (3): 152–3.
Hornsby, J. (1986), 'Physicalist Thinking and Behaviour', in J. McDowell and P. Pettit (eds), *Subject, Thought and Context*, 31–47, Oxford: Oxford University Press.
Hornsby, J. (1993a), 'On What's Intentionally Done', in S. Shute, J. Gardner and J. Horder (eds), *Action and Value in Criminal Law*, 55–74, Oxford: Clarendon Press.
Hornsby, J. ([1993b] 1997), 'Agency and Causal Explanation', in J. Heil and A. R. Mele (eds), *Mental Causation*, 161–88, Oxford: Clarendon Press, 1993; reprinted in her *Simple Mindedness*, 129–53, Cambridge, MA: Harvard University Press, 1997, to which all page references refer.
Hornsby, J. (1997a), *Simple Mindedness: In Defense of Naive Naturalism in the Philosophy of Mind*, Cambridge, MA: Harvard University Press.
Hornsby, J. (1997b), 'Truth: The Identity Theory', *Proceedings of the Aristotelian Society*, 97: 1–24.
Hornsby, J. (1997c), 'Thinkables', in M. Sainsbury (ed), *Thought and Ontology*, 63–80, Milan: Franco Angeli.
Hornsby, J. (1999), 'Anomalousness in Action', in L. E. Hahn (ed), *The Philosophy of Donald Davidson*, Library of Living Philosophers, 623–35, Chicago and La Salle, IL: Open Court Publishing.
Hornsby, J. (2008), 'A Disjunctive Conception of Acting for Reasons', in A. Haddock and F. Macpherson (eds), *Disjunctivism: Perception, Action, Knowledge*, 244–61, Oxford: Oxford University Press.
Hornsby, J. (2010), 'Trying to Act', in T. O'Connor and C. Sandis (eds), *A Companion to the Philosophy of Action*, 18–25, Oxford: Wiley-Blackwell.
Hornsby, J. (2013), 'Basic Activity', *Proceedings of the Aristotelian Society*, 87 (1): 1–18.
Hornsby, J. (2021), 'Verbs of Action and Acting in Time', in C. Bagnoli (ed), *Time in Action: The Temporal Structure of Rational Agency and Practical Thought*, 15–31, London: Routledge.
Houlgate, S. (2005), *Hegel: Freedom, Truth and History*, 2nd edn, Oxford: Blackwell.
Houlgate, S. (2007), 'Hegel's Theory of Tragedy', in S. Houlgate (ed), *Hegel and the Arts*, 146–78, Evanston, IL: Northwestern University Press.
Houlgate, S. (2010), 'Action, Right and Morality in Hegel's *Philosophy of Right*', in A. Laitinen and C. Sandis (eds), *Hegel on Action*, 155–75, London: Palgrave Macmillan.
Hume, D. (1754), *The History of England [HE], Vol. V: From the Invasion of Julius Caesar to The Revolution in 1688*, London: George Bell.
Hume, D. ([1739] 1978), *A Treatise of Human Nature*, 2nd edn, L. A. Selby-Bigge (ed), Oxford: Oxford University Press.
Hurley, P. (2018), 'Consequentialism and the Standard Story of Action', *The Journal of Ethics*, 22 (1): 25–44.
Hursthouse, R. (1991), 'Arational Actions', *Journal of Philosophy*, 88 (2): 57–68.

Hursthouse, R. (1996), 'Normative Virtue Ethics', in R. Crisp (ed), *How Should One Live? Essays on the Virtues*, 19–33, Oxford: Oxford University Press.
Hursthouse, R. (1999), *On Virtue Ethics*, Oxford: Oxford University Press.
Hyman, J. (1999), 'How Knowledge Works', *The Philosophical Quarterly*, 49 (197): 433–51.
Hyman, J. (2010), 'The Road to Larissa', *Ratio*, 23 (4): 393–414.
Hyman, J. (2011), 'Acting for Reasons: Reply to Dancy', *Frontiers of Philosophy in China*, 6 (3); 358–68.
Inwood, M. (1993), 'Introduction and Commentary', in G. W. F. Hegel (ed), *Introductory Lectures on Aesthetics*, ix–xxxvi, trans. B. Bosanquet, London: Penguin.
Isen, A. M. and P. F. Levin (1972), 'Effect of Feeling Good on Helping: Cookies and Kindness', *Journal of Personality and Social Psychology*, 21 (3): 384–8.
Jaeggi, R. (2014), *Alienation*, trans. F. Neuhouser and A. E. Smith, ed. F. Neuhouser, New York, NY: Columbia University Press.
Jay, M. (2005), 'From a View to a Death Revisited', *The Anthony Powell Society Newsletter*, 20: 10.
Jensen, S. J. (2010), *Good and Evil Actions: A Journey Through Saint Thomas Aquinas*, Washington, DC: The Catholic University of America Press.
Johansson, P., L. Hall and S. Sikstrom (2008), 'From Change Blindness to Choice Blindness', *Psychologia*, 51 (2): 142–55.
Joseph, H. W. B. (1931/1933), *Some Problems in Ethics*, 2nd (corrected) impression, Oxford: Clarendon Press.
Jung, C. G. (1933), *Modern Man in Search of a Soul: Essays from the 1920s and 1930s*, trans. C. F. Baynes, London: Routledge and Kegan Paul.
Kane, R. (1996), *The Significance of Free Will*, Oxford: Oxford University Press.
Kant, I. ([1788] 1997), *Critique of Practical Reason*, trans. and ed. M. J. Gregor and A. Reath, Cambridge: Cambridge University Press.
Kaufman, W. (1968), *Tragedy and Philosophy*, Princeton, NJ: Princeton University Press.
Kennett, J. and M. Smith ([1996] 2004), 'Frog and Toad Lose Control', in *Analysis*, 56: 63–73; reprinted in M. Smith, Ethics and the A Priori, 73–83, Cambridge: Cambridge University Press, 2004, to which any page numbers refer.
Kenny, A. J. P. (1963), 'Oratio Obliqua', *Proceedings of the Aristotelian Society Supplementary Volume*, 37: 127–46.
Kenny, A. J. P. (1975), *Will, Freedom and Power*, Oxford: Blackwell.
Kim, J. ([1989] 1997), 'Mechanism, Purpose, and Explanatory Exclusion', *Philosophical Perspectives*, 3: 77–108; reprinted in A. R. Mele (ed), The Philosophy of Action, 256–82, Oxford: Oxford University Press, 1997, to which any page numbers given refer.
Kirkpatrick, K. (2018), 'Beneath the Surface: Whose Phenomenology? Which Art?', in L. Nelstrop and H. Appleton (eds), *Art and Mysticism: Interfaces in the Medieval and Modern Periods*, 27–40, London: Routledge.
Kitto, H. D. F. (1951), *The Greeks*, London: Pelican.
Kitto, H. D. F (1958), *Sophocles: Dramatist and Philosopher*, Oxford: Oxford University Press.
Knobe, J. and S. D. Kelly (2009), 'Can One Act for a Reason Without Acting Intentionally?' in C. Sandis (ed), *New Essays on the Explanation of Action*, 169–83, Basingstoke: Palgrave-Macmillan.
Knowles, D. (2010), 'Hegel on Actions, Reasons, and Causes', in A. Laitinen and C. Sandis (eds), *Hegel on Action*, 42–58, London: Palgrave Macmillan.
Knox, B. (1979), *Word and Action: Essays on the Ancient Theater*, Baltimore, MD: Johns Hopkins University Press.

Knox, B. (1989), *Essays: Ancient and Modern*, Baltimore, MD: Johns Hopkins University Press.
Korsgaard, C. (1993), 'The Reasons We Can Share: An Attack on the Distinction Between Agent-relative and Agent-neutral Values', *Social Philosophy and Policy*, 10 (1): 24–51.
Korsgaard, C. (2009), *Self—Constitution: Agency, Identity, and Integrity*, Oxford: Oxford University Press.
Kramnick, J. (2010), *Actions and Objects from Hobbes to Richardson*, Stanford, CA: Stanford University Press.
Kuhn, T. S. (1962), *The Structure of Scientific Revolutions*, Chicago, IL: University of Chicago Press.
Kundera, M. (2007), *The Curtain: An Essay in Seven Parts*, trans. L. Asher, New York, NY: Harper Collins.
Künne, W. (2003), *Conceptions of Truth*, Oxford: Clarendon Press.
Laitinen, A., E. Mayr and C. Sandis (2019), 'Kant and Hegel on Purposive Action', *Philosophical Explorations*, 21 (1): 90–107; as reprinted in C. Sandis (ed), Philosophy of Action from Suarez to Anscombe, 96–112, London: Routledge.
Laitinen, A. and C. Sandis, eds. (2010a), *Hegel on Action*, London: Palgrave Macmillan.
Laitinen, A. and C. Sandis (2010b), 'Hegel and Contemporary Philosophy of Action', in A. Laitinen and C. Sandis (eds), *Hegel on Action*, 1–21, London: Palgrave Macmillan.
Laitinen, A. and C. Sandis (2019), 'Hegel on Purpose', *Hegel Bulletin*, 40 (3): 444–63.
Lalumera, E. (2014), 'On the Explanatory Value of the Concept-conception Distinction', *Rivista Italiana di Filosofia del Linguaggio*, 8 (3): 73–81.
Lanzmann, C. ([1985] 1995), *Shoah*, extensively corrected and revised edn, New York, NY: Da Capo Press.
Lehrer, K., ed. (1966), *Freedom and Determinism*, New York, NY: Random House.
Lenman, J. (2009), 'Reasons for Action: Justification vs. Explanation', *Stanford Encyclopedia of Philosophy* (Spring 2009 edn), ed. E. N. Zalta. Available online: http://plato.stanford.edu/entries/reasons-just-vs-expl/ (accessed 31 January 2023).
Levinas, E. (1963), 'La trace de l'autre', *Tidischrift voor flosofe*, 25 (3): 605–23.
Levinas, E. ([1972] 2003), *Humanism of the Other* (Humanisme de l'autre home), trans. N. Poller, Urbana and Chicago, IL: University of Illinois Press.
Levy, N. (2011), 'Expressing Who We Are: Moral Responsibility and our Awareness of Our Reasons for Action', *Analytical Philosophy*, 52 (4): 243–61.
Levy, N. (2013), 'The Importance of Awareness', *Australasian Journal of Philosophy*, 91 (2): 211–29.
Levy, N. (2014a), 'Consciousness, Implicit Attitudes and Moral Responsibility', *Noûs*, 48 (1): 21–40.
Levy, N. (2014b), *Consciousness and Moral Responsibility*, Oxford: Oxford University Press.
Lewis, D. (2004), 'Void and Object', in J. Collins, N. Hall and L. A. Paul (eds), *Causation and Counterfactuals*, 277–90, Cambridge, MA: MIT Press.
Liebman, S., ed. (2007), *Claude Lanzmann's Shoah: Key Essays*, Oxford: Oxford University Press.
Littlejohn, C. (2012), *Justification and the Truth Connection*, Cambridge: Cambridge University Press.
Littlejohn, C. and J. Turi (2014), *Epistemic Norms: New Essays on Action, Belief, and Assertion*, Oxford: Oxford University Press.
Locke, J. ([1689] 1975), *An Essay Concerning Human Understanding*, ed. P. H. Nidditch, Oxford: Oxford University Press.

Lowe, E. J. (1981), 'All Actions Occur Inside the Body', *Analysis*, 41 (3): 126–9.
Lowe, E. J. (2003), 'Individuation', in M. J. Loux and D. W. Zimmerman (eds), *The Oxford Handbook of Metaphysics*, 75–95, Oxford: Oxford University Press.
Lowe, E. J. (2010), 'Action Theory and Ontology', in T. O'Connor and C. Sandis (eds), *A Companion to the Philosophy of Action*, 3–9, Chichester: Wiley-Blackwell.
Lowy, C. (1978), 'Gettier's Notion of Justification', *Mind*, 87 (1): 105–8.
Lukes, S. ([1974] 2005), *Power: A Radical View*, 2nd edn, London: Palgrave Macmillan.
Luria, A. R. ([1968] 1987), *The Mind of a Mnemonist: A Little Book About a Vast Memory*, trans. J. S. Bruner, Revised edn, Boston, MA: Harvard University Press.
Macaulay, T. B. (1828), 'History' [Review of The Romance of History by Henry Neele], *Edinburgh Review*, 47 (94): 331–67.
MacIntyre, A. (1967), *A Short History of Ethics*, London: Routledge and Kegan Paul.
MacIntyre, A. (1988), *Whose Justice? Which Rationality?* Notre Dame, IN: University of Notre Dame Press.
Mackie, D. (1997), 'The Individuation of Actions', *The Philosophical Quarterly*, 47 (186): 38–54.
Macmurray, J. (1938), 'What Is Action?', *Proceedings of the Aristotelian Society Supplementary Volume*, 17: 69–85.
Macmurray, J. (1961), *Persons in Relation*, London: Faber and Faber.
Malcolm, N. (1968), 'The Conceivability of Mechanism', *The Philosophical Review*, 77 (1): 45–72.
Marcus, G. (2012), *Rational Causation*, Boston, MA: Harvard University Press.
Margolis, E. and S. Laurence (2014), 'Concepts', in E. N. Zalta (ed), *The Stanford Encyclopedia of Philosophy*, Spring 2014 edn, Berlin: Spring.
Markell, P. (2003), *Bound by Recognition*, Princeton, NJ: Princeton University Press.
Martin, J. L. (2011), *The Explanation of Social Action*, Oxford: Oxford: University Press.
Martin, J. R. (1972), 'Basic Actions and Simple Actions', *American Philosophical Quarterly*, 9 (1): 59–68.
Mason, E. (2019), *Ways to Be Blameworthy*, Oxford: Oxford: University Press.
McCann, H. (1972), 'Is Raising One's Arm a Basic Action?', *Journal of Philosophy*, 64 (9): 235–49.
McCann, H. (1974), 'Volition and Basic Action', *Philosophical Review*, 83: 451–73.
McCann, H. (1979), 'Nominals, Facts, and Two Conceptions of Events', *Philosophical Studies*, 35 (2): 129–49.
McCann, H. (1998), 'Agency, Control, and Causation', in his *The Works of Agency*, 173–9, Ithaca, NY: Cornell University Press.
McDowell, J. ([1994] 1996), *Mind and World*, 2nd edn, Cambridge, MA: Harvard University Press.
McDowell, J. (2009), 'Towards a Reading of Hegel on Action in the "Reason" Chapter of the *Phenomenology*', in his *Having the World in View: Essays on Kant, Hegel, and Sellars*, 166–84, Boston, MA: Harvard University Press.
McEwan, I. (2014), *The Children Act*, London: Vintage.
McGilchrist, I. (2009), *The Master and his Emissary: The Divided Brain and the Making of the Western World*, New Haven, CT: Yale University Press.
McGrath, S. (2005), 'Causation by Omission: A Dilemma', *Philosophical Studies*, 123 (1–2): 125–48.
McNaughton, D. and P. Rawing (2004), 'Duty, Rationality, and Practical Reasons', in A. R. Mele and P. Rawling (eds), *The Oxford Handbook of Rationality*, 110–31, Oxford: Oxford University Press.

Melden, A. I. (1961), *Free Action*, London: Routledge and Kegan Paul.
Mele, A. R., ed. (1997), *The Philosophy of Action*, Oxford: Oxford University Press.
Mele, A. R. (2007), 'Reasonology and False Beliefs', *Philosophical Papers*, 36 (1): 91–118.
Mele, A. R. (2013), 'Actions, Explanations, and Causes', in G. D'Oro and C. Sandis (eds), *Reasons and Causes: Causalism and Anti-Causalism in the Philosophy of Action*, 160–74, Basingstoke: Palgrave Macmillan.
Milgram, S. (1963), 'Behavioral Study of Obedience', *Journal of Abnormal and Social Psychology*, 67 (4): 371–8.
Mill, J. S. ([1861] 1979), *Utilitarianism*, ed. G. Sher, Indianapolis, CA: Hackett Publishing Company.
Millgram, E. (2009), *Hard Truths*, Oxford: Wiley-Blackwell.
Moore, G. E. (1903), *Principia Ethica*, Cambridge: Cambridge University Press.
Moore, R. E. (1979), 'Refraining', *Philosophical Studies*, 36 (4): 407–24.
Moran, R. (2001), *Authority and Estrangement: An Essay on Self-knowledge*, Princeton, NJ: Princeton University Press.
Mourelatos, A. P. D. (1978), 'Events, States, and Processes', *Linguistics and Philosophy*, 2 (3): 415–34.
Moyar, D. (2010), 'Hegel and Agent-Relative Reasons', in A. Laitinen and C. Sandis (eds), *Hegel on Action*, 260–80, London: Palgrave Macmillan.
Mulhall, S. (2002), *On Film*, London: Routledge.
Mulligan, K. (1988), 'From Appropriate Emotions to Values', *The Monist*, 81 (1): 161–88.
Nagel, T. (1970), *The Possibility of Altruism*, Princeton, NJ: Princeton University Press.
Nagel, T. ([1976] 1979), 'Moral Luck', *Proceedings of the Aristotelian Society, Supplementary Volume*, 50: 137–51; as reprinted in his *Mortal Questions*, 24–38, Cambridge: Cambridge University Press, 1979, to which any page numbers refer.
Nagel, T. (1986), *The View From Nowhere*, Cambridge: Cambridge University Press.
Nehamas, A. (1985), *Nietzsche: Life as Literature*, Cambridge, MA: Harvard University Press.
Nietzsche, F. ([1872] 1999), *The Birth of Tragedy – BT* [Die Geburt der Tragödie], *The Birth of Tragedy and Other Writings*, trans. R. Speirs, Cambridge: Cambridge University Press.
Nietzsche, F. ([1874] 1980), *On the Advantage and Disadvantage of History for Life – ADHL* [Vom Nutzen und Nachteil der Historie für das Leben], trans. P. Preuss, Indianapolis, IN: Hackett.
Nietzsche, F. ([1886] 1973), *Beyond Good and Evil – BGE* [Jenseits von Gut und Böse], trans. R. J. Hollingdale, London: Penguin.
Nietzsche, F. ([1888] 1977), *Twilight of the Idols – TI* [Götzen-Dämmerung]; as published in *Twilight of the Idols; and the Anti-Christ*, trans. R. J. Hollingdale, London: Penguin.
Nietzsche, F. ([1901] 1968), *The Will to Power – WTP* [Der Wille zur Macht], trans. W. Kaufmann, New York, NY: Random House.
Nielsen, L. and A. W. Kaszniak (2007), 'Conceptual, Theoretical, and Methodological Issues in Inferring Subjective Emotional Experience: Recommendations for Researchers', in J. J. B. Allen and J. Coan (eds), *The Handbook of Emotion Elicitation and Assessment*, 361–75, New York, NY: Oxford University Press.
Nilsson, M. P. ([1921] 1952), *Den Grekiska Religionens Historia*, published as *A History of Greek Religion*, 2nd edn, trans. F. J. Fielden, Oxford: Oxford University Press.
Nisbett, R. E. and T. D. Wilson (1977), 'Telling More Than We Can Know: Verbal Reports on Mental Processes', *Psychological Review*, 84 (3): 231–59.

Neander, J. A. W. ([1826] 1854), *Allgemeine Geschichte Der Christlichen Religion Und Kirche* [General History of the Christian Religion and Church], Vol. 1, trans. J. Torrey, Boston, MA: Crocker and Brewster.

Neuman, A. (2014), *The Things We Don't Do*, trans. N. Caistor, London: Pushkin Press.

Nussbaum, M. (2001), *The Fragility of Goodness: Luck and Ethics in Greek Tragedy and Philosophy*, revised edn, Cambridge: Cambridge University Press.

Nussbaum, M. (2011), *Philosophical Interventions: 1986–2011*, Oxford: Oxford University Press.

O'Connor, T. (2000), *Persons and Causes: The Metaphysics of Free Will*, Oxford: Oxford University Press.

O'Connor, T. and C. Sandis, eds. (2010), *A Companion to the Philosophy of Action*, Oxford: Wiley-Blackwell.

O'Neill, M. (2014), 'Ludwig Wittgenstein', in D. Reidy and J. Mandle (eds), *The Rawls Lexicon*, 878–80, Cambridge: Cambridge University Press.

O'Neill, O. (1991), 'Kantian Ethics', in P. Singer (ed), *A Companion to Ethics*, 175–85, Oxford: Blackwell.

O'Neill, O. (2013), *Acting on Principle: An Essay on Kantian Ethics*, 2nd edn, Cambridge: Cambridge University Press.

O'Shaughnessy, B. (1972), 'Processes', *Proceedings of the Aristotelian Society, New Series*, 72 (1971–1972): 215–40.

Oudemans, T. C. W. and A. Lardinois (1987), *Tragic Ambiguity: Anthropology, Philosophy and Sophocles' Antigone*, Leiden: Brill.

Owen, D. W. D. (1980), 'Actions and Bodily Movements: Another Move', *Analysis*, 40 (1): 32–5.

Packard, V. ([1957] 2007), *The Hidden Persuaders*, new 50th anniversary edn, New York, NY: IG Publishing.

Paolucci, A. and H. Paolucci, eds. (1962), *Hegel on Tragedy*, New York, NY: Doubleday.

Parfit, D. (1984), *Reasons and Persons*, Oxford: Clarendon Press.

Parfit, D. (2011), *On What Matters*, Vols. I and II, Oxford: Oxford University Press.

Peacocke, C. (2008), *Truly Understood*, Oxford: Oxford University Press.

Pears, D. (1984), *Motivated Irrationality*, Oxford: Clarendon Press.

Pettit, P. (2001), *A Theory of Freedom: From the Psychology to the Politics of Agency*, Cambridge: Polity Press.

Philips, D. Z. (2004), *The Problem of Evil*, Minneapolis, MN: Fortress Press.

Piller, C. (2006), 'Content-Related and Attitude-Related Reasons for Preferences', *Royal Institute of Philosophy Supplement*, 59: 155–81.

Pink, T. (2016), *Self-Determination: The Ethics of Action, Volume I*, Oxford: Oxford University Press.

Pinkard, T. (2000), *Hegel: A Biography*, Cambridge: Cambridge University Press.

Pippin, R. (2010), 'Hegel's Social Theory of Agency: The "Inner-Outer" Problem', in A. Laitinen and C. Sandis (eds), *Hegel on Action*, 59–78, London: Palgrave Macmillan.

Plato (1995), *Phaedrus [P]*, trans. A. Nehamas and P. Woodruf, Indianapolis, IN: Hackett Publishing.

Plato (1973), *Theaetetus [T]*, trans. J. McDowell, Oxford: Clarendon Press.

Poole, A. (2005), *Tragedy: A Very Short Introduction*, Oxford: Oxford University Press.

Pope, A. (1713), *Windsor-Forest*, London: Bernard Lintott.

Powell, A. (1932), *Venusberg [V]*, London: Duckworth.

Powell, A. (1933), *From a View to a Death [FVD]*, London: Duckworth.

Powell, A. (1936), *Agents and Patients [AP]*, London: Duckworth.

Powell, A. (1951-75), *A Dance to the Music of Time*, London: Heinemann, in 12 volumes: A Question of Upbringing [QU], 1951; A Buyer's Market [BM], 1952; The Acceptance World [AW], 1955; At Lady Molly's [LM], 1957; Cassanova's Chinese Restaurant [CCR], 1960; The Kindly Ones [KO], 1962; The Valley of Bones [VB], 1964; The Soldier's Art [SA], 1966; The Military Philosophers [MP], 1968; Books Do Furnish a Room [BDFR], 1971; Temporary Kings [TK], 1973; Hearing Secret Harmonies [HSH], 1975.

Powell, A. (1957), 'Thus Spake Nietzsche' [TSN], *Punch*, 5 June, 720.

Powell, A. (1980), *Faces in My Time [FIMT]*, London: Heinemann.

Powell, A. (1982), *The Strangers All Are Gone [SAAG]*, London: Heinemann.

Powell, A. (1986), *The Fisher King [FK]*, London: Heinemann.

Powell, A. (2000), *A Writer's Notebook [WN]*, London: Heinemann.

Powell, B. (1967), *Knowledge of Actions*, London: George Allen and Unwin.

Price, A. W. (2005), 'Was Aristotle a Particularist?' *Proceedings of the Boston Area Colloquium of Ancient Philosophy*, 21: 191-212.

Price, A. W. (2009), 'Aristotle's Conception of Practical Thinking', in C. Sandis (ed), *New Essays on the Explanation of Action*, 384-95, Basingstoke: Palgrave Macmillan.

Prichard, H. A. ([1932] 2004), 'Duty and Ignorance of Fact', *Proceedings of the Aristotelian Society*; as reprinted in H. A. Prichard, *Moral Writings*, ed. J. MacAdam, 84-101, Oxford: Clarendon Press, 2004, to which any page numbers refer.

Prichard, H. A. ([1945] 2004), 'Acting, Willing, Desiring', as reprinted in H. A. Prichard, *Moral Writings*, ed. J. MacAdam, 272-81, Oxford: Clarendon Press, 2004.

Prichard, H. A. ([1949] 2004), *Moral Obligation*, ed. W. D. Ro, Oxford: Clarendon Press; Reprinted in its entirety in H. A. Prichard, *Moral Writings*, ed. J. MacAdam, Oxford: Clarendon Press, 2004.

Prichard, H. A. (2004), *Moral Writings*, ed. J. MacAdam, Oxford: Clarendon Press.

Prinz, J. (2007), *The Emotional Construction of Morals*, Oxford: Oxford University Press.

Prior, A. N. (1963), 'Oratio Obliqua', *Proceedings of the Aristotelian Society Supplementary Volume*, 37: 115-26.

Prior, A. N. (1971), *The Objects of Thought*, ed. P. T. Geach and A. J. P. Kenny, Oxford: Oxford University Press.

Pronin, E. (2009), 'The Introspection Illusion', in M. P. Zann (ed), *Advances in Experimental Social Psychology*, 41: 1-67.

Proust, M. ([1913] 1992), *Swann's Way*, trans. C. K. S. Moncrieff and T. Kilmartin, rev. D. J. Enright, London: Chatto and Windus.

Quante, M. ([1993] 2004), *Hegel's Concept of Action*, trans. D. Moyer, Cambridge: Cambridge University Press.

Quine, W. V. O. (1960), *Word and Object*, Cambridge, MA: MIT Press.

Railton, P. (2004), 'How to Engage Reason: The Problem of Regress', in R. Wallace, P. Pettit, S. Scheffler and M. Smith (eds), *Reason and Value: Themes from the Moral Philosophy of Joseph Raz*, 176-201, Oxford: Clarendon Press.

Ramsey, F. P. ([1925] 1960), 'Universals', as reprinted in his *The Foundations of Mathematics and Other Logical Essays*, 112-34, Patterson, NJ: Littlefield Adams and Co.

Rand, A. (1964), *The Virtue of Selfishness: A New Concept of Egoism*, New York, NY: New American Library.

Rawls, J. (1974/5), 'The Independence of Moral Theory', *Proceedings and Addresses of the American Philosophical Association*, 48: 5-22.

Rawls, J. ([1975] 1999), *A Theory of Justice*, revised edn, Cambridge, MA: Belknap Press.

Raz, J. (1990), *Practical Reason and Norms*, 2nd edn, Princeton, NJ: Princeton University Press.
Raz, J. (1999), *Engaging Reason: On the Theory of Value and Action*, Oxford: Oxford University Press.
Raz, J. (2008), 'Reason, Reasons and Normativity', in R. Shafer-Landau (ed), *Oxford Studies in Metaethics*, Vol. 5: 5–24, Oxford: Oxford University Press.
Raz, J. (2009), 'Reasons: Explanatory and Normative', in C. Sandis (ed), *New Essays on the Explanation of Action*, 184–202, Basingstoke: Palgrave Macmillan.
Raz, J. (2010), 'Responsibility and the Negligence Standard', *Oxford Journal of Legal Studies*, 30 (1): 1–18.
Raz, J. (2011), *From Normativity to Responsibility*, Oxford: Oxford University Press.
Reader, S. (2010), 'Agency, Patiency, and Personhood', in T. O'Connor and C. Sandis (eds), *A Companion to the Philosophy of Action*, 200–8, Oxford: Wiley-Blackwell.
Reid, T. ([1788] 1969), *Essays on the Active Powers of the Human Mind* [Original title: Essay on the Active Powers of Man], ed. B. A. Brody, Cambridge, MA: MIT Press.
Richardson, S. (1748), *Clarissa; or, The History of a Young Lady*, London: A. Millar.
Richter, D. (2011), *Anscombe's Moral Philosophy*, Lanham, MD: Lexington Books.
Richter, D. (2019), 'Morality and Moral Law: A Reply to James Doyle', *Forma de Vida*, 17 (Anscombe). Available online: https://formadevida.org/dritcherfdv17.
Ricoeur, P. ([1985] 1988), *Temps et récit* [Time and Narrative], Vol. 3, trans. K. Blamey and D. Pellauer, Chicago, IL: University of Chicago Press.
Ricoeur, P. ([1986] 2008), *Du texte à l'action. Essais d'herméneutique II* [From Text to Action: Essays in Hermeneutics, II], trans. K. Blamey and J. Evanston, London: Bloomsbury.
Ricoeur, P. (1992), *Soi-même comme un autre* [Oneself as Another], trans. K. Blamey, Chicago, IL: Chicago University Press.
Ricoeur, P. ([2000] 2004), *La Mémoire, l'Histoire, l'Oubli* [Memory, History, Forgetting], Chicago, IL: University of Chicago Press.
Roche, M. (2005), 'The Greatness and Limits of Hegel's Theory of Tragedy', in R. Bushnell (ed), *A Companion to Tragedy*, 51–67, Oxford: Wiley-Blackwell.
Roche, M. (2006), 'Introduction to Hegel's Theory of Tragedy', *PhaenEx*, 1 (2): 11–20.
Rorty, A. O. (1988), *Mind in Action: Essays in the Philosophy of Mind*, Boston, MA: Beacon Press.
Rorty, R. (1998), *Truth and Progress: Philosophical Papers Volume 3*, Cambridge: Cambridge University Press.
Rorty, R. and P. Engel (2007), *What's the Use of Truth?* New York: Columbia University Press.
Rosenberg, H. (1960), 'The American Action Painters', in his *The Tradition of the New*, 26–8, New York, NY: Da Capo Press.
Ross, L. and R. E. Nisbett (2011), *The Person and the Situation*, 2nd edn, New York, NY: Pinter and Martin.
Ross, W. D. ([1930] 2002), *The Right and the Good*, Oxford: Clarendon Press, revised edn, ed. P. Stratton-Lake, Oxford: Clarendon Press.
Ruben, D.-H. (2003), *Action and its Explanation*, Oxford: Clarendon Press.
Ruben, D.-H. (2009), 'Con-Reasons as Causes', in C. Sandis (ed), *New Essays on the Explanation of Action*, 62–74, Basingstoke: Palgrave Macmillan.
Rumi, J.-D. (1995), *Selected Poems*, trans. C Banks, London: Penguin.
Rundle, B. (1979), *Grammar in Philosophy*, Oxford: Clarendon Press.
Rundle, B. (1993), *Facts*, London: Duckworth.

Russell, B. (1956), 'The Philosophy of Logical Atomism', in R. C. Marsh (ed), *Logic and Knowledge*, 177–281, London: Allen and Unwin.
Ryle, G. (1949), *The Concept of Mind*, London: Hutchinson.
Ryle, G. (1973), 'Negative "Actions"', *Hermathena*, 115 (Summer): 81–93.
Sacks, H. (1984), 'On Doing "Being Ordinary"', in J Maxwell Atkinson and J. Heritage (eds), *Structures of Social Action: Studies in Conversation Analysis*, 413–29, Cambridge: Cambridge University Press.
Sacks, O. ([1973] 1990), *Awakenings*, Revised 1990 edn, New York, NY: Harper Collins.
Sacks, O. (1987), *The Man who Mistook his Wife for a Hat, and Other Clinical Tales*, New York: Harper and Row.
Sandis, C. (2006a), 'When Did the Killing Occur? Donald Davidson on Action Individuation', *Daimon Revista de Filosofía*, 37: 179–86.
Sandis, C. (2006b), 'The Explanation of Action in History', *Essays in Philosophy*, 7 (2): Article 12.
Sandis, C., ed. (2009a), *New Essays on the Explanation of Action*, Basingstoke: Palgrave Macmillan.
Sandis, C. (2009b), 'Hume and the Debate on Motivating Reasons', in C. Pigden (ed), *Hume on Motivation and Virtue: New Essays*, 142–54, Basingstoke: Palgrave Macmillan.
Sandis, C. (2012), *The Things We Do and Why We Do Them*, London: Palgrave Macmillan.
Sandis, C. (2015), 'One Fell Swoop: Small Red Book Historicism Before and After Davidson', *Journal of the Philosophy of History*, 9: 372–92; reprinted in C. Sandis, Wittgenstein on Understanding Others: Strangers in a Strange Land, London: Anthem Press, 2023.
Sandis, C. (2016a), 'He Buttered the Toast While Baking a Fresh Loaf', *Philosophy and Public Issues, Supplementary Volume*, 5 (3): 27–42.
Sandis, C. (2016b), 'Period and Place: Collingwood and Wittgenstein on Understanding Others', *Collingwood and British Idealism Studies*, 22 (1): 167–93.
Sandis, C. (2017a), 'If an Artwork Could Speak', in G. Hagberg (ed), *Wittgenstein on Aesthetic Understanding*, 355–82, London: Palgrave Macmillan.
Sandis, C. (2017b), 'An Honest Display of Fakery', in V. Harrison, G. Kemp and A. Bergqvist (eds), *Philosophy and Museums: Ethics, Aesthetics, and Ontology*, 1–9, Cambridge: Cambridge University Press.
Sandis, C. (2017c), 'Family Resemblance', *The Philosopher's Magazine*, 78 (3rd Quarter): 17–9.
Sandis, C. (2018), 'Robot Reasons', *The Philosopher's Magazine*, 79 (1st Quarter): 22–3.
Sandis, C. (2019a), *Character and Causation: Hume's Philosophy of Action*, London: Routledge.
Sandis, C., ed. (2019b), *Philosophy of Action from Suarez to Anscombe*, London: Routledge.
Sandis, C. (2019c), 'Neo-Anscombians', *Times Literary Supplement*, 24 May.
Sandis, C. (2019d), 'Who Are "We" for Wittgenstein?', in H. Appelqvist (ed), *Wittgenstein and the Limits of Language*, 172–96, London: Routledge.
Sandis, C. (2020), 'Was Jesus a Moral Particularist?', *The Philosophers' Magazine*, 89: 6–8.
Sandis, C. (2021), 'Virtue Ethics and Particularism', *95th Proceedings of the Aristotelian Society Supplementary Volume*, 95: 205–32.
Sartre, J.-P. ([1943] 1956), *Being and Nothingness*, trans. H. E. Barnes, London: Routledge.
Sartre, J.-P. ([1945] 2007), *Existentialism Is a Humanism*, trans. C. Macomber, New Haven, CT: Yale University Press.

Saul, J. M. (2012), *Lying, Misleading, and What Is Said: An Exploration in the Philosophy of Language and Ethics*, Oxford: Oxford University Press.

Scanlon, T. M. (1998), *What We Owe to Each Other*, Cambridge, MA: The Belknap Press.

Scanlon, T. M. (2008), *Moral Dimensions: Permissibility, Meaning, Blame*, Cambridge, MA: Harvard University Press.

Schapiro, T. (2001), 'Three Conceptions of Action in Moral Theory', *Noûs*, 35 (1): 93–117.

Schapiro, T. (2021), 'Kant's Approach to the Theory of Agency', in K. Sylban and R. Chang (eds), *The Routledge Handbook of Practical Reason*, 160–71, Abingdon: Routledge.

Schopenhauer, A. ([1851] 1974), 'Additional Remarks on the Doctrine of the Suffering of the World', and, "Additional Remarks on the Doctrine of the Affirmation and Denial of the Will to Live"', in his *Parerga and Paralipomena*, trans. E. F. J. Payne, Vol. II, 291–305 and 312–23, Oxford: Oxford University Press.

Schroeder, S. (2001), 'Are Reasons Causes?: A Wittgensteinian Response to Davidson', in S. Schroeder (ed), *Wittgenstein and Contemporary Philosophy of Mind*, 50–70, Basingstoke: Palgrave Macmillan.

Schroeder, S. (2010), 'Wittgenstein', in T. O'Connor and C. Sandis (eds), *A Companion to the Philosophy of Action*, 554–61, Oxford: Wiley-Blackwell.

Schueler, G. F. (2001), 'Action Explanations: Causes and Purposes', in B. F. Malle, L. J. Moses and D. A. Baldwin (eds), *Intentions and Intentionality: Foundations of Social Cognition*, 251–64, Cambridge, MA: The MIT Press.

Schueler, G. F. (2003), *Reasons and Purposes*, Oxford: Clarendon Press.

Segal, C. (2001), *Oedipus Tyrannus: Tragic Heroism and the Limits of Knowledge*, Oxford: Oxford University Press.

Sehon, S. R. (1997), 'Deviant Causal Chains and the Irreducibility of Teleological Explanation', *Pacific Philosophical Quarterly*, 78: 195–213.

Sehon, S. R. (2010), 'Teleological Explanation', in T. O'Connor and C. Sandis (eds), *A Companion to the Philosophy of Action*, 121–8, Oxford: Wiley-Blackwell.

Sellars, W. (1966), 'Fatalism and Determinism', in K. Lehrer (ed), *Freedom and Determinism*, 141–74, New York, NY: Random House.

Sellars, W. (1976), 'Volitions Re-affirmed', in M. Brand and W. Walton (eds), *Action Theory*, 47–66, Dordrecht: Reidel Publishing, 1976.

Setiya, K. (2007), *Reasons Without Rationalism*, Princeton, NJ: Princeton University Press.

Shakespeare, W. ([1611] 2007), *The Tempest*, London: Penguin.

Shaw, B. (1903), *Man and Superman*, London: Constable and Company.

Sheppard, J. T. (1911), *Greek Tragedy*, Cambridge: Cambridge University Press.

Sher, G. (2006), *In Praise of Blame*, Oxford: Oxford University Press.

Sher, G. (2009), *Who Knew? Responsibility Without Awareness*, Oxford: Oxford University Press.

Shute, S., J. Gardner and J. Horder, eds. (1993), *Action and Value in Criminal Law*, Oxford: Clarendon Press.

Sidgwick, H. (1874), *The Methods of Ethics*, 7th edn (1907), London: Macmillan.

Silk, M. S. and J. P. Stern (1983), *Nietzsche on Tragedy*, Cambridge: Cambridge University Press.

Simpson, Z. (2012), *Life as Art: Aesthetics and the Creation of the Self*, London: Roman and Littlefield.

Singleton, J. (2002), 'Virtue Ethics, Kantian Ethics, and Consequentialism', *Journal of Philosophical Research*, 17: 537–51.

Sinnott-Armstrong, W. (2015), 'Consequentialism', in E. N. Zalta (ed), *The Stanford Encyclopedia of Philosophy* (Winter 2015 edn). Available online: https://plato.stanford.edu/archives/win2015/entries/consequentialism/ (accessed 31 January 2023).

Skorupski, J. (2010), *The Domain of Reasons*, Oxford: Oxford University Press.

Skow, B. (2016), *Reasons Why*, Oxford: Oxford University Press.

Smith, H. M. (2013), 'Negligence', in H. LaFollette (ed), *The International Encyclopedia of Ethics*, 3665–3570, Oxford: Wiley-Blackwell.

Smith, J. A. (2016), *Samuel Richardson and the Theory of Tragedy: Clarissa's Caesuras*, Manchester: Manchester University Press.

Smith, M. (1987), 'The Humean Theory of Motivation', *Mind*, 96: 36–61.

Smith, M. (1991), 'Realism', in P. Singer (ed), *A Companion to Ethics*, 399–410, Oxford: Blackwell.

Smith, M. (1992), 'Valuing: Desiring or Believing?', in D. Charles and K. Lennon (eds), *Reduction, Explanation, and Realism*, 323–60, Oxford: Oxford University Press.

Smith, M. (1994), *The Moral Problem*, Oxford: Blackwell.

Smith, M. ([1998] 2004), 'The Possibility of Philosophy of Action', in J. Bransen and S. Cuyper (eds), *Human Action, Deliberation and Causation*, 17–41, Dordrecht: Kluwer Academic Publishers; as reprinted in M. Smith (2004: 155–77), to which any page numbers refer.

Smith, M. (2000), 'Moral Realism', in H. LaFollette (ed), *The Blackwell Guide to Ethical Theory*, 17–42, Oxford: Blackwell.

Smith, M. ([2003] 2004), 'Humeanism, Psychologism, and the Normative Story', *Philosophy and Phenomenological Research*, 67 (2): 460–7; as reprinted in M. Smith, *Ethics and the A Priori: Selected Essays on Moral Psychology and Meta-Ethics*, 146–54, Cambridge: Cambridge University Press, 2004, to which any page numbers refer.

Smith, M. (2004), *Ethics and the A Priori: Selected Essays on Moral Psychology and Meta-Ethics*, Cambridge: Cambridge University Press.

Smith, M. (2010), 'Humeanism About Motivation', in T. O'Connor and C. Sandis (eds), *A Companion to the Philosophy of Action*, 153–8, Oxford: Wiley-Blackwell.

Smith, M. and Pettit, P. (1997), 'Parfit's "P"', in J. Dancy (ed), *Reading Parfit*, 71–95, Oxford: Blackwell.

Solomon, D. (1988), 'Internal Objections to Virtue Ethics', *Midwest Studies in Philosophy*, 13: 428–40.

Solomon, D. (2003), 'Virtue Ethics: Radical or Routine?', in L. Zagzebski and M. DePaul (eds), *Intellectual Virtue: Perspectives from Ethics and Epistemology*, 57–80, Oxford: Oxford University Press.

Solomon, D. (2008), 'Elizabeth Anscombe's "Modern Moral Philosophy": Fifty Years Later', *Christian Bioethics*, 14 (2): 109–22.

Sophocles (1982), *The Three Theban Plays (Antigone [A]; Oedipus the King [OT]; Oedipus at Colonus [OC])*, trans. R. Fagles, London: Penguin.

Sorensen, R. A. (1985), 'Self-deception and Scattered Events', *Mind*, 94 (373): 64–9.

Speight, A. (2001), *Hegel, Literature and the Problem of Agency*, Cambridge: Cambridge University Press.

Spurling, H. (1977), *Invitation to the Dance: A Handbook to Anthony Powell's, A Dance to the Music of Time*, London: William Heinemann.

Statman, D. (1993a), *Introduction to Moral Luck*, New York, NY: State University of New York Press.

Statman, D., ed. (1993b), *Moral Luck*, New York, NY: State University of New York Press.

Steiner, G. (1984), *Antigones*, Oxford: Clarendon Press.

Steward, H. (1997), *The Ontology of Mind*, Oxford: Clarendon Press.
Stocker, M. (1968), 'Duty and Supererogation', in N. Rescher (ed), *Studies in Philosophy*, 53–63, American Philosophical Quarterly Monograph Series, Oxford: Blackwell.
Stocker, M. (2004), 'Raz on the Intelligibility of Bad Acts', in R. Wallace, P. Pettit, S. Scheffler and M. Smith (eds), *Reason and Value: Themes from the Moral Philosophy of Joseph Raz*, 303–32, Oxford: Clarendon Press.
Stout, R. (1996), *Things That Happen Because They Should*, Oxford: Oxford University Press.
Stout, R. (1997), 'Processes', *Philosophy*, 72 (279): 19–27.
Stout, R., ed. (2018), *Process, Action and Experience*, Oxford: Oxford University Press.
Stoutland, F. (1968), 'Basic Actions and Causality', *The Journal of Philosophy*, 65 (16): 467–75.
Stoutland, F. (1976), 'The Causation of Behaviour', *Essays on Wittgenstein in Honour of G. H. von Wright, Acta Philosophica Fennica*, 28 (1–3): 286–325.
Stoutland, F. (1998), 'The Real Reasons', in J. Bransen and S. E. Cuypers (eds), *Human Action, Deliberation and Causation*, 43–66, Dordrecht: Kluwer Academic Publishers.
Strawson, G. ([1986] 2010), *Freedom and Belief*, 2nd revised edn, Oxford: Clarendon Press.
Strawson, P. F. (1950), 'Truth', *Proceedings of the Aristotelian Society Supplementary Volume*, 24: 129–57.
Strawson, P. F. ([1966] 2008), 'Aesthetic Appraisal and Works of Art', *The Oxford Review*, 3; as reprinted in his *Freedom and Resentment and Other Essays*, 2nd edn, 178–88, London: Routledge.
Sullivan, R. J. (1989), *Immanuel Kant's Moral Theory*, Cambridge: Cambridge University Press.
Sverdlik, S. (2011), *Motive and Rightness*, Oxford: Oxford University Press.
Swanton, C. (2003), *Virtue Ethics: A Pluralistic View*, Oxford: Oxford University Press.
Swanton, C. (2015), 'A Particularist but Codifiable Virtue Ethics', in M. Timmons (ed), *Oxford Studies in Normative Ethics*, 5: 38–63.
Taleb, N. (2007), *The Black Swan: The Impact of the Highly Improbable*, London: Random House.
Tanney, J. (1995), 'Why Reasons May Not Be Causes', *Mind and Language*, 10 (1/2): 103–26.
Tanney, J. ([2002] 2013), 'Self-knowledge, Normativity, and Construction', in A. O'Hear (ed), *Logic, Thought, and Language, Royal Institute of Philosophy Supplement*, 51: 37–55, Cambridge: Cambridge University Press; as reprinted in her *Rules, Reason and Self-Knowledge*, 300–21, Cambridge, MA: Harvard University Press, 2013, to which any page numbers refer.
Tanney, J. (2005), 'Reason-Explanation and the Contents of Mind', *Ratio*, 18 (3): 338–51.
Tanney, J. (2008), 'Reasons as Non-causal, Context-Placing Explanations', in C. Sandis (ed), *New Essays on the Explanation of Action*, 94–111, Basingstoke: Palgrave Macmillan.
Tappolet, C. (2013), 'Evaluative vs. Deontic Concepts', in H. Lafollette (ed), *The International Encyclopedia of Ethics*, Oxford: Wiley-Blackwell.
Taylor, C. (1964), *The Explanation of Behaviour*, London: Routledge and Kegan Paul.
Taylor, C. (1979), 'Action as Expression', in C. Diamond and J. Teichman (eds), *Intention and Intentionality*, 73–89, Brighton: Harvester Press.
Taylor, C. ([1983] 2010), 'Hegel and the Philosophy of Action', in L. S. Stepelevitch and D. Lamb (eds), *Hegel's Philosophy of Action*, Atlantic Highlands, NJ: Humanities Press; as

reprinted in A. Laitinen and C. Sandis (eds), *Hegel on Action*, 22–41, London: Palgrave Macmillan.
Taylor, C. C. W. (1980), 'Plato, Hare and Davidson on Akrasia', *Mind*, 89 (356): 499–518.
Taylor, C. C. W. (1980), 'Plato, Hare and Davidson on Akrasia', *Mind*, 89 (356): 499–518.
Taylor, R. (1966), *Action and Purpose*, Hoboken, NJ: Prentice Hall.
Teichmann, R. (2008), *The Philosophy of Elizabeth Anscombe*, Oxford: Oxford University Press.
Teichmann, R. (2011), *Nature, Reason, and the Good Life: Ethics for Human Beings*, Oxford: Oxford University Press.
Tenenbaum, S. (2007), *Appearances of the Good*, Cambridge: Cambridge University Press.
Tenenbaum, S., ed. (2010), *Desire, Practical Reason, and the Good*, Oxford: Oxford University Press.
Thagard, P., ed. (2007), *The Philosophy of Psychology and Cognitive Science*, Amsterdam: North Holland.
Thalberg, I. (1977), *Perception, Emotion, and Action: A Component Approach*, Oxford: Blackwell.
Thaler, R. H. and C. R. Sunstein (2008), *Nudge: Improving Decisions about Health, Wealth and Happiness*, London: Penguin.
Thompson, M. (2008), *Life and Action: Elementary Structures of Practice and Practical Thought*, Cambridge, MA: Harvard University Press.
Thomson, J. J. (1971), 'The Time of a Killing', *Journal of Philosophy*, 68 (5): 115–32.
Thomson, J. J. (2003), 'Causation: Omissions', *Philosophy and Phenomenological Research*, 66 (1): 81–103.
Tillich, P. (1957), *Systematic Theology*, Vol. 2, Chicago, IL: University of Chicago Press.
Tolman, E. C. (1932), *Purposive Behavior in Animals and Men*, Berkeley, CA: University of California Press.
Trigg, D. (2014), *The Thing: A Phenomenology of Horror*, Winchester: Zero Books.
Upper, D. (1974), 'The Unsuccessful Self-Treatment of a Case of "Writer's Block"', *Journal of Applied Behavioural Analysis*, 3 (7): 497.
Valency, M. (1987), 'Back to Methuselah: A Tract in Epic Form', in H. Bloom (ed), *Modern Critical Views: George Bernard Shaw*, 167–88, New York, NY: Chelsea House Publishers.
Velleman, J. D. (1989), *Practical Reflection*, Princeton, NJ: Princeton University Press.
Velleman, J. D. ([1992] 2000), 'What Happens When Someone Acts?', *Mind*, 101, 461–81; as reprinted in J. D. Velleman, *The Possibility of Practical Reason*, 123–43, Oxford: Oxford University Press, 2000, to which any page numbers given refer.
Velleman, J. D. (2000), *The Possibility of Practical Reason*, Oxford: Oxford University Press.
Velleman, J. D. (2014), 'Doables', *Philosophical Explorations*, 17 (1): 1–16.
Vendler, Z. (1967), *Linguistics in Philosophy*, Ithaca, NY: Cornell University Press.
Vendler, Z. (1984), 'Agency and Causation', *Midwest Studies in Philosophy*, 9 (1): 371–84.
Vermazen, B. (1985), 'Negative Acts', in B. Vermazen and M. B. Hintikka (eds), *Essays on Davidson: Actions and Events*, 93–104, Oxford: Oxford University Press.
Vermazen, B. and M. B. Hintikka, eds. (1985), *Essays on Davidson: Actions and Events*, Oxford: Oxford University Press.
Vernant, J.-P. (1962), *Les origines de la pensée grecque*, Paris: Librarie François Maspero.
Vernant, J.-P. ([1965] 2006), *Mythe et pensée chez les Grecs: Etudes de psychologie historique*, Paris: Librarie François Maspero; trans. J. Lloyd and J. Fort as *Myth and Thought Among the Greeks*, New York, NY: Zone Books, 2006.

Vernant, J.-P. (1983), 'Ambiguity and Reversal: On the Enigmatic Structure of *Oedipus Rex*', in E. Segal (ed), *Oxford Readings in Greek Tragedy*, 189–209, Oxford: Oxford University Press.
Vernant, J.-P. (1988), *Myth and Tragedy in Ancient Greece*, trans. J. Lloyd, New York, NY: Zone Books.
Vernant, J. P. and P. Vidal-Naquet (1988), *Myth and Tragedy in Ancient Greece*, trans. J. Lloyd, New York, NY: Zone Books.
Vierkant, T. and R. Hardt (2015), 'Explicit Reasons, Implicit Stereotypes and the Direct Control of the Mind', *Ethical Theory and Moral Practice*, 18 (2): 251–65.
Virgil (2003), *The Aeneid*, trans. D. West, London: Penguin Classics.
Vogler, C. (2001), *John Stuart Mill's Deliberative: An Essay in Moral Psychology*, New York, NY: Garland Publishing Inc.
Vogler, C. (2009), *Reasonably Vicious*, Cambridge, MA: Harvard University Press.
Vogt, S. P. (1987), 'Ann and Superman: Type and Archetype', in H. Bloom (ed), *Modern Critical Views: George Bernard Shaw*, 215–32, New York, NY: Chelsea House Publishers.
Von Wright, G. H. (1963), *Norm and Action*, London: Routledge and Kegan Paul.
Von Wright, G. H. (1972), 'On So-Called Practical Inference', *Acta Sociologica*, 15 (1): 39–53.
Von Wright, G. H. (1986), 'Truth, Negation, and Contradiction', *Synthese*, 66 (1): 3–14.
Von Wright, G. H. ([1988] 1998), 'An Essay on Door Knocking', *Rechtstheorie*, 19; as reprinted in his *In the Shadow of Descartes: Essays in the Philosophy of Mind*, 83–96, Dordrecht: Kluwer Academic Publishers, 1998, to which any page references refer.
Wallace, J. (2007), *The Cambridge Introduction to Tragedy*, Cambridge: Cambridge University Press.
Wallace, R. J., P. Pettit, S. Scheffler and M. Smith, eds. (2004), *Reason and Value: Themes from the Moral Philosophy of Joseph Raz*, Oxford: Clarendon Press.
Ward, K. (2007), *Divine Action: Examining God's Role in an Open and Emergent Universe*, 2nd edn, Philadelphia, PA: Templeton Foundation Press.
Watson, G. (1975), 'Free Agency', *The Journal of Philosophy*, 72: 205–20.
Watson, G. (2004), *Agency and Answerability*, Oxford: Oxford University Press.
Watson, J. B. (1919), *Psychology from the Standpoint of a Behaviorist*, Philadelphia, PA: Lippincott.
Wegner, D. (2002), *The Illusion of Conscious Will*, Cambridge, MA: MIT Press.
Weil, V. M. and I. Thalberg (1974), 'The Elements of Basic Action', *Philosophia*, 4 (1): 111–38.
Weil, V. M. and I. Thalberg (1981), 'Basic and Non-basic Actions: "Same" or "Different"?', *Analysis*, 41 (1): 12–17.
Weiner, B. (1992), *Human Motivation: Metaphors, Theories and Research*, Thousand Oaks, CA: Sage Publishers Inc.
Weintraub, R. (2003), 'The Time of a Killing', *Analysis*, 63 (3): 178–82.
Weisbord, M. and S. Janoff (2007), *Don't Just Do Something, Stand There! Ten Principles for Leading Meetings That Matter*, San Francisco, CA: Berrett–Kohler.
Weiskopf, D. and F. Adams (2015), *An Introduction to the Philosophy of Psychology*, Cambridge: Cambridge University Press.
Wesley, J. (1872), *Sermons*, ed. R. P. Heitzenrater and A. C. Outler, 1991, *Anthology*, Oxford: Abingdon Press.
West, D. (2003), 'Introduction', *The Aeneid*, London: Penguin.
Westphal, K. (1994), 'Community as the Basis for Free Individual Action', in M. Daly (ed), *Communitarianism: A New Public Ethics*, 36–40, Belmont, CA: Wadsworth.

Westphal, K. (2003), *Hegel's Epistemology: A Philosophical Introduction to the Phenomenology of Spirit*, Indianapolis, IN: Hackett.
Wetzel, L. (2006), 'Types and Tokens', in E. N. Zalta (ed), *The Stanford Encyclopedia of Philosophy*, Fall 2018 edn. Available online: https://plato.stanford.edu/archives/fall2018/entries/types-tokens.
Whiston, W. (1696), *A New Theory of the Earth*, London: Benjamin Tooke.
White, A. R. (1964), *Attention*, Oxford: Basil Blackwell.
White, A. R. (1970), *Truth*, London: Macmillan and Co.
White, A. R. (1972), 'What We Believe', in N. Rescher (ed), *Studies in the Philosophy of Mind*, APQ monograph series No. 6, 69–84, Oxford: Blackwell.
White, H. (1995), 'Response to Arthur Marwick', *Journal of Contemporary History*, 30 (2): 233–46.
White, N. (2002), *Individual and Conflict in Greek Ethics*, Oxford: Oxford University Press.
Widerker, D. (1995a), 'Libertarianism and Frankfurt's Attack on the Principle of Alternative Possibilities', *Philosophical Review*, 104 (2): 247–61.
Widerker, D. (1995b), 'Libertarian Freedom and the Avoidability of Decisions', *Faith and Philosophy*, 12 (1): 113–8.
Wiggins, D. (2006), *Ethics: Twelve Lectures on the Philosophy of Morality*, Cambridge, MA: Harvard University Press.
Wiland, E. (2012), *Reasons*, London: Continuum.
Williams, B. ([1976] 1981), 'Moral Luck', *Proceedings of the Aristotelian Society Supplementary Volume*, 50: 115–35; as reprinted in his *Moral Luck*, 20–39, Cambridge: Cambridge University Press, 1981.
Williams, B. ([1980] 1981), 'Internal and External Reasons', in R. Harrison (ed), *Rational Action*, Cambridge: Cambridge University Press; as reprinted in his *Moral Luck*, 101–13, Cambridge: Cambridge University Press, 1981, to which any page numbers given refer.
Williams, B. (1981), *Moral Luck*, Cambridge: Cambridge University Press.
Williams, B. (1993), *Shame and Necessity*, Berkeley, CA: University of California Press.
Williams, B. (2006), 'Understanding Homer: Literature, History and Ideal Anthropology', in his *The Sense of the Past*, 60–70, Princeton, NJ: Princeton University Press.
Wilson, T. D. (2002), *Strangers to Ourselves: Discovering the Adaptive Unconscious*, Cambridge, MA: Belknap Press.
Wilson, T. D. and R. E. Nisbett (1978), 'The Accuracy of Verbal Reports about the Effects of Stimuli on Evaluations and Behavior', *Social Psychology*, 41 (2): 118–31.
Winnington-Ingram, R. P. (1948), *Euripides and Dionysus: An Interpretation of the Bacchae*, Cambridge: Cambridge University Press.
Winnington-Ingram, R. P. (1960), 'Hippolytus: A Study in Causation', in O. Reverdin (ed), *Euripide, entretiens sur l'antiquite Classique V*, Geneva: Fondation Hardt.
Wiseman, R. (2016a), *Anscombe's Intention*, London: Routledge.
Wiseman, R. (2016b), 'The Intended and Unintended Consequences of Intention', *American Catholic Philosophical Quarterly*, 90 (2): 207–27.
Wittgenstein, L. ([1922] 1961), *[TLP], Tractatus Logico-Philosophicus*, revised trans. D. F. Pears and B. F. McGuiness, London: Routledge.
Wittgenstein, L. ([1953] 2009), *[PI], Philosophical Investigations*, 4th edn (2009), trans. G. E. M. Anscombe, P. M. S. Hacker and J. Schulte, Oxford: Wiley-Blackwell.
Wittgenstein, L. ([1967] 1981), *[Z], Zettel*, 2nd edn (1981), eds. G. E. M. Anscombe and G. H. von Wright, trans. G. E. M. Anscombe, Oxford: Blackwell.

Wittgenstein, L. ([1977] 1998), *Culture and Value*, ed. G. H. von Wright with H. Nyman, trans. P. Winch, 2nd edn, revised A. Pichler, Oxford: Blackwell.
Wittgenstein, L. (1980), *[RPPII], Remarks on the Philosophy of Psychology*, Vol. II, eds. G. H. von Wright and H. Nyman, trans. C. G. Luckhardt and M. A. E. Aue, Oxford: Blackwell.
Wood, A. W. (1990), *Hegel's Ethical Thought*, Cambridge: Cambridge University Press.
Wood, A. W. (2010), 'Hegel on Responsibility for Actions and Consequences', in A. Laitinen and C. Sandis (eds), *Hegel on Action*, 119–36, London: Palgrave Macmillan.
Woollard, F., *Doing and Allowing Harm*, Oxford: Oxford University Press.
Woollard, F. and D. Howard-Snyder (2016), 'Doing vs. Allowing Harm', *The Stanford Encyclopedia of Philosophy*, Winter 2016 edn, ed. E. N. Zalta. https://plato.stanford.edu/archives/win2016/entries/doing-allowing (accessed 31 January 2023).
Zaidman, L. B. and P. S. Pantel (1992), *Religion in the Ancient Greek City*, trans. P. Cartledge, Cambridge: Cambridge University Press.
Zamir, T. (2007), *Double Vision: Moral Philosophy and Shakespearean Drama*, Princeton, NJ: Princeton University Press.
Zangwill, N. (2008), 'Non-cognitivism and Motivation', in C. Sandis (ed), *New Essays on the Explanation of Action*, 416–24, Basingstoke: Palgrave Macmillan, 2009.
Zimmerman, M. (2008), *Living with Uncertainty*, Cambridge: Cambridge University Press.

Index

*Figures in **bold** refer to diagrams. 'A' refers to the appendix.*

Achinstein, Peter   81–2, 104
action(s), *see also* behaviour
   aspects of   10–15, 19–21, 80
   basic   A203–7
   as cubical volumes   2, 11, 12
   externalism/internalism   10–13, 21, 86, 90, 101, 217 n.7
   individuation   10, 67, 77, 78, 87, 151, A206–8
   mediated   A205
   OED definitions   79–80
   ontologies of   1, 18, 24, 177, 181–2
   qualitative conception of   12
   reflex   73, 75, 146–7
   as repeatables   1, 4, 18, 53, 177, 182
   as spatio-temporal particulars   1, 18, 27, 30, 51, 53, 176–7
actionalism   2, 49, 54
acts   11, 80, 191, 195, 198–9
   act consequentialism   198
   'acts of God'   87, 142, 218 nn.22, 23
   mental   28, A204, 218 n.14
   negative   2, 24–34
   speech   28, 176, 210 n.28, 231 n.21
   as types/tokens   27, 53, 177, 181, 200, 215 nn.9, 10
Adam (biblical character)   170–1
Adams, Robert M.   199
Adventure of the Illustrious Client, The (Doyle)   57
Aegisthus   138, 140
Aeneas   138–9
Aeneid (Virgil)   138–9, 141
Aeschylus   140, 148, 225 n.48
   Oresteia   140, 159, 164 (*see also* *Agamemnon*, *Libation Bearers*)
   Persians   130, 148
   Seven Against Thebes   159

Agamemnon   138, 140, 146, 165, 226 n.55
Agamemnon (Aeschylus)   159
agency   2, 40–1, 129, 133–4, 137, 159, 198, A203
   classical conception   134–6, 225 n.24
   compartmentalized   146–57
   rationalist conception   134
agentialism   103, 124
agents and patients   2, 35–40, 44–5, 48
akrasia   2, 54–63, 131, 138, 148, 166, 198, 216 n.14, *see also* asthenia; *propeteia*
Alvarez, Maria   121–3, 192, 225 nn.35, 44
American Tragedy, An (Dreiser)   155–6, 228 nn.20, 21
Anatomy of Melancholy, The (Burton)   43
Annas, Julia   200
Anscombe, G. E. M.   9–13, 29, 49, 75, 120–2, 151
   contemporary normative ethics   197–201
   Intention   197–8
   'Modern Moral Philosophy'   5, 175, 188–9, 192–201
   moral philosophy before Anscombe   188–92, 201
   three theses   193, 196–8, 234 n.16
anti-disjunctivism/disjunctivism   79, 102, 122, 124, 223 n.20
Antigone   159–66, 174, 229 nn.13, 18
Antigone (Sophocles)   128, 159, 162–3, 229 n.14
anti-psychologism, *see* non-psychologism
Aphrodite/Venus   127–8, 138–41, 143, 225 n.47
Apollo   138, 153, 172–4
apparentism   124
Aquinas, St Thomas   132, 194–5, 232 n.40, 233 n.1, 234 n.25
Aristophanes   171

Aristotle 79, 86, 132, 134, 141, 148–9, 197, 225 n.48
   akrasia 2, 55, 61, 62
   on practical reasoning 2, 49, 54
   on tragedy 128, 130, 158, 164–6
Arjuna 33–4
Artemis 127, 138, 141
asthenia 2, 55, 61–3, 216 n.14
Atossa 148
Audi, Robert 183

Bach, Kent 26–7
Baier, Annette A203, A205–6, 217 n.7, 226 n.51
beards 45, 48, 214 n.15
behaviour 67–83, *see also* action(s)
   causation of 67–77
   Dretske's use of term 67
   indicating stimuli 76–7, **77**
   motionless 78
   non-intentional 73–5
   psychological/non-psychological explanations 71–3
   triggering and structuring causes of 3, 67–77, **72, 74, 76**, 216 nn.4, 6, 217 n.16
behaviourism 68
belief(s) 4, 49–50, 52–4, 81, 111–12, 184–5
   groundless 95
belief-desire pairs 71–7, 109, 122
belief-in-action 53–4
Bennett, Jonathan 178, 207
Bentham, Jeremy 24–5
Bernays, Edward 94–5, 220 n.21
Bhagavad Gītā 1, 2, 22, 33–4
bias 92, 96–7, 219 n.14
Birns, Nicholas 44–5
Blackburn, Simon 142, 226 n.54
Bob Marley example A207–8
bodily movements 18, 31, 39–40, 67, 69, 71–2, **72**, 78, 80, 85
   raising arm 14–15, 27, 39, 76–7, **76**, 79, 85, 233 n.51
   transitive/intransitive sense 78, 85
   turning head 73–5, **74**
Borges, Jorge Luis 23
Bowra, Maurice 145, 153
Bradley, A. C. 161–2, 229 n.11

Brandom, Robert 10–12
Bratman, Michael 136
Burton, R. 43, 213 n.10
Butler, Bishop 193

Carr, E. H. 15
Carroll, Lewis 23
Carruthers, Peter 98–100, 219 n.5
causalism 3, 12, 39, 73, 112, 132–6, 139, 144–5
causation 3, 39, 95, 67–77, 127–45, A204
   double 128–31, 137, 139, 173–4, 230 n.36
causes 82, 119–20
   structuring 3, 67–77, **72, 74, 76**, 216 nn.4, 6, 217 n.16
   triggering 3, 67–77, **72, 74, 76**
Chalmers, David 114
Chappell, V. C. 118
character 43, 90, 136, 175, 183, 201
Charles, David 18, 231 n.13
Charlton, W. 58–9
Children Act, The (McEwan) 25–6
Chisholm, R. M. A205
choice blindness 98
Christian morality 14, 189, 194, 196–7
Churchland, Paul and Patricia 134
cognitivism 2, 49, 101, 103
compartmentalization 150–7
conceptions 114–15, 119, 124
concepts 114–15, 119, 124
conclusions 49–50
conditioning 70
confabulation(s) 3, 88–100, 219 nn.5, 6, 12
   purported 90–5
Conflating View of Behaviour (CVB) 83, 84
   Conflating View of Action (CVA) 84–6, 218 n.18
Conflating View of Motivating Reasons (CVMR) 93, 94
Conflating View of Nesting Reasons (CVNR) 89
Conflating View of Reasons (CVR) 84, 85, 87, 94
Conflating View of Reasons for Action (CVRA) 84–6
consciousness 95–100, 146, 159–60, 166–7

consequences   10, 12, 16–20, 33, 87,
    167–8, 190, 193–201
consequentialism   4–5, 31, 159, 175, 179,
    181, 189, 193–201
considerations   50, 88–90, 97–9, 106,
    110, 113–17, 122
continence   56, 58, 61–2
contractualism   200
Coope, Christopher   195, 200, 234 n.19
Cottingham, John   149–50
Crampton, Georgia Ronan   40–1
Creon   159–66, 171, 229 nn.13, 18
crucifixion, the   13, 209 nn.14–16,
    231 n.22

Dancy, Jonathan   49–54, 85, 89, 101–12,
    117, 122–3, 167, 181–2
  actionalism   2, 49, 52
  enabling conditions   109–10
  non-psychologism   3, 101–3, 105,
    109, 220 n.6, 221 n.14
  Practical Reality   101, 123
  Practical Shape   49–53, 214 n.3
  'The Prichard Point'   50–1, 54,
    214 n.3
Danto, A. C.   26, A203–6, 236 nn.3, 5, 8
D'Arcy, Eric   25
Darius (*Persians*)   130, 148
Davidson, Donald   2–3, 11–12, 26–7,
    29–30, 54, 86, 158, 181, 200
  'Actions, Reasons, and Causes'   118–
    19, 132–4
  akrasia   2, 55–63, 166, 215 n.10
  continence   56, 58, 61–2
  deviant causal chains   73, 77, 118–19,
    156
  objections to   55–6, 58–60
  on Oedipus   150–2, 170
  Patma example   132–3, 224 n.18
Davies, David   186, 187
Davis, N.   199
Davis, Wayne   103–4, 110–11
deconstructivism, analytic   3, 114, 175
deed(s)   79–81, 158, 168, 170, 175–87,
    191–2
  as (leaving of) traces   2, 17
de Merville, Violet   57, 215 n.8
deontology   4, 20, 159, 175, 181, 183,
    199–201

Descartes, René   A204
Description Principle   152
desire(s)   60, 68–77, 132–6, 138–44,
    146–9, 152–7
  first-order   134, 147, 154
  second-order   134, 136, 141, 147–8,
    154, 157
  unconscious   13, 227 n.10
determinism   38, 135, 137, 140, 143–4
Dido   138–9
discoverables   82, 104
disjunctivism/anti-disjunctivism   79,
    102, 122, 124, 223 n.20
divine commands   178, 196, 199
doables   28–31
doctrine of doing and allowing   2, 31,
    198, 200
doctrine of double effect   178, 198, 200
Dodds, E. R.   19–20, 128–31, 149, 153–4,
    164, 172
doing(s)   2, 9, 14, 17–18, 52–3, 80, 190–2
  actions as   29, 80
  vs. deeds   2, 80–1, 175–87
  doing 'being'   28
  doing nothing   22–34
Downton Abbey example   155
Doyle, James   196, 234 n.23
dreadlock example   20
Dreiser, Theodore   155–6
Dretske, Fred   67–77, 216 nn.1–6,
    217 nn.7–16, 218 n.15, 221 n.12
duty   50, 56–7, 159, 161–3, 167, 169–70,
    183–4, 189, 193
Dworkin, Ronald   21, 114, 187
Dylan, Bob   186

Elster, Jon   82
Elton, Geoffrey   15–16
enactivism   10, 11
ends/goals   5, 41, 113, 118, 120, 121
epic   158, 173–4, 224 n.6
Ericsson, K. A.   92
eudaimonia   128, 148
Euripides   226 nn.50, 56
  Bacchae   159
  Hippolytus   127, 140–1, 143
  Iphigenia at Aulis   159
  Medea   148
Evans, Richard   16

Ewing, A. C. 78–9, 176, 188
explanations 68, 74, 83, 84, 101–13, 117
  explananda 68–70, 81–3, 87, 102, 104
  explanantia 68–9, 81–3, 102–6, 112, 116–17, 122–3
  psychological/non-psychological 71–3

facticity/factivism 137, 143–4, 221 n.9, 10, 226 nn.57, 59, 63
Falk, W. D. 119
false belief(s) 101–3, 105–6, 120–3, 147, 152, 223 n.16
falsehoods 94, 102, 105–7, 109, 112, 122
fatalism 43–4, 144
fear of flying example 59–60
Fisher, Carrie 29
Foot, Philippa 193, 197, 198
foresight 10, 19, 20, 190, 194
forgetting 22–3, 25–7, 29, 31–2, 211 n.7
forgiveness 13–14, 25, 209 n.16
Frankfurt, Harry 136–7, 147–8, 157, 217 n.12, 224 n.4, 225 n.35, 228 n.22
free will 44, 97, 137, 140, 143–4, 175
Frege, Gottlob 101, 218 n.13
Freud, Sigmund 13, 94, 134, 150–1, 156, 167, 217 n.11, 230 n.21

Gallie, W. B. 114
Gazzaniga, Michael 97–8, 100
Geach, Mary 195, 197
Geach, Peter 195–6, 199, 232 n.40, 234 n.21
Gettier, Edmund 184
Glock, Hans-Johann 111
God 14, 40, 57, 87, 115, 183, 196
gods, the 127–32, 138–49, 153, 157, 161–2, 165–6, 171–4
Goldman, Alvin I. 26, 132, 134, 135, A204, A207, 225 n.28
Goldschmidt, Tyron 24
Gone without a Trace (Torjussen) 9
Greeks and the Irrational, The (Dodds) 128–9
Greek tragedy 4, 10, 13, 127–31, 137–45, 150–3, 156, 158–67, 170–3, 224 n.6, *see also* Aeschylus; Euripides; Sophocles

Green, O. H. 31
Greenwald, A. G. 96
Grice, P. 57, 107
Griffiths, Clyde 155, 228 n.20

Hacker, Peter 114–15, 220 n.2, 222 n.2
Haidt, Jonathan 95
hamartia 128, 130, 164
Hamlet 29
Handlung 4, 10, 11, 158, 168, 170–1, 230 n.34, 232 n.36
Hanser, Matthew 181, 210 n.31
happening(s) 119, 190, 192, 224 n.4
Hare, R. M. 198
harm 10, 31, 162, 213 n.41
  foreseen/unforeseen 10
Harman, Gilbert 185
Hart, H. L. A. 114, 115
Havel, Václav 163
Hegel, G. W. F. 9–13, 15, 19, 188, 209 n.8, 229 n.11
  Aesthetics 158, 170–1
  Dialectical Synthesis 160–1
  externalism/internalism 10, 11
  Handlung, Tat and *Tun* 4, 10, 11, 158, 168, 170–1, 227 n.16, 230 n.34, 232 n.36
  Philosophy of Right 10, 32, 167, 171, 229 n.18, 233 n.1
  on tragedy 10, 130, 152, 158–74, 228 n.6, 230 n.36
Heidegger, Martin 17, 23, 143, 226 nn.57, 63
Hempel, C. G. 82, 104, 120
Hen Welfare Trust example 179, 180, 182, 185
Herstein, Ori 32, 33
Hidden Persuaders, The (Packard) 93–4
Hippolytus 127, 128, 140, 143
Hippolytus (Euripides) 127, 140–1, 143
history 9, 14
  historical facts 15–16, 210 n.22
  philosophy of 9, 16
hitting a child example 31
Homer 23, 35, 130, 148, 211 n.1
'Homeric man' 128, 129, 136, 146–7, 157, 227 n.3
Homeric Principle 147–8, 157

Hornsby, Jennifer   18, 30, 78, 83, 147,
   176–7, 207, 222 n.9, 223 n.18,
   231 n.24
Houlgate, Stephen   159–60, 165–6, 168–70
Hume, David   132, 135–6, 167, 193,
   209 n.20
   belief-desire pairs   109, 121, 122
hungry rat example   71–2
Hursthouse, Rosalind   121–2, 182,
   191–3, 195, 199–201, 219 n.12
Husserl, Edmund   81, 228 n.2
Hyman, John   106–7, 192, 220 n.5,
   223 n.20
hypnosis   95, 97

Identification Principle   157
inaction   2, 22–34
   in action   24–8
intention(s)   1–4, 10–20, 27–32, 70–7,
   95–7, 132–42, 146–7, 150–8,
   179–81, 197–201
   de re/de dicto   152, 172, 227 n.12
intentionalism   2, 49, 187
internalism, motivational   2, 55, 62
introspection   98, 99

Jenkins   36, 43, 46, 213 nn.5, 9
Jolene murder example   178–9
Joseph, H. W. B.   188, 191, 201, 233 n.8
judgement(s)   54–63
   conditional/unconditional   54, 56–63
Jung, C. G.   150, 151, 153
Jungian Principle   150, 152, 157
justice   114, 153, 166, 192, 194, 222 n.1, 5

kakodaimonia   128
Kant, Immanuel   19, 183–4, 189, 193,
   196, 213 n.42, 232 n.34
Kaszniak, A. W.   99
Kennett, J.   80
Kitto, H. D. F.   129–31, 224 n.9
Knowles, D.   12, 228 n.5
Korsakoff's Syndrome   97
Kramnick, Jonathan   39–40
Krieger, L. H.   96
Kundera, Milan   153, 162–3, 172

Laitinen, Arto   19, 32
Lanzmann, Claude   16

Lenman, James   102
Levinas, E.   16, 210 n.26
Levy, Neil   100, 220 n.20
Lewis, C. S.   115
Lewis, David   24
Libation Bearers (Aeschylus)   140
Littlejohn, Clayton   121–3, 184–5
Locke, John   39, A204
luck   4, 11, 19–20, 41, 144, 169–70, 185,
   211 n.35, 212 n.33
   moral   20, 128, 144, 182–3, 211 n.38,
   214 n.11, 230 n.23
Luke, gospel of   13–14, 209 nn.14–16,
   231 n.22
Lynch, David   5

McCann, Hugh J.   137, 204
McDowell, John   101, 193
McEwan, Ian   25–6
MacIntyre, Alasdair   193, 228 n.6
Macmurray, John   18, 80, 176, 188, 192,
   218 n.22, 231 n.24
Man and Superman (Shaw)   48
meaning   17, 73–7
Medea (Euripides)   148
Medea Principle   148
mental acts   28, A204, 218 n.14
mental contents   71, 72, 77, 99, 100, 139
mental processes   39, 68, 91, 99, 192
mental states   39, 68, 71, 88–9, 98–9, 117,
   132–42
Mill, John Stuart   183, 190, 193–5,
   232 n.35, 233 n.49, 234 nn.15, 17
monism, conceptual   114, 115, 117,
   222 n.11
moods   89–90
Moore, G. E.   59, 188, 193, 201, 234 n.15
Moore's Paradox   59, 109
moral luck   20, 128, 144, 182–3, 211 n.38,
   214 n.11, 230 n.23
moral philosophy   5, 183, 188–9, 193,
   197–202, 233 n.1, 235 n.33
moral psychology   2, 46, 175, 188, 198,
   200, 201
Moran, Richard   99
Moreland, Hugh   37, 41, 47
motivation   55, 62, 75, 77, 88–101,
   128–31, 138–42
   theory of   55, 101, 103, 151

motive(s)   10–20, 93–4, 119, 178–84, 189–92, 197, 200–1
Mourelatos, Alexander   79
Murdoch, Iris   180

Nagel, Thomas   182–3, 218 n.21, 232 n.28
Necker Cubes   **12**, 13, **14**
neglect(ing)   2, 22, 25, 29–34, 211 n.7
negligence   21, 31–3, 213 nn.38, 41
Nehamas, Alexander   187
Nielsen, L.   99
Nietzsche, Friedrich   37–9, 43–5, 134, 143–4, 149, 186–7, 213 nn.7, 8, 226 n.61
  will to power   33, 38, 41
Nilsson, Martin P.   128–31, 136, 146–8
Nisbett, R. E.   90–3, 98–9, 219 n.5
non-facticity/non-factivism   3, 101–12, 117, 123, 124, 221 n.9, 10, see also facticity/factivism
non-psychologism   3, 101–3, 105, 109, 124, 220 n.6, 221 n.14
normative ethics   2, 4, 24, 175–87, 197–201
Nussbaum, Martha   165, 180, 230 n.23

objectivism   167, 189, 193, 195
obligation(s)   50–3, 161–2, 167, 178, 183–4, 193–7
Odyssey (Homer)   23, 35, 138
Oedipus   10, 19, 34, 150–4, 158–9, 165–7, 169–74, 185, 207
Oedipus Rex (Sophocles)   159, 166, 173
omission(s)   2, 24–5, 27–8, 31–2, 78, 134, 178
O'Neil, Onora   183–4, 222 n.1, 232 n.34
On What Matters (Parfit)   21
Oppenheim, P.   82, 104
Oresteia (Aeschylus)   159, 164, see also *Agamemnon*, *Libation Bearers*
Orestes   138, 164
oyster example   191

Packard, Vance   93–4
Paolucci, Anne & Henry   159
Parfit, Derek   21, 185, 199, 211 n.40, 235 n.34
Parmenides   24

Paticca Samuppada   144
Patma example   132–3, 224 n.18
Pavlov's dog example   70
Persians (Aeschylus)   130, 148
perspectivism   11, 19, 25
Pettit, Phillip   114, 117, 217 n.14, 223 n.14
Phaedra   127, 140–1, 143
philosophical psychology   197, 201, 235 n.29
philosophy of mind   145, 197, 198, 235 n.31
  causation in   131–40
philosophy of psychology   188, 190, 192–4, 197–8, 201, 235 n.31
Pinkard, Terry   165
Plato   15, 23, 134, 147–8, 229 n.6
pluralism, conceptual   3, 4, 87, 113–14, 117, 120, 124, 222 n.11
Poole, Adrian   130–1
Pope, Alexander   39, 45
positive/negative acts   2, 24–34
Postcards from the Edge (Fisher)   29
Powell, Anthony   2, 35–48, 213 nn.5, 6, 214 nn.11, 13, 15, 18, 19
  agents and patients   2, 35–40, 44–5, 48
  fatalism   43–4
  Ghost Railway   42
practical reasoning   2, 49–54, 93, 134–5, 214 n.3
Prichard, H. A.   4, 18, 50–1, 54, 167–8, 178, 188, 192, 199–201, 204
  'Prichard Point'   50–1, 54, 214 n.3
prima facie, Davidson *vs.* Ross use of   56
Prinz, Jesse   178
Professor Moody example   89–90
Pronin, Emily   98
propeteia   2, 55, 61–3, 216 n.14
Prospero   153
Proust, Marcel   177, 182, 231 n.10
psychoanalysis   149–50
psychologism   124, see also non-psychologism
psychologists   3, 83–4, 88, 93
psychology   71–3, 77, 88–102, 109, 154, 156, 180–1
  experimental   3, 88
  moral   2, 46, 175, 188, 198, 200, 201
purpose(s)   13, 18, 86, 136, 158, 170, 223 n.15

Index

Railton, Peter   135
raising my arm example   76–7, **76**, 79
Ramsey, Frank   163
Rape of the Lock, The (Pope)   39, 45
rashness   2, 55, 61
Rawls, John   114, 222 nn.1, 3, 235 n.29
Raz, Joseph   134, 135, 213 n.41, 214 n.5, 225 n.25, 227 n.1
Reader, Soran   39
reasoning   2–3, 49–54, *see also* practical reasoning; theoretical reasoning
reasons   3–4, 36–7, 50–2, 71–2, 92, 109
  agential   3, 77, 86, 88–112, 116, 124
  apparent   120–4
  motivating   88, 93, 101, 110–11, 113, 116–23
  nesting   89, 93, 219 n.2
  normative   101, 119, 122–3
  'real'   88–100
  RFAs (reasons for action)   51, 71, 75–6, 84, 86–7, 113–23
reperienda   82, 104
responsibility   4, 19–20, 22–3, 31–3, 100, 137, 146–57, 198
Ricoeur, Paul   2, 9, 11, 17–18, 159, 176, 186, 210 nn.27, 28, 229 n.13
Right and the Good, The (Ross)   56, 167, 189, 233 n.8
rightness   4, 19–20, 178–83
Roche, M.   160–1, 166
Rosenberg, Harold   186–7, 232 n.46
Ross, W. D.   56, 161–2, 164, 167, 172–3, 178, 184, 188–92, 195, 196, 201
Ryle, Gilbert   25–7, 114, 137, A207

Sacks, Harvey   28–9
Sacks, Oliver   23
salad-eaters example   31–2
Sartre, Jean-Paul   143–4, 187, 217 n.11, 226 nn.59–61, 228 n.19
Schopenhauer, A.   25, 211 n.14
Schueler, G. F.   84–5, 217 n.7
Segal, Charles   171
self   149–50, 155, 157
self-consciousness   10, 149, 159, 170–1
Sellars, Wilfred   133–5
Shame and Necessity (Williams)   130
Shaw, George Bernard   35, 48, 214 nn.15, 20

Shoah (Lanzmann)   16
Sidgwick, Henry   188, 193
Silk, M. S.   165
Simon, H. A.   92
Skow, Bradford   120, 223 n.15
Smith, Michael   80, 85, 109, 117, 122–3, 133–4, 216 n.17, 220 n.1, 221 n.14
Socrates   147
Socratic Principle   147, 227 n.12
Sophist (Plato)   23
Sophocles   128–30, 152–3, 158–9, 161, 164, 167, 170–2, 224 n.9, 229 n.14, 230 n.21
soup example   18, 177, 233 n.53
Speight, Allen   165, 209 n.8
Stern, J. P.   165
stockings experiment   90–2
Stout, Rowland   86–7
Stoutland, Frederick   203–5, 217 n.7, 217 n.6
Sverdlik, Steven   20
Swanton, Christine   180
sweating example   86

Tat   4, 10, 11, 158, 168, 170–1
Taylor, C. C. W.   60–2
Taylor, Charles   10, 12, 60–2, 230 n.34
Thalberg, Irving   A207
Theban Trilogy (Sophocles)   158, *see also Antigone* (Sophocles); *Oedipus Rex* (Sophocles)
theoretical reasoning   49, 52–4, 134
Theseus   128, 143
things done   2, 4, 14, 18, 30, 53, 79, 85, 177–87, 191
Through the Looking-Glass (Carroll)   23
Tillich, Paul   143
Tiresias   166, 170
Torjussen, Mary   9
traces   9–11, 150, 176, 186, 209 n.20, 210 nn.21, 26, 27, 33
  on time   2, 11, 14–21
tragedy, Greek   4, 10, 13, 127–31, 137–45, 150–3, 156, 158–67, 170–3, 224 n.6
Trout Quintet example   132
Tun   4, 11, 158, 227 n.16
turmeric example   120–2, 124, 223 n.16

turning my head example   73–5, **74**
typist example   96, 219 n.14

umbrella example   108–9
Upper, Dennis   24
utilitarianism   193, 194, 200–1, 234 n.17, 235 n.42

Velleman, David   28–30
Vendler, Zeno   85
verbal reports   3, 88–100
Vermazen, B.   27
Vermeer, Johannes   133
virtue ethics   4–5, 90, 159, 175, 179–80, 193, 199–201
volition(s)   2, 10, 39, 133–7, 141, 144, 192, A204
   volitional necessity   136–7
voluntariness   67, 132–3, 142, 147, 224 n.17
von Wright, G. H.   18, 49, 78, 192, 211 n.12, 216 n.2, 231 n.13

Wallace, Jennifer   165
weakness of will   38, 58, 62, 134–5, 144, 147, 227 nn.4, 10
Weil, Vivien   A207
Weiner, B.   84

Wesley, John   40–1, 44
West, David   138–9
White, Alan   101, 111–12, 221 n.15
Who's In Charge? (Gazzaniga)   97
Widmerpool   36, 43, 45–7, 214 nn.18, 19
Wiland, Eric   123–4
will   10, 11, 134–7, 140–4, 199, 225 n.48
   in Powell's novels   35–41, 44–8
   weakness of   38, 58, 62, 134–5, 144, 147, 227 nn.4, 10
Williams, Bernard   19, 31–2, 130, 153–4, 172, 185, 226 n.49, 227 n.16, 230 nn.29, 31
willing   10, 38, 39, 136, 149, 169, 211 n.14
Wilson, T. D.   90–4, 98–9, 219 n.5
Winnington-Ingram, R. P.   127–8, 130–1, 137, 139, 227 n.65
Wittgenstein, Ludwig   101, 119, 143, 190–1, 222 nn.1, 6, 233 n.51, 234 n.23
Woman Writing a Letter, with her Maid (Vermeer)   133
Wood, Allen W.   169
worth, moral   19, 183–4

Zeus   138–9, 141, 144, 146
Zouch   45–6

www.ingramcontent.com/pod-product-compliance
Lightning Source LLC
Chambersburg PA
CBHW071811300426
44116CB00009B/1272